# Thomas F. Torrance's Theology of the Ascension

# Re-envisioning Reformed Dogmatics

SERIES EDITORS:

Myk Habets, W. Ross Hastings, and Jacob Samuel Raju

*Re-envisioning Reformed Dogmatics* is a series that explores afresh the rich and diverse dogmatic heritage of the contemporary Reformed tradition. The series will plumb the depths of the riches of the Reformed tradition by engaging in constructive and interdisciplinary study while also challenging assumptions that are sometimes expressed as the Reformed tradition's contemporary consensus. There are in current discussions, contrary trends at work in Reformed Theology. Some are eager to expand Reformed orthodoxy to include all Protestants while others narrow the definition of what is "Reformed" to what characterizes the teachings of, say, the Dutch Reformed Church or the Church in Scotland. *Re-envisioning Reformed Dogmatics* is a series that will explore the rich and complex plurality of thinking in the wider Reformed tradition. The monographs in this series will invite readers to think in fresh ways about various theological loci while exploring constructive developments within this dynamic tradition. They will include subject matter that has been hitherto neglected or excluded from conversations about Reformed theology in an effort to recover the intellectual treasures that once made up the full dogmatic deposit of the confessional era. In this way, the *Re-envisioning Reformed Dogmatics* series is marked by that self-same spirit that once motivated the Reformer's clarion call: *Ad fontes* ("to the sources"). Now, with five hundred years of theological development since this first call was uttered, the authors in this series renew that clarion call. This time, however, the sources to which the authors in this series turn include those of the Reformers and their theological heirs.

EDITORIAL BOARD:

Gijsbert van den Brink, University Research Chair for Theology
    & Science at the Faculty of Theology (Free University of Amsterdam)

Oliver Crisp, Professor of Analytic Theology and Director
    of the Logos Institute for Analytic and Exegetical Theology
    (University of St. Andrews)

Christina Larsen, Professor of Theology (Grand Canyon University)

Paul Nimmo, King's Chair of Systematic Theology (University of Aberdeen)

Carl Trueman, Professor of Biblical & Religious Studies
    (Grove City College)

Adonis Vidu, Professor of Theology
    (Gordon Conwell Theological Seminary)

Willem van Vlastuin, Professor of Theology and Spirituality
    of Reformed Protestantism (Free University of Amsterdam)

# Thomas F. Torrance's Theology of the Ascension

A Constructive Account

STAVAN NARENDRA JOHN

CASCADE *Books* • Eugene, Oregon

THOMAS F. TORRANCE'S THEOLOGY OF THE ASCENSION
A Constructive Account

Re-envisioning Reformed Dogmatics

Copyright © 2025 Stavan Narendra John. All rights reserved. Except for brief quotations in critical publications or reviews, no part of this book may be reproduced in any manner without prior written permission from the publisher. Write: Permissions, Wipf and Stock Publishers, 199 W. 8th Ave., Suite 3, Eugene, OR 97401.

Cascade Books
An Imprint of Wipf and Stock Publishers
199 W. 8th Ave., Suite 3
Eugene, OR 97401

www.wipfandstock.com

PAPERBACK ISBN: 979-8-3852-2143-1
HARDCOVER ISBN: 979-8-3852-2144-8
EBOOK ISBN: 979-8-3852-2145-5

*Cataloguing-in-Publication data:*

Names: John, Stavan Narendra [author].

Title: Thomas F. Torrance's theology of the ascension : a constructive account / Stavan Narendra John.

Description: Eugene, OR: Cascade Books, 2025 | Series: Re-envisioning Reformed Dogmatics | Includes bibliographical references and index.

Identifiers: ISBN 979-8-3852-2143-1 (paperback) | ISBN 979-8-3852-2144-8 (hardcover) | ISBN 979-8-3852-2145-5 (ebook)

Subjects: LCSH: Jesus Christ—Ascension. | Torrance, Thomas F. (Thomas Forsyth), 1913–2007. | Reformed Church—Doctrines.

Classification: BT500 J64 2025 (paperback) | BT500 (ebook)

05/28/25

For Christina, Ishan, and Roshan

# Contents

*Acknowledgments* | ix

1. The Need for a Holistic Theology of the Ascension | 1
2. Introducing T. F. Torrance's Theology of the Ascension | 14
3. The Ontology of the Ascended Christ | 49
4. The Spatiality of the Ascended Christ | 86
5. The Present Ministry of the Ascended Christ | 132
6. A Critical Appraisal and Constructive Account | 178
7. Critical Conclusions | 239

*Bibliography* | 245

*Index* | 259

# Acknowledgments

THE GENESIS OF THIS work was a PhD earned from the Oxford Centre for Mission Studies/Middlesex University, London. I owe a debt of gratitude to my supervisors, Professors Myk Habets and Thomas A. Noble, who enabled me to grow as a theological thinker, writer, and scholar of Torrance's theology. I am also grateful for the kindness and support I received from my examiners, Professors David Fergusson and Paul Molnar. I am thankful to the South Asia Institute of Advanced Christian Studies (SAIACS), Scholar-Leaders International, and the Free Methodist Church for their generous financial scholarship towards my studies.

Dr. Nigel Ajay Kumar, former head in the Theology Department at SAIACS, invested in my all-round academic and spiritual formation through numerous conversations, which greatly impacted me. I also thank other members of the SAIACS leadership team: Drs. Ian Payne, Varughese John, Havilah Dharamraj, and Prabhu Singh, for their encouragement and support. Rev. Dr. Derek Tidball, friend of SAIACS, prayed for me regularly and motivated me to press on in my writing, which I truly appreciate.

My parents, Narendra and Jaya John, together with my sisters Stuti and Sannuthi, cheered me on throughout my writing. I am grateful for their love and encouragement. Since I completed my PhD, my mother went home to be with the Lord, leaving behind a godly legacy of faithful service in the ministry. Together with my father, my mother showed us how to serve the Lord wholeheartedly.

I owe the greatest debt of gratitude to my wife Christina, who worked tirelessly to proofread my work, prayed for me, and along with our sons, Ishan and Roshan—graciously put up with me when I carried work home. I dedicate this work to them.

A special word of thanks is due to Dr. Robin Parry and his editorial team with Cascade Books, who expertly guided me through the process before publication.

# 1

# The Need for a Holistic Theology of the Ascension

## 1. NEGLECT OF A THEOLOGY OF THE ASCENSION

THIS STUDY SITUATES THE relevance of Thomas F. Torrance's doctrine of the ascension in the context of two pressing theological realities. First, more generally, the ascension is a neglected doctrine and must be redressed.[1] While there are notable exceptions, there is a need for more studies on the ascension, particularly on theologians who have contributed significantly to the doctrine in modern theology but are neglected.[2] Torrance is a theologian who has helped recover the underemphasis on the ascension in modern and contemporary theology, but there is still no full-length treatment of his theology of the ascension.[3] This is surprising given that even crit-

---

1. Systematic theologians, biblical scholars, theological ethicists, and practical theologians are all in agreement that the ascension is a neglected theological locus. For more, see Farrow, *Ascension and Ecclesia*, x; Orr, *Christ Absent and Present*, 221–22; Holmes, *Ethics in the Presence of Christ*, 5; Purves, *Reconstructing Pastoral Theology*, 107n7, 108.

2. Some examples of studies on the ascension, generally, are Farrow, *Ascension and Ecclesia*; Farrow, *Ascension Theology*; Dawson, *Jesus Ascended*; Burgess, *Ascension in Karl Barth*; Schreiner, *Ascension of Christ*. In each of these studies, the theology of Torrance is central.

3. See Ortlund, "Explorations," 181, where he correctly observes that Torrancean scholarship has not sufficiently investigated the ascension in Torrance's theology, and he surmises that this is because "in general the focus has been on his [Torrance's] treatment of incarnation, atonement, and resurrection, while his view of the ascension has received relatively little attention." While there is no full-length study on the ascension in Torrance, there are some notable book sections and articles that take up this theme. For more, see Burgess, *Ascension in Karl Barth*, 109–34; Farrow, *Ascension and Ecclesia*,

ics of Torrance's ascension theology acknowledge that it is "one of the few significant twentieth century treatments of Jesus' ascension."[4] Supporters of Torrance's work are no less effusive in their praise: "Torrance's theology of the ascension is one of the richest treatments of the subject in modern theology."[5] This work, therefore, seeks to redress this underemphasis, the doctrine of ascension in general and, in particular, a comprehensive analysis of Torrance's ascension theology, by providing an entire study dedicated to exploring, critically appraising, and constructively developing Torrance's theology of the ascension.

The need for study on the ascension echoes the sentiments of scholars from various confessional traditions and disciplinary perspectives. For instance, Reformed theologian Douglas Kelly (not surprisingly influenced by the work of Torrance) clearly notes that the ascension is an underemphasized doctrine: "For whatever reason, the ascent of the glorified body of Christ bearing our new humanity to the Father's Throne has been generally neglected for centuries in most theological and ecclesiastical traditions."[6] Anthony Kelly, a Roman Catholic theologian, is equally forthright in making a similar assessment: "Theologically speaking, the ascension has suffered some form of benign neglect compared to other aspects of Christian faith."[7] New Testament scholar Peter Orr asserts that there is a lacuna in Pauline scholarship because the humanity of Christ, generally discussed under the broader heading of "Last Adam," is limited to deliberations on his "pre-existence."[8] He goes on to state,

> What is often missing is a more theological engagement with Paul and a consideration of the significance that the exalted Christ's humanity plays in his overall Christology. With the rise of theological interpretation and the increasing recognition of the importance of the *Wirkungsgeschichte* of the Biblical text, it

---

174, 178, 248–49, 252, 262–66; Habets, *Theosis*, 87–91; Fergusson, "Ascension of Christ," 92–107.

4. Burgess, *Ascension in Karl Barth*, 109.

5. Fergusson, "Ascension of Christ," 95.

6. Kelly, "Foreword," in Dawson, *Jesus Ascended*, x. See also Crisp, *Divinity and Humanity*, 133n29, who wonders why the ascension does not feature more in theological works: "Surprisingly few theologians pause to reflect in detail upon this implication of the creed."

7. Kelly, "Ascension," 81. Another Roman Catholic theologian, Oliver Davies, *Theology of Transformation*, 7–8, concurs with such an assessment when he notes that since the Reformation period, "there seems to have been remarkably little interest in reviving or renewing the doctrine of Christ's 'ascension' or exaltation."

8. Orr, *Christ Absent and Present*, 221–22. Cf. Orr, *Exalted Above the Heavens*, for a biblical theological exploration of the ascension.

would seem that the humanity of the exalted Christ is one area that might merit further study.[9]

Christopher R. J. Holmes, writing on theological ethics, acknowledges that the discipline as a whole in recent times lacks an "enduring *theological* foundation," which is evidenced in the fact that "the presence and ongoing ministry of Jesus Christ" is inadequately emphasized in "Christian and/or theological ethics."[10] While many more voices could be added to this list, Albert Collver's observations will suffice to underscore the need for immediate attention to this locus in theology: "While the ascension and the session to the right hand of God are confessed in the ecumenical creeds, they are considered almost as an appendix, or an afterthought."[11]

Contemporary theological scholarship recognizes that the ascension is understated, and while it is too early to declare that the tide is turning, there are promising signs. Theological expositions on the ascension range from highly complex monographs[12] to pastoral[13] and ecclesially-oriented works;[14] and amidst this vast scope are remarkably thorough introductory overviews,[15] interdisciplinary discourses,[16] and biblical and exegetically-themed volumes.[17] However, even within this burgeoning literature, there is still a gap that necessitates further research on the ascension of Jesus. Theological expositions on the ascension of Jesus can be categorized into three broad areas: (1) ontology, (2) spatiality, and (3) present ministry. While there is a healthy discourse with diverse views on each of these subjects,

---

9. Orr, *Christ Absent and Present*, 221–22. See also Green, "What You See," 457, where he argues that theological readings of the ascension in biblical scholarship are not to be considered inferior approaches to the text: "Reading Luke's account with the benefit of hindsight—that is, with interests more reflective of second-century theological reflection than of modern biblical studies—we find theological emphases that speak through the centuries. And we find that those theological emphases cannot be dismissed out of hand as alien intrusions into the Lukan narrative."

10. Holmes, *Ethics*, 5. He goes on to explain on the same page what he perceives to be problematic about contemporary theological reflection on ethics: "Ethics is at times understood to be where individuals or the church begin and, concomitantly, where Jesus leaves off."

11. Collver, "Person of Christ," 9. He goes on to highlight on the same page: "In more recent dogmatics books, the ascension is scarcely mentioned at all."

12. For example, Farrow's *Ascension and Ecclesia*.

13. Cf. Seamands, *Unseen Real*.

14. Cf. Van Driel, *What Is Jesus Doing?*; Presa, *Ascension Theology*.

15. Cf. Schreiner, *Ascension of Christ*.

16. Cf. Harris, "Science."

17. Cf. Bryan and Pao, *Ascent into Heaven*.

there are scarcely any theological works that integrate all three aspects to form a holistic theological account of Jesus's ascension.

To be sure, there are a few exceptions, but generally theologians tend to focus on select aspects of the ascension in their works.[18] Edwin Chr. Van Driel's edited volume entitled *What Is Jesus Doing?* provides a much-needed study on the present ministry of Jesus in light of the ascension, but even he acknowledges at the outset that "a full account of the ascension would therefore need to explore the space the resurrected and ascended Christ inhabits and offers us ways on how to imagine such space in the context of how twenty-first century, scientifically informed believers think about space in general. Such exercise falls outside the scope of this essay."[19]

This work examines the doctrine of the ascension in the thought of Thomas F. Torrance to show that he developed a *holistic* account, taking into consideration the *ontology*, *spatiality*, and *present ministry* of the ascended Jesus. Each of these three areas will be explored to demonstrate that Torrance managed to propel the discussion away from generic affirmations to specific declarations. Jesus's ascended humanity has an ontology that is a composite of body-soul, gender, ethnicity, and he lives an immortal life in creaturely dependence upon God. Jesus's ascended humanity has a spatiality that is defined by a duality, which is a corporeal, human existence as well as a ubiquitous divine existence that cannot be defined by human characteristics. Jesus in his ascended humanity has a present ministry that is active, dynamic, and one which will last into eternity, even when sin and evil have been dealt with.

To do justice to Torrance's holistic theology of the ascension, space will not permit this study to center its attention on several adjoining theological debates, doctrines, methodological approaches, and implications. With respect to debates, it will not focus on Torrance's endorsement of Chalcedonian doctrine. Correspondingly, it will not adjudicate between the various views held in historical and contemporary scholarship on the proper relationship between the divine and human natures in the Person of Christ. Neither can the attention shift to discovering the Alexandrian and Antiochene tendencies present in the Lutheran and Reformed theological traditions, respectively.[20] Doctrines such as Torrance's views on Scripture,

---

18. Farrow's *Ascension and Ecclesia* is an exception to this observation, but even his formidable study on the ascension focuses on the history of thinking on the doctrine, leaving the need for a more in-depth study on select theologians such as T. F. Torrance.

19. Van Driel, "What Is Jesus Doing?," 3n4.

20. It is a common tendency among Reformed and Lutherans to accuse each other of Nestorianism and Eutychianism, respectively. Stephen R. Holmes sheds light on this debate when he writes, "Both Reformed and Lutherans mapped their Christological

pneumatology, and preaching, all of which are related to his exposition on the ascension, deserve independent attention. A sustained focus on each of these areas would stretch the existing work to unmanageable proportions and therefore will not be attempted in this study. Methodological approaches, for instance, Torrance's hermeneutics and use of historical and theological sources, will not be scrutinized in this study, since the focus is on the material content of his doctrine of the ascension, not on his sources or on the hermeneutical approaches that led to his conclusions per se. Since this work centers on Torrance's dogmatic theology, it is beyond the scope of this study to explore the implications from this research to the theology and science discourse. Similarly, apart from tangentially highlighting areas for further dialogue between Torrance's doctrine of the ascension and Christian theology in India, this work will not explore this aspect in detail. These and other issues, however, are areas for fruitful study; while they are beyond the focus of this research, hopefully they will be informed by the present study. The groundwork for such a dialogue is being laid elsewhere.[21]

## 2. THEOLOGY OF THE ASCENSION & REFORMED THEOLOGY

Second, specifically with respect to Reformed theology, Torrance's doctrine of the ascension can serve as a key theological interlocutor within contemporary debates taking place in the tradition on important adjoining loci, such as the beatific vision.[22] In a recent essay for the *Oxford Handbook of Reformed Theology*, Christopher R. J. Holmes avers that Reformed Theology

---

disputes onto the famous patristic debate between Alexandria and Antioch, and the opposing heresies it gave rise to. The mapping was done differently by each side, with the Reformed identifying themselves with the tradition declared orthodox at Chalcedon, and insisting that the Lutherans were Eutychians; and the Lutherans, by contrast, claiming that the Reformed were Nestorian and that they themselves were in fact the heirs of Chalcedon." For more, see Holmes, "Reformed Varieties," 71. This study will not attempt to resolve the historical debate between these two theological traditions that dates to the sixteenth and seventeenth centuries and has continued ever since.

21. Cf. John, "Torrance and Global Evangelicalism."

22. The debate about the beatific vision in contemporary Reformed theology focuses on whether Christ in the eschaton will mediate the vision of God, or whether human beings will be enabled to see God directly. Some contend that the beatific vision will be mediated through Christ, while others argue that Christ's mediation will no longer be necessary, and still others aver that Christ will mediate the beatific vision, but the central focus of this vision will be, not Christ, but the Triune God. Cf. McDonald, "Beholding the Glory"; Strobel, "Jonathan Edwards' Reformed Doctrine"; Gaine, "Thomas Aquinas"; Ortlund, "Will We See."

would benefit from "more thinking . . . in the area of the beatific vision."[23] Torrance's theology of the ascension will be helpful in this endeavor for three main reasons.

Firstly, Torrance is a Reformed[24] theologian par-excellence and therefore can effectively speak to the tradition and offer constructive insights.[25] Secondly, he is a dogmatic theologian, who is not limited to only one theological tradition, and therefore will be able to offer rich insights from the breadth of Christian tradition to Reformed theology. On the one hand, he acknowledges a "great indebtedness" to Reformed theological forbears such as John Calvin, and "to a lesser but significant extent to the Scottish Reformers, John Knox, John Craig, and Robert Bruce, and to the Swiss Reformed theologian, Karl Barth"; but on the other hand, Torrance "also makes considerable appeal to other major figures such as the Greek fathers, St. Cyril of Alexandria and St. Athanasius . . . and also the great mediaeval theologians, St. Anselm . . . and John Duns Scotus."[26] Myk Habets rightly describes Torrance's perspective on Reformed theology as "catholic, broad, and generous,"[27] and it is this aspect that will serve the Reformed tradition in good stead.[28] Thirdly, and most importantly, while Torrance does not answer all the questions about the beatific vision, nor does he offer a substantial exposition on the theme, what he does provide is a consistent Christocentric account, which will serve the Reformed theological tradition well, especially in light of the challenge posed by alternative views, such as the Thomistic account.[29]

Torrance's Christocentric account of the beatific vision is clearly evidenced when he proclaims:

---

23. Holmes, "Last Things," 619.

24. Torrance's Reformed theological thinking can be gleaned from the following sample of his books and articles on the subject: *Calvin's Doctrine of Man*; *Kingdom and Church*; "Deposit of Faith"; "'Substance of Faith'"; "Distinctive Character."

25. Torrance's Reformed theological credentials are widely acknowledged in theological scholarship. Theologians such as Robert J. Palma, Alasdair Heron, and Myk Habets, respectively, provide the following descriptions: (1) it is "clearly situated within the Reformed tradition"; (2) it is "a major representative of that [Reformed] tradition"; and (3) it "is thoroughly and self-consciously Reformed." For more, see Palma, "Thomas F. Torrance's Reformed Theology," 2; Heron, "T. F. Torrance," 31; Habets, *Theology in Transposition*, 18.

26. Palma, "Thomas F. Torrance's Reformed Theology," 2.

27. Habets, *Theology in Transposition*, 19.

28. Torrance is not unique in holding to a theology that is both Reformed and Catholic. Two contemporary works of kindred spirit are Allen and Swain's *Reformed Catholicity* and *Christian Dogmatics*.

29. For Torrance's Christocentric interpretation of the beatific vision, see Torrance, *Apocalypse Today*, 183.

> Certainly it is true that the great reward of all who serve Him here is that they shall ever serve Him there, and see His face, and become like Him. He who has seen Christ, has seen the Father, and that vision more than suffices him. The Father whom we shall see yonder is none other than Him whom we see in Jesus. Yonder we shall see Him in a fullness of vision which is denied to us here, but it will ever be God as revealed to us in Jesus and no other for there is no other. In the heart of transcendent Deity there will still be One like unto the Son of Man, and the light in which we shall see Him will ever be the light of the Lamb.[30]

It is hard to miss the centrality of Christ's mediation of the beatific vision in Torrance's account. In this regard, Torrance can be said to align with theologians such as John Owen who arguably revised the Thomistic account on the beatific vision.[31]

At the core of the debate between Thomists and revisionists, such as John Owen, on the beatific vision is whether the center of this vision at the eschaton will be "the divine essence" or "Christ."[32] In other words, on the one hand there is what can be called a "theocentric" account, where there is an emphasis on "seeing the divine essence," and on the other hand, there is a "Christological" account, wherein there will be a vision of "God in and through Jesus Christ."[33] Torrance's alignment with the revisionist tradition espoused by John Owen is clear, not least because both share a strong Christocentric emphasis. However, Torrance's relevance for the ongoing discussion within contemporary Reformed theology on the beatific vision needs to be underscored.

Torrance's account of the beatific vision is arguably "more consistently christological" than the great Reformer John Calvin's account.[34] It is this claim that highlights the relevance of Torrance for contemporary discussion within the Reformed tradition on this important subject. Calvin's reading

---

30. Torrance, *Apocalypse Today*, 183.

31. For a supporting argument, see Boersma, *Seeing God*, 325; Boersma, "Thomas Aquinas," 139; McDonald, "Beholding the Glory," 144–47. For a contrary account wherein Owen is said to revise not Aquinas, but John Calvin's deficiencies in his theology of the beatific vision, see Gaine, "Beatific Vision," 127–28.

32. Boersma, "Neo-Calvinism," 27.

33. Boersma, "Neo-Calvinism," 27.

34. Boersma, *Seeing God*, 277. To be sure, in this reference, Boersma argues that theologians such as Isaac Ambrose, Thomas Watson, John Owen, and Jonathan Edwards articulate a Christocentric account that far outshines Calvin's account. One can arguably include Torrance in this list as well, because he, too, has a consistent Christocentric emphasis in his theology of the beatific vision.

of the beatific vision is arguably more Thomistic than Reformed.[35] This is evidenced in the way Calvin reads 1 Cor 15:24 ("Christ will deliver the Kingdom to his God and Father") to mean that Christ will divest himself of "the office of Mediator," consequently enabling a vision of God at the eschaton that is not mediated by Christ.[36] In other words, for Calvin, the beatific vision will be "the direct vision of the Godhead," or a "face to face" vision of God.[37] Calvin sheds further light on what he means in his commentary on 1 Cor:

> Christ will then hand back the Kingdom which He has received, so that we may cleave completely to God. This does not mean that He will abdicate from the Kingdom in this way, but will transfer it in some way or other ... from His humanity to His glorious divinity, because then there will open up for us a way of approach, from which we are now kept back by our weakness. In this way, therefore, Christ will be subjected to the Father, because, when the veil has been removed, we will see God plainly, reigning in His majesty, and the humanity of Christ will no longer be in between us to hold us back from a nearer vision of God.[38]

Calvin scholars have been perplexed about how to interpret him at this point, which the section below will briefly highlight.

According to J. F. Jansen, there are three strands of interpretation on this point in the secondary literature: (1) "Those who affirm that for Calvin the humanity [of Christ] will cease," (2) "Those who see this implied but who leave the question somewhat open," and (3) "Those who deny this is Calvin's position."[39] While a detailed analysis of the various interpretive

---

35. Cf. Boersma, "Neo-Calvinism," 27, 28, respectively, where he clarifies (1) that "it is beyond question that Calvin, along with the Western tradition since the high Middle Ages, believed we will one day see the divine majesty or essence"; and (2) that invariably "Reformed" views on the beatific vision are "often Christocentric." Therefore, there is good warrant to state that Calvin is more Thomistic than he is Reformed on the beatific vision. To be sure, there are others like Francis Turretin in the Reformed tradition, whose views also seemingly align more with Thomists on the beatific vision. For more, see Ortlund, "Will We See," 328, where he rightly states that Turretin agrees "that the object of the vision is God's essence," but also observes that "he [Turretin] is more cautious on this point." Ortlund, however, goes on to underscore on p. 328 that Turretin does not "envision Christ as the object of the vision." For more, see Turretin, *Institutes of Elenctic Theology*, 20.8.6, 8, 14 (cited by topic, question, and section numbers, respectively).

36. Calvin, *Institutes* 2.14.3.

37. Calvin, *Institutes* 2.14.3.

38. Calvin, *First Epistle*, 327.

39. See Jansen, "1 Cor. 15.24–28," 556n24, where he lists theologians such as E.

possibilities in Calvin is beyond the scope of this work, theologians such as J. Todd Billings acknowledge that the great Reformer is "ambiguous" on this point in his theology.[40] Others, such as Brannon Ellis, note that "Calvin was not always consistent in his treatment of the incarnational mediation of the *visio Dei*."[41] Myk Habets underscores what he believes is a serious flaw in Calvin's theology at this point: "Calvin's suggestion that Christ's humanity will cease to be the locus of mediation in the *eschaton* . . . that Christ's humanity endures but we know not how or even why, and that humanity will see God and participate in God, but not in any christological way are all highly problematic aspects of his theology."[42] Hans Boersma is more sympathetic, but even he acknowledges that "it is hard to escape the conclusion that for Calvin, the humanity of Christ fails to have a meaningful role in the eschaton."[43]

Calvin, who is otherwise known to espouse a robust theology of the humanity of Christ, not least its corporeality, seems to undermine this very aspect when it comes to his discussion on the beatific vision.[44] To be sure, in other places in his corpus, Calvin does emphasize the need for the resurrection of the body in order to experience the "full *visio Dei*."[45] Therefore, along with Billings, one can reasonably state that "there is, at the very least, tension here with other parts of Calvin's thought."[46] Arguably, there is also an inconsistency in Calvin's theology at this point, which is why there is a need to highlight Reformed theologians, such as Torrance and others, who articulate a consistent Christocentric account with respect to both the ascension and the beatific vision. Such an account is even more pressing considering some contemporary debates with Reformed theology.

---

Emmem, F. W. A. Korff, and A. A. van Ruler to represent the first position, and theologians H. Quistorp and Jürgen Moltmann are said to represent the second position, while G. Berkouwer and E. David Willis are presented as representatives of the third position.

40. Billings, *Union with Christ*, 84.

41. Ellis, *Calvin*, 218n55.

42. Habets, Review of *Holy Spirit as Bond*, 242–43.

43. Boersma, *Seeing God*, 277–78. For a view that argues that Calvin does not undermine the humanity of Christ in the eschaton, see Muller, "Christ in the Eschaton."

44. Compare Calvin, *Institutes* 4.17.26 with 2.14.3 and *First Epistle*, 327.

45. See Tyra, "'Neither the Spirit,'" 180. On p. 180n55, Tyra argues that readers of Calvin's work need to interact with "the *Psychopannychia* and later biblical commentaries" to develop a well-rounded theology of the resurrection of the body and the beatific vision in Calvin's theology.

46. Billings, *Union with Christ*, 83, where he highlights a "tension" between Calvin's overall theology wherein Christ mediates God to humanity and the beatific vision which does not have any role for the mediation of Christ.

Contemporary Reformed theologians such as Michael Allen and Hans Boersma correctly note that the beatific vision is neglected in theology, and therefore through their work, they seek to redress this gap.[47] One aspect that is central to their redressal is a critique of what Allen calls "eschatological naturalism," which basically contends that theologians such as N. T. Wright and Richard Middleton, in particular, are guilty of articulating "the earthy nature of the Christian hope," while neglecting "the spiritual or heavenly reality of our hope."[48] Allen clarifies that his usage of "eschatological naturalism" is a very focused critique of a shortcoming in certain eschatologies, and is not to be read as an overarching assessment of the respective theologies.[49] Specifically, he explains: "With regard to the *telos* or end of our hope, a significant strand of modern theology . . . has articulated that hope in a naturalistic or materialistic manner."[50]

N. T. Wright takes strong objection to Allen's critique by insisting that the latter "simply caricatures" his work.[51] Specifically, Wright contends that the "new-creational eschatology is indeed both biblical and 'centred upon God,'" and furthermore that "Allen uses the rhetoric of 'spiritual' or 'heavenly' to avoid even facing the strong biblical points that I and others have advanced; and his case can in principle be countered by actual biblical exegesis on every front."[52] Middleton's response to Allen is more congenial but even he finds Allen's critique unwarranted when he notes: "I simply do not recognize myself in some of his characterizations of my position."[53] The debate between Allen (along with Boersma) and N. T. Wright (along with Middleton) and others associated with each of the views is far from over.

One could position this as a debate between spiritualist and physicalist eschatologies, but this would be far from accurate, because neither is undermining either physicality or spirituality.[54] However, it is clear that both sides

---

47. Cf. Allen, *Grounded in Heaven*; Allen, "Visibility of the Invisible God"; Allen, "On Bavinck"; Boersma, *Seeing God*.

48. Allen, *Grounded in Heaven*, 7. For more, see the section "On Eschatological Naturalism" (pp. 3–8).

49. Allen, *Grounded in Heaven*, 7.

50. Allen, *Grounded in Heaven*, 7. Cf. Billings, "New View," para. 11, where he finds fault with Wright and Middleton's overemphasis on continuity between creation and new creation. To this end, Billings worries that "such an approach does not generate a cosmic view of God's work in restoring the whole creation (as they [Wright and Middleton] desire), but small, individualized versions of paradise."

51. Wright, "Reconciling the World?," 215.

52. Wright, "Reconciling the World?," 215.

53. Middleton, "Response to Michael Allen," 142n1.

54. Cf. Allen, "Heaven on Earth Perspective," 115–35; Boersma, *Seeing God*, 409–29; Middleton, "Response to Michael Allen," 145–47; Wright, "Reconciling the World?," 215.

of the debate within Reformed theology on the beatific vision would do well to take stock of the nuances of the debate to take the discussion forward in helpful ways.[55] Torrance would be a helpful dialogue partner within the contemporary debate on the beatific vision. Not only does he robustly affirm a redeemed physicality and materiality in his theology of new creation,[56] but he also articulates an "eschatological reserve,"[57] and is reticent in providing too many details about the new creation.[58] Both of these aspects would endear Torrance to proponents of both sides of the divide on this debate within Reformed theology. In contemporary theological debates, Torrance's theology has provided mediating views on some complex issues,[59] so as Reformed theologians continue to debate the specifics of the beatific vision, his theology promises to be a helpful resource that should be critically engaged within the tradition.

A detailed study on the relationship between the ascension and the beatific vision is beyond the scope of this work, but Torrance's theology of the ascension will set the stage for further works that seek to discern the intricate areas in which both doctrines are interconnected. The ascension in Torrance's theology will be the focus of this work, but as the above section has demonstrated, Reformed theology will do well to interact with his theology even in adjoining theological debates such as the beatific vision.

## 3. METHODOLOGY

Torrance's theology of the ascension will be expounded in a manner that is *scientific*, or in other words, that stays true to his own theological impulses. This method can be best described as a work in *constructive dogmatics*, where the goal will be to discover Torrance's theological contribution to the

---

55. One such nuance is whether gender will be retained in the eschaton. Boersma, for instance, is seemingly sympathetic to Gregory of Nyssa's view that in the eschaton there will be "a transformation that will involve the loss of gender, but emphatically not of the body." In other words, this is an eschatological vision of a gender-free human existence. For more, see Boersma, *Seeing God*, 426, 428. Since the debate within the Reformed tradition on the beatific vision is ongoing, it would be helpful for all participants to clearly articulate the details of their views on the beatific vision vis-à-vis gender. Cf. Vale, "Gender Identity," 24–46, for a view that argues that gender will remain even in the eschaton, albeit in its redeemed form.

56. Cf. Torrance, *Apocalypse Today*, 176–77.

57. Torrance, *Space, Time, and Resurrection*, 152, 156, 157.

58. Torrance, *Apocalypse Today*, 176. Cf. MacLean, *Resurrection*, 200.

59. One example is the debate on the *fallen* or *unfallen* humanity of Christ. For the unique mediating view Torrance provides to this debate, see Crisp, "On the Vicarious Humanity," 238.

three loci (ontology, spatiality, and present ministry) and discern ways of constructing his theology in dialogue with contemporary theological interlocutors, with the express goal of clarifying, developing, or refining certain aspects of Torrance's theology.[60] Torrance's work *Space, Time, and Resurrection* will be used as the basis to understand his mature theology of the ascension, supplementing it at various points with keen insights from his wider theological corpus. The goal of this work is to provide a *systematic* and *constructive* study of Torrance's theology of the ascension, not a survey of how his ideas developed over time.

## 4. OVERVIEW OF CHAPTERS

Chapter 2 situates Torrance's theology more generally in the theological landscape and will highlight his distinctive contributions to the locus of the ascension. Most importantly, it will provide important orienting themes that will help one to read his significant contributions to the study of Jesus's ascension. Chapter 3 critically explores Torrance's understanding of Christ's *ontology*, in relation to his theology of the ascension. In chapter 4, Torrance's understanding of Christ's *spatiality* will be examined, in relation to the ascension of Christ. We will then in chapter 5 discern the ways in which the ascended Christ carries out his present ministry on earth vis-à-vis the ascension in Torrance's thought. Chapter 6 studies Torrance's ascension theology by addressing nine criticisms. Such an engagement offers areas for refinement and further development of themes that are underdeveloped in Torrance's theology of the ascension. The conclusion summarizes the study and offers areas for further research.

## 5. CONCLUSION

This chapter has focused on the promise of engaging Torrance's theology of the ascension in a twofold context; first, the underemphasis of the ascension in theological scholarship, specifically in Torrance studies; and second, the potential of Torrance's theology for meaningful dialogue within the Reformed theological tradition on an adjoining theological locus, such as the beatific vision. While a detailed focus on the interrelationship between the

---

60. See two forthcoming essays by me on Torrance's theology of the Ascension, subtitled: "Constructive Theological Masterpiece?" and "Theological Dogmatic Sketch." The first work explores the "constructive" nature of Torrance's theology of the ascension, and second one focuses on the "practical theological" import of his doctrine of the ascension.

ascension and the beatific vision was stated to be beyond the scope of this work, it was shown that Torrance's theology offers promise in addressing both theological loci. Nonetheless, both these aspects were highlighted as key reasons for a book-length work on the ascension in Torrance's thought. While Torrance's views are not without their own set of problems, since his account of the ascension communicates the vast scope of the doctrine, it was reasoned that it would be important to critically interact with it. This chapter laid the groundwork for a detailed exposition of the doctrine of the ascension in the theology of Thomas F. Torrance. The next chapter will introduce Torrance's theology and provide an orientation to his theology of the ascension.

# 2

# Introducing T. F. Torrance's Theology of the Ascension

## 1. INTRODUCTION

MANY HAVE FOUND IT hard not to write about Thomas F. Torrance in a hagiographical way.¹ And for good reason. His life was impressive; the body of literature he left behind is breathtaking in scope,² even if not always systematically presented;³ his accolades are diverse,⁴ and he was recognized

---

1. Daniel Hardy's assessment of much of Torrance scholarship is that it is too "descriptive and analytical"; and he goes on to mention that many scholars "do not challenge his ways and conclusions; only a few go further to probe and challenge his work." The goal of this work, nevertheless, is to be critical and constructive, as well as provide commendation where it is due. For more, see Hardy, "T. F. Torrance," 176.

2. Alister McGrath has identified a total of 610 works that Torrance produced. For more, see McGrath, *Thomas F. Torrance*, xi. Hardy summarizes Torrance's breadth of scholarship: "From God in Christ to God's work in the natural world, from the engagement of orthodoxy with philosophy and the sciences in different eras, from those supportive of Reformed Christianity in ecumenical encounter to those—the greatest number—developing the place of theology among the sciences." For more, see Hardy, "T. F. Torrance," 165.

3. Cf. Hardy, "T. F. Torrance," 165; Habets, *Theology in Transposition*, 26; Colyer, *How to Read*, 15–16.

4. Apart from his significant contribution to the theology and science discourse, Torrance also was at the forefront of ecumenical dialogues with the Orthodox and Roman Catholic Churches on the doctrine of the Trinity; he was also appointed an MBE (Member of the British Empire) for the bravery he displayed as a chaplain in World War II; he was also the Moderator of the General Assembly of the Church of Scotland from 1976–77.

worthy of the highest honors.[5] What is most impressive about Torrance was his faithful Christian discipleship.[6] There is a richness to his theology that inspires those who study it to worship God.[7] Torrance would have welcomed such an assessment, because when he was asked what the central focus of his theology was, he said, "I would claim that it is deeply Nicene and doxological (theology and worship going inextricably together), with its immediate focus on Jesus Christ as Mediator, and its ultimate focus on the Holy Trinity."[8] While for many, Torrance's major accomplishment is his contribution to the theology and science discourse,[9] what stands out the most is his ability to seamlessly integrate *theology* and *doxology*. Many have written eloquent introductions to Torrance the man and his theology, therefore it is not necessary here to repeat what is already common knowledge.[10]

Torrance will be introduced in a way that sheds light on his doctrine of the ascension. Section one of the chapter will focus on introducing Torrance's major theological convictions, contributions, and themes, with the express goal of shedding light on his theology of the ascension. Section two will provide seven orienting themes that will aid in reading Torrance's unique contributions to the doctrine of the ascension. Both sections will lay the foundation for a deeper engagement with three aspects of the ascension in Torrance—the ontology, spatiality, and present ministry of the ascended Christ in the chapters to follow.

## 2. THE THEOLOGIAN THOMAS F. TORRANCE

Regarding Torrance's theology of the ascension, David Fergusson writes, "It registers the impact of both local and ecumenical influences on his work; it expresses his commitment both to Christian dogmatics and theological science; and finally it enables us to identify not only his indebtedness to Karl Barth but also one of his two most critical departures from Barth's theology."[11] Later, Fergusson underscores the centrality of the devotional aspects of Torrance's theology of the ascension: "Torrance particularly stresses the

---

5. In 1978, Torrance was awarded the Templeton Foundation Prize for Progress in Religion.
6. Cf. McGrath, *Thomas F. Torrance*, 13.
7. Cf. Colyer, *How to Read*, 18.
8. Kernohan, "Tom Torrance," 14.
9. Cf. McGrath, *Thomas F. Torrance*, xi.
10. Cf. McGrath, *Thomas F. Torrance*, 3–110; Colyer, *How to Read*, 35–54; Molnar, *Thomas F. Torrance*, 1–30; Habets, *Theology in Transposition*, 7–26.
11. Fergusson, "Ascension of Christ," 93.

liturgical and sacramental significance of the ascension."[12] Joseph Sherrard in a more recent work interacts with the missional thrust of Torrance's theology vis-à-vis the ascension.[13] Therefore, in what follows, Torrance's theological convictions will be introduced by highlighting his ecumenical commitments, his resolve to engage in a *scientific* theology, the influence of Karl Barth on his theology, his commitment to pursue a theology that is transformative in nature, and the missionary nature of all his theological endeavors.

## 2.1 Theological Convictions

### 2.1.1 *Ecumenical Theology*

Torrance engaged in sustained ecumenical efforts with the Roman Catholic, Anglican, and Orthodox Communions.[14] All of these ecumenical efforts were grounded in a deeply Trinitarian theology: "Yet the more deeply we press into the material centre of the Church's faith in Christ and in the Holy Trinity, the greater is the pressure disposing us to reach agreement with one another."[15] Torrance worked hard to see various churches unite over the core Christian doctrines, and to this end he participated in several forums organized by the World Council of Churches:

> He attended the Faith and Order Conference in Lund, Sweden, in 1952 and served on the Faith and Order Commission from 1952 to 1962. Between 1950 and 1958 Torrance participated in the conversations between the Church of Scotland and the Anglican Church. Torrance was also involved in the 1954 meetings of the World Council of Churches in Evanston, Illinois; the Faith and Order Commission in Chicago, Illinois; and the World Alliance of Reformed Churches in Princeton, New Jersey.[16]

While Torrance's Trinitarian theological convictions undergirded his ecumenical initiatives, his family background also sheds important light on his ardent ecumenical efforts. Colyer calls it an "embodied ecumenicity," a phrase he uses to describe the Torrance family's longstanding commitment to an ecumenical spirit not just in the church, but also in their own

---

12. Fergusson, "Ascension of Christ," 95–96.
13. Cf. Sherrard, *T. F. Torrance*.
14. Cf. Colyer, *How to Read*, 46–47.
15. Torrance, *Theology in Reconciliation*, 9.
16. Colyer, *How to Read*, 46.

home.[17] While family members were a part of the Church of Scotland and the Church of England, Torrance notes that his mother, an Anglican, "was a member of the Church of Scotland" for a long time; the same was true of Torrance's own wife who, he notes, had membership in both churches.[18] These family connections to ecumenicity fueled Torrance and his wife "to be really ecumenical in living out the relations between the two churches."[19] The ecumenical pursuit in Torrance can also be attributed to his desire to be a theologian doing theology in "the spirit of the Reformation."[20] Jason Radcliff presciently notes that "Torrance reminds us that Protestants faithful to the Reformation should regularly work towards rapprochement with the other two wings of the One, Holy, Catholic, and Apostolic Church: Roman Catholicism and Eastern Orthodoxy."[21] Radcliff declares that if Protestants do not engage in such efforts, then the whole point of the Reformation will be nullified, since it never intended to start a separate church, but to be "a prophetic movement of reform within it."[22] Failing to accomplish such a task, namely, to work "for reform and rapprochement," ends up giving up all that one holds dear—"we cease to follow the Reformers."[23] Torrance's ecumenical efforts, among many other accomplishments, shows how he was a theologian for whom theology and the practice of it were not disparate realms, and Ray Anderson's commendation of Torrance as a "practical theologian par excellence" is well-deserved praise.[24]

### 2.1.2 Scientific Theology

For Torrance, the notion of "scientific theology" had implications for the study of theology and for theological engagement with science.[25] It is the former that this work is interested in; while the latter is also important, it

---

17. Colyer, *How to Read*, 47.
18. Hesselink, "Pilgrimage," 50.
19. Hesselink, "Pilgrimage," 50.
20. Radcliff, *Thomas F. Torrance*, x.
21. Radcliff, *Thomas F. Torrance*, x.
22. Radcliff, *Thomas F. Torrance*, x.
23. Radcliff, *Thomas F. Torrance*, x.

24. Anderson, "Reading T. F. Torrance," 162. On the same page Anderson goes on to explain what he means by practical theology: "Theology is not simply something to be known; theology is something which is lived and experienced by a particular community."

25. Cf. Habets, *Theology in Transposition*, 27–65.

will not be elaborated upon since this work focuses on Torrance's dogmatic thought.[26] He defined "scientific theology" as follows:

> Scientific theology is active engagement in that cognitive relation to God in obedience to the demands of His reality and self-giving. In it we probe into the problematic condition of the human mind before God and seek to bring knowledge of Him into clear focus, so that the truth of God may shine through to it unhindered by its opacity and the human mind may acquire clear and orderly forms through which to apprehend and conceive His reality. That is to say, we seek to allow God's own eloquent self-evidence to sound through to us in His Logos so that we may know and understand Him out of His own rationality and under the determination of His divine being.[27]

As is evidenced in Torrance's explanation, God sets the terms in which he can be known, and he also sets the methods by which he is to be known. Humans do not set the agenda, but are to be obedient recipients of God's revelation. This way of doing theology was not popular in Torrance's day.[28] In fact, lest one misunderstand what Torrance means by "scientific theology," it is important to underscore what he does not mean by it, as Colyer does here:

> A theology is scientific *not* when it conforms to the presuppositions or procedures of a universal science (there is no universal science in Torrance's perspective), or even of other special sciences (*scientiae speciales*) such as natural science. Rather, in Torrance's mind, theological science, like every special science, *has its own particular requirements and material procedures determined by the unique nature of its object or subject matter.*[29]

In other words, for Torrance there are multiple "scientific" approaches, and not just one; in fact, each discipline can have a "scientific" way of studying it.[30] Therefore, it is important to make a distinction between Torrance's usage of "scientific theology," and the common field of interdisciplinary discourse of "science and theology" on the one hand, and various approaches

---

26. It is common in Torrance scholarship to broadly divide his work into two main categories: his theology and science discussions, and his dogmatic expositions. Cf. Chiarot, *Unassumed Is the Unhealed*, 2.

27. Torrance, *Theological Science*, ix.

28. Webster, "Thomas Forsyth Torrance," 429. Cf. Hardy, "T. F. Torrance," 175.

29. Colyer, *How to Read*, 22.

30. Colyer, *How to Read*, 22.

that believe that a "scientific" approach to a study must conform to "universal" scientific norms.

Were one to do a genealogy of the influences that shaped Torrance's "scientific theology," one would have to divide this list into those that planted seeds of this thought, others that showed how *not* to do it, still others that demonstrated how it could be done but with some necessary modifications, and a few more that provided scientific language that was in consonance with the theological foundation that Torrance was building his project on. Luminaries, such as Daniel Lamont, an early influence on Torrance, showed him what was possible in terms of a robust engagement with theology and science.[31] Therefore, Torrance had theological resources from early on in his career to think of theology and science as friends, not enemies at *war* with each other.[32] Schleiermacher, on the other hand, showed Torrance an example of a "scientific theology," but only in "form" not in "content": "I was captivated by the architectonic form and beauty of Schleiermacher's method and his arrangement of dogmatics into a scientific system of Christian doctrine, but it was clear to me that the whole conception was wrong, for due to its fundamental presuppositions Schleiermacher's approach did not match up to the nature or content of the Christian Gospel."[33] Exposure to Schleiermacher's theology, however, did strengthen Torrance's resolve to produce a theology that was truly scientific in both form and content.[34] To help him with this task, he found in Augustine a good role model, but not a perfect one, as he found "powerful Neoplatonic ingredients" in Augustine that were guiding his thinking, and this for Torrance was unacceptable.[35]

### 2.1.3 Karl Barth's Theology

The pursuit of a *scientific theology* continued for Torrance through readings in Barth's *Church Dogmatics*, which led eventually to doctoral studies under Barth himself.[36] Torrance initially suggested as a PhD topic: "a scientific account of Christian dogmatics from its Christological and soteriological centre and in light of its constitutive trinitarian structure," which Barth declined because he thought it "was too ambitious . . . to undertake at that

---

31. Cf. McGrath, *Thomas F. Torrance*, 33–34.
32. Cf. McGrath, *Thomas F. Torrance*, 199–203.
33. Torrance, *Karl Barth: Theologian*, 121.
34. Torrance, *Karl Barth: Theologian*, 121–22.
35. Torrance, *Karl Barth: Theologian*, 122.
36. Torrance, *Karl Barth: Theologian*, 123.

stage!"[37] Even though Torrance's eventual doctoral thesis focused on "The Doctrine of Grace in the Apostolic Fathers,"[38] one can argue that the pursuit of a "scientific theology" never left Torrance's mind, so much so that a case can be made that "Torrance's theological programme represents precisely such an exploration and application of the scientific nature of theology."[39] To be sure, Torrance and Barth did not see eye to eye on the specifics of the scientific theological enterprise,[40] but what Torrance did glean from Barth were the key essentials that were for him missing in all other so-called "scientific" theologies, namely, the "Trinitarian 'ground and grammar,' the self-revelation of God and the crucial role of the incarnation in this self-revelation of the triune God."[41] Therefore, it is important to note that Barth's theology had a significant impact on Torrance, but with Alister McGrath and others one must also acknowledge that "it is quite improper" to declare Torrance an "uncritical" expositor of Barth's theology.[42] Furthermore, while scholarship tends to rightly focus on Barth's impact on Torrance, it is also important to note the significant role Torrance played through his work on the translation of *Church Dogmatics* from German to English on Barth studies.[43] Torrance was "a major figure in relation to English-language Barth-reception" and must be given the credit he deserves for the lasting impact on theology he has made along with others who worked with him in translating and critically engaging with Barth's theology in the English speaking contexts.[44]

### 2.1.4 Transformative Theology

Torrance was "'pastorally academic.'"[45] The critique of being an *armchair* theologian would certainly not apply to him. Before teaching theology, he served for a whole decade in pastoral ministry, out of which two years were dedicated to serving as a chaplain with the army; these experiences, both in the parish and out on the battlefield facing extreme danger, were formative because they "reinforced the need for complete harmony between theology,

   37. Torrance, *Karl Barth: Theologian*, 123.
   38. Torrance, *Karl Barth: Theologian*, 124.
   39. McGrath, *Thomas F. Torrance*, 112.
   40. Cf. Molnar, *Thomas F. Torrance*, 94.
   41. Habets, *Theology in Transposition*, 28.
   42. McGrath, *Thomas F. Torrance*, 117.
   43. Cf. McGrath, *Thomas F. Torrance*, 113–45.
   44. McGrath, *T. F. Torrance*, 117.
   45. Habets, *Theology in Transposition*, 25.

# INTRODUCING T. F. TORRANCE'S THEOLOGY OF THE ASCENSION

preaching, and daily life."[46] When theology failed to be true to the Bible, to "evangelical" convictions, to the range of life experiences, especially circumstances like death and despair, Torrance, according to his brother David W. Torrance, labelled it "'paper theology.'"[47] As such, Torrance placed a great premium on maintaining that "theology must be tested and born [sic] out in the Christian life."[48] Experiences in practical ministry exposed him to the burning questions of people, such as "is God really like Jesus?"[49]—and this question in particular, one could argue, Torrance spent the rest of his theological career seeking to answer.[50] Critics of Torrance's theology claim that he neglected ethics and focused primarily on God's relationship with human beings. While there is some merit in this criticism, recent works on Torrance are seeking to redress such a reading of his theology, and chapter 6 of this work will engage with this aspect in detail.

### 2.1.5 Missionary Theology

At the core of Torrance's theological convictions, one could argue, was a missionary impulse.[51] Even though he did not go to Tibet as he had originally planned,[52] he saw his work in the academy as a missionary one.[53] His missionary parents impacted his life greatly and among many other qualities "bequeathed to Torrance a permanently missionary attitude and vocation."[54] Throughout the course of his life Torrance did not shy away from his missionary upbringing, nor from his conviction that people and whole systems of thought need to be evangelized with the gospel.[55] Torrance self-consciously saw his "theological work as a form of missionary activity,"[56]

---

46. D. W. Torrance, "Thomas Forsyth Torrance," 17.
47. D. W. Torrance, "Thomas Forsyth Torrance," 17.
48. D. W. Torrance, "Thomas Forsyth Torrance," 13.
49. McGrath, *Thomas F. Torrance*, 74.
50. Munchin, *Is Theology a Science?*, x.
51. Hesselink, "Pilgrimage," 49. Cf. Colyer, *How to Read*, 51: "I view Thomas F. Torrance as an evangelical missionary who became a theologian without ever ceasing to be an evangelist." Cf. Torrance, "Thomas Torrance Responds," 304.
52. Hesselink, "Pilgrimage," 49.
53. Hesselink, "Pilgrimage," 60.
54. Webster, "Thomas Forsyth Torrance," 418.
55. Cf. Stein, "Editor's Introduction," 2.
56. Torrance, "Thomas Torrance Responds," 304.

and one that was mainly concerned "to help evangelize the foundations of modern scientific culture."[57]

Each of these five theological convictions—ecumenical, scientific, the influence of Karl Barth, transformative, and missionary— shows how Torrance's theology is multifaceted and informed at many points by his own biography, but deeply interested in knowing God according to the way in which he believed God wants himself to be known. These five theological convictions also anticipate theological emphases in Torrance's theology of the ascension. In the next subsection, Torrance's main contributions to theology will be considered vis-à-vis their relation to the doctrine of the ascension in his theology.

## 2.2 Main Contributions to Theology

Torrance's contribution to theology is manifold. Five main kinds of contribution, however, serve to introduce the way he expounds his theology of the ascension. Torrance develops his whole theology in a *scientific* manner, and no introduction to Torrance's theology will be complete without a reference to this methodological starting point. Theology is always profound and intended to lead one to worship God as Father, Son, and Holy Spirit; in other words, theology for Torrance is always wedded to *doxology*. The apophatic nature of certain parts of Torrance's theology are not as emphasized in Torrance scholarship, and therefore, one of the unique contributions of this whole project is to bring to the forefront a neglected but important theme, namely, Torrance's rhetoric on the ascension. The constructive nature of Torrance's whole theological edifice is important, as it also shapes the intended goal of this work. The missionary nature of Torrance's whole theology promises to shed keen insights on the application of the theme of ascension in his theology. In other words, the ascension is a doctrine that beckons one to proclaim and indeed respond to the gospel of the risen and ascended Lord, who will come again to rule and to reign over the whole world.

### 2.2.1 Theology as Science

Torrance's scientific theology emphasizes a thoroughgoing dependence on God to know God's revelation in a manner that is in consonance with who God is and how he wants to be known. There are several places in his

---

57. Stein, "Editor's Introduction," 2.

theology of the ascension that are unexplored because Torrance believes that there is insufficient biblical revelation on those topics. Therefore, at points readers are frustrated that Torrance has not chosen a mode more adept to theological speculation on important questions, but he has provided sufficient seed ideas in those places for his readers to build on his theology. Theology as science in relation to the ascension entails following the biblical revelation and affirming truths that Scripture affirms—namely, that the ascension is a real event, that Jesus is in heaven at the right hand of God as a human with a body, that Jesus is presently king, who is interceding for his followers and the world, and who will return just as he went to heaven. There are aspects that Torrance affirms without going into details—for example, he does not give a detailed picture of the resurrected body, heaven, or the new heavens and the new earth. He does this because he believes he is being scientific in such an endeavor.[58]

## 2.2.2 *Theology as Doxology*

According to Torrance, all reality and truth is stratified, such that we can say there are, broadly speaking, three levels in the theologizing process, where the goal is to move from an experience of God to the ultimate truth about God via the way in which God has revealed himself in Jesus Christ.[59] The first level is called "*the evangelical and doxological level*" and is in the setting of personal encounter with Jesus at both individual and corporate worship that one first learns to do theology.[60] With the first level still intact, one moves onto the second level, "*the theological level*," wherein one focuses on knowing how God has revealed himself in Jesus Christ.[61] The third level builds on the first and second levels and is called the "*higher theological level*"; at this level, one probes deeper into the reality of God as Triune. This reality of God as Triune was always present in the first level, but it became clearer in the second level, and in the third much more pronounced.[62] These levels of theology are crucial for Torrance, as Colyer points out: "The Holy Trinity can only be known evangelically and doxologically, in a transformative encounter with the love of God through the grace of Christ and in the communion of the Holy Spirit which includes personal faith, thanksgiving,

---

58. Cf. MacLean, *Resurrection*, 200, for an explanation for why Torrance did not explore certain theological topics.

59. Torrance, *Christian Doctrine of God*, 88–111.

60. Torrance, *Christian Doctrine of God*, 88–91.

61. Torrance, *Christian Doctrine of God*, 91–98.

62. Torrance, *Christian Doctrine of God*, 98–107.

worship and prayer, first in the vicarious humanity of Christ and then in us."[63] Theology and doxology are integral aspects in the thought of Thomas F. Torrance.

### 2.2.3 Theology as Missionary Enterprise

Torrance's missional aim was no less than "to evangelize the foundations . . . of scientific culture, so that a dogmatics can take root in that kind of structure."[64] Aside from his missionary upbringing and influence which played a pivotal role in Torrance's formation, "from Hugh Ross Mackintosh Torrance learned the supreme importance of the centrality of Christ, the atonement and the missionary cause."[65] Much of Torrance's efforts were targeted at countering faulty conceptions of thinking, or in other words "he set himself the task of removing all *a priori* dualisms that have crept into contemporary theology."[66] Torrance's whole theological enterprise serves as a good missionary model, worthy of emulation. What must not be missed, and scholars will do well to note the same, is that "Torrance's missional biography needs to be considered not as distinct from, but integral to his theological output."[67] Torrance's missionary zeal never faded, and this is evidenced in the fact that even in the twilight of his career he carried on his missionary activity, which tellingly "provides a fitting reminder that he was, first and foremost, a theologian of the church and for the church."[68] Theology is, therefore, a missionary enterprise for Torrance.

### 2.2.4 Theology as Constructive Endeavor

George Hunsinger aptly notes that Torrance "generally placed himself somewhere between Calvin and Barth, though also moving well beyond them."[69] Elsewhere, Hunsinger importantly observes that "Torrance thought with Barth and through Barth, while also going beyond him and against him. Barth himself had more than one occasion to remark . . . Torrance shows

---

63. Colyer, *How to Read*, 287.
64. Hesselink, "Pilgrimage," 60.
65. Habets, *Theology in Transposition*, 11.
66. Habets, *Theology in Transposition*, 14.
67. Seed et al., "Thomas F. Torrance," 1.
68. Habets, *Theology in Transposition*, 17.
69. Hunsinger, "Foreword," xiii.

himself to be a true 'Barthian,' because Barth would have it no other way."[70] It is this insight that is crucial for this study. Torrance critically built on and extended on the works of other theologians, and many examples could be given on this point.[71] There are places in Torrance's theology that he provides unique insights that are especially helpful, but at times he does not fully develop these insights, and therefore in this work the goal will be to extend his theology by connecting the dots.[72]

### 2.2.5 Theology as Apophatic

One must be careful in describing Torrance's theology as "apophatic" because it is only a qualified point that he wishes to make.[73] Says Torrance,

> What I am concerned to emphasize in these references to the "mystical" is much the same point made by St. Anselm when he spoke of God as infinitely greater than we can ever conceive or express. And stated otherwise, echoing Job, that there are moments in his knowing of him and speaking of him and worshipping him, when a theologian can only clap his hand on his mouth, for what God is or who God is, is quite inexpressible.[74]

Torrance's theology, as he himself clarifies, does not place a premium on an "apophatic" approach to theology, but it is nevertheless an important feature in certain places in his theology.[75] The ascension is one of these areas where one cannot fully appreciate what Torrance is doing without

---

70. Hunsinger, "Foreword," xvi.

71. See for instance, the unique way in which Torrance's used the *an/en hypostasis*. For more, see Walker, "Innovative Fruitfulness," 189–206.

72. With respect to this study, Torrance articulates a robust doctrine of the humanity of the ascended Christ, but he does not always spell out all the details of this humanity. Similarly, regarding the spatiality of the ascended Jesus, Torrance affirms the physicality but does not enumerate on the details of the location. Finally, regarding the present ministry of the ascended Christ, Torrance's theology of the *triplex munus* is underdeveloped and does not flesh out the eschatological outworking of the ministry of Christ to one's satisfaction. The onus of such constructive works falls on readers of Torrance's theology.

73. Cf. Torrance, "Thomas Torrance Responds," 329: "Nor do I operate with some mystical theology, but simply endeavor or try to show that at certain crucial and decisive points where humility in thinking, or, if you like, some form of apophatic thinking, is in place."

74. Torrance, "Thomas Torrance Responds," 328.

75. Torrance, "Thomas Torrance Responds," 328–29.

understanding the apophatic dimensions of his thought, which in this work is categorized as an *artistic* way of theologizing.[76]

## 3. KEY THEMES IN TORRANCE'S THEOLOGY

Major themes in Torrance's theology find resonances here as well. Trinitarian, Christocentric, ecclesiological, among many other themes rightly describe Torrance's theology. This study highlights minor themes such as eschatology and theological anthropology that are important in illuminating Torrance's unique contribution to a theology of the ascension. Each of these themes are expounded in relation to Torrance's theology of the ascension, and as such provide a helpful overview of key aspects that inform his doctrine of the ascension.

### 3.1 Trinity

The doctrine of the Trinity is at the very center of Torrance's theology.[77] With respect to the relationship between the ascension and the Trinity, there is a pertinent question that must be addressed. A repeated refrain in Torrance's theology is how the ascension of Jesus takes humanity into the very presence of God—this is the ultimate destiny for humankind:[78] "It is the ascension in which our humanity in Christ is taken up into the full Communion of Father, Son and Holy Spirit in life and love."[79] How is one to make sense of this ontologically? Is there a sense in which the humanity of Jesus now is part of the Trinity? Answering this question is complex, but for Torrance the answer is in the negative: humanity is not part of the Godhead. This can be explained by pointing to the hypostatic union in Jesus, wherein the human and divine natures do not get confused in the person of Christ but remain distinct. Based on this reality, one can deduce that while humanity is in communion with the Triune God in Christ through his ascension, it is not part of the Godhead, nor does this suggest that there is a co-mingling of divinity with humanity.[80] Habets's point, while made in another context,[81]

---

76. See section 4.5, "Artistic," in this chapter, and chapter 4 for more on this point.

77. See, for instance, Molnar, *Thomas F. Torrance*, 2, 31.

78. See Torrance, *Space, Time, and Resurrection*, 135.

79. Torrance, *Space, Time, and Resurrection*, 133. See also Torrance, *Conflict and Agreement*, 2:117; Torrance, *When Christ Comes*, 150.

80. See Torrance, *Space, Time, and Resurrection*, 135.

81. Habets explains how the use of the *homoousion* by Torrance is meant to reveal God, but not to such an extent that God overrides humanity in the incarnation, nor does humanity co-opt God in the incarnation. For more, see Habets, "Essence," xxvii.

can be used to substantiate the present argument: "Neither God nor human nature is changed by this fellowship . . . however, as the one Person of Christ remains the same in the incarnation despite the union of the two natures . . . so in the union . . . of humanity and God in salvation neither is changed ontologically but each relates to the other in a 'real' way."[82] It is important to note that for Torrance God's ontology does not change because of the ascension; correspondingly, human ontology does not change either.

## 3.2 Christology

The ascension in the first instance for Torrance declares the kingship of Jesus.[83] It also plays an integral role in Torrance's Christology, so much so that it "must be understood in a correlation with the incarnation, as the *anabasis* (ascent) of the Son of God corresponding to his *katabasis* (descent)."[84] In other words, the ascension is the climax of Jesus's ministry, according to Torrance, just as the incarnation was the commencement of his ministry. As such, it "is considered as integral to the atoning redemption of Christ; it too has saving significance."[85] What does this mean? According to Torrance, the atonement does not climax on the cross but in the ascension,[86] which basically means this kind of thinking interprets "Jesus's ascension to 'God's place' as the final step in the movement of reconciling fallen creatures to the Creator and recreating humanity in union with him."[87] It is also, importantly, "the final step of the work of salvation . . . in which He offers Himself in the Father's presence."[88] The answer to the question of how exactly the ascension has "saving significance" is found in Torrance's understanding of the "vicarious humanity of Christ," which he states is the "cutting edge of 'my theology,'" and explains as follows: "The fact that Jesus Christ even in His humanity takes our place in faith, prayer, worship, mediating all we are and do in His name toward the Father—but really believing, praying and

---

82. Habets, "Essence," xxvii.
83. Torrance, *Space, Time, and Resurrection*, 106.
84. Torrance, *Space, Time, and Resurrection*, 123.
85. Habets, *Theosis*, 87.
86. Cf. Moffit, *Atonement*, makes a biblical case for the climax of the atonement, not on the cross, but in the ascension, where Jesus offers himself as a sacrifice in heaven; this logic corresponds well, Moffit argues, with how the Levitical sacrifices were climaxed not when the animal was killed, but when its blood was taken into the holy of holies. Cf. Burgess, "Ascension," 379.
87. Burgess, "Ascension," 377.
88. Burgess, *Ascension in Karl Barth*, 110.

worshipping Him in our place in such a way that He is our worship, and our faith is a sharing in His faith and our prayer a sharing in His prayer."[89]

Jesus's vicarious life does not end with his death but continues even after his resurrection and ascension. Therefore, the focus in Torrance's understanding of the vicarious humanity of Christ is on the entirety of Christ's life that is vicariously lived out for humankind. "What is important here is that the whole life of Christ, from birth to ascension, was a life which Christ offered up to God in our place and on our behalf, so that his birth from above was our new birth, his life of righteousness our righteousness, his death our death, and his ascension our ascension."[90] The influence of Athanasius is writ large in Torrance's understanding of the vicarious humanity of Christ, because in the thinking of Athanasius, "Jesus' entire life was one of vicarious representation in which human nature itself and as a whole was saved in the sense that our sin and self-will were overcome in and through his entire sinless life of obedience to the Father."[91] It is important to highlight, for Torrance, that the vicarious humanity of Christ is central even in his ascension.

## 3.3 Ecclesiology

The commission to the church, in light of the ascension, is to intercession: "So far as the Church in history and on earth is concerned, therefore, the great connecting link between world history and the heavenly session of Christ is to be found in *prayer and intercession*."[92] Jesus's intercession, which the church through the Spirit is allowed to participate in, will prevail against "the forces of darkness," so the church can participate in this activity knowing that victory is guaranteed; and therefore, it is the church's "most important service" to the world.[93] In the Eucharist, according to Torrance, believers participate in the future Kingdom "of the risen and ascended and advent Christ."[94] The presence of Jesus in the Eucharist, for Torrance, is "the *real presence*,"[95] by which he means through the Spirit the presence of Christ can be experienced.[96] The importance of the Eucharist is also existentially meaningful: "He lives from week to week, by drawing his life and strength

---

89. Kernohan, "Tom Torrance," 14.
90. D. W. Torrance, "Introduction," 5.
91. Molnar, *Thomas F. Torrance*, 138.
92. Torrance, *Space, Time, and Resurrection*, 138.
93. Torrance, *Space, Time, and Resurrection*, 138–39.
94. Torrance, *Space, Time, and Resurrection*, 101.
95. Torrance, *Space, Time, and Resurrection*, 102.
96. Torrance, *Space, Time, and Resurrection*, 147.

from the bread and wine of the Lord's Supper, nourished by the body and blood of Christ, and in the strength of that communion he must live and work until Christ comes again."[97] Ecclesiology, therefore, is a central aspect of Torrance's doctrine of the ascension.

## 3.4 Eschatology

Torrance is keen to maintain, in line with the promise given in Acts 1:11 ("This same Jesus will come again"), the continuity between the incarnate and ascended Jesus with the Jesus who returns.[98] In this return, all that Jesus has done from the ascension onward will be revealed, and it will be the "unveiling of the perfected reality of what Christ has done."[99] The scope of this eschatological renewal is important to point out. For Torrance, "Eschatology has . . . a teleological relation to the whole realm of created existence, and leads into the doctrine of 'the new heaven and the new earth.' God does not abandon his creation when he has saved man, for all creation, together with man, will be renewed when Christ comes again."[100] While this is a future reality that is guaranteed by the "pledge" that God has given in Christ's resurrection from the dead,[101] the time between now and this future reality is a time God has graciously given the world "to repent and believe."[102] Eschatology is a key theme in Torrance's exposition of the ascension.

## 3.5 Theological Anthropology

The ultimate destiny for humankind, in Torrance's theology, is participation in God, which is interpreted to mean either participation (union and communion) or *theosis*. According to Habets: "Without using technical vocabulary, Torrance states that the goal of the incarnation is *theosis* and this is finally achieved by the ascension of Jesus Christ."[103] What this means is that the destiny for humankind is a majestic reality, where "we really are gathered into the communion of the Son with the Father and of the Father with

---

97. Torrance, *Space, Time, and Resurrection*, 158.
98. Torrance, *Space, Time, and Resurrection*, 144–45.
99. Torrance, *Space, Time, and Resurrection*, 152.
100. Torrance, *Space, Time, and Resurrection*, 155. Torrance uses "man" in a gender inclusive way, given the social conventions of his day. Today, however, we would write "humanity" or "humankind."
101. Torrance, *Space, Time, and Resurrection*, 155.
102. Torrance, *Space, Time, and Resurrection*, 146–47.
103. Habets, *Theosis*, 89.

the Son, and really are taken up through the Spirit to share in the divine life and love that have overflowed to us in Jesus Christ."[104] Torrance is careful to maintain that in *theosis*, where human beings "are exalted in Christ to partake of the divine nature," the human remains distinct from the divine, and the basis for this confidence in the continuity of humanity even in *theosis* is the "hypostatic union of divine and human natures in Jesus"; all of which means that humans "share in the life of God while remaining what we were made to be, men and not gods."[105] In other words, eschatology, for Torrance, entails an affirmation of humanity, because human beings will continue to exist as humans in the eschaton.

## 4. INTRODUCTION TO TORRANCE'S THEOLOGY OF THE ASCENSION

Seven orienting aspects shed light on how to read Torrance's theology of the ascension. Given all that has been highlighted in the sections above it will be no surprise that aspects such as Biblical, Holistic, Scientific, Patristic, Reformed, Ecumenical, and Global feature in this orientation to Torrance's theology of the ascension. This section provides important tools to read Torrance's unique contribution to the ascension; it also highlights aspects that are underexplored in his theology and are therefore important to recover to better appreciate his theology. Torrance's theology of the ascension promises to be an important resource for global theology, and while this study does not expound this theme in detail, the future of Torrance studies promises to highlight the global relevance of his theological contributions at large.

### 4.1 Biblical

Torrance's doctrine of the ascension is grounded in a *theological interpretation of Scripture*.[106] In other words, his exposition can be described through the words of Robert Walker as "effectively an extended theological

---

104. Torrance, *Space, Time, and Resurrection*, 135.

105. Torrance, *Space, Time, and Resurrection*, 136.

106. For Torrance's theological interpretation of Scripture, see Habets, "Theological Interpretation," 43–69. Biblical scholars are appreciating the value of theological reception history with regard to the doctrine of the ascension. See, for example, Green, "What You See," 455, where he argues that the theological reception history of the "second-century" (p. 452) on the ascension is a legitimate method that could "generate interesting and important interpretive insights" on the ascension texts.

commentary on the bible."[107] More specifically, Walker provides a threefold explanation of Torrance's understanding of the relationship between his theology and the Bible, which can be used to shed light on how to interpret his theological interpretation of Scripture:

> i) it thinks with all the saints in the tradition of the church and in faithfulness to apostolic tradition, church creeds and ecumenical decisions on doctrine, ii) Christian dogmatics recognises that church tradition, creeds and dogma must always be subject to scripture and open to further development or amendment in the light of scripture; iii) it endeavours to express faithfully the doctrine of Christ and to bring all doctrine, preaching and ministry of the church into agreement with scripture and above all with Christ.[108]

Myk Habets avers that these three points unambiguously attest that "the central tenets of a theological interpretation of Scripture" are upheld.[109]

One can use the three points Walker highlights to explain how Torrance's doctrine of the ascension is an example of a theological interpretation of Scripture. First, among many theological resources Torrance depends upon, he arguably shapes his doctrine in line with the theology of Irenaeus to affirm the physicality of the ascended Christ,[110] with Calvin's theology of the spatiality of the ascension to simultaneously affirm the comprehensibility ("ascension into the heavens") and incomprehensibility of the event ("ascension beyond the heaven of heavens"),[111] and along with William Milligan to affirm the agency and ongoing ministry of the ascended Christ.[112]

---

107. See Walker, "Editor's Foreword," xi. Walker provides this explanation to illuminate Torrance's Edinburgh Dogmatic Lectures, but they equally apply to his doctrine of the ascension, since it is found in one of the volumes of these lectures: *Atonement*, 265–314; and in *Space, Time, and Resurrection*, 106–58. Fergusson, "Ascension of Christ," 96–97, keenly observes that the expositions on the ascension from both books "are almost identical, save for the more extensive footnoting in the latter." He goes on to add, "We can conclude from this that the latter volume, published in 1976, was based on New College lectures that he had developed over many years."

108. Walker, "Editor's Introduction," xxiii.

109. Habets, "Theological Interpretation," 50.

110. See Torrance, *Space, Time, and Resurrection*, 133n11, where he provides a quote from Irenaeus, *Against Heresies* 1.10.1 that affirms among other things: "the ascension into heaven in the flesh of the beloved Christ Jesus."

111. Torrance, *Space, Time, and Resurrection*, 128. On p. 128n7, Torrance provides the following sources from Calvin to substantiate his point: "*Comm. on Ephesians*, 1. 20 (tr. By T. H. L. Parker, p. 136f.), 4. 10 (p. 176f.); *Commen. On Hebrews*, 6. 26 (tr. By W. B. Johnston, p. 102); *Institute*, 2. 16. 14f."

112. See Torrance, *Space, Time, and Resurrection*, 111n5, where he informs readers

Second, Torrance's willingness to critique, among others, luminaries such as Origen and Augustine for their *Platonic* tendencies vis-à-vis the ascension shows that he is not uncritically appropriating theological reception history but is focused on being faithful to the Bible.[113] Third, the second point noted above would apply to the third aspect that Walker provides to shed light on how Torrance's theology interacts with Scripture.

A further observation may be made, however, which pertains to how one can argue that Torrance is being biblical when there is minimal exegetical engagement with various biblical texts. Arguably, Torrance is following a method of theological writing he learned from John Calvin, in whose work there is a "symbiotic relationship"[114] between the *Institutes* and the *Biblical Commentaries* such that detailed expositions on biblical texts found in *Institutes* will not be duplicated in *Commentaries*.[115] In the introduction to his *Institutes*, Calvin informs readers about this interrelationship between both kinds of works:

> If, after this road has, as it were, been paved, I shall publish any interpretations of Scripture, I shall always condense them, because I shall have no need to undertake long doctrinal discussions, and to digress into commonplaces. In this way the godly reader will be spared great annoyance and boredom, provided he approach Scripture armed with a knowledge of the present work, as a necessary tool.[116]

Without being too dogmatic, it is plausible that Torrance is doing something similar in his works. In his case, the relationship is potentially between his theological writings and Calvin's commentaries.[117] Calvin's *Institutes* was deeply formative in Torrance's ministry, as he himself explains, "While I was a minister, it was Calvin to whom I repeatedly turned. His

---

that his own interpretation of the "three-fold office of Christ" in his ascension depends on two of William Milligan's works: *Resurrection of Our Lord*, 136–52; and *Ascension*, 61–226.

113. See Torrance, *Space, Time, and Resurrection*, 140, especially nn13–14.

114. Gordon, *Calvin*, 108.

115. The inspiration for this constructive suggestion is Habets, "Theological Interpretation," 49: "It is in this tradition [Calvin and Augustine] of theological interpretation of Scripture that Thomas Torrance stands. Torrance echoes similar thoughts to Calvin in the way he defines Christian dogmatics and its relation to Scripture."

116. Calvin, "John Calvin to the Reader," 4–5.

117. Torrance's sermon volumes, such as *When Christ Comes and Comes Again*, provide a good example of his engagement with the biblical texts. One wishes his academic theological works did the same more often.

*Institutes* and his commentaries . . . were in my hands continually."[118] Paul Molnar says that it was Torrance's ordination service at "Alyth Barony Parish Church" that "his father attended and presented him with a full set of Calvin's commentaries which proved useful to Torrance in preparing his sermons."[119] Therefore, while one wishes that Torrance engaged in more extended exegetical work with various biblical texts that shape his doctrine of the ascension, it is likely that following Calvin, he expected his readers to be aware of and consult works that were deeply formative in his own theological thinking. In Torrance's case, it is perhaps particularly his sermons that he eventually expected his readers to consult to discover the biblical grounding for his theological expositions.[120] However, since his sermon volumes were not widely accessible, it is plausible that until they became more easily available, Torrance expected readers to consult commentaries (Calvin's and others) as a supplement to his theological writings. Alternatively, it is also plausible that Torrance may have expected his audience to be more informed about the various biblical texts he was alluding to, considering his own familiarity with Scripture.

## 4.2 Holistic

Torrance's theology of the ascension is a remarkable contribution to scholarship that can be captured best by the term *holistic*. It is holistic in the sense that it has a vast scope. Jeremy Begbie's assessment of Torrance's *Space, Time, and Resurrection* in a 2018 lecture can also aptly describe his theology of the ascension: "I was gripped by the sheer audacious sweep of this text. It seemed to cover the creation of all things to the re-creation of all things."[121] Torrance's doctrine of the ascension is embedded within *Space, Time, and Resurrection*, and offers clear corroboration of Begbie's claim, because it is deeply interconnected with several theological loci, ranging from

118. Bauman, "Thomas Torrance," 112.

119. Molnar, *Thomas F. Torrance*, 9.

120. For a small selection of biblical texts that are important to Torrance's theology of the ascension, see Torrance, *Space, Time, and Resurrection*, 106n1: "Neither St. Matthew nor St. John speaks about the ascension in their Gospels; St. Mark alludes to it, at least in the addendum to his Gospel, 16:19, but a fuller account is given by St. Luke, 24: 50–53, Acts 1: 9–11. There are, however, references to it elsewhere as in the early *kerygma* reported in the Acts of the Apostles (2: 23f.; 5: 30f.), etc., and in the epistles (Phil. 2: 6–9, 3: 20; Eph. 4: 8–10; 1 Tim. 3: 16; 1 Peter 3: 22; Heb. 2: 9, 12: 2; cf. also Rom. 8: 34; Col. 3: 1; 1 Peter 1: 21)."

121. Begbie, "Incarnation, Creation, and New Creation," 02:23–02:32. Begbie has subsequently published this work in *Participatio* as "Incarnation, Creation, and New Creation."

Christology to theological anthropology, Trinity to ecclesiology, pneumatology to epistemology, and eschatology to doxology, to name but a few. It is this holistic nature of Torrance's account of the ascension that distinguishes his work in an intellectual milieu that either dismisses the doctrine of the ascension altogether, or when it is seriously explored, with some exceptions, it is mostly done with a limited focus on specific aspects of the doctrine, for example, the present ministry of the ascended Jesus. When Torrance's doctrine of the ascension is examined closely, his work is unique because of its holistic scope—it expounds the *ontology, spatiality,* and *present ministry* of the ascended Christ, and therefore provides a robust account of the ascension that deserves wide reception and critical engagement.

## 4.3 Scientific

Kate Tyler helpfully appropriates three aspects of Torrance's scientific theology that are particularly germane to understanding his "dogmatic theology": (1) "the kataphysic method," (2) "the rejection of dualism," and (3) "the importance of personal knowledge."[122] These three categories serve well to provide an orientation to the intricate way Torrance's theology of the ascension is expounded in a scientific manner.

### 4.3.1 *Kataphysic*

There are two specific exhortations Torrance issues with respect to the *kataphysic*[123] nature of the ascension. First, he underscores the centrality of God's revelation in Jesus: "The ascension . . . sends us back to the incarnation, and to the historical Jesus, and so to a Word and Act of God inseparably implicated in our space and time."[124] While Torrance is highlighting the importance of God's historical revelation in Jesus, his theology of the ascension is grounded in a continuation of the importance of God's revelation and the need for human beings to allow God to set the agenda for how he will reveal himself in and through the ascension. This is clearly enunciated in the way Torrance espouses a *relational* understanding of God's relationship to space and time.[125] In theologizing in such a way, Torrance is clearly working out

---

122. Tyler, *Ecclesiology*, 9.

123. *Kataphysic* is a term that refers to a study that is done "according to the nature or reality of things." For more, see McGrath, *Thomas F. Torrance*, 211.

124. Torrance, *Space, Time, and Resurrection*, 134.

125. Torrance, *Space, Time, and Resurrection*, 126.

his ascension doctrine in a *kataphysic* manner. Second, he contends that human beings should recognize their limitation in understanding certain aspects of the ascension:

> Here also, then, in respect of the ascension we must say with Calvin that the ascension is an event which we must speak of, on the one hand, through its relation with space and time as we know it on earth and in history, and within creaturely existence, but, on the other hand, we must speak of it as transcending all that, and as an event infinitely beyond the boundaries of our space and time or anything we could conceive in terms of them.[126]

Both aspects are crucial to understanding the scientific nature of Torrance's doctrine of the ascension, which will be fleshed out in more detail in the way he expounds it in *non-dualistic* and *personal* terms.

### 4.3.2 Non-Dualistic

Torrance is particularly keen to avoid two kinds of dualisms vis-à-vis the ascended Christ. First, he eschews any dualism of body and spirit in his theology of the ascension. Unlike Origen's theology that denied the bodily nature of the ascended Jesus,[127] Torrance categorically affirmed its physicality and corporeality because he contended that "to be a spiritual body is not to be less body but more truly and completely body."[128] Theological traditions that espouse views on the ascended Christ's ontology in primarily spiritualistic categories, Torrance asserts, are moving beyond the pale of biblical revelation: "But this is to fail to observe the proper theological reserve at the boundary of the eschatological; we inevitably fall into error as soon as we transgress the limits set by the Word."[129] Second, he wants to avoid creating a dualism between the divinity and humanity of Jesus in the ascension, and in doing so is arguing for something similar to what he argued for in the incarnation.[130] In other words, when God became incarnate, he did not give up his divinity, and therefore, when he ascended into heaven, he did not give up his humanity.[131] Torrance's explanation is memorable: "As in

---

126. Torrance, *Space, Time, and Resurrection*, 132.
127. Torrance, *Space, Time, and Resurrection*, 140.
128. Torrance, *Space, Time, and Resurrection*, 141.
129. Torrance, *Space, Time, and Resurrection*, 140.
130. Torrance, *Space, Time, and Resurrection*, 129.
131. Torrance, *Space, Time, and Resurrection*, 129.

the incarnation we have to think of God the Son becoming man without ceasing to be transcended God, so in his ascension we have to think of Christ as ascending above all space and time without ceasing to be man or without any diminishment of his physical, historical existence."[132] Torrance's resistance to two kinds of dualisms can be seen clearly in the way he articulates his views on body and spirit and the divine and human natures in the person of Jesus.

### 4.3.3 Personal

Torrance makes two central arguments about how one must *personally* encounter the ascended Christ. First, he asserts that the ascended Christ does not rule out the need for the historical Jesus. On the contrary, through the ascension "Christ sends us back to the historical Jesus Christ as the *covenanted place* on earth and in time which God has appointed for meeting between man and himself."[133] For Torrance, personal knowledge of the ascended Christ cannot happen directly, by bypassing the historical Jesus. On this point Torrance is firm: "We cannot and must not try to go behind the back of Jesus Christ, to some kind of *theologia gloriae* reached by direct speculation of the divine majesty."[134] Second, he highlights the crucial role of the cross and the Holy Spirit in knowing the ascended Christ. He clarifies that the only proper way to know the exalted Christ is to first encounter the "crucified Jesus."[135] The only way for one to make this kind of connection, Torrance explains, is *"through the Spirit"*; furthermore, it is the Spirit who helps one make sense both of the absence and presence of Christ: "It is through the Spirit that things infinitely disconnected—disconnected by the 'distance' of the ascension—are nevertheless infinitely closely related."[136] The role of the Holy Spirit, therefore, is crucial in personally encountering the ascended Jesus.

---

132. Torrance, *Space, Time, and Resurrection*, 129.
133. Torrance, *Space, Time, and Resurrection*, 133.
134. Torrance, *Space, Time, and Resurrection*, 134.
135. Torrance, *Space, Time, and Resurrection*, 134.
136. Torrance, *Space, Time, and Resurrection*, 135.

## 4.4 Patristic and Reformed

Torrance's theology of the ascension is influenced by several theologians. Three theologians are particularly relevant to Torrance's theology of the ascension and will be briefly introduced below.

### 4.4.1 Irenaeus

Torrance not only affirms a bodily resurrection; he also believes in a bodily ascension and in doing so aligns himself with Irenaeus (not Origen) and the tradition he bequeathed to theology.[137] The force of the bodily ascension is accentuated well by Douglas Farrow when he clarifies why the body of the ascended Jesus is important, and in doing so he draws from Irenaeus:

> We are not wanting to assert that the physical body is the most significant aspect of human personhood, identity or presence, whether in the eucharistic situation or even at the parousia. But we do want to side with Irenaeus: "As therefore, when that which is perfect is come, we shall not see another Father, but him whom we now desire to see . . . , neither shall we look for another Christ and Son of God, but him who [was born] of the Virgin Mary, who also suffered, in whom we trust, and whom we love" (*AH* [*Against Heresies*] 4.9.2; cf. 5.1.4.4).[138]

Such a view resonates with Torrance's own views on the matter of the body of the ascended Jesus:

> But even the *parousia* in that future aspect, at the second or final advent of Christ, will nevertheless be a *parousia* of essentially the same texture as that of the historical Jesus in the incarnation and the risen Jesus of Easter and the ascension. "This same Jesus will come again," it was said on the day of ascension, "in the same way as you have seen him going into heaven" (Acts 1:11).[139]

Torrance's views stress continuity between the incarnation, resurrection, ascension, and the return of Christ. His views clearly align with Irenaeus's views on the subject.[140]

---

137. Cf. chapters 3 and 4 of Farrow's *Ascension and Ecclesia*, 41–164. See also chapter 3 of this work for more.
138. Farrow, *Ascension and Ecclesia*, 268n48.
139. Torrance, *Space, Time, and Resurrection*, 144–45.
140. For more on Torrance's views on Irenaeus, see Baker, "Place of St. Irenaeus."

### 4.4.2 Calvin

There are many aspects of Calvin's influence pertinent to Torrance's theology of the ascension, but one is illustrative at this stage. Calvin clearly underscores the physicality of the ascended Jesus when he argues for locating the body of the ascended Christ in heaven: "the body of Christ from the time of his resurrection was finite, and is contained in heaven even to the Last Day."[141] Torrance is unequivocal in his affirmation of the physicality of the ascended Jesus, evidenced in vivid statements such as: "It is as our Brother, wearing our humanity, that He has ascended, presenting Himself eternally before the face of the Father, and presenting us in Himself."[142] Furthermore, key phrases he uses throughout his corpus underscore Christ's physicality in Torrance's thought: "bone of our bone and flesh of our flesh";[143] "having entered it in our flesh";[144] "Man";[145] "ascended wearing our humanity";[146] "the Continuous Living Reality of the Lord Jesus after the Resurrection";[147] "we must never let go of the physical incarnated reality of Jesus";[148] and "ascension of Jesus Christ in the self-same body which was born of the Virgin Mary, and was crucified, dead and buried and which rose again."[149] While Torrance does draw from Calvin and would affirm in essence Calvin's point, interestingly he does not reiterate Calvin's insights about the location of the body of the ascended Christ. One must look closely and deduce such a conclusion from Torrance's writings.[150] Perhaps Torrance does not repeat Calvin's assertions because he expects the reader to know Torrance's other writings and come to such a conclusion based on his entire corpus.[151] Perhaps there is also some caution he is exercising in the way he articulates his position in a culture that is scientifically attuned. Be this as it may, some of

---

141. Calvin, *Institutes* 4.17.26.
142. Torrance, *Royal Priesthood*, 14–15.
143. Torrance, "Christ Who Loves Us," 18.
144. Torrance, *Kingdom and Church*, 103.
145. Torrance, *Conflict and Agreement*, 1:99.
146. Torrance, *When Christ Comes*, 151.
147. Torrance, *Doctrine of Jesus Christ*, 191.
148. Torrance, *Doctrine of Jesus Christ*, 191.
149. Torrance, *Scottish Theology*, 21.

150. See Torrance, *Space, Time, and Resurrection*, 124–25, where Torrance states, "If a receptacle view of space or place is held, how are we to think of the Body of Christ as contained in the host, in every part of it, and in a multitude of hosts at the same time, *and how can we think of it as being contained without any relation between the dimensions of the Body of Christ and the space of the place that contains him?*" (emphasis added).

151. Torrance, *Space, Time, and Resurrection*, 129.

INTRODUCING T. F. TORRANCE'S THEOLOGY OF THE ASCENSION   39

Torrance's own views on the physicality of the ascended Christ are certainly preempted by Calvin.

An aspect of Calvin's thought that deserves closer scrutiny but which is beyond the scope of this exploration is the potential neglect of eschatology in his view on the ascension. Douglas Farrow, inspired by Torrance,[152] points out a weakness in ascension scholarship, which can be historically traced back to Calvin: "Calvin handled the dialectic of presence and absence almost exclusively in spatial terms, and hence (what has already been said about the parousia notwithstanding) in a non-eschatological fashion."[153] The underlying issue in such a preoccupation for Farrow is "if we do not speak of a *temporal* as well as a spatial opposition, the reality of our putative union with Christ is confined to the hidden sphere of the soul."[154] In other words, Farrow's main concern is that if the temporal gap until Christ's bodily return along with the spatial distance vis-à-vis the ascension is not considered, then there is the danger that one could think that the fullness of relating to Christ is only spiritual, with the concomitant effect that "the body itself is not involved."[155] Michael Horton agrees with Farrow's critique of Calvin and wishes to embark on a similar project: "Pushing this account in a more eschatological direction will be one of my main goals."[156] Others like Adrian Langdon argue that when the ascension is not understood as both spatial and temporal, we "submit theological mysteries to philosophical and scientific problems (which, nonetheless, ought to be dealt with) and miss the theological import of Christ's absence."[157] The ascension must be viewed in both spatial and temporal terms, and Torrance's theology, which will be articulated in chapter 4, provides just such an account.

*4.4.3 Barth*

Karl Barth affirms the humanity of Christ in the ascension. To this end, Barth writes that "the human essence of Jesus Christ, without becoming divine, in its very creatureliness, is placed at the side of the Creator. . . . It is a clothing which He does not put off. It is His temple which He does

---

152. Cf. Farrow, *Ascension and Ecclesia*, 263n24.
153. Farrow, *Ascension and Ecclesia*, 178.
154. Farrow, *Ascension and Ecclesia*, 179.
155. Farrow, *Ascension and Ecclesia*, 179.
156. Horton, *People and Place*, 10.
157. Langdon, *God the Eternal Contemporary*, 144–45. On p. 144, Langdon asserts that the ascension is "both a spatial-temporal event and a theological statement."

not leave. It is the form which He does not lose."[158] Commenting on this passage, Douglas Farrow writes, "The ascension is no longer a device for the undoing of Jesus' humanity, but for its establishment."[159] Torrance's theology of the ascension is similar to Barth's, and this is a point that Andrew Burgess does well to underscore.[160] Burgess also highlights the dissimilarities between the two theologians correctly: "The most significant difference lies in the adoption of a sequential reading of humiliation and exaltation."[161] David Fergusson distills the similarities between Barth and Torrance on the ascension in the following manner: "The positive appropriation of ascension language over against strategies of demythologizing, the prioritizing of the once-for-all work of Christ, the integration of his person and work, and the enabling condition of the ascension for church proclamation."[162] He avers that the differences can best be seen in the manner in which Torrance places "stress on the doxological and sacramental significance of the eternal ministry of the ascended Christ," while Barth does not.[163] A further area that distinguishes the two theologians, according to Fergusson, is in the emphasis Barth places on "the ethical and political significance of the ascension," which is conspicuously missing in Torrance.[164] An area that is not interrogated as much in scholarship on the ascension is the differences between how the eschatologies of these two eminent theologians differ vastly. For example, how each one answers the question about the future of humanity is shaped by their theologies of the ascension. While Torrance's answer would be an unequivocal "yes,"[165] Barth's answer is more difficult to discern, leaving some skeptical about the future of humanity in Barth's eschatology.[166]

It will be argued in chapter 6 that Torrance's eschatology, while embryonic in many parts, has the resources to affirm the ongoing existence of human beings at the eschaton. This is an aspect that distinguishes Torrance from Barth, at least according to some common criticisms of Barth's

---

158. Barth, *Church Dogmatics*, 4/2:100–101.

159. Farrow, *Ascension and Ecclesia*, 242.

160. Cf. Burgess, *Ascension in Karl Barth*, 122–34.

161. Burgess, *Ascension in Karl Barth*, 133.

162. Fergusson, "Ascension of Christ," 105.

163. Fergusson, "Ascension of Christ," 105.

164. Fergusson, "Ascension of Christ," 106. A similar critique is leveled by Webster. Cf. Webster, "Thomas Forsyth Torrance," 427. See Speidell, *Fully Human in Christ*. See also Molnar, "Rejoinder," 83–88, for a response to Torrance's neglect of ethics and political engagement.

165. Torrance, *Space, Time, and Resurrection*, 135.

166. See Hitchcock, *Karl Barth*, xv; Cortez, *Resourcing Theological Anthropology*, 245–58, particularly 253–58.

eschatology in contemporary Barth scholarship. Therefore, along with a host of Torrance scholars, ably represented by Paul Molnar and David Fergusson, one has to acknowledge more generally that Torrance is "not [an] uncritical" exponent of the theology of Karl Barth,[167] and specifically with respect to the ascension that Torrance provides "significant adjustments to Barth's theology in the area of church, sacraments, and ministry."[168] To this list of differences between Torrance and Barth that Fergusson correctly notes, in light of this study on the ascension, one must also add eschatology and theological anthropology as areas for further investigation in the ongoing dialogue between Torrance and Barth studies.

## 4.5 Artistic

Torrance's rhetoric is a neglected area in scholarship, but this is an aspect that promises to pay rich dividends.[169] It can be argued that Torrance depends on *artistic* language to speak about realities that are beyond human ken, with the ascension as one key area in which this is evidenced.[170] In making a case for viewing Torrance's theology of the ascension as *artistic* it must be acknowledged that Torrance himself perhaps would not endorse such language. However, observing how Torrance addresses certain subjects, it is hard not to conclude that he is operating with some sort of artistic approach, as opposed to an analytical or deductive one. To highlight this aspect, one must first note that Torrance acknowledges that there is mystery after a certain point in theology. Torrance follows Calvin in this regard when he observes that the former was not "above all a logician" but one who repeatedly "was content to leave the ends of his theological thinking loose for the precise reason that theology runs out always to the point of wonder where we can only clap our hands on our mouths and remember that we are humble creatures."[171] Torrance followed such an approach consistently

---

167  Molnar, "Thomas F. Torrance," 3:232.

168. Fergusson, "Barth and T. F. Torrance," 2.665.

169. There is no full-length monograph on Torrance's rhetoric. Karl Barth's theology, on the other hand, has been analyzed through the rhetorical perspective, and there are insights from such a work that could prove fruitful for a similar study on Torrance's rhetoric in his theology. For more, see Webb, *Re-figuring Theology*.

170. This is an idea shared by Torrance scholar Myk Habets, but he has not published anything on Torrance as a theological artist. In what follows, I am building on Habets's ideas to make a case for viewing Torrance, among other things, also as a theological artist.

171. Torrance, *Conflict and Agreement*, 1:92.

in his theology and acknowledged mystery at various points,[172] including in his exposition on the spatiality of the ascension.[173] It is at these points in his theology, where human words are inadequate to the task because the realities being discussed are beyond the human ability to grasp that Torrance, we contend, resorts to language that can be described as *artistic*. While the details of this argument will be fleshed out in chapter 4, at this stage it must be noted that such a view is like C. S. Lewis's argument about how metaphors play an intrinsic role in language. To anyone who thinks otherwise, he would respond by stating, "The man who does not consciously use metaphors talks without meaning. We might even formulate a rule: the meaning in any given composition is in inverse ratio to the author's belief in his own literalness."[174] In other words, there are limits to how much deductive language can communicate on certain subjects. While Lewis insisted in the inevitability of "metaphors" to accurately communicate, Torrance, arguably, resorted to the language of mystery.[175]

## 4.6 Rich Resource for Ecumenical Dialogue

Torrance's theology has established impressive credentials for bolstering ecumenical dialogue and appropriation.[176] Joel Scandrett clearly highlights

---

172. A few examples where Torrance practices this approach is in the context of expressing his views on the *Scotist Hypothesis*, the atonement, and the Ontological Trinity. For more, see Torrance, *Christian Doctrine of God*, 210: "Hence, while clapping our hands upon our mouth, without knowing what we say, we may nevertheless feel urged to say that in his eternal purpose the immeasurable Love of God overflowing freely beyond himself which brought the creation into existence would have become incarnate within the creation even if we and our world were not in need of his redeeming grace." See also Torrance, *Atonement*, 2: "That means that the innermost mystery of atonement and intercession remains mystery: it cannot be spelled out, and it cannot be spied out. That is the ultimate mystery of the blood of Christ, the blood of God incarnate, a holy and infinite mystery which is more to be adored than expressed. Here we tread the holy ground of the garden of Gethsemane and Calvary and here we must clap our hand upon our mouth again and again for we have no words adequate to match the infinitely holy import of atonement." Also see Torrance, *Christian Doctrine of God*, 110: "To speak like this of God's inner Being, we cannot but feel to be a sacrilegious intrusion into the inner holy of holies of God's incomprehensible Mystery, before which we ought rather to cover our faces and clap our hands upon our mouths, for God is utterly ineffable in the transcendence and majesty of his eternal Being."

173. See Torrance, *Space, Time, and Resurrection*, 127–32.

174. Lewis, "Bluspels and Flalansfers," 262.

175. Lewis, "Bluspels and Flalansfers," 262; see also chapter 4 of this study for more on this topic.

176. For an overview and assessment of Torrance's theological contribution to ecumenical theology, see Scandrett, "Thomas F. Torrance," 51–66.

the continuing ecumenical purchase of Torrance's theology by noting the impressive array of theological interlocutors:

> Both Orthodox theologian Matthew Baker and Anglican theologian Jason Radcliff endorse Torrance's work as a bridge for Protestant-Orthodox relations. Baptist theologian Myk Habets appropriates Torrance's thought in his consideration of the doctrine of *theosis*. Reformed theologian George Hunsinger demonstrates Torrance's continuing ecumenical relevance in his appropriation of Torrance's eucharistic theology. And Roman Catholic theologian Paul Molnar elevates the ecumenical potential of Torrance's sacramental theology.[177]

Scandrett importantly goes on to assess the ongoing significance of Torrance's theology as follows: "Insofar as these treatments and others indicate a new season of engagement with Torrance's work, his ecumenical theology may yet be of service to the task of Christian unity."[178] Two specific subjects vis-à-vis the ascension promise to further ecumenical dialogue, namely, Torrance's contribution to the discussion about Christ's "fallen" human nature, and his views on the *extra Calvinisticum* are some potential areas for dialogue between Reformed and Lutheran theology.

### 4.6.1 Fallen or Unfallen Humanity of Christ

Christians from different theological traditions are indeed finding in Torrance an important theological interlocutor as has been demonstrated above, whose insights provide clarity and even solutions at times to theological conundrums. A recent example among others is the contribution from an appreciative critic, Oliver Crisp, on the ongoing debate on the kind of human nature Jesus had in the incarnation—*fallen* or *unfallen*. Crisp finds in Torrance's theology of *the vicarious humanity of Christ* a means to provide a solution to the existing divide between both views:

> This vicarious humanity view is, I think, a kind of theological olive branch—that is, a way of construing the notion of assumption such that it grants to the defenders of the fallenness view what they regard as essential for Christ to act on our behalf, healing our human natures. Yet it also preserves what I think is non-negotiable from a more Augustinian perspective, namely, that the human nature possessed by the Word is sinless from the

---

177. Scandrett, "Thomas F. Torrance," 64–65.
178. Scandrett, "Thomas F. Torrance," 65.

moment he assumes it. In other words, it is a kind of theological *via media*. Perhaps it may provide a dogmatic resolution to a rather vexed christological matter.[179]

Crisp's statements are significant and highlights the relevance of Torrance's theology for ecumenical dialogue on contentious theological subjects. In what follows, Torrance's potential ecumenical contribution vis-à-vis the *extra Calvinisticum* with respect to the Reformed and Lutheran traditions will be noted.

### 4.6.2 Reformed, Lutherans, and the Extra Calvinisticum

David Fergusson correctly observes that Torrance's commitment to the *extra Calvinisticum* is not just limited to the period of the incarnation, but also extends to the ascension: "He commits himself to the so-called *extra Calvinisticum*, the Reformed view that the ascended body of Christian [sic] is located in heaven and so is not ubiquitous, as classical Lutheran theology had taught, through its union with the Word of God."[180] Fergusson's observation is an important one because Torrancean scholarship has not explored the various facets of Torrance's ascension theology in depth, and there can be a tendency to interpret Torrance in Lutheran rather than Reformed categories vis-à-vis the ascended body of Christ.[181] However, Fergusson also believes that Torrance missed an opportunity to find commonality between the two theological traditions—Reformed and Lutheran—perhaps because he did not make a clear distinction between Luther and Bultmann:

> Torrance detects this Lutheran tendency in Bultmann's demythologizing project, which eliminates the bodily resurrection and ascension of Jesus. In some respects this is regrettable, since it may have prevented him from a fuller appreciation of Luther's stress on the *totus Christus*. At a time of greater ecumenical convergence, we should recognise that both Reformed and Lutheran theologies were seeking to protect vital elements of the incarnation of the Word of God, as understood in Chalcedonian Christology. For the Reformed, Christ's assumption of humanity was never absorbed by his divine ubiquity; for the Lutherans, the union of the Word of God with our humanity is more than apparent and continues forever.[182]

---

179. Crisp, "On the Vicarious Humanity," 238.
180. Fergusson, "He Ascended into Heaven," 37.
181. See chapter 4 for an exploration of this point.
182. Fergusson, "He Ascended into Heaven," 37n11.

While there is merit in Fergusson's assessment of the debate, it must be mentioned that there may be further nuances to the debate between Lutheran and Reformed theologians that are not sufficiently interrogated in contemporary scholarship. For instance, the historical debate between Reformed and Lutheran theologians has not been explored through the differing cosmologies they each adopted—Ptolemaic for the former and Copernican for the latter.[183] How much their differing cosmologies should shape the current reception of the debate between both theological groups on the *extra Calvinisticum* is a task that is incomplete in contemporary scholarship and may prove to be an area that is ripe for ecumenical dialogue.

## 4.7 Potential for Global Theological Dialogue

Torrance's theology has a global appeal,[184] and in recent times majority world theologians are appreciatively interacting with his theology.[185] In what follows, only Torrance's potential contribution to Indian theology vis-à-vis his theology of the ascension will be briefly highlighted. In contemporary Indian theological scholarship Torrance is not a major interlocutor.[186] However, Steven Tsoukalas has recently brought Torrance's theology of *theosis* into conversation with the eminent Hindu philosopher of the eleventh and twelfth centuries, Ramanuja.[187] While Tsoukalas's work is only suggestive, in that it is very brief, it does show potential for more substantive works of an interreligious nature between Torrance and other Indian philosophers and theologians. Specifically, with reference to the ascension there are three potentially fruitful areas for further exploration.

First, missiologist Herbert Hoeffer in his article entitled "Gospel Proclamation of the Ascended Lord" advocates for an approach to evangelization in the majority world that begins with the ascension rather than the cross.[188] Such an approach basically seeks to mirror Paul's conversion experience, wherein the experience of the ascension precedes the cross: "First personal

183. I thank Dr. Kerry Magruder for sharing this insight with me in a personal correspondence.

184. The recent *T&T Clark Handbook of Thomas F. Torrance* contains critical appraisals of Torrance's theology from scholars who reside in three different continents.

185. A few examples are: Eugenio, *Communion with the Triune God*; Wei, "Theological Anthropology"; Magezi and Magezi, "Healing and Coping"; Magezi and Magezi, "Christ Also Ours."

186. There are some exceptions, however. Cf. Prasadam, "Beyond Conscientization," 363–89; Philipose P. M., "Critical Exploration."

187. See Tsoukalas, "Theōsis."

188. Hoeffer, "Gospel Proclamation."

experience of the ascended Lord and then intellectual conviction about his suffering, death, and resurrection."[189] This missiological approach has pedagogical[190] as well as evangelistic appeal and is ripe for further dialogue and practical appropriation. Second, the discourse on the appropriateness of the term avatāras for Jesus's incarnation has a long reception history in Indian theological scholarship.[191] While classical Indian theologians are aware of how the ongoing humanity of Jesus post-resurrection should shape the use of the term avatāras,[192] on the whole Christian literature on avatāras does not explore the ascension and the ongoing humanity of Christ sufficiently. Furthermore, there is a need to explore how Jesus's ascended humanity compares, contrasts, and dialogues with the Hindu concept of "eternal" avatāras in "Bengal *Vaiṣṇavism*."[193] Within Hinduism "eternal" avatāras are the exception to the normal understanding of deities who take on humanity temporarily and then return to their former states because "the *avatāra* always has the form and never discards it."[194] Such a comparative study offers an interesting parallel to Jesus's own retention of his humanity after his resurrection and ascension. Third, Torrance's connection to Indian Christian theology is an area that needs to be explored further from a historical perspective. Torrance was one of the PhD mentors to Robin Boyd, whose work on *Indian Christian Theology*[195] is still used as a "standard textbook"[196] in many Indian theological seminaries. It would be interesting to discern the Torrancean influence on Boyd's theology (and perhaps vice versa as well), and more broadly the influence of the Torrances on the ministers who trained under them, who then came to India to serve as missionaries in various capacities.[197]

189. Hoeffer, "Gospel Proclamation," 435.

190. The ascension is a subject that can seem esoteric, but Hoeffer's article shows how it is practically relevant and exhorts the church to be sensitive to appropriating evangelistic approaches that are better suited to majority world contexts.

191. Cf. Raj, "Why Jesus"; Sheth, "Hindu Avatāra"; Tsoukalas, *Kṛṣṇa and Christ*; Lipner, "Avatāra and Incarnation?"

192. Cf. Boyd, "Indian Christian Interpretations."

193. Sheth, "Hindu Avatāra" 106.

194. Sheth, "Hindu Avatāra," 106–7.

195. Boyd, *Indian Christian Theology*.

196. See Arles, "State of Mission Studies," 157.

197. I thank Professor Christopher Hancock for suggesting this research focus to me in a personal correspondence.

## 5. CONCLUSION

This chapter introduced Torrance's theology with a view to orienting readers to his doctrine of the ascension. It also explained that the methodology used to study Torrance would be *constructive dogmatics*. Major theological themes common to introductions to Torrance's theology found resonances in this account as well, such as Trinitarian, christological, ecclesiological, ecumenical, scientific, missionary, transformation-oriented, and doxological. Furthermore, the influence of major theological thinkers, such as Irenaeus, Athanasius, Calvin, and Barth, among others, on Torrance's doctrine of the ascension was noted. Minor theological themes that may not feature in other works as prominently as they do in this work are eschatology, theological anthropology, and the significance of theological language. The chapter pointed out that each of these aspects shed light on Torrance's doctrine of the ascension and has not been sufficiently interrogated in contemporary Torrancean scholarship. Torrance's eschatology, while embryonic in many parts, has the resources to affirm the ongoing existence of human beings in the eschaton. This is an aspect, it was observed, that distinguishes Torrance from Barth, at least according to some common criticisms of Barth's eschatology in contemporary Barthian scholarship. Therefore, along with a number of Torrance scholars, ably represented by Paul Molnar and David Fergusson, it was acknowledged more generally that Torrance is "not [an] uncritical" exponent of the theology of Karl Barth,[198] and specifically with respect to the ascension that Torrance provides "significant adjustments to Barth's theology in the area of church, sacraments, and ministry."[199] To this list of differences between Torrance and Barth that Fergusson correctly notes, in light of this study on the ascension, it was highlighted, that one must also add eschatology and theological anthropology as areas for further investigation in the ongoing dialogue between Torrance and Barth studies.

Regarding theological language, it was noted that Torrance uses *artistic* language in his description of the ascension, by which is meant that there is a mysterious aspect to the ascension that analytical language cannot fully capture, but which the language of art through icons, for example, can better communicate. Torrance uses such language to communicate truths about the ascension, and such an emphasis on Torrance's rhetoric, it was noted, promises to tread ground that is underexplored in studies of Torrance. Seven orienting aspects were then offered to introduce Torrance's theology of the ascension. Apart from common themes like biblical, scientific,

---

198. Molnar, "Thomas F. Torrance," 3:232.
199. Fergusson, "Barth and T. F. Torrance," 2:665.

ecumenical, and in addition to the artistic language, Torrance's holistic account, his Reformed theological convictions, as well as the potential for dialogue with global theologies, for example with Indian Christian theology, were highlighted as aspects that promise to shed new light on Torrance's theology of the ascension.

With respect to methodology, while Torrance studies are divided more generally according to major doctrinal, historical, methodological, ecumenical, or theology-science emphases, this work aligns itself with the doctrinal emphasis, with an added specific focus on *constructive* dogmatics. Arguably, such a work is not new as it represents what Torrance did in his own theology (and what many Torrance scholars are also doing), wherein he interacted with several theologians but always added his own layer of nuance and specificity according to the needs of his own context. As such, the goal of this study has been to expound faithfully Torrance's theology of the ascension, constructively building on areas that are underexplored or in need of theological refinement. The next three chapters (3–5) will form the heart of the theological exposition of this study of Torrance's doctrine of the ascension, by focusing on the *ontology*, *spatiality*, and *present ministry* of the ascended Jesus.

# 3

# The Ontology of the Ascended Christ

## 1. INTRODUCTION

TORRANCE IS KNOWN AS a theologian who is able to "summarize a thousand years of thought in one paragraph."[1] While no claims to being able to do the same are made in this chapter, at the outset what Torrance has to say about Jesus's risen and ascended ontology can be summarized in one condensed yet theologically rich statement: the ascended Jesus is still a corporeal human being, but he is in a humanity that is free from corruption and decay that characterized the *fallen* humanity that he assumed in the incarnation. This is a theologically loaded statement that needs to be unpacked and critically interrogated, but in short, it clearly indicates that Torrance is keenly interested in *ontology* vis-à-vis his exposition of Jesus's risen and ascended being. In what follows, Torrance's theology of the ascended being of Jesus will be critically expounded and developed constructively.

## 2. ONTOLOGY OF THE ASCENDED JESUS

Since Torrance scatters his writings on the ascension across his oeuvre, his theology must be read and interpreted considering the broader corpus of his work. To provide clarity and structure for each of the next three chapters, the focus will be on Jesus's ascended (1) *ontology,* (2) *spatiality,* and (3) *present ministry*. Torrance's mature theological work, *Space, Time, and Resurrection*, will provide an overview of and orientation to Torrance's thought, incorporating work from across his corpus to shed further light,

---

1. Molnar, *Thomas F. Torrance*, 39.

before proceeding to analyze and critically evaluate it. Torrance explicates his theology of Christ's ascended ontology in *Space, Time, and Resurrection* in integral relationship with other theological loci, and therefore to be faithful to his theology, one must follow his approach. Torrance unpacks his theology of Christ's ascended ontology in relationship to (1) theological anthropology, (2) ecclesiology, and (3) Christology proper. In what follows, each of these areas will be critically expounded, after which they will be constructively developed.

## 2.1 Jesus's Ascended Ontology and Theological Anthropology

In a section of *Space, Time, and Resurrection* entitled "The Material Implications of the Doctrine of the Ascension," Torrance makes three main points: (1) Jesus's ascension "means the exaltation of man into the life of God and on to the throne of God";[2] (2) Jesus's ascension provides the foundation for the church to be rooted "in history, within space and time on the historical foundation of the Apostles and Prophets";[3] and (3) Jesus's ascension "and his session at the right hand of God the Father is the mystery of world history."[4] Each aspect will be considered below.

### 2.1.1 Jesus's Ascension and the Exaltation of Human Beings

In the first point Torrance makes clear connections between the ascended ontology of Jesus and theological anthropology, and in what follows, this integral relationship will be highlighted. Torrance makes one main assertion, followed by an important clarification. He asserts unequivocally how significant the ascension is in his theology—nothing less than the *telos* of the incarnation and human existence is accomplished through it: "In the ascension the Son of Man, New Man in Christ, is given to partake of divine nature. There we reach the goal of the incarnation, in our great *Prodomos* or Forerunner at the right hand of God. We are with Jesus beside God, for we are gathered up in him and included in his own self-presentation before the Father."[5]

The integral relationship between the incarnation and the ascension will be articulated in more detail in the next chapter, but at this stage what

---

2. Torrance, *Space, Time, and Resurrection*, 135.
3. Torrance, *Space, Time, and Resurrection*, 136.
4. Torrance, *Space, Time, and Resurrection*, 137–39.
5. Torrance, *Space, Time, and Resurrection*, 135.

needs to be underscored is the interrelationship between Christology and theological anthropology; in other words, there is a direct relationship between what happens to the humanity of the ascended Jesus and what will happen to human beings. This aspect is evidenced most clearly in Torrance's clarification about what the exaltation of Jesus does *not* accomplish for human beings.

## 2.1.2 *Humans Will Remain Human*

Jesus's ascension and exaltation does not amount to a negation or reduction of humanity within the being of the God-man. On the contrary, Jesus remains human in his ascension, and, by direct implication, human beings will continue to be human in their eschatological existence.[6] In an earlier work, the title for the section in which he articulates these themes is: "*The preservation of human nature and creaturely being*," highlighting the consistency in his thought.[7] Torrance's articulation on the retention of humanity in the eschatological existence because of Jesus's ascension is clearly evidenced in the following declaration: "The staggering thing about this is that the exaltation of human nature into the life of God does not mean the disappearance of man or the swallowing up of human and creaturely being in the infinite ocean of divine Being, but rather that human nature, remaining creaturely and human, is yet exalted in Christ to share in God's life and glory."[8]

Jesus's retention of his full and genuine humanity in his ascension not only shapes how theological anthropology is to be construed as robustly human and physical in its eschatological state, but for Torrance it also provides the key to interpreting passages of Scripture that may suggest non-bodily types of interpretations. For example, Matt 22:30 is a passage of Scripture that declares that the eschatological existence for humans is to be devoid of marriage and to be like angels. Torrance explains this passage to mean (considering Jesus's ascension) that it "cannot be interpreted to imply any denigration of the flesh, on the ground that in the resurrection we will put off the flesh and take on a bodiless angelic nature, for the resurrection does not mean a transformation into another nature, but rather the establishment of human nature in an imperishable state."[9]

---

6. Torrance, *Space, Time, and Resurrection*, 135–36; see also Torrance, *Atonement*, 294–95.

7. Torrance, *Atonement*, 294.

8. Torrance, *Space, Time, and Resurrection*, 135.

9. Torrance, *Space, Time, and Resurrection*, 135n12.

The destiny for humankind is proleptically actualized in Jesus Christ, according to Torrance, and as already intimated earlier, Jesus's ascension as a human "is the ultimate end of creation and redemption."[10] The certainty that such a state of affairs will obtain, Torrance explains, is the reality of Jesus's ascended existence; but for human beings, this is assured by the bestowal of the Holy Spirit "upon us by the ascended man from the throne of God."[11] The Holy Spirit provides one with an immediate experience of the benefits of Christ's ascended reality, but since Torrance does not affirm an overrealized eschatology, he declares that *all* the benefits of Christ's ascension will be fully realized "in the resurrection and redemption of the body."[12]

### 2.1.3 Participating in the Divine Nature

Torrance expands the focus of his discussion to address how *not* to interpret the manner in which humans "partake of the divine nature."[13] In doing so, Torrance provides the reader with additional details of his theological anthropology, which in other places he describes as "*theosis.*"[14] Torrance interprets *theosis* negatively to mean "it has nothing to do with the *divinization* of man," and positively to mean that "creatures though we are, men on earth, in the Spirit we are made to participate in saving acts that are abruptly and absolutely divine, election, adoption, regeneration or sanctification and we participate in them by grace alone."[15] In *Space, Time, and Resurrection*, Torrance can be said to be keen to avoid two erroneous kinds of theological anthropologies, namely, the interpretation of "mystics and pantheists" because they both "tend to identify their own ultimate being with the divine Being."[16] In other words, in these two kinds of interpretations, there is no eschatological existence for humankind because it is subsumed into God's existence. For Torrance, affirming such a view "would be the exact antithesis of what the Christian Gospel teaches," and he goes on to argue his point by maintaining: "for the exaltation of man into sharing the divine life and love, affirms the reality of his humble creaturely being, by making him live out

---

10. Torrance, *Space, Time, and Resurrection*, 135–36.
11. Torrance, *Space, Time, and Resurrection*, 136.
12. Torrance, *Space, Time, and Resurrection*, 136.
13. Torrance, *Space, Time, and Resurrection*, 136.
14. Torrance, *Theology in Reconstruction*, 243.
15. Torrance, *Theology in Reconstruction*, 243. For a recent study on Torrance's doctrine of *theosis*, see Habets, *Theosis*.
16. Torrance, *Space, Time, and Resurrection*, 136.

of the transcendence of God in and through Jesus alone."[17] Two important points need to be underscored, from Torrance's perspective: (1) humans will remain human in their eschatological existence, and (2) human participation in the divine nature is via the mediation of the humanity of Christ.[18] Both of these points are grounded, for Torrance, in the "hypostatic union of divine and human natures in Jesus" because he believes what the hypostatic union testifies to in unmistakable terms is that "Jesus preserves the human and creaturely being he took from us, and it is in and through our sharing in that human and creaturely being, sanctified and blessed in him, that we share in the life of God while remaining what we were made to be, men and not gods."[19]

In making these assertions, Torrance is radically distancing himself, as Habets helpfully notes, from any "Neoplatonic ideas of divinisation," wherein "the creature literally becomes divine in its essence"; and furthermore, he is also making an important distinction between Jesus and the believer: "The eternal Son is 'deified' by nature; the believer in Christ is 'deified' by grace."[20] In making such a clarification, one may wonder what kind of deification happens to Jesus if it is different from what happens in human beings. One can answer this by stating that while there is a distinction between Jesus and the believer, Torrance makes it clear that the principles of Chalcedon apply to Jesus, as evidenced in Torrance's affirmation: "Jesus preserves the human and creaturely being he took from us."[21] Therefore, one cannot conclude that Jesus in his ascension has only a divine nature, but he continues to have two natures—divine and human—in a "hypostatic union."[22]

### 2.1.4 Torrance's Broader Corpus

With respect to the relationship between the ascended ontology of Jesus and theological anthropology, what can be gleaned from the above exposition from *Space, Time, and Resurrection* is that *humans will remain human because Jesus continues to be a human*, and that *humans will participate in the divine nature only through the mediation of the humanity of Jesus*. In other places, Torrance sheds further light on what humanity will be like at the

---

17. Torrance, *Space, Time, and Resurrection*, 136.
18. Torrance, *Space, Time, and Resurrection*, 136.
19. Torrance, *Space, Time, and Resurrection*, 136.
20. Habets, *Theosis*, 193. Nonetheless, Habets still finds a robust doctrine of *theosis* in the work of Torrance.
21. Torrance, *Space, Time, and Resurrection*, 136.
22. Torrance, *Space, Time, and Resurrection*, 136.

eschaton, and because Torrance derives his theological anthropology from his Christology (not the other way around), it can be deduced that the ascended Christ instantiates these properties in the first instance. Humankind at the eschaton will be: (1) creaturely and finite, (2) a composite of body and soul, and (3) biologically differentiated as male and female.[23]

### 2.1.4.1 Creaturely and Finite

For Torrance, there is no aspect of the human being that is not creaturely and finite. A fundamental theological conviction undergirding such a resolve in Torrance is: "If to be divine and uncreated is to be intrinsically immortal, then to be creaturely and human is to be intrinsically mortal."[24] Torrance makes these convictions clear in the context of illuminating the nature of the soul in the human being. In contrast to Greek thinking where the soul possesses an eternal nature, Torrance makes unequivocally clear that "the Christian view, however, is that the soul is a creature no less than the body.... Considered in itself, the soul can only pass away: it is intrinsically mortal and not immortal."[25] With this said, it must be clarified that Torrance does believe that human beings will live eternally at the eschaton, but attributes life eternal, not to anything intrinsic within the human, but to God alone: "Human immortality can only be conceived as a gift of God's grace within a relation between the creature and God which God will not terminate but brings to a fruition in what the New Testament calls 'eternal life.'"[26] In another place, Torrance notes, that resurrection life for human beings will be "creaturely participation in the uncreated eternal Life of God."[27] This confirms the consistency in Torrance's thought regarding how human beings will remain human and creaturely in the eschaton.

### 2.1.4.2 Composite of Body and Soul

Humanity is to be understood, Torrance declares, in a "non-dualist" way, and shaped by "the Hebrew view of humanity."[28] In such a view, "man's body and soul were regarded as forming an integrated unity, with man's body

---

23. See Torrance: "Soul and Person"; Torrance, "Immortality and Light."
24. Torrance, "Immortality and Light," 149.
25. Torrance, "Immortality and Light," 149.
26. Torrance, "Immortality and Light," 151.
27. Torrance, "Soul and Person," 106.
28. Torrance, *Christian Frame of Mind*, 35.

as body of his soul and his soul as soul of his body."[29] Both aspects, soul and body, together make up a human being, and there is no room for any conception wherein they are "regarded as antithetical."[30] With such an integrated nature of human beings firmly in place, Torrance highlights how central the body is in the equation of what constitutes a human being: "A Christian understanding of man's continuing personal life after death has to take the body into its basic equation."[31] To be sure, both body and soul are important, but the central place for the body needed to be highlighted because a Christian theological anthropology had to be forged, Torrance explains, in an intellectual milieu that had a strong disdain for the physical body.[32]

### 2.1.4.3 Biologically Differentiated as Male and Female

Gender and sexual differentiation, for Torrance, are ontological categories, not functional ones. In other words, "difference in sex is not simply a feature of the body, merely adventitious or accidental to the soul, but is intrinsic to the human soul which, far from being neutral, *is* either male or female."[33] To be either male or female, Torrance declares, is an intrinsic, nonnegotiable feature of what it means to be human. This aspect, Torrance acknowledges, was not popular in patristic theology because a patriarchal understanding was predominant.[34] The biblical teaching, however, would not entertain any patriarchal understanding, according to Torrance, because of "the 'goodness' of what God had created, together with its rejection of dualist and

---

29. Torrance, *Christian Frame of Mind*, 35.

30. Torrance, "Immortality and Light," 151. Here, Torrance explains that the phraseology "body of his soul and soul of his body" is taken from a Drew lecture given by James Denney in 1910.

31. Torrance, "Immortality and Light," 151.

32. Torrance explains that a "Greek or Oriental" kind of thinking of a human being would perceive "the end of his [human being] physical existence as the release of his spirit." For more, see Torrance, "Immortality and Light," 151. See also Torrance, *Christian Frame of Mind*, 35, where he observes that "Greek and Roman views of humanity" affirmed "a radical dualism of body and soul (or mind), the soul being regarded as but loosely related to the body in which it is temporally imprisoned."

33. Torrance, "Soul and Person," 108–9.

34. Torrance, "Soul and Person," 109: it was a "generally accepted [in patristic theology] biological idea that it is in the male sperm alone that the whole 'seed' of human being is contained, with the female supplying only the womb to shelter its germination and nourish its growth into infancy."

Manichaeistic denigration of the body as evil."[35] Such a biblical belief led to the conclusion that "sexuality thus determines the innermost being of people, making them either male or female in themselves."[36] Importantly, the reason for the creation of male and female, Torrance highlights, was for *relationships*: "man *is* man only in relation to woman, and woman *is* woman only in relation to man."[37] In the resurrection, human beings will continue to exist as male and female, Torrance underscores: "It should be pointed out that this divinely instituted union between man and woman is a characteristic not only of their creation but of their life in the resurrection in which their creation as man and woman will be brought to its ultimate completion."[38] Torrance clarifies that there will be no sexual procreation in the resurrection between the two sexes, as Jesus made clear, "but the bond of union between man and woman remains intact—far from being dissolved by the resurrection, it will be perfected and eternalized."[39] This aspect remains controversial in contemporary scholarship, and Torrance's reasons for such a view will be elaborated in more detail below.[40] It will pay to return to Torrance's *Space, Time, and Resurrection*, to discern more about the ontology of the ascended Jesus, this time vis-à-vis ecclesiology.

## 2.2 Jesus's Ascended Ontology and Ecclesiology

Torrance's presentation in *Space, Time, and Resurrection* proceeds to highlight the integral relationship between the ascended Jesus and ecclesiology, and this is evidenced in points (2) and (3) in his section on "The Material Implications of the Doctrine of the Ascension."[41]

---

35. Torrance, "Soul and Person," 109.
36. Torrance, "Soul and Person," 109.
37. Torrance, "Soul and Person," 109.
38. Torrance, "Soul and Person," 109.
39. Torrance, "Soul and Person," 109.
40. See section 3.1, entitled "Jesus's Ascended Ontology and Theological Anthropology: Not Gregory of Nyssa's View," for more on this point. Torrance's views on gender and sexuality are controversial for at least two reasons: (1) his binary understanding of humanity as male or female will be challenged by the sexuality, gender, and identity politics of the current intellectual milieu; and (2) his affirmation of an egalitarian understanding of human persons differs from patristic theologians who affirmed patriarchy on the one hand and others who envisioned the eschatological state of the human person as non-gendered. For an overview of two kinds of theologies on whether there will be gender in the eschaton, see Vale, "Cappadocian or Augustinian?"
41. See Torrance, *Space, Time, and Resurrection*, 136–39.

## 2.2.1 Jesus's Ascension and the Historical Church

Jesus's ascension has real implications for the way in which ecclesiology should be construed. Torrance makes one main declaration, and fleshes this out in two specific ways. His declaration is that the church is to be rooted "within space and time on the historical foundation of the Apostles and Prophets."[42] It is this community, the church, with its identity rooted in historical events of decisive significance, that is called to be located historically in various contexts of the earth. Jesus's ascension, rather than dismissing the importance for the church to be grounded in "processes and structured patterns of history as a coherent Body," underscores its centrality.[43] In other words, the church is commissioned to the task of carrying out Jesus's mission *on earth*, which means that it will have to deal with the vicissitudes involved in having to necessarily adopt "this-worldly forms of life as they develop among the nations and peoples and kingdoms of historical existence."[44] Torrance fleshes this central declaration out in two specific ways.

### 2.2.1.1 SCRIPTURE AND CHURCH PRACTICES

For Torrance, the church is rooted in a specific tradition that goes all the way back to the historical Jesus, to his disciples, and further still to God's revelation in and through Israel.[45] This grounding is evidenced in both the "Holy Scriptures" and specific church practices that originated with the "apostolic tradition" and passed on ever since.[46] Torrance contends that "the Church's life, worship and prayer can no more be spaceless and timeless than its historical existence can be detached from historical relation to its historical roots in Jesus Christ," and in doing so makes it clear that just as there is to be no docetic conception of Christ's ascended being, so too is there no room for any docetic conception of the church of Jesus Christ.[47] Torrance further elaborates on how the church is to be grounded in various church practices but not tied to them so dogmatically that these structures are taken to be the ultimate reality.[48]

---

42. Torrance, *Space, Time, and Resurrection*, 136.
43. Torrance, *Space, Time, and Resurrection*, 136–37.
44. Torrance, *Space, Time, and Resurrection*, 137.
45. Torrance, *Space, Time, and Resurrection*, 137, 161, 178.
46. Torrance, *Space, Time, and Resurrection*, 137.
47. Torrance, *Space, Time, and Resurrection*, 137.
48. Torrance, *Space, Time, and Resurrection*, 137.

### 2.2.1.2 Church Structures Are to be Held Loosely

Torrance holds two aspects in tension. On the one hand, church structures are important because they testify to its historical rooting, but on the other hand, dogmatic allegiance to such structures do not bode well with truths that the "resurrection and ascension" declare, namely, that "the full reality of the new humanity of the Church as the Body of Christ will be unveiled" only at the eschaton.[49] Therefore, in the current period church structures are to be viewed "more like scaffolding," which is important but only for a period of time, until the more permanent structure is established.[50] Torrance's exposition on the relationship between the ascension and ecclesiology point to important insights; namely, the *now-and-not-yet* aspects of the church, which will be discussed further in another section of this chapter.[51]

### 2.2.2 *Jesus's Ascension, Session, and Its Implications on Earth*

With respect to the ascension, the session, and its implications, Torrance makes one main point, and illuminates it in two ways. Principally, he argues that the ascension and session provide the proper perspective to interpreting "world history."[52] Central to this perspective is the current reality of the Lordship of Christ *on earth*.[53] Torrance will not entertain any idea of viewing the ascension "in the old manner of idealistic Christianity as a flight from history," but instead it must be viewed emphatically "as the invasion of history by the Kingdom of Christ through the everlasting Gospel."[54] Such a perspective is available even now, Torrance explains, to one who has "the eyes of faith," and therefore is able to put things in proper perspective and see the victory that God in Jesus Christ is bringing about, even when it does not seem like it, through various events in the world.[55] This point about the victory of Christ while presented from a human vantage point (from the point of view of those who have faith), is re-presented next by Torrance from the perspective of the risen and ascended Christ.

---

49. Torrance, *Space, Time, and Resurrection*, 137.
50. Torrance, *Space, Time, and Resurrection*, 137.
51. See section 2.2.3.2, "Ethical Implications," for more on this point.
52. Torrance, *Space, Time, and Resurrection*, 137; see also Torrance, *Atonement*, 296.
53. Torrance, *Space, Time, and Resurrection*, 137–38.
54. Torrance, *Space, Time, and Resurrection*, 138.
55. Torrance, *Space, Time, and Resurrection*, 138.

## 2.2.2.1 The Ascended Christ's Perspective

For Torrance, the period "from resurrection to final advent" is called "*millennium-time*"—and this belongs to the risen and ascended Lord, who is now able to see all earthly events from the vantage point of an already accomplished victory.[56] Torrance calls this period "history seen from the point of the triumph of the risen Lamb of God who subornes [*sic*] all world events to serve God's saving purpose."[57] This victorious perspective is shaped by a crucicentrism, by which is meant that retrospectively it was *through* the cross that God accomplished this "salvation of mankind," and prospectively that God will bring about "the new creation" by the "same Cross."[58] The ascended Christ's perspective, Torrance urges, should be adopted as it assures one about the eventuality of Christ's reign: "for it is what he has done and is that will prevail until all history is subdued and brought into conformity to his saving Will."[59] For Torrance, the church's ministry of intercession proleptically declares on earth today Christ's eventual victory.

## 2.2.2.2 The Ascended Christ and the Church's Participation in Intercession

The ascended Christ's victory should cause the church to take seriously the work of intercession, primarily because it is "the great connecting link between world history and the heavenly session of Christ" and also because it is a practice of proleptic eschatology.[60] The ministry of intercession is crucial, Torrance explains, because according to him the New Testament deems it the church's "most important service" to the world, and also because by engaging in it one is not only in one accord with the ascended Lord, one is also in concert with him against "the forces of darkness."[61] Since the victory over such powers has already been achieved by the crucified and risen Lord Jesus in the ministry of intercession, the church is engaging in a proleptic-eschatological kind of prayer, wherein "prayer is already a participation in the final victory of the Kingdom of Christ."[62]

---

56. Torrance, *Space, Time, and Resurrection*, 138. This position can best be described as the classic Reformed Amillennial view.
57. Torrance, *Space, Time, and Resurrection*, 138.
58. Torrance, *Space, Time, and Resurrection*, 138.
59. Torrance, *Space, Time, and Resurrection*, 138.
60. Torrance, *Space, Time, and Resurrection*, 138–39.
61. Torrance, *Space, Time, and Resurrection*, 138.
62. Torrance, *Space, Time, and Resurrection*, 139.

## 2.2.3 Torrance's Broader Corpus

The integral relationship between the ascended ontology of Jesus and ecclesiology is illustrated in the above section *by the physicality of both the ascended Christ and his church*. In other words, just as the incarnate existence of Christ continues in his bodily ascension, so too the church has an incarnational existence, and as such manifests itself on the earth through its historical situatedness, the tangible Scriptures, church structures, and specific practices like intercession.[63] Torrance underscores these themes succinctly when he states: "As the Word of God became irrevocably involved with a physical event, so in the Church the same Word is involved in a physical event. In other language, the Church extends the corporeality of the Word and mediates it to a corporeal world through such physical events as the Bible, Preaching, the Sacraments, etc., and the physical society of those who belong to the Church."[64] Two further aspects are highlighted in the following section, namely, the ontological relationship between the ascended Christ and his church and the ethical implications of the ontology of the ascended Jesus for the church.

### 2.2.3.1 The Ontological Relationship Between the Ascended Christ and His Church

Is there any sense of an ontological equating of Christ with the church or Eucharist, in Torrance's thinking? The answer is a resolute no, but before expositing this rejection, there are places where Torrance does highlight the ontological relationship between Christ and the church that need to be considered. For instance: "When we speak of the Church as Christ's Body we are certainly using analogical language, but we are speaking nevertheless of an ontological fact, that is, of a relation of *being* between the Church and Christ."[65] Elsewhere, Torrance writes about the close relationship between Christ and the church, especially in the act of the Eucharist, as follows: "Christ has become bone of our bone and flesh of our flesh, but in the Eucharist we become bone of His bone and flesh of His flesh. No union, save that of the Persons of the Holy Trinity, could be closer, without passing into absolute identity, than that between Christ and His Church as enacted in the Holy Eucharist."[66]

---

63. See also Torrance, *Conflict and Agreement*, 1:206–7.
64. Torrance, *Conflict and Agreement*, 1:206–7.
65. Torrance, *Royal Priesthood*, 29.
66. Torrance, *Conflict and Agreement*, 2:188–89.

Does this, then, amount to an ontological equating of Christ with the church or the Eucharist? As mentioned above, the answer is no, and resolutely so for Torrance, because he believes that "when St. Paul speaks of the Church as the Body of Christ, He is expressly *distinguishing* the Church from Christ, although the being of the Church is grounded in the oneness of the love between the Father and the Son."[67] Lest there are any lingering doubts, Torrance further explains, "While the Church is one Body with Christ it is in no sense an extension of His Personality (surely an un-Biblical conception) or an extension of His incarnation, not to speak of a reincarnation of the Risen Lord."[68] As if these explanations were not sufficient, Torrance quotes from Ian Muirhead to provide a more robust expansion of such a negation: "She is not Christ continued, the Incarnation continued. One cannot pass without interruption from Christ to the Church. The Cross stands between. In being the Body of Christ, the Church meets her Lord; she does not prolong Him, but she expresses Him here and now. She does not replace Him, but makes Him visible, demonstrates Him without being confounded with Him."[69] As is evidenced, for Torrance, there is a close relationship between Christ and the church and Eucharist, but there is no fusion between them, such that the ascended Christ gets lost. The distinct identities of the ascended Christ and the church remain.

### 2.2.3.2 Ethical Implications of the Ontology of the Ascended Jesus for the Church

The ontology of the ascended Jesus has theological and practical (ethical) implications for Torrance. Theologically, "it is the advent which reminds the Church that although it is already one Body with Christ through the Spirit, it has yet to be made one Body with Him in the consummation of His Kingdom."[70] What will be purified in the church at the eschaton, Torrance explains, will not only be its own sin but also the temporary structures within the church, and inclusive within this are the "Bible" and "Sacrament," of which, Torrance avers, "there will be no need . . . for the Word and Lamb Himself will be in the midst of His Church."[71] While this is the theological longing with which the church is to live, Torrance drawing from Calvin, makes a more immediate, practical point about the need for ethics in the

---

67. Torrance, *Royal Priesthood*, 31.
68. Torrance, *Royal Priesthood*, 31.
69. Torrance, *Royal Priesthood*, 31.
70. Torrance, *Conflict and Agreement*, 1:115.
71. Torrance, *Conflict and Agreement*, 1:115.

church: "union with the humanity of Christ means that here and now we must live out that humanity from day to day in the midst of the earth—that is why Calvin's sermons are always pressing home to the Church the need to be concerned with *humanité* in every aspect of its life and work."[72] There is, as it were, both a forward looking impulse within the church, but also a present focus, to live out the future realities that the ascended Jesus represents for the church. Both these aspects are equally important for the church.

As evidenced in the explication above, Torrance describes Christ's risen ontology not just in relationship to Christology but to theological anthropology, to ecclesiology, and to eschatology. He does focus more on Christology, to be sure, true to the nature of his christocentric theology, but even in such a section, there are implications for how the Eucharist is to be viewed, and therefore, having critically explicated Torrance's section entitled "The Material Implications of the Doctrine of the Ascension," transitioning to discerning what he states about the interrelationship between the resurrection and ascension will be important.

## 2.3 Jesus's Ascended Ontology and Christology

### 2.3.1 Interrelationship Between Resurrection and Ascension

Torrance declares that there is an integral relationship between the resurrection and ascension, which can be explained both biblically and theologically. Biblically, he draws insights from Hebrews and John's writings to declare that the resurrection and ascension can be understood "in the perspective of Christ's victory over the powers of darkness and over the evil that separates creation from its Creator," or as "the triumph of light over darkness."[73] Does such an affirmation endorse viewing Christ's resurrected and ascended humanity "as transfused with light, and as perfectly transparent?"[74] As will be demonstrated momentarily, Torrance asks this question with the intention of answering it in terms of its ontological and relational aspects. Ontologically, for Torrance, Jesus's resurrected and ascended body does not transfuse into a spirit being: "This is not to say that the Body of Christ in the resurrection and ascension was transmuted into pure spirit."[75] Relationally, Christ's resurrected and ascended humanity is

---

72. Torrance, *Conflict and Agreement*, 1:99.
73. Torrance, *Space, Time, and Resurrection*, 139.
74. Torrance, *Space, Time, and Resurrection*, 139.
75. Torrance, *Space, Time, and Resurrection*, 139.

vicariously in perfect communion with God: "The opaqueness and darkness that come from separation from God are utterly overcome and put away."[76] Torrance elaborates on both the ontological and relational aspects and it will be highlighted in what follows, but not before underscoring his theological reasons for maintaining the close relationship between the resurrection and ascension. Theologically, both the resurrection and ascension are important because they together testify that the doctrine of "creation" is integrally related to the doctrine of "recreation" or "redemption," and by this is meant that the telos for humankind is achieved in the humanity of the risen and ascended Christ.[77] In the resurrection and ascension, Torrance declares that Jesus accomplishes the removal of "all darkness (our darkness into which Christ descended) . . . and even the human nature he took from our dark and fallen existence is completely and finally restored to the light of God (2 Cor. 4: 6)."[78] In other words, for Torrance, the ascension accomplishes the vicarious cleansing of our humanity.

### 2.3.1.1 Ontology, Relationality, and Epistemology

For Torrance, ontology, relationality, and epistemology are integrally related when it comes to a theology of Jesus's resurrected and ascended being. An epistemological humility must be exercised from a human point of view, Torrance asserts, because in essence, the resurrected and ascended Jesus is not in a "fallen" humanity anymore, while all other human beings are.[79] Therefore, understandably, Torrance reckons that the early disciples were not able to fully understand the postresurrection appearances of Jesus, not least Jesus's ability to appear and disappear at will, as the disciples at Emmaus experienced.[80] Nor were the disciples able to completely grasp Jesus's ascension, and this must be the case, Torrance avers, because the disciples did not have the conceptual tools in their own experience to make sense of either event.[81] Even the tools of history would not be adequate for such a task, because its resources, Torrance explains, would be adept to understanding only a "historiography accommodated to this fallen existence."[82] Torrance states categorically that it is "only when we are redeemed in body

---

76. Torrance, *Space, Time, and Resurrection*, 139.
77. Torrance, *Space, Time, and Resurrection*, 139.
78. Torrance, *Space, Time, and Resurrection*, 139.
79. Torrance, *Space, Time, and Resurrection*, 139–40.
80. Torrance, *Space, Time, and Resurrection*, 139.
81. Torrance, *Space, Time, and Resurrection*, 139–40.
82. Torrance, *Space, Time, and Resurrection*, 140.

ourselves, in the fullness of humanity, when our eyes are truly and finally pure, that we will be able to see Christ in all his risen and transcendent glory."[83] With these epistemological insights serving as a guide, Torrance tackles the ontological question, and it will pay to focus on this aspect.

### 2.3.1.2 Ontology

The corporeality of the risen and ascended Jesus is important for Torrance. Put differently, Jesus has a resurrected and ascended *body*. There is no room for any kind of evaporation of this body, for Torrance, as already highlighted earlier, but at this stage Torrance expounds this view in more detail by taking on those readings that he believes undermine the body of the risen and ascended Jesus. Torrance first defines such a view, before going on to show why it is not tenable. His definition of the view is as follows:

> The idea of the spiritualization and transparency of the risen and ascended humanity of Christ through its complete impregnation with divine light developed in Origenist circles in the early Church. Apparently "the spiritual body" of the resurrection was regarded as an incorporeal orb of radiant light (this was partly in accordance with the Platonic idea that the essential form of the real was the "mathematical" sphere)—traces of this idea appear centuries later in Dante, and in the picturesque mythologizing of the drama of salvation that is found in the stained glass of many Mediaeval Cathedrals.[84]

Torrance does not fully lay the blame for such a view on Origen, but neither does he declare him free from guilt.[85] Augustine, too, is brought under Torrance's theological scanner, for his Platonic tendencies: "St. Augustine, who, under the influence of Plato, held that the incorruptible bodies of the saints are like the ethereal bodies of the stars."[86] With this said, it must be underscored that Torrance rejects the "spiritualization" (or non-corporeal/non-physical) interpretation for Christ's resurrected and ascended state for three reasons: (1) it does not practice proper epistemic humility; (2) it does not properly interpret the "spiritual body" of the resurrected and ascended

---

83. Torrance, *Space, Time, and Resurrection*, 140.
84. Torrance, *Space, Time, and Resurrection*, 140.
85. Torrance, *Space, Time, and Resurrection*, 140n13.
86. Torrance, *Space, Time, and Resurrection*, 140n14.

Christ; and (3) it does not take into proper account the "*empty tomb*" of Jesus.[87]

### 2.3.1.2.1 Epistemic Humility

It is Torrance's contention that those who interpret the resurrected and ascended body of Jesus in non-corporeal and non-physical terms are making a twofold error: (1) they are not exercising a "proper theological reserve at the boundary of the eschatological," and (2) they are not remaining within "the limits set by the Word."[88] Torrance has already underscored the importance of recognizing the human inability to understand the fullness of the resurrected and ascended humanity of Jesus because he is not in a "fallen" state anymore, while the rest of humankind are. It is only at the eschaton where the fullness of Jesus will be revealed, and it is this theological reality, Torrance avers, that should provide sufficient caution to anyone claiming that Jesus possesses an ontology composed only of spirit in his risen and ascended state.[89] Furthermore, Torrance also believes that scriptural witness would not corroborate any notion of Jesus being in a non-physical state in his resurrection and ascension, and it is this point that he further develops by interpreting what is meant by "spiritual body" and the "empty tomb."

### 2.3.1.2.2 A Spiritual Body

While Torrance does not explicitly mention it at this stage of his argument in *Space, Time, and Resurrection*, he is in essence providing an interpretation of the "spiritual body" of Jesus that is found in 1 Cor 15. As it will be demonstrated from within Torrance's theology momentarily, he does not create a divide between the so-called Lukan and Pauline trajectories, one emphasizing continuity and the other highlighting discontinuity between the earthly and ascended Jesus.[90] For Torrance, both these trajectories (Lu-

---

87. Torrance, *Space, Time, and Resurrection*, 140–41.
88. Torrance, *Space, Time, and Resurrection*, 140.
89. Torrance, *Space, Time, and Resurrection*, 140.
90. Harris, "Science," 212, highlights how both these perspectives, Lukan and Pauline, are pitted against each other in biblical and theological scholarship. He endorses a view that takes in insights from both the Lukan and Pauline perspectives. From Torrance's perspective, however, there is both continuity and discontinuity between the earthly Jesus and the resurrected and ascended Jesus, and as such both so-called Lukan and Pauline views need not be mutually exclusive.

kan and Pauline) are not mutually exclusive as will be evidenced in the way Torrance interprets "spiritual body":

> The resurrection of the body to be a "spiritual body" no more means that the body is resolved away into spirit than the fact that we are made "spiritual men" in Christ means that our humanity is dissolved away in him. To be a spiritual man is to be not less than man but more fully and truly man. To be a spiritual body is not to be less body but more truly and completely body, for by the Spirit physical existence is redeemed from all that corrupts and undermines it, and from all or any privation of being.[91]

Torrance underscores one point in three different ways in the passage above about what it means to have a "spiritual body": (1) it is still physical, (2) it is still human, in fact, it is completely human, and (3) it is physical, human, and by the Holy Spirit's work, free from all corruption and decay.[92] Torrance underscores each of these points by referring to the reality of the empty tomb.

### 2.3.1.2.3 The Empty Tomb

The empty tomb of Jesus, Torrance emphasizes, must be taken "quite seriously" because it attests to two central truths. First, it asserts that the resurrection must be interpreted in *bodily* terms, and therefore "spiritual body" cannot mean anything less than a body that is physical, corporeal, and free from corruption and decay: "The body of Jesus Christ was raised, certainly a spiritual body, but it was no less body because it was a body healed and quickened by the Spirit in which all corruption had been overcome."[93] Second, the resurrection of the body of Jesus happened *on earth*, and this is significant for Torrance because it testifies to "the triumph of Christ over the space-time of our fallen world."[94] In other words, Christ was victorious over the grave in the earth that we inhabit, not in the heavens where we can

---

91. Torrance, *Space, Time, and Resurrection*, 140–41.

92. Torrance, *Space, Time, and Resurrection*, 140–41. Cf. Wright, *Resurrection*, 477–78, where Wright uses the term "Transphysical" to describe the resurrected ontology of Jesus, thereby underscoring "that the early Christians envisaged a body which was still robustly physical but also significantly different from the present one. If anything—since the main difference they seem to have envisaged is that the new body will not be corruptible—we might say not that it will be *less* physical, as though it were some kind of ghost or apparition, but more."

93. Torrance, *Space, Time, and Resurrection*, 141.

94. Torrance, *Space, Time, and Resurrection*, 141.

have no tangible sign of it. While there is cause for confidence because the empty tomb is an *"empirical correlate in statements about the resurrection of Christ,"*[95] Torrance provides one admonishment, followed by a clarification about the resurrection.

The admonishment highlights how humans are incapable of fully understanding the inner workings of a miracle, like the resurrection or the act of creation: "We cannot observe or pin down in our grasp the process of resurrecting any more than we can observe or pin down in our grasp the process of creating."[96] The clarification focuses on how the resurrected being of Jesus, just like other aspects of creation, could be seen by the disciples, but the manner in which this seeing was to take place was "by faith": "as the created reality is observable, so the resurrected reality was apprehensible to the disciples, apprehensible, of course in a mode appropriate to its nature, i.e. by faith."[97] From all that is stated above, there can be no mistaking what Torrance means *ontologically* about the resurrected and ascended body of Jesus. He goes on to substantiate the *relational* and *epistemological* aspects of Jesus's resurrected and ascended being.

### 2.3.1.2.4 Relationality and Epistemology

Torrance, in the conclusion of his section on the relationship between the resurrection and ascension in *Space, Time, and Resurrection*, reiterates a theme that he has already discussed, namely, the relational aspects of the resurrected and ascended Jesus. However, he also sheds further light on the epistemological role the Holy Spirit plays in the period from the ascension to the eschaton, and finally concludes with an illustration of how the Eucharist testifies to a holistic understanding of salvation.[98] Torrance does not explicitly mention that he is underscoring the relational aspects of Jesus's ascended being when he states the following: "There is, however, a deep element of truth in the doctrine of the transparency of the new creation in Christ—its utter lack of all opacity and darkness."[99] However, based on what he stated earlier in the section, one can be confident that he is highlighting the relational dimensions of the new creation already realized in Christ.[100]

- 95. Torrance, *Space, Time, and Resurrection*, 141.
- 96. Torrance, *Space, Time, and Resurrection*, 141.
- 97. Torrance, *Space, Time, and Resurrection*, 141.
- 98. Torrance, *Space, Time, and Resurrection*, 141–42.
- 99. Torrance, *Space, Time, and Resurrection*, 141.

100. See, for example, Torrance, *Space, Time, and Resurrection*, 139, where he describes Jesus's resurrected and ascended body as follows: "The opaqueness and darkness that come from separation from God are utterly overcome and put away."

In other words, the ascended Christ is not in a "fallen" humanity anymore, and therefore is vicariously in a perfect relationship with God. However, understanding all that this entails is beyond human ability to grasp until the eschaton, when the bodily resurrection of all people will take place.[101] This is why the epistemological role of the Holy Spirit becomes crucial.

The Holy Spirit, according to Torrance, is not only sent "by the risen and ascended Lord" but he also "creates in us the capacity to discern and understand beyond what we are naturalistically capable of in ourselves," and he is additionally the one responsible to help us "know the reality of God himself in Christ in such a way as to distinguish it from our own objective states and conditions."[102] Crucially, it is the Holy Spirit who enables one to "apprehend Christ in his actuality as resurrected in the body and thus as the First-fruits of the new *creation* and the First-born of every *creature*."[103] In other words, the Holy Spirit testifies not only to Jesus's resurrected reality but also attests to the future resurrection of every other person.[104] He elucidates this point through an analogy about human childbirth taken from the early church fathers to underscore the certainty of the future resurrection of all persons: "When a baby is born it is usually born head first, but when the head is born the whole body follows naturally, for it is the birth of the head that is the most difficult part."[105] In the analogy, Christ's resurrection body is likened to the head of a baby and, just as the rest of the body proceeds after the head, Torrance assures, so, too, will the resurrection of all other people follow suit.[106] Torrance highlights a point here that must not be missed: "We who are incorporated with him as his Body will rise with him and be born into the new creation in our *physical* as well as our *spiritual* existence."[107] The resurrection existence of Christ is composed of both physical aspects (ontology), as well as spiritual aspects (relational), and both these aspects will in turn be present in all other human beings. Returning to this point about the reality of the future resurrection in the body based on Christ's own resurrection, Torrance highlights how the Eucharist testifies to this reality now.

The Eucharist contains in miniature form a testimony about how human salvation at the resurrection is to be understood in holistic terms. In other words, the physicality of the elements of bread and wine digested in

---

101. Torrance, *Space, Time, and Resurrection*, 141.
102. Torrance, *Space, Time, and Resurrection*, 141–42.
103. Torrance, *Space, Time, and Resurrection*, 142.
104. Torrance, *Space, Time, and Resurrection*, 142.
105. Torrance, *Space, Time, and Resurrection*, 142.
106. Torrance, *Space, Time, and Resurrection*, 142.
107. Torrance, *Space, Time, and Resurrection*, 142 (emphasis added).

the act of the Eucharist testifies, according to Torrance, to the physicality of the future resurrection of the body.[108] By participating in the Eucharist with such a theology, Torrance explains, one is tangibly proclaiming the future resurrection, and he muses: "No wonder early Christians could speak of the Eucharist as 'the medicine of immortality.'"[109] Such a phrase vividly captures the physicality of the future resurrection.

## 2.3.2 Torrance's Broader Corpus

The ascended ontology of Jesus in the above section can be described as (1) physical and human, (2) in a perfect relationship with God, and (3) beyond fallen human ken to grasp until the resurrection. In other places, Torrance provides (4) the creedal and theological influences behind his view, (5) crucial pastoral implications, and (6) an affirmation of the Jewish identity of the ascended Jesus.

### 2.3.2.1 CREEDAL AND THEOLOGICAL SOURCES

In *Space, Time, and Incarnation*, which is the companion volume to *Space, Time, and Resurrection*, Torrance writes about the permanence of Jesus's embodied existence from the incarnation onwards and even into eternity.[110] He asserts as follows: "But the addition to the Creed of the words 'whose Kingdom shall have no end' crowned the conviction that the assumption of our corporeal existence by the Son of God was not '*only* economic,' i.e. a temporary episode, for the involvement of the Son of God in our human and creaturely being, even after His resurrection, ascension, and *parousia*, must be maintained without reserve."[111] In another source, *Scottish Theology: From John Knox to John McLeod Campbell*, Torrance concurs with John Knox's views on the bodily nature of Jesus's ascension, with the emphasis on the continuity of Jesus from one phase of his life to the other: "Knox laid unusually strong emphasis on the ascension of Jesus Christ in the self-same body which was born of the Virgin Mary, and was crucified, dead and

---

108. Torrance, *Space, Time, and Resurrection*, 142.

109. Torrance, *Space, Time, and Resurrection*, 142. Torrance refers to the works of Ignatius, Serapion, and Clement of Alexandria to substantiate his quotation. He provides the following citations on p. 142n7: "Ignatius, *Epistle to the Ephesians*, 20.2; Serapion, *Euchologion*, 17.2; cf. Clement of Alexandria, *Protrepticos*, 10."

110. Torrance, *Space, Time, and Incarnation*, 3–4.

111. Torrance, *Space, Time, and Incarnation*, 3–4.

buried and which rose again, and very rightly."[112] In his 1938–39 Auburn lectures on Christology, Torrance's stress on the duration of Jesus's embodiment in human form post-incarnation comes across, perhaps, most clearly:

> Let us remember that what the Nicene Bishops and Theologians called "the hypostatic union of God and man" in the Lord Jesus, of the union of eternal Word of God with the humanity of the Lord Jesus, was/is eternal and never-ending. If Jesus Christ is also Man, and precisely as *Man* rose from the dead, then there must still be a proper place for our steady understanding of him in theology.[113]

Torrance draws on various theological resources to affirm the humanity of Jesus in his ascension; in fact, he goes on to affirm Jesus's humanity for eternity.

#### 2.3.2.2 Pastoral Implications

Torrance highlights the incompleteness of a christocentric theology if it does not take into account the ongoing humanity of Christ.[114] The immense pastoral dimensions of these truths also come to bear in Torrance's work when he highlights the fact that there is in heaven one who was ontologically bonded with humankind on earth, and *still is* in heaven: "There is a *MAN* in heaven today, one who knows all about us, one who suffered with us and for us, one who was tempted in all points as we are, and knows all our infirmities, trials and temptations, and who nevertheless came through them all and ascended to the very right hand of God the Father to be *our* representative before him for ever."[115] The continuity in the identity of Jesus from his earthly life to his ascended life, for Torrance, provides significant pastoral and existential comfort to followers of Jesus.

#### 2.3.2.3 The Ascended Jesus as a Jew

One can confidently assert that for Torrance, Jesus is still a Jew in his ascension because of what he states in an article entitled "Salvation Is of the Jews." Says Torrance: "The knowledge of God and the Jews are bound up together, so that when God came into this world He came as a Jew. And to this very

---

112. Torrance, *Scottish Theology*, 21.
113. Torrance, *Doctrine of Jesus Christ*, 190.
114. Torrance, *Doctrine of Jesus Christ*, 190.
115. Torrance, *Doctrine of Jesus Christ*, 193.

day Jesus remains a Jew while still the eternal Son of God."[116] Stan MacLean sheds further light on what Torrance means when he states, "Jesus' Jewish ethnicity, cultural, and religious background are not just incidental aspects of the incarnation. We need to see Jesus 'as he really is,' and that means 'as a Jew.' We need to think of him [Jesus] as such not only at Christmas but all the time, since the resurrection and bodily ascension of Jesus mean that 'to this very day' he 'remains a Jew while still the eternal Son of God.'"[117] The Jewishness of Jesus, according to Torrance, continues even after his resurrection and ascension.

## 2.4 Section Summary

In the above section, Torrance's theology of Christ's ascended ontology was critically expounded in relation to (1) theological anthropology, (2) ecclesiology, and (3) Christology. In relation to theological anthropology, it was observed that Torrance affirms the existence of humans *as* humans in the eschaton because Jesus retains his humanity. Furthermore, for Torrance, humanity is not generic but specific, which means that it is creaturely, composed of body and soul, and biologically differentiated as male and female.

Regarding ecclesiology, there is an "earthiness"[118] to the church, in Torrance's theology, by which is meant that there is no sense of a docetic understanding of the church, but a firm grounding of the church on the earth. This grounding is evidenced in specific tangible aspects, like Scripture and specific church practices, not least the work of intercession for the world, in concert with the ascended Jesus. By way of clarification, it was also emphasized that for Torrance, while there is an integral relationship between the ascended Christ and the church and Eucharist, there is no subsuming of one into the other. The distinct identities of Christ and the church and Eucharist remain intact.

Perhaps most importantly, what the ascended ontology states about Torrance's Christology is that Jesus remains both human and divine in his ascension. More specifically, it was demonstrated that for Torrance the "spiritual body" of Jesus does not diminish Jesus's humanity in the least; in fact, it adds to it. Jesus is still human, but there are continuities and discontinuities that need to be investigated further. The continuities from what was described in the sections above are that the ascended Jesus is still a human,

---

116. Torrance, "Salvation," 166.

117. MacLean, "'Salvation,'" 2. MacLean in this part of his article quotes two of Torrance's works: *Mediation of Christ*, 20; and "Salvation," 166.

118. See Harris, "Science," 212.

and by this is meant very specific things, like a being composed of both body and soul, biologically gendered as a male, and that he remains a Jew. In the next section of this chapter, Torrance's theology of Christ's ascended ontology will be constructively developed.

## 3. ONTOLOGY OF THE ASCENDED CHRIST: A CONSTRUCTIVE DEVELOPMENT

The main goal in this section is to bring Torrance into conversation with various theological interlocutors. As such, with respect to theological anthropology, Torrance's views will be shown to align with Augustine, who affirms gender at the eschaton as opposed to Gregory of Nyssa, who rejects it. Furthermore, regarding ecclesiology, Torrance's reservations about using analogies for the relationship between Christ and the church that end up stating that it is akin to a biological entity will be highlighted. Lastly, in relation to Christology, it will be shown that Torrance does not make any distinctions between a so-called Lukan and Pauline interpretation of the resurrection, with the former affirming a corporeal body and the latter rejecting it.

### 3.1 The Ontology of the Ascended Jesus and Theological Anthropology: Not Gregory of Nyssa's View

Torrance clearly affirms the maleness of Jesus in his resurrected and ascended being.[119] Humans beings, too, will retain their biological gender in the eschaton, according to Torrance.[120] In making such a clear affirmation, Torrance is rejecting the views of those like Gregory of Nyssa, who declare that biological gender is a temporary phenomenon, which will be eliminated in the eschaton.[121] Such a belief is promulgated by Gregory, Marc Cortez explains, for three main reasons, which can be stated in the form of: (1) a biblical argument, (2) a contingency argument, and (3) a union argument. The biblical argument is encapsulated in the belief that human beings were intended originally to be created without sexual differentiation as male

---

119. See section 2.1.4.3, "Biologically Differentiated as Male and Female," for more on this point.

120. See section 2.1.4.3, "Biologically Differentiated as Male and Female," for more on this point.

121. For more information on this view, see Cortez, *Christological Anthropology*, 31–55; Vale, "Cappadocian or Augustinian?," 184–92.

and female, and at the eschaton this will finally be realized.[122] This biblical argument is founded on the premise that Gen 1:26 should be understood as God's "original intention for humanity," while Gen 1:27 communicates "the historical outworking of that intention."[123] In other words, the "image of God," which is described in Gen 1:26, is God's blueprint for humanity, but Gen 1:27 that describes the creation of sexually differentiated beings, male and female, is not God's original design for humankind.[124] This is all based on the underlying conviction that in God there is a logical separation between the "original intention" for humankind and the way things eventually materialized.[125]

This leads nicely to what is being called the contingency argument, which Cortez captures well through the following explanation: "In his foreknowledge, God knew that humanity would fall into sin and that the fall would endanger their continuation as his creatures."[126] Therefore, sexual differentiation was for the purpose of procreation, so that after the fall humankind would not become extinct, but such an allowance would be needed only until the eschaton, as "biological procreation . . . will be done away with in the resurrection."[127] The third reason Cortez provides can be called the union argument, which basically affirms that all forms of division will be nullified at the eschaton, including the division of humanity that is caused by the existence of sexually differentiated beings.[128] Cortez summarizes the force of this point as follows: "Gregory's third argument for the necessity of a christological transformation of humanity's biological sexuality is that it is among those things that divide us and prevents our complete unity in Christ," and therefore, humanity will no longer be divided as male and female in the eschaton.[129]

Torrance would disagree fundamentally with each of the points stated above. In response to (1) above, the biblical argument, Torrance would counter it by highlighting "the Biblical teaching about the 'goodness' of what God had created,"[130] and further contend that human sexuality is an

---

122. Cortez, *Christological Anthropology*, 45–46.
123. Cortez, *Christological Anthropology*, 46.
124. Cortez, *Christological Anthropology*, 46.
125. Cortez, *Christological Anthropology*, 46.
126. Cortez, *Christological Anthropology*, 48.
127. Cortez, *Christological Anthropology*, 48–49.
128. Cortez, *Christological Anthropology*, 49.
129. Cortez, *Christological Anthropology*, 49.
130. Torrance, "Soul and Person," 109.

essential part of what defines human beings in the first place.[131] Therefore, for Torrance, the correct biblical view on human beings would not just posit sexual differentiation as part of God's original intention, but would go so far as to assert that biological gender is an "intrinsic" part of the human soul itself, by God's design.[132] Geordie Ziegler correctly notes that Torrance at this point is influenced by Barth's relational anthropology,[133] but Eric Flett is also right to state that "Torrance's anthropology . . . is underdeveloped."[134] Flett is dissatisfied with the lack of specificity regarding the ethical outworking of Torrance's anthropology that is otherwise clearly characterized by a strong relationality between the male and female sexes.[135] The merits of Flett's observations will be interrogated in a later part of this study,[136] but one must note that Torrance's insights on the gendered nature of the soul (apart from the relational emphases) are a unique contribution to modern theology. Torrance does not reveal his theological interlocutors, but it would not be surprising if in the background lay Thomas Aquinas's theology. Torrance's views can be distinguished from that of Aquinas in that he argues for gender to be attributed not just externally (to human bodies), but also internally, to the very soul.[137] Aquinas, on the other hand, can be said to argue for gender to be attributed to body and not to the soul.[138]

Considering Torrance's strong affirmation of human sexuality, one can imagine how he would respond to (2) the contingency argument. Sexual differentiation, far from being a contingency plan in Torrance's theology, forms the bedrock definition of human beings: "sexual difference . . . [is] constitutive of human nature."[139] Torrance's relational theology sheds further light on why he argues in the way he does. He explains: "The essential human nucleus, is neither man by himself nor woman by herself, but only man and woman," and he goes on to assert that such a relationship will

---

131. Torrance, "Soul and Person," 108–9. See section 2.1.4.3 for more on this point.

132. Torrance, "Soul and Person," 108–9.

133. Ziegler, *Trinitarian Grace*, 160.

134. Flett, "Priest of Creation," 11.

135. Flett, "Priest of Creation," 11.

136. Chapter 6 will engage with the broader criticism of a lack of ethics in Torrance's theology of the ascension.

137. Torrance, "Soul and Person," 109.

138. John Finley, however, believes that latent within Aquinas's theology is also an affirmation of how the soul is gendered, not just the body, although he acknowledges that Aquinas explicitly argues for the attribution of gender to the body, not the soul. For more, see Finley, "Metaphysics of Gender." For a critique of Finley's assessment and constructive contribution, see Newton, "Aquinas's Metaphysics."

139. Torrance, "Soul and Person," 109.

continue even in the eschaton.[140] In these relationships between male and female, Torrance explains, "there is imaged the ineffable personal relations of the Holy Trinity."[141] Insofar as God in himself is relational, human sexual differentiation as male and female is to mirror God's own relationship, and therefore, Torrance's reasons are deeply Trinitarian in nature. With respect to point (3) the union argument, Torrance would take issue with the removal of sexual differentiation at the eschaton, but would affirm that there are divisions between the sexes caused by the fall that will indeed be removed.[142] In other words, as far as sexual ontology is concerned, male and female will continue to exist in a biologically differentiated manner, but the relational fallout of the primal human rebellion will be healed.[143] Torrance states this in his own words in the context of affirming that both male and female are equally created in God's image and the incarnation testifies to this as follows: "The Incarnation . . . [is] the saving assumption of the whole human being, male and female, and as the healing of our complete human nature. This must surely be understood as involving the healing of any divisive relation between male and female due to the curse imposed upon them at the fall (Gen 3:16), while sanctifying the distinction between them."[144]

Torrance's argument can be likened to Augustine's position on gender and sexuality in the eschaton.[145] Two points need to be highlighted, one of which is explicitly shared by Augustine and Torrance, and another which is not explicit but implicit. What is without question found in both is the relational aspect that biological gender and sexuality testify to, and Felipe do Vale explains Augustine's view well when he observes,

> Human beings are . . . social, and what their sociability is supposed to point us to . . . [is] the soteriological and storied significance of Christ and the church. So human beings were created to be social so as to point to this component of the narrative of redemption, which finds its culmination in the resurrection. So, we retain our genders in order to continue pointing to the deepest soteriological realities of God's narrative.[146]

Torrance essentially makes the same argument, although he does not nuance it in the same way. By pointing to the Trinitarian relationship that

140. Torrance, "Soul and Person," 109.
141. Torrance, "Soul and Person," 109–10.
142. Torrance, *Gospel*, 207, 219.
143. Torrance, *Gospel*, 207, 219.
144. Torrance, *Gospel*, 207.
145. See Vale, "Cappadocian or Augustinian?," 192–98.
146. Vale, "Cappadocian or Augustinian?," 195–96.

human biological differentiation points to, one can claim that Torrance, too, would agree with all that Augustine affirms. What is not as explicit in Torrance, but is implicit nonetheless, is what Augustine can be said to explain as the reason for the existence of gender in the eschaton, and once again do Vale's comments are insightful. He explains, "We need gender in the resurrection because it is only then that the miseries of this world (including its pernicious constructions of gender) will be seen for what they are, and gendered life lived as it was supposed to be."[147] This argument, do Vale states, leads to "a view of gender in the resurrection that offers justice for the miseries of the world for which we can strive in faith, hope and love."[148] While Torrance does not use this argument in his own affirmation of gender and sexuality in the resurrection, the teleological and eschatological orientation of his theology would be able to easily adopt such an Augustinian view. More could be said about the similarities between Augustine and Torrance, but it is sufficient to highlight what Torrance affirms, along with similar views.

## 3.2 The Ontology of the Ascended Jesus and Ecclesiology: The Appropriateness of Biological Analogies

David Fergusson in the context of Torrance's strong stand against Lutheran theology in their rejection of the *extra Calvinisticum* rues a missed opportunity on Torrance's part to gain "a fuller appreciation of Luther's stress on the *totus Christus*."[149] One way in which Torrance scholarship can make amends is through a dialogue with Lutheran theology on the *totus Christus*. From an ecclesiological perspective, Torrance is unequivocal. He declares that *"the Church is the Body of Christ."*[150] But he is equally unreserved in clarifying that the term *Body of Christ* "is not a term to be understood and expounded in biological language as organism."[151] Torrance underscores the distinction between Christ and the church in order to avoid any notion of the "Church as the extension of the Incarnation," or in other words he seeks to avoid any idea that the church replaces Christ.[152] Contemporary Lutheran scholar Ian McFarland has articulated an ecclesial vision that utilizes the *totus Christus* without equating the church with Christ in the process. It will be important

---

147. Vale, "Cappadocian or Augustinian?," 198.
148. Vale, "Cappadocian or Augustinian?," 183.
149. Fergusson, "He Ascended into Heaven," 37n11.
150. Torrance, "What Is the Church?," 6.
151. Torrance, "What Is the Church?," 6.
152. Torrance, "What Is the Church?," 9.

for contemporary Torrancean scholarship to dialogue with McFarland's insights, particularly because of the potential for ecumenical exchange.

McFarland highlights the intimate relationship between Christology and ecclesiology, first, by pointing out two dangerous approaches that must be conceptually and practically avoided, and second, by providing a different model that conceives of the relationship in more healthy terms.[153] In terms of dangerous approaches to the relationship between Christ and the church, McFarland identifies on the one hand among theological works a *total* rejection of Christ's presence in the church, to avoid any pretense of the church thinking she is Lord, not Christ;[154] on the other hand, he points out a tendency in scholarship of a *complete* acceptance of Christ's presence in the church, to make sense of the "location" of Christ's risen existence, and to affirm the continuation of Christ's work on earth.[155]

Both these views are termed extreme by McFarland, and he instead proposes a view which takes the best of both positions, by incorporating insights from a communications concept—namely, "second-" and "third-person encounter."[156] By "second-person encounters," he means connecting with someone verbally, through "word and deed."[157] By "third-person encounters" is meant something non-verbal, or what he terms, "mere fact of my physical presence."[158] He goes on to mention that both kinds of communication are important for meaningful knowing to happen.[159] Notably, he connects both kinds of "encounter" to how Christ is related to the church, yet distinct.[160] He does so through the use of Eph 4:14–16, where there is a distinction made between Christ, who is the head, and the church, which is the body, all the while making clear that both head and body constitute the whole.[161] He connects the "second-person encounters" to the relationship between Christ and the church, by stating that when there is communication

153. For more see McFarland, "Body of Christ."

154. McFarland identifies such a tendency in the work of Karl Barth. He says of Barth: "Barth's concern for divine freedom causes him to accentuate the distinction between head and members to the point of positing two churches." For more, see McFarland, "Body of Christ," 225, 228.

155. McFarland, "Body of Christ," 233. McFarland on p. 225 identifies such a tendency in Robert Jenson: "Jenson's stress on Christ's objective presence in the world risks collapsing Christ into the church."

156. McFarland, "Body of Christ," 237–43.

157. McFarland, "Body of Christ," 240.

158. McFarland, "Body of Christ," 240.

159. McFarland, "Body of Christ," 240–43.

160. McFarland, "Body of Christ," 242.

161. McFarland, "Body of Christ," 238–39.

involved, through "word and sacrament,"[162] then one has encountered the "head" of the body.[163] A "third-person encounter" takes place through encounter with members of the church, without any verbal communication, because the body of Christ, verbally and linguistically by way of analogy, constitutes the body as well as the head.[164] In this way, through the use of his linguistic analogy, McFarland seeks to bring the best of both positions and apply it to the relationship between Christology and ecclesiology.

While McFarland makes a sound argument that does not end up equating Christ with the church or vice versa, Torrance would be wary of theological language that suggests that the body constitutes the head, as if it was one biological substance. For Torrance, one must always guard against ecclesiological attempts that "try to usurp His [Christ's] place."[165] Nonetheless, McFarland as a Lutheran theologian offers keen insights that future Torrance scholars must dialogue with to further the ecumenical dialogue between the Reformed and Lutheran theological traditions on the *totus Christus*, as there were missed opportunities in the past for dialogue and mutual appreciation that must not be repeated. A fuller exploration of the relationship between Christology and ecclesiology will be addressed in chapter 6.

---

162. McFarland, "Body of Christ," 241.

163. McFarland, "Body of Christ," 241.

164. McFarland, "Body of Christ," 240–42. To make this distinction between both "second-" and "third-person encounters" clearer, on p. 242 McFarland states, "Having invoked the model of second-person encounter to emphasize with Barth the distinction between the heavenly head and the earthly-historical body (thereby forestalling the conclusion that the church's speech and action were in every respect and in itself Jesus' own), one may also use the model of third-person address to agree with Jenson that in every one of the church's members Christ is at every instance encountered both genuinely and directly. This distinction with respect to the mode of encounter is necessary as a means of avoiding either conflation or separation of head and members. Encountering Christ in the church's members is distinct from encountering him in word and sacrament not because anything less than Christ is encountered, but because Christ is encountered in the sheer physical presence of his body's earthly members rather than through direct address. Such a distinction is possible because as much as Christ is the head of the body, he is not himself the whole body and is therefore genuinely encountered in its various members independently of whether or not they are being used by him as instruments of second-person self-disclosure."

165. Torrance, "What Is the Church?," 11.

## 3.3 The Ontology of the Ascended Jesus and Christology: Torrance on the So-Called Lukan and Pauline Ontologies of the Ascended Jesus

It is common in biblical and theological studies to discern a strong contrast between Luke and Paul on the resurrected and ascended body of Jesus. Where does Torrance stand on this matter? While he does not directly address this issue in terms of the apparent rift between Luke and Paul, what he does state about the "spiritual body" of the resurrected Jesus strongly suggests that he does not discern any unbridgeable divide between both positions. In what follows, the focus will be on first highlighting how both these views are understood in contemporary scholarship, and then, pointing out how Torrance would speak into this debate.

Mark Harris describes the Pauline and Lukan views on the ontology of the resurrected Jesus as follows:

> Paul's description of the resurrection body in 1 Corinthians 15 . . . [is] that of a mysterious eschatological *transformation* of which we can say little with any confidence (e.g. vv. 35–54). Luke, on the other hand, insists upon the earthy, material reality of the risen Jesus: the risen Jesus is flesh and bones like the disciples (Luke 24:39), eats broiled fish (vv. 41–43), and is "carried up" into heaven (v. 51); Luke's risen Jesus is rather more like us than is Paul's, at least in terms of bodily reality.[166]

While the Lukan view is easily discernible from the above quotation, the Pauline view remains elusive. What Harris goes on to state clarifies what the Pauline view stands for, namely, "Jesus' transformed *otherness* as an eschatological reality" and "the intangibility of eschatological transformation."[167] Therefore, the contrast to be made between Luke and Paul, as Harris presents it, is between the *physicality* and the *non-physicality* of the resurrection body, or to put it more positively, between the corporeality and the *beyond* corporeality of the resurrection body of Jesus.[168] Interestingly, Harris opines that the discipline of theology generally has gravitated toward the Pauline view, while the discipline of science would be more interested in the Lukan perspective: "For while theology might share Paul's concern to emphasize Jesus' transformed *otherness* as an eschatological reality, science has a more *immediate* view that parallels Luke's concern to emphasize Jesus'

---

166. Harris, "Science," 212.
167. Harris, "Science," 212.
168. Harris, "Science," 212.

earthiness."[169] Harris is not wrong to make this sweeping observation, but there are exceptions to this within theology, and Torrance is one of them.[170]

Torrance's own view, as presented in the section above, summarizes the resurrected and ascended ontology of Jesus as follows: "To be a spiritual man is to be not less than man but more fully and truly man. To be a spiritual body is not to be less body but more truly and completely body."[171] Such a statement suggests that Torrance does not believe that the Lukan and Pauline views are mutually exclusive. One can find an indirect substantiation of this point, especially when Torrance explicitly denies that Christ's body underwent some change ontologically into a spirit being during the forty days between the resurrection and ascension:

> One of the lessons to be learned from "the forty days" between the resurrection and the ascension . . . [is that] they had nothing to do, as is sometimes alleged, with a progressive spiritualization or immaterialization of the body of Christ, but with the training of the disciples through a manifestation of Christ in which the thoughts of suffering and glory, of humiliation and exaltation, were bound together in his own Person in indissoluble union.[172]

Torrance is essentially agreeing with Scottish theologian William Milligan in what he states above.[173] Specifically, Torrance is underscoring two points: (1) the resurrected Jesus is the *same* Jesus who suffered and died, and (2) the path to glory is *through* suffering.[174]

At this stage, it is helpful to point out that Torrance's own views on the ontology of the resurrected Jesus are more in line with what N. T. Wright states than with the views of Turid Karslen Seim. A case in point will be how both scholars interpret 1 Cor 15:50, which states that "flesh and blood will not inherit the kingdom of God and the perishable cannot inherit the imperishable." According to Turid Karlsen Seim, this verse entails that earthly bodies are not designed to inhabit heavenly spaces, so the only way for an earthly body to enter heavenly space is through the "transformation of flesh

---

169. Harris, "Science," 212.

170. Douglas Farrow, Gerrit Dawson, and N. T. Wright, among others, could be added to this list. For more, see John, "Risen and Ascended Humanity," 4–5.

171. Torrance, *Space, Time, and Resurrection*, 141.

172. Torrance, *Space, Time, and Resurrection*, 123.

173. Torrance, *Space, Time, and Resurrection*, 123n1, points to Milligan, *Ascension*, 5.

174. Torrance, *Space, Time, and Resurrection*, 123. Torrance is essentially in agreement with what Milligan states in *Ascension*, 4–5.

to glory."[175] It must be noted that 1 Cor 15:50 need not only be interpreted in the way that Seim and others have suggested. According to N. T. Wright, "'flesh and blood' is a way of referring to ordinary, corruptible, decaying human existence,"[176] so what is being denied access into heaven is a humanity that is corruptible, not humanity per se.[177] Douglas Farrow sheds further light on the passage by stating: "Paul did not mean to exclude flesh and blood from the kingdom (a most un-Jewish idea) but rather to make clear to Jews, and Gentiles too, that access to the kingdom does not come by human strength, or by ethnic identity, or by any means available to man."[178]

Torrance's view on the matter comports well with N. T. Wright and Douglas Farrow, because he, too, like them believes that the resurrection must be interpreted in light of the Jewish worldview, not the Greek one.[179] In the latter perspective, death was the end of bodily existence, such that "it is the moment when, and the means by which, the immortal soul is set free from the prison-house of the physical body."[180] As a result, "Those who followed Plato . . . did not want a body again" after death.[181] As seen in the section above, the body is central to Torrance's theological anthropology, and it is equally central to Torrance's conception of the resurrected and ascended being of Jesus. Torrance strongly believes this because for him anything other than bodily resurrection and bodily ascension amounts to speculation and going beyond the bounds of Scriptural testimony.[182]

## 3.4 Section Summary

In this section, Torrance's theology was developed constructively in three areas: (1) theological anthropology, (2) ecclesiology, and (3) Christology proper. With respect to theological anthropology, Torrance's views are shown to be radically opposed to Gregory of Nyssa's views and are more in line with Augustine's views, insofar as Torrance affirms the continuation

---

175. Seim, "Resurrected Body," 31.
176. Wright, *Resurrection*, 359.
177. See also Farrow, "Resurrection and Immortality," 216.
178. Farrow, "Resurrection and Immortality," 216. Cf. the following critical commentaries of the New Testament which support such a reading: Fee, *First Epistle to the Corinthians*, 775–95; Thiselton, *First Epistle to the Corinthians*, 1276–306; Garland, *1 Corinthians*, 725–38.
179. See Torrance, *Space, Time, and Resurrection*, 41–45.
180. Wright, *Resurrection*, 48.
181. Wright, *Resurrection*, 60.
182. See Torrance, *Space, Time, and Resurrection*, 140.

of biological differentiation of humankind as male and female, even in the eschaton. On ecclesiology, Torrance maintains a close relationship between Christ and the church, but is wary of thinking of this relationship through biological analogies that can equate the two or even replace Christ with the church. With respect to Christology, in Torrance there is no radical divide between the Lukan and Pauline perspectives on Christ's resurrected and ascended ontology. Fidelity to the Hebraic and Jewish background of the resurrection, together with a desire to remain faithful to the boundaries prescribed by Scripture, and a disdain for any kind of speculation, are Torrance's reasons for affirming the robustly physical account of Christ's resurrected and ascended humanity. He desires to make clear that Christ remains human in his resurrection and ascension.

## 4. CRITIQUE

Torrance's ontology of the ascended Christ will be critically evaluated in chapter 6. At this stage, it will be helpful to note the specific critiques that will be addressed in more detail in chapter 6.

### 4.1 Ascended Ontology and Theological Anthropology

The following question with respect to Torrance's theological anthropology will be addressed in chapter 6: Does Torrance's theological anthropology affirm an eschatological existence for human beings?[183] While Torrance is not specifically critiqued concerning the continuation of humanity in his eschatology, Barth is sternly critiqued on this point by Nathan Hitchcock.[184] Hitchcock's basic contention is that there is no genuine human existence *as human* in Barth's eschatology, and he lays down the gauntlet for other theologians influenced by Barth to pay heed to these warnings and take stock of the critique. It is his firm belief that "any reconfiguration of the doctrine of the resurrection in terms of a 'relational ontology' is a project laden with serious difficulties."[185] This is a critique that will apply to Torrance as well, since his is a *relational ontology*, but it will be argued in chapter 6 that Torrance is not culpable of the accusation that may rightly apply to Barth because in contradistinction to Barth, Torrance has a robust eschatology, with room for both an embodied Jesus and embodied human beings.

---

183. See section 2.1.1, "Critique #1," in chapter 6 for more on this point.
184. See Hitchcock, *Karl Barth*.
185. Hitchcock, *Karl Barth*, xvi.

## 4.2 Ascended Ontology and Ecclesiology

With respect to ecclesiology, the following question becomes pertinent and will be addressed in chapter 6: Does Torrance make clear distinctions ontologically between Christ and the church?[186] Torrance does not equate the ascended Christ with the church or Eucharist, as this chapter has sought to demonstrate. However, not all scholars are convinced that Torrance has succeeded in these efforts. Stanley MacLean, for instance, contends that Torrance "presses . . . [the] Body image too far, so that the relationship between Christ and the church becomes too close."[187] The force of his critique lies in his assertion that "the end result is that we cannot think of the church *only* as the Body of Christ. 'Christ *is* the Church.' He is both 'the One and the Many.'"[188] Arguing with Paul Molnar, MacLean's arguments will be rebutted as in the final instance untenable because it "fails to take account of the reasons why Torrance rejected identifying the church as Christ's body with Christ as its head, as happens when the church is thought of as an extension or continuation of the incarnation."[189]

## 4.3 Ascended Ontology and Christology

On Christology, the following question will be explored in chapter 6: Does Torrance's Christology avoid succumbing to some form of kenoticism?[190] Torrance's Christology with respect to the ascension is scrutinized by Andrew Burgess because he believes Torrance's affirmation of the hypostatic union eventually has to succumb to some form of "*kenotic* theory."[191] He asserts such a weakness in Torrance because of the affirmation "that perfect humanity is only united to divinity in the ascension."[192] Burgess finds this problematic because it seems to imply that Jesus did not have a perfect relationship with the Father while on earth.[193] While this is an important issue that will be unpacked in chapter 6, with Sandra Fach it can be argued that Burgess does not pay sufficient heed to the importance of Christ's vicarious redemption of "our" fallen humanity: "Fallen humanity is in need of

---

186. See section 2.1.2, "Critique #2," in chapter 6 for more on this point.
187. MacLean, *Resurrection*, 197.
188. MacLean, *Resurrection*, 197.
189. Molnar, "Introduction," li.
190. See section 2.1.3, "Critique #3," in chapter 6 for more on this point.
191. Burgess, *Ascension in Karl Barth*, 131.
192. Burgess, *Ascension in Karl Barth*, 131.
193. Burgess, *Ascension in Karl Barth*, 131.

perfection. If fallen humanity is made perfect at the point of the incarnation, then the events of Jesus' life are rendered meaningless."[194]

## 5. CONCLUSION

This chapter focused on exegeting and *constructively* building on Torrance's *theological* thought on the ontology of the ascended Jesus. It highlighted the integral relationship that the ontology of Jesus's ascension has to theological anthropology, to ecclesiology, and to Christology proper, after which Torrance's thought in these three areas were constructively developed by bringing him into dialogue with contemporary discussions. Theologically, for Torrance, the ascended Jesus is still human and divine, and his view can be said to extend the logic of the Chalcedonian Definition to the ascension and on into eternity as well. Torrance's views are not only shaped theologically, but grounded in exegetical convictions, where the "spiritual body" of 1 Cor 15 is interpreted as an affirmation, not a negation, of the physical body, with the addition of the gift of perfect communion with the Triune God and "immortality"—both of which are guaranteed by the ascension of the God-man Jesus to heaven and the gift of the Holy Spirit. Such a christological conviction has a direct bearing on theological anthropology for Torrance, wherein human beings are promised an eschatological existence *as humans*. Human beings will be resurrected at the eschaton with specific aspects including bodies and souls, biological gender, ethnicity, and as creatures dependent upon God. The implication for ecclesiology is an exhortation to be grounded in Christ's commission to the church, without confusing it with Christ. Additionally, she is called to keep her focus on seeking to live out the eschatological future now and await the day when Christ will fully perfect the church at the eschaton.

Constructively building on Torrance's thought, the chapter showed how Torrance's theological anthropology aligns itself with Augustine's perspective, where the eschatological human being has gender, as opposed to Gregory of Nyssa, who argues that there will be no gender in the eschaton. Furthermore, ecclesiologically, it was observed that while Torrance uses "Body of Christ" language for the church, he seeks to distance himself from biological conceptions of "head" and "body" that end up believing they both constitute one biological entity. Christologically, Torrance would reject any difference between so-called Lukan perspectives, which affirm a physical and corporeal Christ, and interpretations of Paul that deny any notion of corporeality. Torrance reads 1 Cor 15 as an unequivocal affirmation of

---

194. Fach, "Answering the Upwards Call," 225.

corporeality at the final resurrection, but a corporeality that is freed from any kind of physical corruption; as such, Torrance's views on the matter do not see Luke's and Paul's interpretation of the resurrection and ascension to be mutually exclusive. Having explored the ontology of the ascended Jesus in Torrance's corpus, the next chapter will explore the theme of spatiality in his theology of the ascension.

# 4

# The Spatiality of the Ascended Christ

## 1. INTRODUCTION

TORRANCE ARTICULATED HIS THEOLOGY of spatiality in the wake of the work of Albert Einstein in physics, who showed that spatial entities are intrinsically also temporal. This is important to note as one begins to critically expound and constructively develop Torrance's thought in this area. Torrance's exposition on the spatiality of the ascension is commended for being more advanced than most treatments of the topic in biblical studies because of its engagement with spatial theology.[1] Surprisingly, even in this area, his major contribution to the subject of God's relationship to space, *Space, Time, and Incarnation,* has not been sufficiently critically appraised.[2] Within Torrancean scholarship, however, Paul Molnar and Chan Ho Park, among others, commendably explore the various facets of God's relationship to space with regard to the incarnation that Torrance unpacks in *Space, Time, and Incarnation.*[3] What needs to be explored further is Torrance's theology of the spatiality and temporality of the ascension,[4] and therefore in what follows addressing these aspects will be the focus.

---

1. Cf. Sleeman, *Geography*, 19, where he acknowledges Torrance's contribution to the spatiality of Jesus's ascension: "T. F. Torrance's articulations of space, a legacy which has helped systematic theology move ahead of biblical studies in understanding Christ's ascension."

2. Nesteruk, "Universe, Incarnation, and Humanity," 213–14.

3. See Torrance, *Space, Time, and Incarnation*; cf. Molnar: *Thomas F. Torrance*, 124–36, 314–18; Molnar, "Introduction," xvii–lv; see also Park, *Transcendence and Spatiality*, 32–39, 81–94.

4. Two exceptions to this lacuna are found in the following sources: Purves, "End of Ministry," 280–83; Fergusson, "He Ascended into Heaven," 37–38.

Torrance's thought on the subject is deeply integrated, and therefore it is challenging to break it down into theological layers that can be clearly expounded and critically evaluated. Kevin Chiarot, however, makes a general observation about the threefold layers in Torrance's theological work that fits well in breaking down the various levels in his theology of the ascension vis-à-vis space and time. Chiarot explains, "Torrance is always a Christian dogmatician working from an integrating center in the incarnate Word. From this center his thought moves upstream to a fully Trinitarian theology and downstream to the doctrines of the church, the sacraments, and the Christian life."[5] As the ensuing exposition will clearly demonstrate, there are three specific aspects to Torrance's understanding of the spatiality of the ascension: (1) a christological level, (2) a Trinitarian level, and (3) an epistemological level that focuses on the proper use of theological language for God. There is a disproportionate emphasis on the first and third levels, while the Trinitarian level is left in an embryonic form, which must be developed through insights from Torrance's wider oeuvre. *Space, Time, and Resurrection* contains Torrance's discourse on spatiality vis-à-vis the ascension and therefore will serve as an orienting guide in the first section of the chapter, supplementing it with insights from his broader corpus. The second section will then constructively develop the three levels in Torrance's thought, after which a third section will briefly highlight points of criticism leveled against Torrance that will be engaged further in chapter 6.

## 2. SPATIALITY OF THE ASCENDED JESUS

### 2.1 Christology and Spatiality

#### 2.1.1 Ascension and Incarnation

There is an integral relationship between the incarnation and the ascension for Torrance, such that the former's spatial issues are directly related to the latter's—or, in Torrance's words, "[the ascension] is the other pole of the question as to the relation of the incarnation to space and time."[6] Torrance repeatedly uses the spatial issues that arose because of the incarnation as a heuristic to explain the spatial complexities involved in the ascension, and he begins with the issue of the *extra Calvinisticum*.[7] Torrance's engagement

---

5. See Chiarot, *Unassumed Is the Unhealed*, 1.

6. Torrance, *Space, Time, and Resurrection*, 123.

7. Torrance, *Space, Time, and Resurrection*, 124–26. Torrance also uses the example of how Jesus is the "Temple of God" because of the incarnation, as an additional example to explain what is happening in the ascension. For more, see the point on "Ontology and Spatiality" enumerated below, and *Space, Time, and Resurrection*, 128–30.

with the *extra Calvinisticum* is presented in the form of a polemic against those who reject it, especially Lutherans. He insists that for the latter, God's relationship to space and time is conceived through a "receptacle view of space," by which is meant that, in the incarnation, the Son "left the bosom of the Father" to come down to earth and be "resolved into this Jesus without remainder."[8] Other interpretations of the incarnation, such as those offered by Calvin which exclaimed that "Christ . . . became man born of the Virgin's womb without leaving heaven or the government of the world," were rejected outrightly by the Lutherans.[9] For Lutherans, according to Torrance, Calvin's views were understood to mean that there was only a partial incarnation: "In the incarnation only part of the Word was contained in the babe of Bethlehem or wrapped in the swaddling clothes in the cradle, and that something was left 'outside' (extra)," which is what resulted in the pejorative title "'Calvinist extra.'"[10] Torrance lauds Luther's intention in seeking to affirm a genuine incarnation but still finds his rejection of the *extra Calvinisticum* problematic on many fronts.[11] Contemporary Scottish theologian David Fergusson, however, believes that Torrance could have appreciated Luther's intentions more than he actually did, and in not doing so missed an opportunity to recognize the strengths of Luther's view and the possibility for "ecumenical convergence" in the process.[12]

Torrance goes on to contend that two insurmountable problems obtain for Lutherans who reject the *extra Calvinisticum*: (1) "metaphysical *kenōsis*," and (2) "demythologizing" conclusions.[13] He seeks to maintain both these assertions by asking a question that was also asked during the eucharistic controversies of the sixteenth century, namely, "How are we to think of the Body of Christ as contained in the host, in every part of it, and in a multitude of hosts at the same time, and how can we think of it as being contained without any relation between the dimensions of the Body of Christ and the space of the place that contains him?"[14] The Lutheran answer to this question, Torrance emphasizes, was like the transubstantiation doctrine. He notes this similarity because their answer affirmed an "artificial distinction . . . between the substance and the accidents of the elements," and while appropriating this teaching to form "kenotic theories" that affirmed an

---

8. Torrance, *Space, Time, and Resurrection*, 124, 126.
9. Torrance, *Space, Time, and Resurrection*, 124.
10. Torrance, *Space, Time, and Resurrection*, 124.
11. Torrance, *Space, Time, and Resurrection*, 124–26.
12. Fergusson, "He Ascended into Heaven," 37n11.
13. Torrance, *Space, Time, and Resurrection*, 126.
14. Torrance, *Space, Time, and Resurrection*, 124–25.

incarnation in which the Son either gave up attributes "that were incompatible with creaturely existence or that their use was restricted in the incarnate state," ended up being only lip service.[15] In actuality, Torrance maintains, the Lutheran response could not but state that the "human receptacle" could "contain the divine," seen for instance in "the doctrine of the ubiquity of the body of Christ."[16] Or, they had to resort to a form of demythologization, which affirmed "a radical disjunction between the divine and the human in which there was no interaction between them."[17] In the case of the former, Torrance contends that it amounts to "a form of monophysitism," and in the case of the latter, God's historical interaction with human beings in space and time is given up in favor of a relationship that is only superficial and intellectual. Or, as Torrance puts it, God interacts with human beings "only tangentially at the point called 'Jesus' whose historical existence is then only a sort of springboard for a constant leap in existential decision that leaves history behind."[18] Torrance commends Luther's intentions, but believes strongly that a "receptacle view of space" will not do justice to both the natures of Jesus, divine and human, and therefore a refined view of space and time is needed that will take both aspects into consideration in its spatial theology.[19]

## 2.1.2 Relational Space and Time

For Torrance, a *"relational view of space and time"* emerges not because of human speculation but from a desire to pursue theology as "a science," specifically by being "faithful to the nature of Christ as very God and very Man."[20] What results from such a *relational* approach, Torrance argues, is not just that it does justice to both natures of Jesus, but it does so without the negative kenotic consequences, such as demythologization.[21] A relational view of space and time, for Torrance, means one thinks "differentially or variationally related to God and man" in regard to their interaction with space and time, and one way of doing this would be by considering what it means to state that "God exists" in contrast to what it means to affirm

---

15. Torrance, *Space, Time, and Resurrection*, 125.
16. Torrance, *Space, Time, and Resurrection*, 125.
17. Torrance, *Space, Time, and Resurrection*, 125.
18. Torrance, *Space, Time, and Resurrection*, 125.
19. Torrance, *Space, Time, and Resurrection*, 126.
20. Torrance, *Space, Time, and Resurrection*, 126.
21. Torrance, *Space, Time, and Resurrection*, 126.

that "man exists."²² When one affirms God's "existence," Torrance explains, one can only rightly interpret such a statement if one then goes on also to interpret it in line with "the nature of God," and end up with an affirmation that "divine existence is of an utterly unique and transcendent kind."²³ In contrast, human existence is of the kind which is not transcendent, but located within "space and time."²⁴ With Jesus, both God and man's relationship to space and time will have to be considered simultaneously and differently, because in Jesus both divine and human natures reside hypostatically, Torrance maintains.²⁵ When such a relational view of space and time is used to think of Jesus vis-à-vis the ascension, there are further nuances to consider, to think rightly and scientifically, according to Torrance.

The ascension of Jesus qualifies the relational view with an additional layer of nuance, for Torrance. If the relational view of space and time with regard to God and human beings operates like a stereoscope with one lens depicting God's transcendence and the other lens portraying human finitude, the ascension of Jesus qualifies the human lens with another twofold image that must be viewed simultaneously as well: (1) fallen space-time, and (2) redeemed space-time.²⁶ Fallen space-time can be described as "the on-going existence of this passing world," while redeemed space-time is best captured through the phrase "recreated or renewed" space and time.²⁷ To be sure, with regard to the humanity of the ascended Jesus, Torrance wishes to maintain a perspectival approach that does justice to human beings of the "passing world" and Jesus's ascended human perspective, wherein "space and time" are "redeemed . . . from all corruption and privation of being,

---

22. Torrance, *Space, Time, and Resurrection*, 126–27.

23. Torrance, *Space, Time, and Resurrection*, 126–27.

24. Torrance, *Space, Time, and Resurrection*, 127.

25. Torrance, *Space, Time, and Resurrection*, 127. This is the logical outworking of the Chalcedonian doctrine that Torrance consistently affirmed in his theological writing and therefore is not something that is idiosyncratic to Torrance.

26. Torrance, *Space, Time, and Resurrection*, 127.

27. Torrance, *Space, Time, and Resurrection*, 127. Ritchie, *T. F. Torrance*, 187, uses the phrase "bad time" to communicate what Torrance means by fallen time and he explains its significance as follows: "It conveys more of the brokenness of a sin-affected cosmos. Moreover, it powerfully expresses the notion that fallen created order has lost the very possibility of having being and existence at all." He goes on to describe redeemed space on p. 188 as "totally 'new time,' freshly minted and brought into being for us, by the event of the triumph of Jesus Christ through his resurrection and ascension." While Torrance argues for the existence of both times (fallen and redeemed) simultaneously until the new creation, Ritchie avers that after the resurrection and ascension, only one time exists—"new time." This is explained further on pp. 188–90 of Ritchie's book.

and every threat of death or nothingness."[28] In other words, on the one hand, Torrance maintains that the ascension of Jesus is not illogical from a this-worldly human perspective, but on the other hand, he also contends that human language is utterly unable to fully grasp new creation realities that are inaugurated by Jesus's resurrection and ascension.[29] With respect to this latter point, Torrance honestly acknowledges human shortcomings: "We have no adequate language to describe this, and can speak of it only in apocalyptic language, that is, in language that breaks down in its very using, but which must break down if it really is to point us to this new reality beyond, which cannot be captured or enclosed in the language of this fallen world."[30] Lest one get lost in the complexity of the issue at hand, Torrance simplifies what he is arguing for with a twofold affirmation. (1) Jesus's resurrected and ascended humanity, while free from "all decay and corruption" is still "fully and truly human" and therefore "creaturely space and time, far from being dissolved are confirmed in their reality before God."[31] (2) Jesus's ascension is ultimately beyond human ken to grasp entirely, and therefore it must be acknowledged that the ascension "cannot ultimately be expressed in categories of space and time, or at least cannot be enclosed within categories of this kind."[32] Therefore, one must exercise caution and not be overly dogmatic in one's affirmations about these topics.

## 2.1.3 Ontology and Spatiality

Torrance recognizes that much of his explication of *relational space and time* is stated in negative terms, and therefore he puts his theology of spatiality more positively, once again with reference to the incarnation.[33] God-incarnate, Jesus Christ, is the fulfillment of the function the temple played in the Old Testament of providing a meeting place for God and human beings.[34] Jesus Christ, according to Torrance, is now the definitive "*place* in this physical world of space and time where God and man meet, and where they have communion with one another."[35] He accentuates his argument further by asserting that Jesus Christ "is the place where heaven and earth meet,"

28. Torrance, *Space, Time, and Resurrection*, 127.
29. Torrance, *Space, Time, and Resurrection*, 127.
30. Torrance, *Space, Time, and Resurrection*, 127.
31. Torrance, *Space, Time, and Resurrection*, 127.
32. Torrance, *Space, Time, and Resurrection*, 128.
33. Torrance, *Space, Time, and Resurrection*, 128–30.
34. Torrance, *Space, Time, and Resurrection*, 128–29.
35. Torrance, *Space, Time, and Resurrection*, 128.

and furthermore that he is "the place of reconciliation within our historical existence in flesh and blood."[36] Through the incarnation, God's spatiality is ontologically located, as it were in the person of Jesus Christ, and since Torrance does not subscribe to a *receptacle* notion of space, this must not be read to mean that the being of God is exhaustively captured in the human body of Jesus. What it does mean is that the divinity of Jesus assures one that it is in his being that one fully encounters God—or, in other words, it is in his person alone that God and humanity are fully united. Torrance then applies this theo-logic to the ascension.

According to Torrance, two important things happen in Jesus's ascension. First, Torrance repeats a point he has already adumbrated, namely, that Jesus remains human in his ascension. This follows from applying the theo-logic of the *extra Calvinisticum* consistently to both the incarnation and the ascension, resulting in the following affirmation:[37] "As in the incarnation we have to think of God the Son becoming man without ceasing to be transcendent God, so in his ascension we have to think of Christ as ascending above all space and time without ceasing to be man or without any diminishment of his physical, historical existence."[38] Second, Torrance affirms the transformation of heaven because of the ascension. Jesus makes God's presence in heaven accessible to and inhabitable by human beings.[39] Torrance is essentially making a soteriological point about heaven when he argues in such a fashion, and in making his case he is drawing insights from both Karl Rahner and Joseph Ratzinger.[40] Torrance's own argument is captured in the following words: "For the ascension of the incarnate, crucified and risen Jesus Christ inevitably transforms 'heaven': something quite new has been effected in the heavenlies which must alter its material content in our understanding of what heaven is."[41]

Torrance is specifically referring to Rahner's explication of "heaven," in what he states above. Rahner avers that "the occurrence of his [Jesus's]

---

36. Torrance, *Space, Time, and Resurrection*, 129.

37. Torrance clearly uses the *extra Calvinisticum* for the ascension but he does not explicitly elaborate on the point. Torrancean scholars have usually not explored this connection, although Fergusson acknowledges that Torrance is operating with a belief in the *extra* even for the ascension. See Fergusson, "He Ascended into Heaven," 37. One place where Torrance arguably uses the *extra Calvinisticum* for the ascension can be gleaned from how he uses Byzantine art to communicate a relational way of thinking about God's relationship to space and time in the incarnation and ascension. Cf. Torrance, "Relation of the Incarnation," 69.

38. Torrance, *Space, Time, and Resurrection*, 129.

39. See Ortlund, "Explorations," 184.

40. See Torrance, *Space, Time, and Resurrection*, 129n9, 130n10.

41. Torrance, *Space, Time, and Resurrection*, 129.

resurrection created 'heaven' (to the extent that this implies more than a purely spiritual process) and taken together with the ascension (which fundamentally is an element in the resurrection), is not merely an entry into an already existing heaven."[42] In the broader context of this statement, Rahner is connecting Christology and soteriology by arguing that Jesus's resurrection is the basis for the resurrection of all humankind and the transformation of creation.[43] Therefore, similarly, his views on how Jesus in his resurrection and ascension "created 'heaven'" are to be understood in like manner—humans one day can go into heaven because Jesus has gone there for them.[44] This is exactly the point Torrance is underscoring as well, and it is a soteriological one. Torrance later uses insights from Joseph Ratzinger's work to underscore this same theme: "What the 'Ascension' tells us about heaven is that it is the dimension of divine and human fellowship which is based upon the resurrection and exaltation of Jesus. Henceforth it designates the 'place' (in the strictly ontological sense) in which man can have eternal life."[45]

While Christology is central to Torrance's spatiality of the ascension, this spatiality is also to be ecclesially construed. In other words, for Torrance, God's presence, while definitively found only in Jesus, is mediated by the Holy Spirit "in the Church" with the result that the church, firmly located in the "space-time of this world, is the 'place' where God and man are appointed to meet."[46] There is another aspect to the ontology of Torrance's spatiality, which is its eschatological dimensions; this is clearly intimated

---

42. Rahner and Schmitt, "Resurrection," section D ("Theology"), para. 4; cf. Torrance, *Space, Time, and Resurrection*, 129n9.

43. See Rahner and Schmitt, "Resurrection," section D ("Theology"), para. 3, where for instance, Rahner states, "Jesus' resurrection is not only in the ideal order an 'exemplary cause' of the resurrection of all, but objectively is the beginning of the transfiguration of the world as an ontologically interconnected occurrence. In this beginning the destiny of the world is already in principle decided and has already begun." Cf. Torrance, *Space, Time, and Resurrection*, 129n9.

44. See for example what Rahner states in the following: "On the basis of these reflections systematic theology might then show why Jesus as pledge and beginning of the perfect fulfilment of the world, as representative of the new cosmos, as dispenser of the Spirit, head of the Church, dispenser of the sacraments (above all in the Eucharist), as heavenly mediator and goal of hope, can only be fully grasped if he is known throughout as the risen Lord, *and if his resurrection is not thought of as his private destiny after a work which alone had soteriological significance*" (emphasis mine). For more, see Rahner and Schmitt, "Resurrection," section D ("Theology"), para. 5; cf. Torrance, *Space, Time, and Resurrection*, 129n9.

45. Ratzinger, "Ascension of Christ," para. 6; cf. Torrance, *Space, Time, and Resurrection*, 130n10.

46. Torrance, *Space, Time, and Resurrection*, 129.

through Torrance's reference to the beginning of the Lord's prayer: "'Our Father who art in heaven, hallowed be thy name. Thy kingdom come, thy will be done *on earth* as it is in heaven.'"[47] While Torrance does not flesh out the eschatological aspects of his spatial theology here in any detail, what he wishes to convey is that "God's place" (heaven) and "man's place" (earth) "through the Spirit . . . are not separated from one another (they were not spatially related in any case),"[48] and that when God's will is fully realized, as is invoked in the Lord's prayer, it will happen "on earth," and therefore the human "space-time of this world" will not disintegrate in the least.[49] In other words, at the eschaton, there will be human beings and a new creation, because Jesus's ascension to heaven affirms rather than removes his own humanity and the space-time of creation.[50]

### 2.1.4 Torrance's Broader Corpus

Torrance's exposition on the christological aspects in *Space, Time, and Resurrection* underscores the centrality of the *extra Calvinisticum*, the *relational* way one must think about space, and crucially the retention of space and time in God's schema for his creation. In other places in his corpus, he lists the areas of disagreement in the historical debate between Reformed and Lutherans on the spatial aspects of the ascension, the essentially soteriological nature of his exposition on the ascension in relation to space and time, and the thoroughgoing eschatological thrust of his account on the ascension.

#### 2.1.4.1 Historical

Torrance contends that in the historical debate in the sixteenth century, the Reformed and Lutherans disagreed over three specific aspects vis-à-vis their spatial theologies of the incarnation and ascension.[51] In all three areas, Torrance explains that the main divergence can be attributed to whether one affirms a *relational* or a *receptacle* view of space and time.[52] First, the Reformed theologians, according to Torrance, affirmed the *extra*

---

47. Torrance, *Space, Time, and Resurrection*, 130.
48. Torrance, *Space, Time, and Resurrection*, 129–30.
49. Torrance, *Space, Time, and Resurrection*, 130.
50. Torrance, *Space, Time, and Resurrection*, 129–30.
51. Torrance, *Space, Time, and Incarnation*, 30–31.
52. Torrance, *Space, Time, and Incarnation*, 31–32.

*Calvinisticum* because they believed it did justice to the *relational* conception of space adopted by the "early church," evidenced in the non-spatial ways in which the two natures in Christ (divine and human) related to one another.[53] In other words, Reformed theologians believed that their *relational* spatiality concurrently allowed them to think of the Son as genuinely incarnate and embodied on earth, but also present in heaven.[54] In diametric opposition to the Reformed, Torrance explains, the Lutheran theologians contended that only a "container notion," in which the Son was absolutely circumscribed in a body, could amount to a genuine incarnation.[55] Second, the Lutherans parted company with the Reformed, because they believed that the latter's affirmation of the presence of "Christ's body in heaven" could only mean circumscribing the presence of Christ in heaven.[56] Such a conclusion, Torrance argues, did not sufficiently appreciate the polyvalent ways in which the Reformed were conceptualizing space. On the one hand they were affirming the transcendent aspects present in the ascension, but they were also insisting, on the other hand, its humanity-affirming aspects, notably in the assertion that "Christ did not lose dimensional character or reality as a human body."[57] Third, discerning the way Christ can be present in the Eucharist divided Reformed and Lutherans. The Reformed argued that the eucharistic presence of Christ had to be tempered with an equal recognition of the presence of Christ at the eschaton, while the Lutherans did not make such a distinction, maintaining Christ's actual bodily presence in the eucharistic sacrament.[58] In other words, Reformed theologians argued that the Eucharist is a form of proleptic eschatology, not a fully realized one, while Lutheran theologians contended that "the full actuality of the real presence of Christ" was present in the Eucharist.[59] As the above section has shown, Torrance clearly aligns himself with the Reformed, not the Lutherans, and this aspect is important to bear in mind, as the underdeveloped aspects of Torrance's spatial theology of the ascension will need to be developed in a thoroughly Reformed manner.

---

53. Torrance, *Space, Time, and Incarnation*, 31. For a critique of Torrance's interpretation that the early church held on to a *relational* view of space and time, see Luoma, *Incarnation and Physics*, 57.

54. Torrance, *Space, Time, and Incarnation*, 31.

55. Torrance, *Space, Time, and Incarnation*, 31.

56. Torrance, *Space, Time, and Incarnation*, 32.

57. Torrance, *Space, Time, and Incarnation*, 31.

58. Torrance, *Space, Time, and Incarnation*, 32.

59. Torrance, *Space, Time, and Incarnation*, 32.

## 2.1.4.2 Soteriological

Torrance is more interested in highlighting the soteriological ramifications of the ascension than in providing a robust cosmology. One can explain such a stance in one of two ways. First, Torrance, it can be argued, is following Calvin in prioritizing the work of Christ and staying clear of the cosmological details that the ascension throws up: "Calvin very rightly and wisely remarked that we must think of these events as speaking of the function or work of Christ rather than understand them in terms of strict space-time categories—for example 'sitting at the right hand of the Father.'"[60] Second, when Torrance does address the cosmological questions of the ascension, he resorts to mystery as the best answer: "Christ the risen and ascended Lord is in a place that is beyond definition and delimitation."[61] Torrance shows no such reticence, however, when he is interpreting the spatiality of the ascension in soteriological terms: "The conditions created for and intended for humanity must continue in eternity for man, inasmuch as he is redeemed precisely as man and by a Saviour who was human as well as divine."[62]

Torrance's strong soteriological accent in his discussion on the spatiality of the ascension is further illumined in two respects, which are clearly evidenced in the way Bruce Ritchie interprets the significance Torrance gives to the ascension vis-à-vis time.[63] Rightly, Ritchie explains that "time should never be considered apart from space,"[64] and therefore his interpretation of Torrance with respect to ascension and time can be extrapolated to shed light on the spatial dimensions of the ascension as well. First, Ritchie views the ascension of Jesus to heaven, in Torrance's theology, as an act that finally achieves restoration between God and the fallen Adamic race. He brings out this redemptive aspect well when he interprets Torrance's statement, "It is as our Brother, wearing our humanity, that He has ascended, presenting Himself eternally before the face of the Father, and presenting us in Himself,"[65] to mean Jesus "reverses the expulsion from Eden."[66] Second, Ritchie brings out the salvific-ontological implications of the ascension when he notes the universal scope of the transformation Jesus brings about, according to Torrance: "In the same risen humanity, the ascended Christ

---

60. Torrance, *Doctrine of Jesus Christ*, 191.
61. Torrance, *Gospel, Church, and Ministry*, 100.
62. Torrance, *Doctrine of Jesus Christ*, 192.
63. Ritchie, *T. F. Torrance*, 187–88.
64. Ritchie, *T. F. Torrance*, 186. Cf. Torrance, *Space, Time, and Resurrection*, 131.
65. Torrance, *Royal Priesthood*, 14–15.
66. Ritchie, *T. F. Torrance*, 187.

... penetrates every corner of created existence, past, present, and future."[67] While Ritchie substantiates his interpretation by pointing to the climactic role the ascension plays in Torrance's theology, particularly in guaranteeing eschatological salvation,[68] perhaps, he could have also used the incarnation as a heuristic to illuminate the ontological-salvific implications of the ascension for all time (and space). Regarding the implications of the incarnation for time, Torrance declares,

> Christian theology thus thinks of the Incarnation of the Creator Logos of God as penetrating back through created time to the very beginning unravelling the twisted skein of evil, recapitulating all things in himself, as St Paul expressed it, in order to liberate us from the tyranny of the guilt-conditioned irreversibility in which our existence has become trapped, and so to heal our existence of disorder and direct it forward to the renewal and consummation of all things in the Creator.[69]

The redemptive aspects of the incarnation can be applied to the ascension with the clarification that it is the ascension that confirms its realization.[70] Torrance's stress on the salvation of space-time, therefore, is hard to miss. Soteriology and eschatology are closely related as well to the christological aspects of the spatiality of the ascension.

### 2.1.4.3 ESCHATOLOGICAL

The tone and tenor of Torrance's eschatology in general is shaped by his Christology, as he himself insists: "Eschatology properly speaking is the application of Christology to the Kingdom of Christ and to the work of the Church in history."[71] It is no wonder then that there is a strong interrelationship between Christology and eschatology regarding the spatiality of the ascension. This interrelationship can be explained by what Torrance wishes to unequivocally affirm and correspondingly what he wants to oppose. For Torrance, God's eschatological plan for his creation is already realized in Christ, evidenced in his assertion that "Christ is already the new man in

67. Ritchie, *T. F. Torrance*, 187.
68. Ritchie points to how the ascension brings the work of salvation to its culmination, notably in Jesus's victorious homecoming and in the start of his priestly ministry in heaven. He also observes how the ascension brings about the redemption of "human time." For more, see Ritchie, *T. F. Torrance*, 187–88.
69. Torrance, *Theological and Natural Science*, 52.
70. See Torrance, *Atonement*, 429.
71. Torrance, *Royal Priesthood*, 43.

whom all things are become new, and in whom we have proleptically even now the consummation of the divine purpose of creation."[72] The specific point in which the fullness of God's plan is realized is "in the resurrection of Christ and His ascension to fill all things (Eph. 1.23; 4.10)."[73] It is these events that give Jesus the title "New Man, the Last Adam, the Head of a new race."[74] Stanley MacLean explains why Torrance gives such significance to Jesus's resurrected and ascended humanity: "When Torrance spoke of the 'humanity of Christ,' he was referring to the new vicarious humanity of *the risen and ascended* Christ. This humanity is the key to the salvation of our humanity. It is Christ, the 'New Man,' who gathers up humanity in himself through his movement from descent to ascent."[75] While Torrance clearly insists that Christ's ascension is the realization of God's salvific intentions for his creation, how one interprets the implications of this reality for the world and church becomes complex. It is here that Torrance wishes to avoid two specific kinds of interpretations, maintaining that what is already actualized in Christ will be actualized in the world and church—but only in the new creation.[76]

On the one hand, he opposes what he calls a "Realised teleology," by which he means that one is claiming a "perfected union of the eternal and the temporal."[77] In other words, new creation, it is alleged, is the result of the natural way in which the world can be ordered, akin to "communism" and "a secularized eschatology" that asserts that a structured human society will eventually be "the realisation of the kingdom of God."[78] On the other hand, Torrance rejects what he calls a "Realised eschatology," which he interprets in terms of a "tension between the new and the old."[79] Otherwise stated, in this view in Jesus, "The Kingdom of God has already come," and "there is no eschatological expectation left."[80] Opposing both views, Torrance comes up with a corrective that he believes allows one to believe in both "eschatology" and "teleology" in a balanced and mutually-conditioning manner:

---

72. Torrance, *Incarnation*, 330.

73. Torrance, *Royal Priesthood*, 25.

74. Torrance, *Royal Priesthood*, 25.

75. MacLean, "Torrance's Recovery," 201.

76. For more on what the new creation will be like, according to Torrance, see Torrance, *Apocalypse Today*, 173–83.

77. Torrance, *Incarnation*, 336.

78. Torrance, *Incarnation*, 329.

79. Torrance, *Incarnation*, 336.

80. Torrance, *Incarnation*, 320.

> It is because the teleological end must be interpreted eschatologically, placing the decisive event in the birth, death and resurrection of Jesus Christ, that we must reject all liberal doctrines of a kingdom of progress. It is because the eschatological end must be interpreted teleologically that we must reject equally the view that the *parousia* is past and gone and the kingdom fully present because it has been completely realised in the resurrection and ascension of Christ.[81]

Torrance does not want God's new creation to be viewed as (1) something humans can bring about by themselves, and (2) something that is not going to happen in the world that humans live in. Shaped by biblical thinking, Torrance emphasizes "the kingdom as bound up with creation, and yet as the pure act of God."[82] Torrance's sermons crystallize these beliefs memorably:

> God's original creation will be fully restored in redemption. It is a redemption, however, that transcends that original creation in glory though it is not divorced from it . . . the perfection of the Christian life involves the perfection of earth as well as heaven. The Christian hope is fulfilled only in a new heaven and a new earth peopled with human beings living in holy and loving fellowship with God, with one another, and in harmony with the fullness of creation.[83]

In the final analysis, for Torrance, the details of the spatiality of the ascended Christ may be mysterious, but what the ascension signifies for eschatology is indeed spatial in nature—namely "the new heaven and new earth."[84]

## 2.2 Trinity and Spatiality

### 2.2.1 Ascension and Dual Affirmations

Torrance concludes his theology of the spatiality of the ascended Jesus in *Space, Time, and Resurrection* by asserting the importance of simultaneously holding on to two convictions: "(i) In the ascension Jesus Christ ascends from man's place to God's place; (ii) By his ascension Jesus Christ has

---

81. Torrance, *Incarnation*, 337.
82. Torrance, *Incarnation*, 314.
83. Torrance, *Apocalypse Today*, 177.
84. Torrance, *Incarnation*, 330. See MacLean, "Torrance's Recovery," 189–206, for a detailed exposition of the spatial aspect of Torrance's eschatology.

established man in man's place in time and space."[85] The first point begins to discuss the Trinitarian aspects of spatiality that the ascension brings to the surface, while the second point illuminates the epistemological and theological use of language that is necessary to do justice to complex doctrines like the ascension.

### 2.2.2 God's Space and Time

Torrance first wishes to declutter the discussion from "abstract" or unscientific conceptions of both time and space.[86] Instead of thinking of both space and time as *static* conceptions, he clarifies that their relationship is an intrinsic and inseparable one: "Space and time are relational and variational concepts defined in accordance with the nature of the force that gives them their field of determination. In modern thought we cannot separate space and time but think of space-time in a four dimensional continuum."[87] While Torrance acknowledges that there are differences in one sense between space and time,[88] he believes in the final analysis "we cannot separate space from time, or location from time—temporal relation belongs to location."[89] With this Einsteinian[90] thinking about space-time, where if something is spatial it is also necessarily temporal, Torrance moves on to consider how this applies to thinking about the differences between human *space-time* and God's *space-time*.[91] He notes that there is no possibility of correlating

85. Torrance, *Space, Time, and Resurrection*, 130.

86. Torrance, *Space, Time, and Resurrection*, 130–31.

87. Torrance, *Space, Time, and Resurrection*, 130–31.

88. Torrance explains this difference as follows: "Whereas space is three-dimensional, time is one directional or irreversible." See Torrance, *Space, Time, and Resurrection*, 131.

89. Torrance, *Space, Time, and Resurrection*, 131.

90. Cf. Torrance, *Theological and Natural Science*, 69–73, where he engages with Einstein's work vis-à-vis space and time. Some of the sources Torrance provides on Albert Einstein on p. 69n79 are: "*The Evolution of Physics, From early concepts to relativity and quanta*, Albert Einstein and Leopold Infeld, New York, 1938; *Ideas and Opinions*, Albert Einstein, New York, 1954; and *The Born-Einstein Letters*, Max Born, London, 1971." Apart from Einstein, Torrance finds the works of several other scientists like "Katsir, Landsberg, Prigogine" helpful in illustrating the relational understanding of space and time, particularly how God redeems time. For more, see Torrance, *Theological and Natural Science*, 52–53. In contemporary scholarship, Stephen Hawking's work evinces a *relational* space-time model akin to one developed by Einstein. In terms of the interface of theology and science that considers a *relational* view of space-time, see Wilkinson, *Christian Eschatology*.

91. Torrance rejects the traditional assumption that God is in "eternity" which entails timelessness. Torrance affirms "*the reality of time* even for God." He explains his

human space-time conceptions, which are marked by "the field of change and the sequence of coherent structures in which he lives his life . . . as a creature of this physical world," with conceptions about God's space-time realities, as the latter's is transcendent and operates out of its own notions of space and time.[92] To this end, Torrance writes, "We do not speak of space-time in relation to God, but we must speak of the 'place' and 'time' of God in terms of his own eternal life and his eternal purpose in the divine love, where he wills his life and love to overflow to us whom he has made to share with him his life and love."[93] In other words, what Torrance is stating could be interpreted to mean that God has his own space and time, and when this is understood through Torrance's scientific theology, this would mean that one would have to seek to discern what God's space and time is and how it must be understood from God's perspective. Human notions of space and time cannot be extrapolated to interpret God's space and time.[94]

Torrance explains God's space and time well when he states: "'Time' for God himself can only be defined by the uncreated and creative life of God, and 'place' for God can only be defined by the communion of the Persons in the Divine life—that is why doctrinally we speak of the *'perichorēsis'* (from *chora* meaning space or room) or mutual indwelling of the Father, Son and Holy Spirit in the Triunity of God."[95] It is important to note that one cannot superimpose human notions of space-time onto conceptions of God's space-time. Torrance's explanation above interprets God's space and time from theological concepts that help shed light on the being of God.

### 2.2.3 *Torrance's Broader Corpus*

While Torrance leaves the reader wishing for a more robust explication of Trinitarian space and time, he clarifies that God's own space and time is distinct from humans' space and time. One cannot univocally read human conceptions of space and time into God's experience of these aspects. In other places, Torrance elaborates on the Trinitarian aspects of space and time by underscoring the centrality of relationality, and elaborates on how

---

rationale as follows: "If the Word is made flesh, then it is also made time, and not to take that seriously is docetic heresy." For more, see Torrance, *Incarnation*, 273. This position is akin to the "sempiternal" or "everlasting" view of God's relationship to time.

92. Torrance, *Space, Time, and Resurrection*, 131.
93. Torrance, *Space, Time, and Resurrection*, 131.
94. Torrance, *Space, Time, and Resurrection*, 131.
95. Torrance, *Space, Time, and Resurrection*, 131.

God's experience of space and time is different from how human beings experience these realities.

#### 2.2.3.1 Relational

Torrance minimally expounds the doctrine of *perichoresis* in *Space, Time, and Resurrection*. Elsewhere, he provides a more detailed exploration of how *perichoresis* should be understood with reference to the Trinity.[96] While all the details are not germane to this discussion, three specific insights on *perichoresis* can be extrapolated to shed light on the spatiality of the ascension vis-à-vis the Trinity. First, for Torrance *perichoresis* underscores the intimacy and relationality the persons of the Trinity share with one another, such that their relationships with one another constitute their personal identities without diminishing their particularity as persons, nor undermining the oneness of God.[97] Writes Torrance,

> The Father, the Son and the Holy Spirit are distinctive Persons each with his own incommunicable properties . . . they dwell *in* one another, not only *with* one another, in such an intimate way . . . that their individual characteristics instead of dividing them from one another unite them indivisibly together, the Father in the Son and the Spirit, the Son in the Father and the Spirit, and the Spirit in the Father and the Son . . . each is who he is in his wholeness as true God of true God in the wholeness of the other two who are each true God of true God, and yet in the mystery of their perichoretic inter-relations they are not three Gods but one only God, the Blessed and Holy Trinity.[98]

Second, Torrance has both a Trinitarian and a soteriological accent to *perichoresis*. Both these aspects are clearly evidenced when he explains, "*perichoresis* is not a static but a dynamic concept, for it refers to an eternal movement in the Love of the Father, the Son and the Holy Spirit for one another, which flows outward unceasingly toward us."[99] In other words, he argues that there is a perfect accord between the intra-Trinitarian relationship of love that the persons of the Trinity share with one another and its soteriological outworking toward human beings in Jesus.[100] With respect to

---

96. See Torrance, *Christian Doctrine of God*, 173–202.
97. Torrance, *Christian Doctrine of God*, 172.
98. Torrance, *Christian Doctrine of God*, 172.
99. Torrance, *Christian Doctrine of God*, 172.
100. Torrance, *Christian Doctrine of God*, 172.

soteriology, Torrance avers "that *perichoresis* is not a speculative concept. It expresses the soteriological truth of the identity between God himself and the content of his saving revelation in Jesus Christ and in the Holy Spirit, and thereby assures us that what God is toward us in Jesus Christ and in his Spirit he is inherently and eternally in himself."[101] Torrance clearly insists, as evidenced in what he states, that in and through Jesus Christ human beings are welcomed into the same relationship of love that exists between the persons of the Trinity.[102]

Third, Torrance maintains that while not every aspect of the economic Trinity can be univocally applied to the ontological Trinity, the "coactivity of the Father, the Son and the Holy Spirit" can indeed be said to represent who God is ontologically.[103] Torrance is essentially asserting that both the *being* and the *work* of the Triune God are characterized by *perichoresis*: "They are not only Triune in Being but are Triune in Activity."[104] Importantly, this means that there is not a single aspect of Christ's life and work, including the ascension, in which the other persons of the Trinity were not involved:

> We cannot but say that both the Father and the Spirit participated in ways appropriate to their distinctive natures and properties in the birth of Jesus, in his servant ministry as Son of Man, in his atoning sacrifice on the Cross for sin, in his triumphant resurrection, in his ascension to the Father, in his heavenly intercession for us, and his rule over all things at God's right hand. And so we cannot but hold that the Father and the Spirit continue to participate in the saving work of God's Love, and will participate with Christ in the consummation of all things at the final judgment and resurrection.[105]

The oneness and intimacy the persons of the Trinity share with one another, not only in their being but also in their work, comes across clearly in the above explanation from Torrance.

## 2.2.3.2 SPATIO-TEMPORAL

Torrance's exposition of God's space and time has a thick soteriological accent, and therefore it is hard to decipher what his own views are on space

---

101. Torrance, *Christian Doctrine of God*, 172.
102. Torrance, *Christian Doctrine of God*, 172.
103. Torrance, *Christian Doctrine of God*, 198.
104. Torrance, *Christian Doctrine of God*, 197.
105. Torrance, *Christian Doctrine of God*, 199.

and time in relation to the being of God.[106] Nonetheless, Torrance unequivocally affirms that God experiences time when he asserts that "the creation of the world out of nothing is something *new even for God*."[107] Importantly, Torrance does not mean that God is in time as if he were contained by it, but that there are "new" events that God has in his life. Other events as well, including the crucifixion, resurrection and Pentecost, Torrance maintains, are "utterly new even for God."[108] When Torrance makes such an argument, he is distancing himself from docetism[109] and aligning himself with what he believes to be the teaching of the Scriptures; namely, "the New Testament teaching of an imminent advent of the kingdom *in time*."[110] Furthermore, Torrance is subscribing to the theology that Barth held on to in the latter part of his career—namely, one that had a "realist attitude to time and history."[111]

In light of such a perspective, one can confidently aver with R. T. Mullins that Torrance affirms a view of time called *divine temporalism*, which asserts that "God exists without beginning and without end" and furthermore insists that "God does have succession in His life."[112] While God does experience time in his own being, without thinking of this in terms of container notions, Torrance clarifies that there is a difference between God's time and human time; namely, while God experiences in his own being "uncreated 'time,'" humans experience "created time" that "has a beginning and an end."[113] Stated differently, one can explain the difference as Mullins does: "The difference between our [human] now and God's eternal now is that God never came into existence. The now of physical time had a beginning, and it need not exist, whereas God necessarily exists."[114] With respect to time, one must affirm that Torrance aligns himself with divine temporalism, not any view of timelessness. What about the Triune God's relationship to space?

For Torrance, with regard to God's spatiality, because of the incarnation there is an important dialectic at work—God is spatial but not enclosed

---

106. Cf. Torrance, *Theological and Natural Science*, 50–52.
107. Torrance, *Christian Doctrine of God*, 208.
108. Torrance, *Christian Doctrine of God*, 238.
109. Cf. Torrance, *Incarnation*, 273: "If the Word is made flesh, then it is also made time, and not to take that seriously is docetic heresy. . . . We must take time seriously in respect of both the first advent of Christ and of his second advent."
110. Torrance, *Incarnation*, 273.
111. See Torrance, *Incarnation*, 272–74.
112. Mullins, *Timeless God*, 31.
113. See Torrance, *Theological and Natural Science*, 50.
114. Mullins, *Timeless God*, 35.

within space: "While the Incarnation does not mean that God is limited by space and time, it asserts the reality of space and time for God in the actuality of His relations with us."[115] Jonathan Hill interprets this duality in Torrance's discussion to mean that he is a *"simple atemporalist."*[116] By *simple atemporalism*, Hill means that "the Son remains 'outside' time, even during the incarnation."[117] He goes on to explain, "Whatever relation exists between Jesus, who lived during an identifiable period of history, and the Son, it is a relation between something temporal and something atemporal."[118] Hill arguably correctly identifies a duality in the way God experiences space and time because of the incarnation, but incorrectly attributes this to mean Torrance affirms simple atemporalism.[119] Instead, it would be more accurate to state that Torrance affirms the *extra Calvinisticum* through such a duality, and posits a distinction in the way the divine and human natures in Christ's person experience space and time differently. In other words, from Torrance's perspective it is important to assert that "elements in the incarnate economy such as the time pattern of human life in this world . . . may not be read back into the eternal Life of God."[120] Furthermore, he would contend that "the *homoousion* does not allow us indiscriminately to read back into God what is human and finite."[121] Spatially speaking, one must conclude that while God's being is not embodied, Christ's human nature still is embodied while his divine nature is not.[122]

## 2.3 Epistemology, Theological Language, and Spatiality

### 2.3.1 Theology of Ascension Through Byzantine Art

Through a particular piece of Byzantine art, Torrance brilliantly captures how "Christ stands in bounded space and time, but at the other end he

115. Torrance, *Space, Time, and Incarnation*, 67.
116. Hill, "Incarnation, Timelessness, and Exaltation," 22.
117. Hill, "Incarnation, Timelessness, and Exaltation," 22.
118. Hill, "Incarnation, Timelessness, and Exaltation," 22.
119. It may be the case that this is a matter of nuance and interpretation. Torrance would clearly make a distinction between how the two natures of Christ (divine and human) experience space and time. Instead of "simple atemporalism," Torrance would argue that Christ's divine nature experiences "uncreated time," while the human nature experiences "created time." See Torrance, *Theological and Natural Science*, 50.
120. Torrance, *Christian Doctrine of God*, 109.
121. Torrance, *Christian Doctrine of God*, 99.
122. This is an extension of the logic of the *extra Calvinisticum*, which Torrance affirms. Cf. Torrance, *Space, Time, and Resurrection*, 123–26.

transcends all such limitations."[123] This Byzantine artwork, for Torrance, clearly conveys how two kinds of spatiality are operative in the person of Jesus because he has two natures that hypostatically reside within his being.[124] After this pictorial depiction of his theology of the ascension,[125] as it were, Torrance makes two points, one relating to epistemology and the other to spatiality. In terms of epistemology, Torrance cautions against any kind of *receptacle* epistemological thinking—"God or Christ" cannot be fully comprehended, and certainly cannot be mastered and captured by human intelligence.[126] In terms of spatiality, Torrance speaks of how Jesus's ascension to God's presence entails his absence on earth, in terms of his humanity, but because God is both transcendent and immanent, Jesus is still present.[127]

### 2.3.2 Two Different Times Operating Simultaneously

Torrance contends that the ascension is the occasion for thinking of two kinds of time simultaneously. First, there is the time that is characterized by fallenness: "The time of the old man . . . the corruptible existence which we still wear and in which we are fully implicated."[128] Second, there is the time of perfection and telos, which is already inaugurated by Jesus's ascension because "it is ascension in which our humanity in Christ is taken up into the full Communion of Father, Son and Holy Spirit in life and love."[129] While Torrance does not spell it out here, in an earlier section of *Space, Time, and Resurrection* he enumerates how these two different conceptions of time apply to believers after death. Perspectival differences emerge, according to Torrance, about what actually happens to a believer upon his or her death: "Looked at from the perspective of the new creation there is no gap between the death of the believer and the *Parousia* of Christ, but looked at from the perspective of time that decays and crumbles away, there is a lapse in time between them."[130] While this difficult passage will be expounded in

123. Torrance, *Space, Time, and Resurrection*, 132. Torrance provides an illustration of what this looks like in "Relation of the Incarnation," 69.

124. Torrance, *Space, Time, and Resurrection*, 132.

125. Torrance generally uses this illustration of the Byzantine art to highlight how one must think of the incarnation and arguably also the ascension. Here, the illustration is used in the context of explicating the spatiality of the ascension. See Torrance, *Space, Time, and Resurrection*, 132.

126. Torrance, *Space, Time, and Resurrection*, 132.

127. Torrance, *Space, Time, and Resurrection*, 132.

128. Torrance, *Space, Time, and Resurrection*, 133.

129. Torrance, *Space, Time, and Resurrection*, 133.

130. Torrance, *Space, Time, and Resurrection*, 102.

chapter 6, at this stage it must be noted that the genesis of Torrance's twofold categorization of time (fallen and redeemed time) originates in Barth.[131]

## 2.3.3 Importance of Space and Time

Torrance bookends this last point he makes about the spatiality and temporality of the ascended Jesus in *Space, Time, and Resurrection*, by affirming on the one hand the absence of Jesus on earth, but on the other hand his presence through the Holy Spirit.[132] The absence of Jesus on earth, for Torrance, interestingly entails two positive affirmations: (1) the oneness between the earthly Jesus and the ascended Jesus, and (2) the oneness between God and Jesus Christ.[133] With regard to the oneness between the ascended Jesus and the earthly Jesus, Torrance makes this clear by affirming, even in spite of the ascension and an absent Jesus, that one's knowledge of Jesus today is in the first instance always through the historical Jesus: "The withdrawal of Christ from visible and physical contact with us in our space-time existence on earth and in history means that Jesus Christ insists in making contact with us, not first directly and immediately in his risen humanity, but first and foremost through his historical involvement with us in his incarnation and crucifixion."[134]

In fact, Torrance goes to the extent of stating that all knowledge of Jesus will always be only through the historical Jesus: "The ascension thus means that to all eternity God insists on speaking to us through the historical Jesus."[135] Torrance confidently asserts this because he is certain that Jesus is God: "*Jesus speaks as God and God speaks as Jesus.*"[136] Therefore, for Torrance, it is epistemically imperative to know the ascended Jesus *through* the historical Jesus, in order to avoid two negative consequences. First, since God has chosen to reveal himself concretely in history, Torrance wants to avoid any kind of "demythologizing" tendencies, which undermine the historicity of God's revelation and also undercut the oneness between God's *being* and *act*.[137] Second, Torrance underscores the centrality of the cross in order to avoid any "*a priori*" approaches to God, and also because he believes

---

131. See Torrance, *Karl Barth: Introduction*, 79.
132. Torrance, *Space, Time, and Resurrection*, 133–35.
133. Torrance, *Space, Time, and Resurrection*, 133–34.
134. Torrance, *Space, Time, and Resurrection*, 133.
135. Torrance, *Space, Time, and Resurrection*, 133.
136. Torrance, *Space, Time, and Resurrection*, 133–34.
137. Torrance, *Space, Time, and Resurrection*, 134.

in the oneness between the historical Jesus and the ascended Jesus.[138] The Holy Spirit, for Torrance, answers all the epistemic quandaries. The Spirit, because he is sent by the ascended Jesus, assures one that there is a oneness between the historical Jesus and the ascended Jesus.[139] Furthermore, it is the Spirit that enables one to make sense of the duality present in the *relational* account of the ascension vis-à-vis God and human beings' space-time, and it is also the Spirit who mediates the presence of the ascended and absent Jesus: "It is through the Spirit that things infinitely disconnected—disconnected by the 'distance' of the ascension—are nevertheless infinitely closely related."[140] In other words, the Holy Spirit, Torrance contends, provides the answers to all the difficult questions that the ascension raises.

## 2.3.4 *Torrance's Broader Corpus*

Torrance highlights the importance of using artistic analogies that communicate theological truths about the transcendence of God. Furthermore, he avers that a dual use of language is needed when talking about space-time and the ascension. Lastly, he underscores the epistemological centrality of God's historical revelation. There are four other pertinent aspects of Torrance's theological language vis-à-vis the spatiality of the ascension.

### 2.3.4.1 ANALOGICAL LANGUAGE

First, Torrance draws upon Athanasius's theology to acknowledge that language is "analogical."[141] With respect to the incarnation and spatial language, Torrance argues that literal kinds of understanding represented by "receptacle" models miss the mark, while analogical ways of thinking are more helpful.[142] With Athanasius, Torrance avers that Christ's relationship with the believer and the Father cannot be construed literally in a spatial manner but only analogically: "Christ is 'in' us through sharing our bodily existence, but He is also 'in' the Father through His oneness with Him, but how are we to work out the relation between these two 'in's? Athanasius offered an analogical account of the relationship."[143] Habets helpfully explains

---

138. Torrance, *Space, Time, and Resurrection*, 134.
139. Torrance, *Space, Time, and Resurrection*, 135.
140. Torrance, *Space, Time, and Resurrection*, 135.
141. Torrance, *Space, Time, and Incarnation*, 16.
142. See Torrance, *Space, Time, and Incarnation*, 15–17.
143. Torrance, *Space, Time, and Incarnation*, 16.

the meaning of "analogical" in this passage when he states, "By respecting both the divine and the human nature we can see that to be 'in' the other (Christ *in* the Father and men and women *in* Christ), applies not to *place* but to *nature*."[144] In other words, Habets maintains that since "nothing is far from God" with respect to space, "the phrase, 'we are in Christ Jesus'" cannot be interpreted to mean a spatial location; on the contrary, it "points analogically to the fact that we are in a relationship with him."[145] Torrance does something similar with respect to the ascension and spatiality, when he makes a soteriological and relational point, not a cosmological one. This is evidenced when he asserts, "Whatever else 'heaven' is for us it is the 'place' where Christ is in God."[146] In effect, Torrance is insisting that Christ's ascension means that God's presence in heaven is accessible to and inhabitable by human beings.[147]

David Fergusson brings out the various nuances in Torrance's explication of heaven well when he writes: "For Torrance, heaven is not an empty or partially inhabited space into which the ascended Jesus is admitted. Instead, the shape or form that heaven takes is itself determined by the action of the ascended Lord. Again the language is apocalyptic and baffling, but it signals the intention to think of heaven as Christ-shaped, as ensuring a place in the eternal life of God for creatures."[148] What Christ does in his ascension, for Torrance, has immense soteriological and relational implications, which Gavin Ortlund memorably captures when he reasons, "Because the ascension does not subtract or dilute any of God the Son's creaturely reality, it reveals heaven as the place of God to be a place that is friendly to creaturely existence *as creaturely*—for instance, bodily and spatiotemporal existence."[149] Both Fergusson and Ortlund highlight the soteriological significance that lay behind Torrance's language on Jesus's ascension to heaven.

## 2.3.4.2 STRATIFIED LANGUAGE

Second, Torrance points out that reality is *stratified*. With respect to the ascension, one is moving from the *economic* to the *ontological* levels of Torrance's theology.[150] Therefore, for Torrance, it is inevitable that human

144. Habets, *Theosis*, 64.
145. Habets, *Theosis*, 64.
146. Torrance, *Atonement*, 288.
147. See Ortlund, "Explorations," 184.
148. Fergusson, "Ascension of Christ," 100.
149. Ortlund, "Explorations," 184.
150. For an overview of Torrance's levels of theological thinking, see Colyer, *How to Read*, 291–300.

language becomes inadequate to the task as "statements regarding the ascension are *closed at man's end* (because bounded within the space-time limits of man's existence on earth) but are *infinitely open at God's end*, open to God's own eternal being and the infinite room of his divine life."[151] In other words, understanding what is happening in the ascension is impossible to capture fully in human words. The bankruptcy of human language is particularly noticeable, for Torrance, when one is moving to the highest level of his theological thinking, the *ontological* level, because it is here that "All true theological concepts and statements inevitably fall short of the God to whom they refer, so that . . . their fragility and their inadequacy, as concepts and as human statements about God must be regarded as part of the correctness and truthfulness of their reference to God."[152]

Torrance applies the same principle to studying the spatiality of the ascension vis-à-vis God and insists that humility not hubris is the proper attitude to adopt: "Only when categories of space and time break off and point beyond themselves altogether to what is ineffable and inconceivable in modes of our space and time" is one beginning to rightly speak about the ascension in relation to God.[153] The impoverishment of existing human language, for example, is instanced in the manner in which Torrance writes about what happens to believers after they die.[154] While God-talk at the ontological level, in particular, in order to be accurate, will inevitably be couched in mystery, this does not mean that one has to succumb to "merely apophatic or negative contemplation."[155] Torrance's particular understanding of *apophatic* is important to note as another feature of his theological language.

### 2.3.4.3 Apophatic Language

Third, Torrance utilizes *apophatic* speech in his theology. By this is meant that Torrance acknowledges that there is mystery after a certain point in theology.[156] It is no wonder that he expresses what can best be described as an "apophatic reticence"[157] with regard to the spatiality of the ascension

---

151. Torrance, *Atonement*, 290.
152. Torrance, *Christian Doctrine of God*, 110–11.
153. Torrance, *Atonement*, 287.
154. Torrance, *Atonement*, 260.
155. Torrance, *Christian Doctrine of God*, 111.
156. See Richardson, "Revelation"; Torrance, "Thomas Torrance Responds," especially pp. 324–29. See also section 4.5, "Artistic," in chapter 2 for more on this point.
157. Habets uses this phrase in *Theosis*, 154. I am using it here to convey the idea

when he declares: "Precisely because we pass here into the future it is not within our reach at all to say how much of this is metaphorical or figurative and how much literal fact."[158] Torrance's apophatic language can best be described as a practice of proper epistemic humility, or as he himself would call it, "holy moments," because it is at this point that one acknowledges that one cannot know all there is to know about God.[159]

### 2.3.4.4 EXAGGERATED LANGUAGE

Fourth, Torrance utilizes the rhetorical device of hyperbole to make a point. For instance, he states repeatedly in one of his works that "God loves us more than he loves himself."[160] Myk Habets opines that Torrance perhaps uses this phrase to communicate the "*ecstatic*" nature of God's love for human beings, and not that "God's love for sinners . . . [is] greater than the Father's love for the Son."[161] However, in using such phrases, Habets believes that Torrance is using "provocative language" to express "the love of God exhibited at the cross," but Habets also weighs in on such language by stating that Torrance "could have done so in less ambiguous terms that would not have the potential to implicitly undermine his own theology."[162]

There are other places as well where Torrance seems to exaggerate to make an emphatic point in his theology.[163] David Fergusson, in his critique

---

that Torrance acknowledges human limitation and mystery regarding various aspects of the ascension.

158. Torrance, *Doctrine of Jesus Christ*, 192. See also Torrance, *Space, Time, and Resurrection*, 127.

159. Torrance, "Thomas Torrance Responds," 328.

160. Torrance, "Christ Who Loves Us," 14, where he underscores this phrase twice. See also pp. 8 and 9 of this work where Torrance repeats this phrase.

161. Habets, *Theosis*, 85, 86.

162. Habets, *Theosis*, 87.

163. For instance, Torrance, *Theology in Reconstruction*, 160, writes: "Justification has been fulfilled subjectively as well as objectively in Jesus Christ, but that objective and subjective justification is objective to us." For some such a statement could be read to mean that Torrance is affirming universalism. While Robert Letham, "Triune God," 454, does not specifically refer to this passage from Torrance, he may be thinking of it when he critiques Torrance as follows: "It is simply incoherent for Torrance to say what he says about the definitive justification and reconciliation for all people and yet to deny universal salvation. Moreover, if it is possible for people to reject Christ and what he has done, it cannot be definitive and effective for them and cannot have been complete in Christ's person. It simply will not do to dismiss criticism on this point by the assertion that Torrance's claims stem from a center in God and that the critics have an uncrucified epistemology; this is to break down rational discourse on the basis of a privileged and precocious gnosis." For Torrance's explicit rejection of universalism, see

of Torrance, confirms the use of exaggerated language at certain points in his theology of the ascension. Says Fergusson, "Torrance perhaps underplays the extent to which our discourse is inevitably tentative, broken, and provisional in this area of dogmatic thought. The apparent resolution of problems may be too premature in places."[164] While Fergusson rightly acknowledges a certain exaggeration in Torrance's language on the ascension, which may indeed need to be addressed, perhaps an aspect that is not sufficiently considered is what Torrance is trying to accomplish through such language. Namely, as will be expounded in more detail momentarily, Torrance is arguably resorting to artistic language when words and concepts are inadequate to the task of theologizing about realities that are beyond human speech.

## 2.4 Section Summary

Torrance's concern in his exposition on the spatiality of the ascension is clearly christologically oriented, Trinitarian (but only suggestively explicated), and worked out with a keen interest to document theological truths through an appropriate theological epistemology and language. Specifically, the christological level emphasizes soteriological and eschatological truths, respectively. Torrance insists that Christ's ascension promises humanity access into the very presence of God as human beings; furthermore, he avers that the ascension looks forward to the goal for creation, which is the gift of new creation. The Trinitarian level affirms both *oneness* and *threeness* in the Triune being of God, which underscores the intimate and genuine relationality among the persons of the Trinity. Importantly, in and through Christ human beings are welcomed into the communion of love that exists among the persons of the Trinity. With respect to epistemology and theological language, Torrance affirms the need to use language that appropriately conveys various mysteries associated with the ascension. Through an analysis of Torrance's rhetoric, it was argued that he uses what can be called *artistic* language that acknowledges mystery at key places in his theology, with the ascension as an example of this feature in his theology.

---

Torrance, "Universalism or Election?" For a secondary source that shows why Torrance does not affirm universalism, see Molnar, "Problem of Universalism." For a contrary view, see Crisp, "T. F. Torrance." To be sure, Torrance's point about atonement can be made clearer to avoid misunderstanding him as a universalist when one distinguishes between the "corporate" level of atonement, wherein Christ died "for all," and the "personal" level of atonement, wherein one must appropriate the gift of atonement by the power of the Holy Spirit who does not work irresistibly.

164. Fergusson, "Ascension of Christ," 106.

Each of these three levels in Torrance's thinking about the spatiality of the ascension will be constructively developed in what follows. First, christologically, the goal will be to make a case for the use of the *extra Calvinisticum* as a heuristic to think not just about the incarnation, but also about the spatiality of the ascended Jesus. Second, since Torrance's theology of space in light of the Trinity is only present in nascent form, the goal will be to develop it further in conversation with other theologians. Third, *artistic* language will be used as a descriptor to shed light on the idiosyncrasies of Torrance's use of theological language in his discourse on the ascension vis-à-vis space and time.

## 3. SPATIALITY OF THE ASCENDED CHRIST: A CONSTRUCTIVE DEVELOPMENT

### 3.1 Ascension and the *Extra Calvinisticum*

Torrancean scholarship has not always explored the implications of the *extra Calvinisticum* for the ascension of Christ. Fergusson clearly believes that Torrance affirmed it but does not explore it in detail.[165] Paul Molnar does not directly address the connection between the ascension and the *extra Calvinisticum*. When Molnar exposits Barth's theology of the ascension, he maintains that "Barth insists, however, that he [Jesus] did not cease to be a creature because of the ascension but that he clearly showed himself to be man who lives now 'on the God-ward side of the universe, sharing his throne, *existing and acting in the mode of God, and therefore to be remembered as such*' (CD III/2, 454)."[166] Since Molnar does not directly comment on this topic (the use of the *extra Calvinisticum* for the ascension), it would be unfair to pigeonhole him to one view or another, but from his other works on Torrance's theology vis-à-vis the ascension one can conclude that he does not directly address this theme.[167]

One can make a case for the use of the *extra Calvinisticum* for the ascension in Torrance's theology by noting his strong Reformed as opposed to Lutheran theological convictions about the ascension. Torrance clearly rejected a Lutheran understanding of the transferring of properties

165. See Fergusson, "He Ascended into Heaven," 37.

166. Molnar, *Incarnation and Resurrection*, 28 (emphasis mine).

167. See Molnar, "Introduction," xliii–xlvi, where he dedicates a section to introducing the theme of the *extra Calvinisticum* in Torrance's *Space, Time, and Resurrection*. In this section, while he acknowledges that Torrance discusses the *extra Calvinisticum* in the context of expositing the spatial issues involved in the ascension, the ensuing exposition focuses more on the incarnation.

(*communicatio idiomatum*) from the human nature to the divine nature and vice versa. Instead, he affirmed a Reformed perspective (*communio idiomata*) on this subject.[168] Habets helpfully explains the difference between both positions as follows: "A Reformed account of the *communio idiomata* (communion of properties) differs substantially from a Lutheran account of a *communicatio idiomata* (communication of properties), in that in the former, the idioms of each nature are now true of the one Person of the incarnate Son, whilst in the latter account, attributes of the two natures are transferable across the natures."[169] Torrance rejected a Lutheran interpretation because he believed it entailed serious theological problems like "monophysitism,"[170] and a literal divinizing of all humankind,[171] to name but a few serious objections he raises against it.

In addition to Torrance's Reformed convictions, one can also maintain that Torrance never gives up the heuristic value of the *extra Calvinisticum*. Ortlund can be said to illustrate this emphasis when he avers that "Torrance conceives of the ascension as a sort of photographic negative to the *extra Calvinisticum*."[172] What he goes on to state is crucial: "For Torrance, the *extra Calvinisticum* establishes a kind of mode of thinking that must be maintained in considering the remainder of Christ's incarnate life."[173] It goes without saying that Ortlund includes the ascension as part of Christ's incarnate life because in Torrance's theology Christ does not give up his humanity in the ascension: "As the *extra* serves to preserve the full deity of Christ in his descending to us, the bodily and space-time nature of the ascension serves to preserve his full humanity in his ascending from us."[174] Since the ascension is a neglected area within Torrance studies, it is hard to find resonances for the perspective offered here.[175] However, there are two reservations one may express for not wanting to adopt the model that is being suggested here.

---

168. See Habets, "Fallen Humanity of Christ," 41n97.

169. Habets, "Fallen Humanity of Christ," 41n97.

170. Torrance, *Space, Time, and Resurrection*, 125.

171. "But when we remember that the humanity assumed by the Son of God is that in which we are given to share, how can we stop short at applying those divine attributes to the individual humanity of Jesus and not to humanity in general?" For more, see Torrance, *Theology in Reconstruction*, 70–71.

172. Ortlund, "Explorations," 183.

173. Ortlund, "Explorations," 183.

174. Ortlund, "Explorations," 183.

175. For the lack of in-depth studies on the ascension within Torrance scholarship, see Ortlund, "Explorations," 181.

### 3.1.1 No God Behind the Back of Jesus

An affirmation of the *extra* for the ascension would have to posit, like in the incarnation, that the Son of God is genuinely embodied in Jesus but not exhaustively contained in the body of Jesus. One may fear that in affirming such a view for the ascension (not just the incarnation), there would be a danger of denying a fundamental tenet in Torrance's Christology—that there is "no God behind the back of Jesus."[176] Since Torrance affirms a genuine incarnation and believes that the incarnate state continues into eternity, this necessitates thinking of God now only through Jesus Christ, one may retort. Torrance clearly explains this when he states,

> It is utterly—indeed, divinely—impossible for us to probe behind the revelation with which God has once and for all clothed himself in Jesus Christ, or ever to set it aside in trying to think or speak of God apart from or outside of what he is in Jesus Christ, for in him God and man are now indissolubly and eternally one. We cannot go behind the incarnation, for there is in fact no God behind the back of Jesus Christ, and no God apart from his own self-revelation.[177]

To make any internal distinctions (even in Chalcedonian terms) regarding the person of the Son in the ascension, as the *extra Calvinisticum* necessitates, would perhaps raise alarm bells in some quarters. A likely cause for this is the fear that one might be treading on dangerous theological ground and slipping into denying the divinity of Jesus. However, is this fear warranted?

To insist that the Son of God exists in two states simultaneously is only echoing what classical orthodoxy has always affirmed.[178] To express fears about there being a *God behind the back of Jesus* in the ascension, if one affirms the *extra*, would also mean that one must find fault with its use for the incarnation. Torrance certainly affirmed the *extra Calvinisticum* for the incarnation and implicitly for the ascension, and therefore his views are only endorsing the Reformed perspective on the incarnation and the ascension, not the Lutheran one, thereby rendering this fear unwarranted.[179]

---

176. Torrance, "Christian Apprehension," 136.

177. Torrance, "Christian Apprehension," 136.

178. Cf. Willis, *Calvin's Catholic Christology*, 60, who argues that the "extra Calvinisticum" could equally be called either "extra Catholicum" or "extra Patristicum" because "it was in fact almost universally confessed—from Origen and Theodore of Mopsuestia, to Athanasius and Cyril, to St. Thomas and Gabriel Biel."

179. Cf. Torrance, *Space, Time, and Resurrection*, 123–26.

### 3.1.2 The Danger of Nestorianism

Avoiding Nestorianism might be another fear behind not wanting to affirm the *extra Calvinisticum* for the ascended being of Jesus. Torrance's own views on the union between the two natures in Christ might provide ample ammunition to sustain such a fear. In the context of explaining the Reformed understanding of the *communicatio idiomatum*, Torrance explains how both natures work in concert with each other, but not by sharing the distinct properties of each nature, such that the result of an action can always be attributed to the person of Christ. He explains this view, which he calls "*communicatio operationum*," as follows:

> In him [Christ] there takes place such a union and communion between his divine and human natures, that the divine acts are acts in his human nature, and the human acts are acts in his divine person. Each nature in communion with the other performs acts appropriate to it, but performs them as acts of the one person who embraces both natures, and is the one subject of all divine and human acts.[180]

Torrance is not stating that the union between the natures results in a transference of properties across the natures. He does not believe this is what happens: "What is the property of one nature is by no means common to the other one, because of the essential and eternal difference between the natures, though it is common to the person, and to one of the natures in the person."[181] What he is arguing for is a functional (not ontological) "co-operation" between both natures, in ways that are proper to each nature, in accomplishing the mediatorial mission, but the end result is that there is only one actor in this mission—"the person of Christ."[182] Torrance's affirmation of the communion between both natures, such that there is only one actor of any action—*the person of Christ*—may lead one to believe that to affirm the *extra* for the ascension would divide the person of Christ in a Nestorian manner.

James Gordon engages with the critique of the *extra Calvinisticum* as Nestorian in detail, and his response to it is instructive for our purposes.[183] He essentially argues that the allegation of Nestorianism is effectively rebutted when one provides a model of the incarnation that does not posit the existence of two persons as a result of the incarnation—a divine person

---

180. Torrance, *Incarnation*, 226.
181. Torrance, *Incarnation*, 226.
182. Torrance, *Incarnation*, 226.
183. Gordon, *Holy One*, 58–71.

(Son) and a divine-human person (Jesus Christ)—but only one person, the "eternal Son."[184] He finds in a metaphysical model of the incarnation called "subsistence" or "compositionalism" exactly these kinds of resources.[185]

This view asserts that in the incarnation "the Word assumes a human nature that is a substance in itself. Jesus Christ is therefore a composite substance composed of a human nature and a divine nature, both of which subsist in the one person of the Word."[186] Gordon then uses insights from two different types of "compositionalism" that Thomas Flint proposes, one of which is called "Model T" and the other "Model A."[187] Gordon explains that while "Model A" affirms the notion that "the composite that arises as a result of the assumption of the concrete human nature *is not identical to the Son*," "Model T" rejects this, and in so doing posits a "strict numerical identity between Jesus Christ and the Son."[188] As a result, he believes that "Model A" is compatible with the *extra Calvinisticum*, while "Model T" is not.[189] The argument in favor of how "Model A" does not end up in Nestorianism can be stated succinctly as follows: "There is, then, quite literally just one person who is the subject of the incarnation, namely, the eternal Son, who, in addition to being the subject of all of Jesus's actions also exercises rule and reign beyond Christ's body in sustaining the entire cosmos. Model A, therefore, is not guilty of the Nestorian objection."[190] While there are more nuances to the critique and further rebuttals, the above response is sufficient to show that the *extra Calvinisticum* does not lead to Nestorianism.[191]

### 3.1.2.1 A Torrancean Construction

Torrance himself does not explicitly articulate a constructive proposal on how the *extra Calvinisticum* applies to the identity of the ascended Jesus, although there are resources in his theology to make such a connection. One Torrance scholar has done this in his brief yet thought-provoking article

---

184. Gordon, *Holy One*, 67.
185. Gordon, *Holy One*, 59, 62, 64.
186. Gordon, *Holy One*, 63–64.
187. Gordon, *Holy One*, 64–67.
188. Gordon, *Holy One*, 65. To be sure, Torrance himself would have been satisfied with mystery as the answer to various theological conundrums and would find the analytic conceptualization adopted by Gordon inappropriate.
189. Gordon, *Holy One*, 65.
190. Gordon, *Holy One*, 66–67.
191. For more, see Gordon, *Holy One*, 58–71.

entitled "Who's in Heaven?"[192] Aimed at a popular audience, he enumerates four possible options of conceptualizing the identity of Jesus in heaven, but affirms the fourth option: "Father, Son, Jesus Christ, and Spirit are in heaven."[193] While Habets is right to extend the theo-logic of Torrance's Reformed convictions into a constructive account of the person of the Son that upholds the *extra Calvinisticum* even after the ascension, his theological grammar may need to be modified to circumvent the critique of Nestorianism. One way to do this is to affirm his options 3 and 4, but in *different* ways. Option 3, which states that "Father, Jesus Christ = Son, and Spirit are in heaven,"[194] can be taken to affirm that there are only 3 *persons* in the Trinity, while Option 4 can be used to highlight that one of the three persons, the Son, exists in two states simultaneously, and in doing so insists that the Son is not "numerically identical"[195] with Jesus. To be sure, this is what Habets does in the latter part of his article, so in some ways this suggestion is only a semantic one, not a theological one.[196] With this in mind, a combination

---

192. Habets, "Who's in Heaven?," 7, 13.

193. "Option 1: Father, Son and Spirit are in heaven"; "Option 2: Father, Jesus Christ, and Spirit are in heaven"; "Option 3: Father, Jesus Christ = Son, and Spirit are in heaven"; and "Option 4: Father, Son, Jesus Christ, and Spirit are in heaven." Habets believes, rightly in our view, that the first 3 options are problematic, because they either neglect the humanity of Jesus (Option 1), or neglect his divinity (Option 2), or do not take sufficient account of the internal distinctions between the two natures in the Son—divine and human (Option 3). Habets believes only Option 4 is biblically and theologically accurate. For more, see Habets, "Who's in Heaven?," 7, 13.

194. Habets critiques Option 3 because it does not take account of the natures of Christ—divine and human: "But being the same person is different from the state that one exists in. The eternal Son does not have a body; like the Father and the Spirit he is pure spirit and thus immaterial. Jesus Christ, however, is a man, and as such he is localised in one place at one time, and has a *human* mind, will, and emotions. Thus to equate Jesus Christ and the eternal Son in the way this option does is to fail to adequately distinguish between the Son as God and Jesus as God the Son incarnate." Habets, "Who's in Heaven?," 7, 13.

195. Cf. Gordon, *Holy One*, 65.

196. Habets in his article clearly affirms the *extra Calvinisticum* and works this out in the distinctions he makes between the Son and Jesus in terms of their ontologies, but he maintains that there is only *one person*: "Of the eternal Son we affirm that he is God almighty, equal with the Father and the Spirit, that he is the creator and sustainer of the universe, that he is spirit, and that he is in an indissoluble bond of love and being with the Father and the Spirit both in eternity past, in the present, and into eternity future. Of Jesus Christ we affirm that the second person of the Trinity, the eternal Son, took on human flesh in becoming man, without ceasing to be God, and lived a sinless life, died a sinner's death for us, was bodily resurrected, and then ascended to the right hand of the throne of the Father in heaven, where he sent the Spirit on the Day of Pentecost, currently reigns, and from where he will return at his second coming." Habets, "Who's in Heaven?," 7, 13.

of options 3 and 4 would lead to the following: *Option 5: Father, Son = Jesus (the Son is > Jesus but Jesus is not < the Son), Spirit are in heaven.* While this constructive proposal is complex, it is important not to end up with a view of the ascended Christ that collapses Jesus's humanity into his divinity, resulting in a Lutheran account of the ubiquity of the human body of Christ. Torrance consistently maintained the *extra Calvinisticum*, and therefore one must interpret him in Reformed categories, not Lutheran ones. This is an attempt, and however fragile it may be, it is following in the spirit of Torrance himself who was not averse to taking risks in his theology to communicate important theological truths.[197]

## 3.2 Space, Time, and the Trinity

Torrance's exposition on the Trinitarian aspects of the spatiality of the ascension are only present in embryonic form.[198] This is in stark contrast to the manner in which he expounds the christological and epistemological aspects of the ascension vis-à-vis space and time.[199] David Wilkinson complains, "For someone who specifically states that he wants to explore this issue in both theological and scientific terms, Torrance is then disappointing in actually describing what it means for space-time to be healed and restored."[200] While Wilkinson makes this observation in the context of the lack of specificity in Torrance's account of the spatiality of the new creation, arguably, one can conclude something very similar with regard to the Trinitarian aspects of the spatiality of the ascension. However, one must be fair to Torrance and acknowledge that any lack on his part is deliberate "because of his emphasis on the need for eschatological reserve when discussing these matters."[201] Torrance provides important clues, however, when he asserts

---

197. Cf. Fergusson, "Ascension of Christ," 97–98, for one instance of Torrance's willingness to take risks in his theology to communicate important theological truths.

198. Cf. Torrance, *Space, Time, and Resurrection*, 131, where Torrance explains how space and time apply to the Triune God in a sentence. One wishes Torrance expanded on this statement to provide a more robust exposition of the Trinitarian aspects of the spatiality of the ascension.

199. See Torrance, *Space, Time, and Resurrection*, 123–35, in which one can find his mature theological views on the ascension vis-à-vis space and time. Most of the exposition, arguably, is focused only on the christological and epistemological aspects, while the Trinitarian aspects are underdeveloped.

200. Wilkinson, *Christian Eschatology*, 131.

201. Purves, "Torrance and Eschatology," 282. While Purves provides this rebuttal to Wilkinson in the context of space and time in the new creation, the same insight can be applied to the Trinitarian aspects of spatiality as well.

that "the resurrection means the *redemption of space and time*"[202]—and it is based on this important theme of redemption that one can provisionally begin to think about the Trinitarian aspects of the spatiality of the ascension.

### 3.2.1 Redemption of Space

There is a theological and a teleological point that needs to be underscored with respect to how one must think about the *redemption of space* from a Trinitarian perspective. Theologically, Torrance's account of Trinitarian space is enveloped in relationality, which importantly maintains the distinctiveness of each person within the Triune being without compromising the oneness of God.[203] Murray Rae makes a similar observation about Barth's theology of space when he avers, "Space is, on Barth's account, a condition by which one person is differentiated from another—in God first!"[204] He goes on to explain that "proximity and distance are essential to the distinction of and the communion between the divine persons."[205] John Webster in his own theological reflection on the spatiality of the Trinity insists that the God-human (vertical) and the human-human (horizontal) relationship is premised on the existence of "distance and proximity."[206] Webster asserts: "This spatial distance is precisely the condition for mutuality and togetherness"—instantiated in the first instance between God and human beings, but should work itself out in the way human beings interact with one another.[207] Teleologically, in Torrance's theology, the whole of space is redeemed by Jesus's life and work, and while he does not unpack all of the implications, he would unequivocally affirm that all the negative consequences of human sin that darken all of space have been redeemed by Jesus.[208] Webster clearly enunciates what can be categorized as the teleological orientation of all of space when he exclaims,

> He [Jesus] has set an end to the wicked project of spatial autonomy. In him all creaturely places are reordered, by being claimed with the full authority of the one who is Lord of heaven and earth, as the spaces in which we are to discover the presence of God. And being so claimed, they are also made into places of

---

202. Torrance, *Space, Time, and Resurrection*, 90.
203. Torrance, *Christian Doctrine of God*, 172.
204. Rae, "Spatiality of God," 79.
205. Rae, "Spatiality of God," 79.
206. Webster, *Confessing God*, 105.
207. Webster, *Confessing God*, 105.
208. See Webster, *Confessing God*, 106–7.

adjacency to other creatures ... in Jesus Christ, now present to all places through the Spirit's power, space is made a medium of fellowship.[209]

While Torrance does not explicitly state what Webster does, one can conclude that he would affirm it, given the strong emphasis on relationality within the Trinity and by implication also to all of creation in his theology.

## 3.2.2 Redemption of Time

Torrance's remarks about God's time in relation to the ascension are rather cryptic. Nonetheless, in dialogue with other theologians, one can infer two main views that Torrance would affirm as well. First, Wilkinson, in the context of envisioning what a biblical picture of redeemed space and time will look like, declares that "God's transcendence" is a non-negotiable tenet.[210] Differently stated, he is keen on maintaining the distinction "between God and new creation," such that "heaven cannot be equated with God."[211] The "transcendence of God" is central to Torrance's theology of space and time, and even though he does not explicitly assert it in relation to the new creation, there is nothing to suggest that he would not do so. Torrance uses the "hypostatic union" as an analogy to think of God's time and the time of new creation which Jesus's resurrection inaugurates, and within this analogy one can argue that Torrance is always maintaining the distinction between God and human beings.[212] Says Torrance, "In the risen Christ, in whom hypostatic union between God and Man is carried through to its *telos*, there is involved an hypostatic union between eternity and time, eternity and redeemed and sanctified time, and therefore between eternity and new time."[213]

Second, apart from insisting on God's transcendence, Torrance would want to affirm the importance of eschatology and proleptic theology.[214] In other words, Torrance eschews an *overrealized* eschatology and an *underrealized* one. He believes instead, because of the resurrection and ascension, that new creation is already a reality, but it is not yet revealed in its fullness

---

209. Webster, *Confessing God*, 106–7.
210. Wilkinson, *Christian Eschatology*, 133.
211. Wilkinson, *Christian Eschatology*, 133.
212. Torrance, *Space, Time, and Resurrection*, 98.
213. Torrance, *Space, Time, and Resurrection*, 98.
214. Torrance, *Space, Time, and Resurrection*, 98–99.

for all to see with their naked eyes.[215] Torrance believes that these twin truths exist concurrently, and phrases it as follows: as "the taking up of *human time* into God," on the one hand, and on the other hand, "this time of the new creation in Christ is hidden from us . . . until in the mercy of God Jesus Christ comes again to judge and renew all his creation."[216] What this means for a theological conception of time, therefore, is that currently (until Jesus returns) there is both "decay" and "new creation" existing simultaneously.[217]

Bruce Ritchie avers that when Torrance acknowledges both kinds of time existing simultaneously until the new creation, he does not sufficiently address the negative effects of human sin and rebellion "into the structures of creation."[218] Ritchie goes on to explain: "Because of the Fall, nature needs to die and be recreated. It cannot exist. . . . As such, the only time which can exist now, and the only time which does exist now, is the time of Jesus Christ, crucified, risen, and ascended."[219] Therefore, Ritchie proposes a model of redeemed time in which there is no duality but only a singularity; or, in other words, because of the "resurrection and ascension" only one kind of time can exist.[220] In essence, Ritchie distinguishes himself from Torrance's own position when he reasons,

> In Torrance's preferred model, God upholds "old time" but drives the "new time" of Christ's triumph into every corner of it. In the alternative model, God does not hold onto "old time." In Torrance's model "old time" is redeemed. In the alternative model "old time" is replaced. It has gone . . . in the alternative model, this "new time" does not interpenetrate, reclaim, or redeem, previously existing "old time." Instead, it generates, within itself, the very time—the only time—within which history occurs or can occur.[221]

Ritchie does acknowledge that Torrance's model is "coherent and consistent" but perhaps not radical enough.[222] One does have to ask whether Ritchie's own model is transgressing the dialectic between the *now* and the *not-yet* of the new creation that Torrance clearly affirms.[223] Eschatology and

---

215. Torrance, *Space, Time, and Resurrection*, 98.
216. Torrance, *Space, Time, and Resurrection*, 98.
217. Torrance, *Space, Time, and Resurrection*, 98.
218. Ritchie, *T. F. Torrance*, 190.
219. Ritchie, *T. F. Torrance*, 190.
220. Ritchie, *T. F. Torrance*, 188.
221. Ritchie, *T. F. Torrance*, 188–89.
222. Ritchie, *T. F. Torrance*, 190.
223. Cf. Torrance, *Incarnation*, 315.

a proleptic theological conviction undergird Torrance's theology of time, and both aspects must be maintained.

## 3.3 Theological Language for God

Arguably, Torrance's language on the spatiality of the ascension can be described as *artistic*. By this is meant that he begins to speak through images rather than precise analytic concepts because those words and concepts cannot fully describe the realities being discussed. It is at these points that one must resist the desire to use analytical and precise language, choosing instead the language of art, because it can capture what words sometimes cannot. A case in point is Torrance's use of Byzantine art, as already discussed, to communicate truths about the spatiality of the ascension.[224] Torrance himself may have expressed reservations about the category of art to describe parts of his theology, but he uses it in crucial places.[225] Therefore, it is appropriate to use the descriptor of *artistic language* to describe what Torrance is doing in his exposition on the spatiality of the ascended Jesus.

One may respond, however, by arguing that Torrance is known to be a theological scientist not a theological artist, and therefore it is inappropriate to describe his theology as artistic. Geordie Ziegler captures the force of this argument well when he explains,

> Torrance's wholism enables him perhaps more than most to keep his attention on the incredible acts of God in Christ and in the Spirit, and thus to maintain a mood in his theology which, while certainly analytic, is never far from praise and wonder. Yet Torrance's wonder is rarely poetic. Torrance is more naturally a scientist than a poet, a cartographer than an artist. Given a literary style designed to present theology in a truly scientific form, simplicity of concepts are not to be found, which has posed difficulties to wide reception. Torrance's writings have been characterized as a semantically undisciplined "verbal jungle," "densely packed and replete with jargon," "a cobweb of different doctrines and notions," "dense to the point of obscurity," "stylistically turbulent," and full of "great intellectual constructions," which "make hard going and by the end seem to have lost their bite." The difficulty for readers is so great according to Stamps

---

224. Torrance, *Space, Time, and Resurrection*, 131–32. Cf. Torrance, "Relation of the Incarnation," 69–70.

225. *Artistic* is a word that is used to communicate Torrance's willingness to acknowledge mystery at certain places in his theology. Cf. Torrance, "Thomas Torrance Responds," 324–29.

that they may be inclined to disregard Torrance's doctrine "not for its sheer realism, but for its sheer complexity."[226]

Ziegler is voicing the concerns of many scholars. Other scholars, however, would disagree with such an assessment of Torrance, and insist that his sermons show clear evidence to the contrary.[227] To be fair to Ziegler, he is not categorically asserting that Torrance is *not* an artist, but that he is "rarely" one, and he substantiates his comment through Roger Newell's work.[228]

Newell believes that Torrance's theology in comparison to C. S. Lewis's is not artistic, and his argument can be succinctly stated in two main points. First, he believes that Lewis focuses on *emotive* aspects in his theological writings, while Torrance does not.[229] Second, Torrance's writings, unlike Lewis's, do not evidence a primary concern for the audience reading his work. In other words, "communication" in ways suitable to the audience is not Torrance's main concern whereas it is Lewis's, and there are many arguments Newell puts forward to defend this assertion.[230] With respect to Torrance's articulation on the ascension, particularly on the spatiality of the ascension, one can counter both of Newell's arguments.

In response to his argument that Torrance's theology is not artistic[231] because it does not always move one's emotions, one can readily respond by stating that Torrance's ascension theology does address one's emotions deeply. These emotive aspects are summarized well by Fergusson when he declares,

> For all its semantic and technical detail, Torrance's theology of the ascension offers some significant existential and pastoral gains by offering a strong reading of a classical article from

---

226. Ziegler, *Trinitarian Grace*, xvii–xviii. On these pages Ziegler provides the following references for his quotations: "Donald M. McKay, 'Review of *Divine and Contingent Order* by T. F. Torrance, ChrG 35, 2 (1982),' 38–39"; "David L. Anderson, 'Review of *Divine and Contingent Order* by T. F. Torrance, Bloomsbury, 2005,' 502"; "Lee, *Union*, 6"; "Colyer, *How to Read*, 16"; "Walter Thorson, 'Review of *Reality and Scientific Theology* by T. F. Torrance,' PSCF 38, no. 2 (1986): 212–14"; "Ronald Lunt, 'Review of *Theology of Reconciliation* by T. F. Torrance,' *Expository Times*, 87 (1975–76): 379"; "Stamps, *Sacrament*, 290." The shortened references are to: Lee, *Living in Union with Christ*; Stamps, *Sacrament of the Word Made Flesh*.

227. Cf. Habets, "*Theologia Is Eusebia*," 259: "[Torrance's] sermons by contrast are immensely and attractively readable and accessible."

228. Ziegler, *Trinitarian Grace*, xvii.

229. See Newell, "Participatory Knowledge," 537–41.

230. See Newell, "Participatory Knowledge," 541–55.

231. In what follows, while Newell himself does not equate the two, we will be using "artistic" as a synonym for "theology as art."

Scripture and the creeds. Here we are given the theological space within which to make sense of quite simple but powerful notions: God is with us; we are not left alone; our future is guaranteed by God's love; our surest proxy for the life to come is the risen Christ, who continues to be present and active in the church. These are secured by a theology of the ascension that is unrivalled in recent theology and that continues to repay our study. In this rich account, Torrance displays the ways in which church and academy, prayer and study, and the heart and intellect are united in the vocation of the theologian.[232]

It is hard to read such words and come away without being emotionally moved. Nonetheless, were one to focus on many of Torrance's writing that are dense, it is easy to conclude that his writings lack the necessary emotive appeal that is part of theology as art, but when Torrance's whole corpus is considered, especially his dogmatic theology, Newell's point can be effectively countered.[233] Additionally, it is important to note that Torrance had a deep appreciation for the "architectonic form and beauty" present in Schleiermacher's theology, even if he fundamentally disagreed with its content.[234] Torrance found in Barth what was missing in Schleiermacher, namely, the symmetry between form and content, beautifully constructed in a scientific manner.[235] Torrance's whole dogmatics is a work of scientific theology,[236] which is beautiful in its own right. In other words, beauty in theology, as in life, *is in the eye of the beholder.*

In response to Newell's second argument that Torrance is not as interested in communicating to the audience as Lewis was, it is important to clarify the differences between the genres of theologies being discussed. Lewis made it a point to address lay audiences through his writings. Many of his written pieces were originally radio broadcasts, talks to soldiers during wartime, and even pieces written for magazines. Therefore, it is unfair to compare Lewis's popular writings with Torrance's academic theology. A more accurate rendering would be to compare Lewis's written work on medieval literature with Torrance's dogmatic theology.[237] Until such a work

232. Fergusson, "Ascension of Christ," 107.

233. A few examples among many are where Torrance can be said to appeal emotively to his readers are: *Christian Doctrine of God*, 110, 210; *Atonement*, 2; "Christ Who Loves Us," 8, 9, 14; *Mediation of Christ*, 59–62; *Doctrine of Jesus Christ*, 194.

234. See Torrance, "My Interaction," 52.

235. Torrance, "My Interaction," 53–55.

236. McGrath, *Thomas F. Torrance*, 112.

237. Fleming, "Literary Critic," suggests the following resources from Lewis that can be categorized as his academic works: *Allegory of Love, Preface to Paradise Lost,*

is done, it would be unfair to compare them. Additionally, even when one compares their writings across different genres, one will notice that Torrance is keen on communicating well with his audience. One does not have to go farther than Torrance's artistic depictions of what is happening in the ascension. This is perhaps most clearly portrayed in Torrance's articulation of *relational space* through the way in which Byzantine art was able to communicate what words cannot—the simultaneous affirmation of the transcendence and immanence of God in Jesus:

> This is why again and again when Byzantine art sought to express this iconically it deliberately reversed the natural perspective of the dais upon which the figure of the incarnate, risen, and ascended Lord was represented.... The Son of God become man could not be presented as one so confined in the limits of the body that the universe was left empty of His government. He could not be represented, therefore, as captured by lines (AB and CD), which when produced upward met at some point in finite space, but only within lines (A′ B′ and C′ D′), which when infinitely produced never meet, for on either side they reach out into the absolute openness and eternity of transcendent God.[238]

In using Eastern icons, Torrance is effectively communicating in ways that try to do justice to the complexity of the spatiality of the ascension event.[239] Therefore, while a more in-depth analysis of Torrance's writings is needed to rebut the points Newell makes, there are ways in which one can affirm the descriptor *artistic* for Torrance's theology of the ascension. While Torrance should be viewed as an artist, there are important contrasts to be made between him and Lewis, not least their different genres.

One may respond, however, by acknowledging that there may be some substance to the argument that is being made, but *artistic* language is not the best description for it. Instead, taking one's cues from Stephen Webb's work on Barth's rhetoric in theology, perhaps *rhetoric* may be a better description for what Torrance is doing in his own theology. It would take a more expansive work on Torrance's rhetoric to establish the usefulness or lack thereof of *artistic* language to describe what he is doing at key places in his theology, where words are inadequate. Perhaps rhetoric could be the larger category

---

*Discarded Image, English Literature, Studies in Medieval and Renaissance Literature,* and *Spenser's Images of Life*. Comparing the rhetoric and artistic components of these academic works of Lewis with Torrance's dogmatic theology would be a good place to begin for those interested in contrasting the works of both these influential figures.

238. Torrance, "Relation of the Incarnation," 69–70.

239. Cf. Sleeman, *Geography*, 19, who commends Torrance's views on the spatiality of the ascension.

under which artistic language is one way in which Torrance communicates, among many other modes of communication he utilizes in his theology. Webb's insightful work on Barth's rhetoric is helpful, among other reasons, for two specific aspects.

First, his work endorses the use of rhetoric in theology not just as an extraneous feature, but for "the use of rhetoric as an explanatory tool in theology."[240] Torrance's theology has not been studied through this prism, and therefore this is an important area to add to the existing areas of lacunae in Torrance scholarship. Second, Webb helpfully traces a movement in Barth's rhetoric from "Expressionism"[241] that can characterize his early theology, especially in "*The Epistle to the Romans*"[242] to "Barth's later theology" which "can be understood rhetorically as a kind of realism."[243] A similar study of Torrance's work is needed. It would be helpful to study Torrance's vast corpus through a rhetorical perspective; while such a work is needed, it is beyond the scope of this study. While the use of *artistic* language is a helpful way to understand what Torrance is doing at key places in his theology, the use of *rhetoric* may perhaps be a more prescient term, but only a fuller study of Torrance's rhetoric can establish this aspect.

## 3.4 Section Summary

In this section, Torrance's theology was constructively developed in three specific ways. First, christologically, it was argued that there are sound reasons to claim that Torrance would affirm the use of the *extra Calvinisticum* as a heuristic for the ascension. Such an affirmation, it was maintained, does not need to include some form of Nestorianism. Second, from a Trinitarian perspective vis-à-vis space and time, while Torrance does not expound

240. Webb, *Re-figuring Theology*, 7.

241. Webb acknowledges that *expressionism* is a "term that is notoriously difficult to define and its range of application can be so broad as to force it to hold more meaning than is good for any such label." Webb goes on to highlight certain aspects of "expressionism" as follows: "Its memetic practice, however, was not concerned with accuracy of representation. Instead, it wanted to distort, extend and even fragment and shatter the surface of reality in order to uncover something even more hidden beneath the surface. Several scholars have pointed to exaggeration as one of its techniques." Webb notes that the use of *expressionism* to study Barth's rhetoric has "both its benefits and its limitations." For more, see Webb, *Re-figuring Theology*, 11–12.

242. Webb, *Re-figuring Theology*, 8.

243. Webb, *Re-figuring Theology*, 149. Webb explains *realism* as follows: "In realism language is representational or mimetic; it serves a preexisting reality. It is not, however, a slave to reality; language is still creative in the way in which it responds to reality, but it is primarily responsive, not creative." For more, Webb, *Re-figuring Theology*, 154.

these aspects in much detail, it was shown that Torrance affirms both the redemption of space and time, without transgressing the *now* and *not-yet* aspects of eschatology. Third, through a brief rhetorical analysis of Torrance's work on the ascension, it was suggested that Torrance's theology can be considered as a work of theological art and beauty, not just as a work in *theological science*.

## 4. CRITIQUE

The criticisms in each of the three aspects of Torrance's spatiality of the ascension will be briefly highlighted in what follows, but each of them will be substantively interrogated in chapter 6.

### 4.1 Christology and Spatiality

On the relationship between Christology and spatiality, the following question will be raised and addressed in chapter 6: Does Torrance's theology suffer from an overrealized individual eschatology?[244] Torrance's christological emphasis has much that one can commend, but it is light on some eschatological details that pertain to space and time. For instance, it is unclear whether Torrance affirms an *intermediate* state or believes in an *instantaneous* resurrection. While Torrancean scholars touch on this topic,[245] much more work needs to be done to clarify Torrance's views on matters pertaining to eschatology and the spatial issues that emerge because of the ascension. Stanley MacLean's work is helpful in this regard, along with N. T. Wright's contributions to the subject from the perspective of biblical studies.[246]

### 4.2 Trinity and Spatiality

On Trinity and spatiality, the following question will be addressed in chapter 6: Does Torrance have an embryonic Trinitarian spatial theology that can be developed?[247]

---

244. See section 2.2.1, "Critique #4," in chapter 6 for more on this point.

245. Anderson, *Theology, Death, and Dying*, 117–18.

246. Among many other works, the following will be especially helpful: Wright, *Surprised by Hope*; Wright, *Resurrection*.

247. See section 2.2.2, "Critique #5," in chapter 6 for more on this point.

Chan Ho Park in his work contends that Torrance does not develop the Trinitarian insights of God's spatiality enough.[248] This is a correct assessment, and to address it, there are helpful constructive accounts by Jeremy Begbie, among others, on a spatiality influenced by the Trinity. His account will be helpful in articulating Torrance's spatiality of the ascension in a substantively Trinitarian manner.[249]

## 4.3 Epistemology, Theological Language, and Spatiality

On the relationship between epistemology, theological language and spatiality, the following question will be addressed in chapter 6: Does Torrance provide specific details about the location of the ascended Christ?[250] Oliver Crisp claims that Torrance is too vague in his description about where the resurrected and ascended body of Jesus is.[251] While Crisp is right to critique Torrance on this aspect, perhaps he does not sufficiently acknowledge why Torrance does not provide such details. Nonetheless, dialoguing with Crisp, who represents the best of contemporary analytic theology, will be fruitful for Torrance studies more generally, but will also provide some options about how one can respond on behalf of Torrance to the allegation that he is evading giving details about the spatiality of the ascended Jesus.[252]

## 5. CONCLUSION

This chapter theologically expounded Torrance's contribution by noting a threefold aspect to his discussion on the spatiality of the ascension. First, a christological aspect highlighted Torrance's soteriological and eschatological accent to the discussion about spatiality. Soteriologically, through Christ's ascension Torrance affirms that humanity is guaranteed access into the very presence of God as *human beings* because Jesus is still human in his ascension. Eschatologically, the spatiality of the ascension points to the ultimate telos of God's purposes for his creation in a "new heavens and a new earth" that will have both (*redeemed*) space and (*redeemed*) time. Second, a Trinitarian aspect to spatiality, for Torrance, underscores the need to think

---

248. Park, *Transcendence and Spatiality*, 94.
249. Begbie, "'Semblance More Lucid.'"
250. See section 2.2.3, "Critique #6," in chapter 6 for more on this point.
251. Crisp, *Analyzing Doctrine*, 218.
252. Crisp, *Analyzing Doctrine*. The T. F. Torrance Fellowship invited Oliver D. Crisp to present the keynote address at their Annual Meeting on November 22, 2019. The address was entitled "T. F. Torrance on Theosis and Universal Salvation."

of God's space and time as distinct from human space and time. Fundamentally, however, there is a *oneness* and *threeness* in the Triune being of God that sheds light on how one must think about the meaning of space and time vis-à-vis the Trinity. When one does this, there is an intimate relationality between the persons of the Trinity that affirms unity and distinction, and it is into this communion of love that human beings are welcomed to participate through Christ. Third, an epistemological and theological language aspect informs Torrance's views on the spatiality of the ascended Christ. Essentially, it was observed that Torrance highlights the importance of using theological speech commensurate with the varied mysteries associated with the ascension, not least the dualities present in thinking of space and time (God's space-time vs. human space-time; redeemed space-time vs. fallen space-time, etc.). Torrance acknowledges the need to resort to mystery at certain points in his theology, but also encourages expanding the meaning of theological concepts to shed light on these mysteries, and arguably one way he does this, it was noted, is through *artistic* language.

Constructing on Torrancean foundations, the chapter explored how the *extra Calvinisticum* illuminates the christological aspect of Torrance's thinking on the spatiality of the ascension. In other words, it was argued that just as Torrance used the *extra Calvinisticum* as a heuristic to explain a genuine incarnation without undermining divine transcendence, similarly, in the ascension, while affirming divine transcendence, one could also affirm the retention of the human body-soul composite of Jesus. Arguably, it was suggested that Torrance himself uses the *extra* for the ascension but does so implicitly. This section showed the need to expand the logic of Torrance's implicit acknowledgement (of the *extra* for the ascension) into a full-fledged affirmation to interpret his views in Reformed, not Lutheran, categories. The aspect of Trinitarian spatiality sought to emphasize how Torrance would conceptualize space and time in light of the Trinity. Torrance offers clues more than a clear roadmap, it was noted, but since he affirms both *oneness* and *threeness* within the Triune being of God, one can infer a theology of spatiality that affirms genuine relationality at the God-human level as well, and in turn an exhortation to think about the human-human level as a space for mutual relationships. The epistemological and theological language aspects argued that while Torrance himself may not endorse the use of *artistic* language to describe any aspect of his theology, there is strong case for viewing his acknowledgement of mystery at various points in his exposition of the ascension as an example of theological art. Not all Torrancean scholars would welcome such a suggestion, it was observed, as Torrance is known as a theological "scientist" not an artist; but by juxtaposing Torrance with C. S. Lewis, the section argued that one can make a case for viewing Torrance's work (specifically on the ascension) as a work of art and beauty, much like many of Lewis's writings. The next chapter will explore the theme of Torrance's theology of the present ministry of the ascended Jesus.

# 5

# The Present Ministry of the Ascended Christ

## 1. INTRODUCTION

FOR TORRANCE, THE ASCENDED Jesus is not only in a transformed physical body (chapter 3), he is also residing simultaneously in heaven and everywhere, provided these dual locations are conceptualized in Chalcedonian categories (chapter 4). Moreover, he is also actively and personally involved in ministry to the world and church. Importantly, according to Torrance, this ministry can be described in *tensed* terms—the ascended Jesus is presently involved in ministry. Far from being a passive bystander to current events until the eschaton, Christ, for Torrance, is intimately involved in the details of world affairs, using his church to point the world to himself in and through the power of the Holy Spirit, to the praise of God the Father.

Torrance describes the ascended ministry of Jesus by using the framework of the *triplex munus*, and to his credit, unlike many other Reformed theologians, begins to think about the ministry of Jesus in light of the ascension.[1] As such, Torrance is unafraid of confronting the frontiers of theology, and as this chapter will demonstrate, he has commendably provided a roadmap in some areas (particularly regarding the priestly ministry). However, he has left his thinking largely embryonic in others (to a certain extent, both the kingly ministry and the prophetic ministry), pointing to the need for theological construction in ways that are faithful to his overall theology.

---

1. See Liston, "Eschatology," 325–27, where Liston lists luminaries such as John Calvin, Louis Berkhof, Donald McKim, Daniel Migliore, and Robert Sherman, all of whom expound the *triplex munus* primarily in light of the earthly ministry of Jesus.

This chapter will critically explore, constructively develop, and briefly evaluate Torrance's theology; as such, it comprises three main sections. Section one introduces Torrance's methodology for understanding and interpreting biblical terms, followed by a detailed exposition of the three offices of Christ. Section two develops constructively Torrance's contribution to the *triplex munus*, building on his theology through ecumenical theological exchanges at points as well as developing embryonic ideas at other times. Section three highlights important areas of criticism that Torrance's theology of the present ministry of the ascended Jesus faces—all of which will be substantially addressed in the next chapter. Torrance's contribution to the ministry of the ascended Jesus is at times novel, at other times too brief, but it is nevertheless stimulating and worthy of critical engagement, and it is to this task that one's attention must now shift.

## 2. PRESENT MINISTRY OF THE ASCENDED JESUS

### 2.1 Theological Significance of Words Used for Ascension

Torrance notes that there are principally four Greek verbs used for the ascension in the New Testament: "*anabainein*," "*kathizein*," "*analambanein*," and "*hupsoun*."[2] While these words are not unique to the New Testament, in that they are also used in non-biblical sources, Torrance is interested in identifying the "theological and cultic significance" of each of these words that the biblical authors give to them at key points.[3] He notes that he is focused on the meaning of these words at this "deeper" level.[4]

While *anabaino* simply means "to go up,"[5] according to Torrance with respect to the ascension passages like Acts 2:34; John 3:13, 6:62, 20:17; and Eph 4:8–10 he observes three theologically significant points.[6] They are: (1) an emphasis on regal notions like the "ascent of the king . . . enthronement of Jahweh"; (2) an emphasis on priestly notions like "ascent to the Temple . . . for priestly service"; and (3) an emphasis on cultic notions like "ascent to God of the whole burnt offering . . . more generally of prayer."[7] *Kathizo*, Torrance states, generally means "to sit down,"[8] and points to passages such

---

2. Torrance, *Space, Time, and Resurrection*, 107.
3. Torrance, *Space, Time, and Resurrection*, 107.
4. Torrance, *Space, Time, and Resurrection*, 107.
5. Torrance, *Space, Time, and Resurrection*, 107.
6. Torrance, *Space, Time, and Resurrection*, 108.
7. Torrance, *Space, Time, and Resurrection*, 108.
8. Torrance, *Space, Time, and Resurrection*, 107.

as Eph 1:20; Heb 1:3, 8:1, 10:12, 12:12; and Rev 3:21.[9] The theologically significant meaning of this word is tied closely to the symbolism behind the "mercy seat" in the holiest of places in the temple.[10] This word, for Torrance, underscores Jesus's "enthronement" in his ascension wherein he "dispenses the divine mercy and peace."[11] *Analambano*, according to Torrance, means "to take up,"[12] but its meaning vis-à-vis the ascension, he concedes, "is not so straightforward" because of verses like "Mark 16:19; Acts 1:2; 11:22; Tim. 3:16"[13] and other passages in which the idea of being taken up in the Old Testament do not communicate an "assumption" at one's "*death*."[14] However, this is the exact idea that is communicated in Luke 9:51 when the noun form of the word, *analēmpsis*, is used, Torrance contends, which leads him to conclude, "The combination of noun and verb thus indicates that the ascension of Christ to heaven began with his lifting up on the Cross."[15]

*Hupsoo* means "to exalt," but with reference to the ascension, on the basis of passages such as Acts 2:32 and 5:31 and especially Johannine texts like John 3:14; 8:28; and 12:32, 34, Torrance observes that this word is used explicitly in reference to "the *death* of Christ."[16] In light of this, Torrance reiterates: "the glorification of Christ begins not with his actual ascension or resurrection, but with his crucifixion."[17] He further emphasizes that the theological import of "the unity of crucifixion and ascension" entails "that the sacrifice of Christ falls also within the eternal sphere, within the presence of God himself."[18] David Moffitt, a contemporary biblical scholar, supports Torrance's interpretation in his exegetical work on the book of Hebrews. With Torrance, he argues that the atonement is fully realized at the ascension, not the cross, because it fulfills the pattern of the Old Testament sacrifices, which were incomplete when the animal was killed and only finally complete when that same animal's blood was offered to God inside the "sanctuary."[19]

---

9. Torrance, *Space, Time, and Resurrection*, 108.

10. Torrance, *Space, Time, and Resurrection*, 108.

11. Torrance, *Space, Time, and Resurrection*, 109.

12. Torrance, *Space, Time, and Resurrection*, 107.

13. Torrance, *Space, Time, and Resurrection*, 109. Acts 11:22 seems to be a typo on Torrance's part. The verses should be Acts 1:11, 22. The reference from Timothy is to 1 Tim 3:16.

14. Torrance, *Space, Time, and Resurrection*, 109.

15. Torrance, *Space, Time, and Resurrection*, 109.

16. Torrance, *Space, Time, and Resurrection*, 110.

17. Torrance, *Space, Time, and Resurrection*, 110.

18. Torrance, *Space, Time, and Resurrection*, 110.

19. See Burgess, "Ascension," 379, who helpfully explains the larger point Moffitt

Cumulatively, each of these four words convey an important theological message for Torrance: "The ascension of Christ in this sense is his exaltation to power and glory but *through the cross*, certainly an exaltation from humiliation to royal majesty, but through crucifixion and sacrifice, for the power and glory of the Royal Priest are bound up with his self-offering in death and resurrection."[20] Torrance's reasons for underscoring the integral relationship between the crucifixion, resurrection, and ascension of Jesus include: (1) maintaining continuity in Jesus's identity, (2) fidelity to Jesus's teachings about receiving glory only after suffering, and (3) the centrality of the historical revelation of God's work in Christ.[21] Torrance discusses points one and two clearly in his *Space, Time, and Resurrection*,[22] while he succinctly underscores the importance of point three in another work when he avers, "Had Jesus continued visibly in the succession of history the Cross would doubtless have been relegated to a mere incident of bygone history, perhaps to be forgotten, so the very fact of His Ascension affirms as nothing else could the essential historical foundation of faith and knowledge in Him."[23] For Torrance, the ascension, far from undermining significant historical events, underscores its importance.

### 2.1.1 Torrance's Broader Corpus

Torrance's understanding of the ministry of the ascended Christ is not only informed by a theological understanding of the terms above but is also grounded in three key Old Testament terms which together form the basis of a holistic understanding of the atonement.[24] These terms are: "*padah, kipper* and *go'el*," which are all equally important in understanding the

---

makes when he states, "Central to his work is the argument that in the Old Testament sacrificial liturgy the death of the animal was not the culmination but a necessary step in the movement, with the offering of the 'life' of the animal in the sanctuary marking the peak of atoning action. So Jesus's ascension to the Father as the 'lamb who was slain' and presentation of his life as sacrifice, in the true sanctuary, mark the peak of his atoning work. Moffitt argues for a similar understanding in Luke-Acts, claiming that the well-known lack of sacrificial language in relation to the cross in these writings is explained by Luke's understanding of atonement taking place in the final movement—Christ's presentation of himself as the atoning sacrifice in the presence of the Father." For more on Moffitt's argument, see his *Atonement* and "Atonement at the Right Hand."

20. Torrance, *Space, Time, and Resurrection*, 111.

21. For more on the first two points, see Torrance, *Space, Time, and Resurrection*, 123; and for more on the third point, see Torrance, *Conflict and Agreement*, 1:213.

22. Torrance, *Space, Time, and Resurrection*, 123.

23. Torrance, *Conflict and Agreement*, 1:213.

24. See Torrance, *Atonement*, 26–60.

variegated meaning of the atonement.[25] Torrance applies his theological methodology to these terms when he prioritizes the manner in which these terms find their ultimate meaning—not in the way they are used in their respective Old Testament contexts but in relation to Christ's "sacrifice."[26] Says Torrance, "These concepts are radically re-interpreted by the New Testament in its very use of them to speak of the unique sacrifice of Christ, and that ultimately therefore it is from their application to him and not merely from their linguistic history that the terms have doctrinal significance for us."[27] When interpreted christologically, therefore, Torrance explains, *padah* conveys the power of God which manifests itself in "the holiness of Christ" not least in "his obedience unto the death of the cross."[28] Christ's victory has the twofold effect of defeating "evil" powers and also providing a way "out of judgment and death."[29] *Kipper* highlights Christ's "sacrifice," or substitution—"Christ's life for our life," and the ensuing benefits for human beings: "restoration to fellowship with God."[30] With *goel*, Torrance notes, the one seeking to save someone shares a "blood tie or covenant bond" with that person; furthermore, the undergirding impulse in the act of saving is "pure love" and the manner by which salvation is accomplished is integrally related to the "nature of the redeemer."[31] All three "aspects" are essential for Torrance: "the *dramatic*," "the *cultic-forensic*," and "the *ontological*," which corresponds to *padah, kipper,* and *goel,* respectively.[32]

Torrance clearly rules out any prioritization of one aspect over another when he appeals to his readers: "We cannot afford to neglect any aspect. All three aspects are to be held together like the three strands of a single rope."[33] Furthermore, he insists, "We need to recover the wholeness of the biblical understanding of atoning redemption."[34] Torrance eschews thinking of the atonement in terms of "theories" because, he believes, there can be a tendency for views to compete with one another for predominance, resulting in incomplete perspectives.[35] Torrance commends thinking, in-

---

25. Torrance, *Atonement*, 26, 50–56.
26. Torrance, *Atonement*, 27.
27. Torrance, *Atonement*, 27.
28. Torrance, *Atonement*, 51.
29. Torrance, *Atonement*, 51.
30. Torrance, *Atonement*, 52.
31. Torrance, *Atonement*, 52.
32. Torrance, *Atonement*, 53.
33. Torrance, *Atonement*, 55.
34. Torrance, *Atonement*, 55.
35. Torrance, *Atonement*, 56.

stead, in terms of "aspects" of the atonement because such a view fosters "inter-connections" or integration between the views, producing a more holistic account as a result.[36] Keeping Torrance's overarching goal in mind is essential in order to accurately and fairly assess his use of biblical terms and also evaluate the connections he makes between the three Hebrew terms and the *triplex munus*.

Torrance, as a Reformed theologian, affirms the *triplex munus*, which he explains originates more from theological reception history than the text of the Scriptures, to luminaries such as "Justin Martyr, Hippolytus . . . Chrysostom and Cyril of Alexandria . . . including Aquinas" but quintessentially to "Calvin at the Reformation."[37] The theological innovation, Torrance avers, is the addition of the "prophetic office" to the more common biblical and theological usage, even in Calvin's early works of the "*duplex munus*."[38] This insight may offer some reasons why Torrance does not expound the prophetic office in much detail in his work, but for now, it is important to highlight that Torrance uniquely connects the three "aspects" of atonement to the *triplex munus* when he attaches the prophetic office to the "*goel aspect of redemption*," the priestly office to the "*kipper aspect of redemption*," and the kingly office to the "*padah aspect of redemption*."[39] He goes on to uniquely integrate the office of prophet with the "*incarnational assumption of our fallen humanity*" in order to underscore the oneness of *being* and *act*; the office of priest with Christ's "*passive obedience*," accentuating the "self-offering" involved in the sacrifice of Christ; and finally, the office of king is associated with "*the active obedience* of Christ" to stress that "the holiness of Jesus' life" accomplished salvation for human beings.[40]

It is imperative, Torrance exclaims, for one to take into account all three aspects in order to properly and holistically theologize on the atonement: "In this way we get a far better and richer apprehension of the doctrine of the atonement than by merely following through the historical theories

---

36. Torrance, *Atonement*, 56.

37. Torrance, *Atonement*, 59.

38. Torrance, *Atonement*, 58–59. Cf. A. J. Torrance, "Reclaiming the Continuing Priesthood," 188: "It wasn't until the 1545 edition of his *Institutio* that Calvin opted for a threefold office over a twofold office. Until then and throughout his commentaries, Calvin (appears to have) considered Christ's prophetic role as included within his priesthood—and there was biblical justification for that. Jesus Christ faithfully communicated God's word in his person as the true priest—a separate prophetic office was superfluous."

39. Torrance, *Atonement*, 59.

40. Torrance, *Atonement*, 59–60.

in the traditional way."[41] Ian Ramsey's work *Models and Mystery* helpfully sheds light on Torrance's particular approach to the atonement.[42] Torrance in another context commends Ramsey's work for the distinction it makes between "*disclosure models*" and "*picturing models*," and for the way it thinks the former is superior to the latter, because it refrains from attempting to exhaustively describe a reality, choosing instead to only point to it.[43] In Torrance's rejection of "theories" of the atonement, his aversion to overconfident theologies comes to the fore. Nonetheless, while Torrance's biblical methodology is legitimately critiqued at points, he must be commended for favoring "aspects" rather than "theories" to understand the atonement. In doing so, he anticipates the way in which much contemporary biblical scholarship expounds a theology of the atonement in a multifaceted manner.[44] These methodological insights serve as an important backdrop to understand the theology of the present ministry of the ascended Christ in Torrance's work, which he articulates by using the *triplex munus*.

## 2.2 The Kingship of the Ascended Jesus

Torrance notes "the nature of the kingship" of Jesus in his ascension, before he goes on to underscore the identity of Jesus as the ascended king.[45] Differently put, *how* Jesus exercises his kingship is integrally tied up with *who* Jesus is as king.[46] In order to highlight the way in which Jesus exercises his kingship, Torrance points out that the theological words used for the ascension provide a telling summary.[47] More specifically, he explains that two biblical images reveal the manner in which Jesus is king, namely, Jesus is "the Lion of the tribe of Judah" and "the Lamb as it had been slain" in accordance with the account provided in Revelation.[48] Torrance captures this same idea through two key words, "grace and omnipotence," but also clarifies that while the ascended Jesus already exists in a state of "unveiled

---

41. Torrance, *Atonement*, 60.
42. Ramsey, *Models and Mystery*.
43. Torrance, *Theology in Reconstruction*, 92.
44. Cf. Baker and Green, *Recovering the Scandal*. Cf. Crisp, "Methodological Issues," 315: "The consensus among modern theologians is that the New Testament does not offer a single explanation of Christ's atoning work."
45. Torrance, *Space, Time, and Resurrection*, 112.
46. Torrance, *Space, Time, and Resurrection*, 112.
47. Torrance, *Space, Time, and Resurrection*, 112.
48. Torrance, *Space, Time, and Resurrection*, 112. The specific reference Torrance provides is Rev 5:1–14.

majesty and power" this is concealed from human beings for the moment until he returns again.⁴⁹ Therefore, Jesus exercises his kingship in a manner that is commensurate with both aspects, as Torrance eloquently renders: "Even in ascension the power of Christ is exercised through his sacrifice, through his atoning expiation of guilt, through his priestly mediation before God."⁵⁰

The manner in which Jesus in his ascension exercises his lordship is important for Torrance to highlight the identity of Jesus as the ascended king.⁵¹ Torrance wants to make unmistakably clear that there is *continuity* in Jesus's identity.⁵² In order to establish this point, he draws the reader's attention to narrative details in Jesus's life and their theological significance now in the ascension.⁵³ In other words, the Jesus who became incarnate and who suffered is the same Jesus who is now ascended, and through this act is "installed as Head of the New Humanity, the Prince of the New Creation, and the King of the Kingdom."⁵⁴ Jesus's identity is key for Torrance, and he makes this evident when he states that "the ascension is the enthronement of *that Christ* at the right hand of the Father in the sovereignty of Grace."⁵⁵ He then concludes his brief exposition on Jesus's kingship with a statement that is at once theologically rich in symbolism, regally potent in its universal scope and present activity, and pastorally sensitive: "Henceforth all things are directed from the mercy-seat of God, by the enthroned and exalted Lamb, who reigns not only over the Church, but over all creation."⁵⁶

### 2.2.1 *Torrance's Broader Corpus*

In other parts of his oeuvre, Torrance declares that the ascended Jesus is sovereign and is accomplishing God's plans for his creation even during times of crisis. Writing a few months before the Second World War and its devastating consequences, Torrance declares the truth of Jesus's kingship to offer hope to his readers:

---

49. Torrance, *Space, Time, and Resurrection*, 112. Elsewhere, Torrance explains that the reason for this concealment is because the fullness of Jesus's majesty would mean the final judgment. See *Space, Time, and Resurrection*, 145–47, for more.
50. Torrance, *Space, Time, and Resurrection*, 112.
51. Torrance, *Space, Time, and Resurrection*, 112.
52. Torrance, *Space, Time, and Resurrection*, 112.
53. Torrance, *Space, Time, and Resurrection*, 112.
54. Torrance, *Space, Time, and Resurrection*, 112.
55. Torrance, *Space, Time, and Resurrection*, 112 (emphasis mine).
56. Torrance, *Space, Time, and Resurrection*, 112.

> We may not now understand all that happens and can happen in the world of today. . . . [I]t is black—and when has it been blacker than this very moment? (i.e. 1939)—but of this we are assured by the Ascension that the Lord Jesus Christ is reigning over the kingdoms and nations of the world and working out his redeeming purpose for redemption. He Reigns, he is King and Lord, and all things are made by him to work together for good to them that love the Lord and are called according to his purpose (Romans 8:28).[57]

While Jesus's kingship in his ascension offers immense hope and pastoral care, for Torrance, it also points to two other important truths. First, the ascended Jesus exercises his kingship on earth now "through the Church," wherein "Christ the King is fulfilling his purpose to actualize his redeeming purpose for all mankind, by renewing them and raising them to the very footstool of God, the Lord and Creator."[58] Second, the hiddenness of Jesus's kingship on earth is due to "the patience of his Grace."[59] In other words, were Jesus to fully reveal "the Majesty of his risen Glory," the necessary consequences would be final judgment, and this would be troubling news for those who have rejected the gospel.[60] The interim period before Jesus's final return, Torrance explains, is a "time for decision; time to face up to the proclamation of the Gospel, the urgent message of the crucified Christ, before they meet him as the King in his risen power and Holiness."[61]

## 2.3 The Priestly Ministry of the Ascended Jesus

Torrance prefaces his threefold theological exposition on the priestly ministry of the ascended Christ with an extended introduction.[62] In this introduction, he situates the priestly ministry of Christ within the Old Testament context, after which he highlights how Christ is the fulfillment of the Old Testament priestly longing. He then goes on to underscore the uniqueness of Christ's priesthood, in that it is ontological in nature, not merely symbolic, and finally emphasizes the dynamic nature of the ascended Christ's priesthood.[63] Each of these four aspects capture what is at the heart of Christ's

57. Torrance, *Doctrine of Jesus Christ*, 194.
58. Torrance, *Doctrine of Jesus Christ*, 194.
59. Torrance, *Doctrine of Jesus Christ*, 196.
60. Torrance, *Doctrine of Jesus Christ*, 196.
61. Torrance, *Doctrine of Jesus Christ*, 196.
62. Torrance, *Space, Time, and Resurrection*, 112–15.
63. Torrance, *Space, Time, and Resurrection*, 112–15.

priestly ministry, according to Torrance, and they also provide a helpful orientation to the more substantial exposition on the priestly ministry of Christ that is to follow.

The Old Testament, Torrance explains, expected the priestly ministry to function in a particular order, with preeminence given to "the Word from God to man," and the role of attesting to the truth of God's Word was given to "the liturgical priesthood," wherein "cultic acts of mediation through oblation and sacrifice" were offered.[64] While God's Word to human beings was represented by Moses, the latter ("liturgical priesthood") was known after Aaron's priesthood, and both these persons represented central aspects of the priesthood.[65] The issue with priesthood arose in the Old Testament whenever this order was circumvented, and this is exactly what happened in the time of "the prophets" when "the primacy of [the] Torah" was undermined and needed to be asserted again over the cultic aspects of the priestly ministry.[66] In Jesus's own day, Torrance notes, this same tension played out in a different manner; only this time, the priests and the scribes were unwilling to recognize in Jesus's own person the fulfillment of the Mosaic aspect of the priesthood.[67] Instead of the priests and scribes offering proper attestation through a "liturgy of praise and thanksgiving" to the "Word of God," "sinners and little children" offered it instead, much to the chagrin of the religious leaders.[68]

Torrance reads the New Testament account of Jesus as priest to be a fulfillment of the twofold priestly ministry of the Old Testament: Jesus is "both . . . *Apostle from God* and . . . *our High Priest* (Heb. 3: 1f)."[69] He captures how Christ fulfills in his own person the Old Testament priestly longing when he asserts, "He himself is the Word come down into our midst, and himself the perfect response of man to that Word in his obedient self-offering in life and death."[70] It is at the ascension, Torrance contends, that "both aspects come fully and finally together" because Jesus has entered "through the veil into the Holy of Holies."[71] While Torrance does not always make the connections evident, what he is arguing is basically akin to what David Moffitt has

---

64. Torrance, *Space, Time, and Resurrection*, 112–13.
65. Torrance, *Space, Time, and Resurrection*, 113.
66. Torrance, *Space, Time, and Resurrection*, 113.
67. Torrance, *Space, Time, and Resurrection*, 113.
68. Torrance, *Space, Time, and Resurrection*, 113.
69. Torrance, *Space, Time, and Resurrection*, 113.
70. Torrance, *Space, Time, and Resurrection*, 114.
71. Torrance, *Space, Time, and Resurrection*, 114.

recently argued in his work on the book of Hebrews: the atonement finds its climax not on the cross but in the ascension.[72]

Torrance closely follows William Milligan's work on the ascension in his own exposition on the priestly ministry of the ascended Jesus. Milligan (1821–93), a founder of the Scottish Church Society and Professor of Biblical Criticism, strove to add to the existing literature "on the Incarnation by expounding the doctrines of the Resurrection and Ascension."[73] Interestingly, even in the nineteenth century, he firmly believed that "the continuing heavenly ministry of Christ as high priest" was a neglected theme.[74] David Fergusson rightly observes that "Torrance frequently commended" Milligan's "work on the significance of the ascended Christ in worship,"[75] as Milligan's insights are writ large in Torrance's whole work on the ministry of the ascended Jesus. Milligan, writing in the latter part of the nineteenth century, makes a similar point that Moffitt more recently makes, and one can be confident that Torrance is arguing in a similar manner.[76] Milligan renders his own argument as follows:

> For, according to that law, the death of the animal selected for sacrifice did not atone for sin . . . Another step, however, had to be taken before atonement was made. The blood obtained by slaughtering was given either upon ordinary occasions to the priest, who smeared it upon the horns of the altar; or upon the great Day of Atonement to the high-priest, who sprinkled it upon the Mercy-seat, that he might thus bring it into the closest contact with God. Not till this was done was the atonement perfected, sin covered, and the broken covenant restored.

---

72. Moffitt, "Blood, Life, and Atonement," 211–12: "To put the issue more bluntly, I argue that Jesus' death on the cross is not the place or the primary means of atonement for the author of Hebrews. Rather, when the writer claims in 8:4 that Jesus can only serve as a high priest in heaven, he intends to say that the great redemptive moment of the Christ event occurred not when Jesus was crucified, but after he was resurrected and ascended into heaven. There he presented himself alive and incorruptible before God. Just as Yom Kippur does not focus on the slaughter of the victim, but the presentation of its blood—that is, its life—before God, so also the author of Hebrews thinks in terms of the presentation of Jesus' indestructible life before God as the central act that effects atonement." Cf. Milgrom, *Leviticus*, whose analysis concurs with Moffitt's.

73. Murray, "Milligan, William," 566.

74. Murray, "Milligan, William," 566.

75. Fergusson, "Thomas F. Torrance," 41.

76. Cf. Torrance, *Space, Time, and Resurrection*, 111n5, where Torrance commends readers to Milligan's two works on the resurrection and ascension, respectively. Torrance's own exposition on the priestly ministry of Jesus in his ascension follows the threefold exposition that Milligan offers, but with differences, which will be explained in the section to follow. Cf. Milligan, *Ascension*, 113–65.

Atonement, in short, was found, not in death for sin, but in the use afterwards made of the blood thus shed in death.[77]

Torrance highlights how Jesus's priesthood in his ascension is unique because it is not "merely symbolic" like Aaron's priesthood was, but is ontological in nature.[78] By this he means that Jesus qualifies to act perfectly on God's behalf and in humanity's stead; but he also asserts that the efficacy of Jesus's priesthood is finally guaranteed to deal with the problem that the Aaronic priesthood was never able to address.[79] Aaron's priesthood is superseded by Christ's priesthood because it is based on "his own endless Life" and, further still, due to the fact that in Jesus is a "priesthood in which Word and Act are identical," which is why what he "does on our behalf is actually fulfilled with final power."[80]

Torrance concludes his introductory comments on the priesthood of Christ in his ascension with an emphatic assertion that the priesthood of Christ is active and *ongoing* in his ascension, and not "over and done with."[81] He highlights two ways in which Christ continues to function as priest based on the teachings of Hebrews, namely, as *Prodromos* and *Leitourgos*.[82] Or in other words, as the pioneer who has paved the pathway "into the heavenly sanctuary," and the "Leader of the Heavenly Worship."[83] With this detailed introduction, Torrance commences his threefold exposition on what Christ does as priest in his ascension, and it is on these aspects that the spotlight will now shine.

### 2.3.1 The Endless Self-Oblation of the Ascended Jesus

Torrance's exposition on this aspect is very brief, but this does not mean that what he has to offer is any less important. In fact, it is almost as if Torrance expects his reader to know what sources are informing his thought at this point, which is perhaps why he does not provide a more detailed discussion.[84] Andrew Burgess rightly recognizes Torrance's indebtedness to William Milligan's work on the resurrection and ascension, but he also

77. Milligan, *Ascension*, 131–32.
78. Torrance, *Space, Time, and Resurrection*, 114.
79. Torrance, *Space, Time, and Resurrection*, 114.
80. Torrance, *Space, Time, and Resurrection*, 114.
81. Torrance, *Space, Time, and Resurrection*, 114–15.
82. Torrance, *Space, Time, and Resurrection*, 115.
83. Torrance, *Space, Time, and Resurrection*, 115.
84. Cf. Burgess, *Ascension in Karl Barth*, 116–21.

importantly notes that Torrance is not uncritical in his appropriation of Milligan's insights on the priestly work of the ascended Christ. Burgess avers that Torrance does not fully agree with Milligan in asserting that Christ's priestly work only properly begins at the ascension.[85] On closer examination of Milligan's work on the ascension, one can easily notice that Torrance is drawing insights from him, and this should be no surprise because Torrance has already pointed readers to his work for more a more detailed exposition on the ideas he is offering.[86] In light of Milligan's work, Torrance can be said to highlight two main aspects in his explication of the priestly work of Christ as an *"endless self-oblation."*[87]

First, Torrance emphasizes a soteriological aspect through his emphasis on the *endless self-oblation* of the humanity of the ascended Christ.[88] The ontological being of the ascended Christ in heaven serves to highlight the ontological nature of salvation—past, present and future.[89] Theologically rich terms such as "Offering," "Redeemer," "Brother," "consecrated," "perfected"—all underscore the deeply ontological nature of salvation that Christ has brought about for humankind, and in the ascension, in the ontological being of Christ before the Father, this salvation is attested in a way that provides surety for eternity.[90] Milligan makes this same point in a much more poignant manner:

> As an offering of life our Lord's offering embraces in its efficacy the whole life of man. When as our High Priest and representative Jesus offers His life to God, that life touches not only individual acts of our life, it covers it in every one of its departments. There is no portion of the life lived by us in which, by the fact that He had lived a human life, the Redeemer of the world had not shared. Must we labour? He had laboured. Must we suffer? He had suffered. Must we be tempted? He had been tempted. Must we at one time have solitary hours, at another move in social circles? He had spent hours alone upon the mountain

---

85. Burgess, *Ascension in Karl Barth*, 118–19.

86. Torrance, *Space, Time, and Resurrection*, 111n5, where Torrance points readers to two works by Milligan for more on the *Triplex Munus*: "*The Resurrection of our Lord*, pp. 136–52; and *The Ascension and Heavenly Priesthood of our Lord*, pp. 61–226." Burgess rightly picks up on this reference and explores Milligan's work to better understand what Torrance may be highlighting in his own exposition. Cf. Burgess, *Ascension in Karl Barth*, 116–21.

87. Torrance, *Space, Time, and Resurrection*, 115.

88. Torrance, *Space, Time, and Resurrection*, 115.

89. Torrance, *Space, Time, and Resurrection*, 115.

90. Torrance, *Space, Time, and Resurrection*, 115.

top, and He had mingled with His disciples as companions and friends. Must we die? He had died. Must we rise from the grave? He had risen from it on the third morning. Must we appear before the Almighty as our Judge? He had appeared before Him who "sent" Him with the record of all that He had accomplished. Must we enter into eternity? He has entered it before us, and eternity is now passing over Him. More even than this has to be said. For our High-priest had not only moved in every one of the scenes in which we move. In each He had been a conqueror, and that for us; so that, when He presents His life to the Father, the conquest which He had gained in each is included in His offering, and we may be of good cheer because He has overcome. As the offering which He makes in His perfected human life, our whole human life is brought in Him within the scope of His consecrating power, and every part of it is presented to God as a trophy of His victory.[91]

Christ's ascended human life is not just victorious, but vicarious, and this is the point that Torrance is making in his soteriological emphasis, and one can notice through Milligan's quotation the theological impulse behind Torrance's as well.

Second, Torrance is stressing a teleological aspect through Jesus's *endless self-oblation*.[92] He does not provide all the details, so once again Milligan's work is helpful to fill in the gaps. What Torrance does explicitly affirm is that Jesus continues to present an offering to the Father, and that his offering is not to be construed as only something he did in the past: "Here we think of the ascension as the act of Christ's self-offering to the Father in which his self-sacrifice on the Cross is backed up by his own resurrection and endless Life, and made an offering to God through Eternal Spirit."[93] Therefore, the cross, resurrection, ascension, and ongoing life of Jesus are all presented to the Father as an offering, in Torrance's conception.[94] Torrance provides an important clue that the point he is making is a teleological one, when he provides "the Old Testament conception of the *minhah*, the thank-offering" as a means of illuminating the significance of this *endless self-oblation*.[95] Milligan again proves to be especially insightful. In Milligan's schematization of the Old Testament sacrificial ritual, there were three essential parts: (1) the animal sacrifice, (2) the animal's blood used after death

---

91. Milligan, *Ascension*, 148–49.
92. Torrance, *Space, Time, and Resurrection*, 115.
93. Torrance, *Space, Time, and Resurrection*, 115.
94. Torrance, *Space, Time, and Resurrection*, 115.
95. Torrance, *Space, Time, and Resurrection*, 115.

for ritual cleansing and reconciliation, and (3) the completion of this sacrifice through a life of thanksgiving.[96] Milligan explains how Jesus fulfills each of these three aspects perfectly:

> On the cross He gave Himself for us, the just for the unjust, so that when we identify ourselves with Him as the Victim upon which our help is laid, we behold in Him the law vindicated, our sins expiated, and our admission to the Divine presence and favour secured. This, however, is no more than the first part of the one great step taken for us by our heavenly High-priest. A second part followed. As the blood, or, in other words, the life, of an animal was liberated in death in order that by the sprinkling a union might be effected between the offerer and God, so the blood, or, in other words, the life, of Christ was liberated on the cross in order that our life in His might be united to the Father in the closest communion and fellowship, and that the broken covenant might be replaced by one that should last for ever. A third part still remained, depending upon these two, naturally resulting from them, and necessary to the completion of the issue to which they were designed to lead. The life thus united to God was actually surrendered to Him in a perpetual service of love and praise.[97]

The life of thanksgiving, according to Milligan, is presented as the climax of the sacrificial ritual, and since Torrance points to this particular aspect to shed light on what Jesus offers to the Father eternally, it is reasonable to conclude that Torrance is following Milligan on this point. In essence, Torrance is underscoring the importance of the joyful submission of one's life to God as the telos for which humankind was made in the first place and which is now fulfilled in the ascended humanity of Jesus.[98]

### 2.3.2 *The Eternal Intercession of the Ascended Jesus*

Three salient points illuminate Torrance's understanding of Jesus's intercession in his ascension. First, he highlights the ontological nature of the ascended Jesus's intercession.[99] Akin to how the atonement is to be understood in ontological categories, for Torrance, Jesus's intercession in his

---

96. Milligan, *Ascension*, 131–32, 139.
97. Milligan, *Ascension*, 139.
98. Milligan, *Ascension*, 117, 136–37, 139.
99. Torrance, *Space, Time, and Resurrection*, 115–17.

ascension is to be thought of in similar ways.[100] In other words, Torrance is advocating an understanding of Jesus's intercession that is not episodic in nature but exhaustive: "The whole existence of the incarnate Son was both the fulfilled intervention of God among men and the fulfilled response of men toward God."[101] Just as Jesus was in his being the "divine-human intervention or intercession" in his "life, work, crucifixion, resurrection," so too, now in his ascension he continues to function in this role.[102] What must not be missed is that for Torrance, as David Fergusson rightly notes, Christ's "work is never detachable from descriptions of his person."[103] This is exactly what Torrance intends to communicate when he declares, "It is with that ontological content of his Advocacy on our behalf that we are concerned here. It is an Advocacy in which his Word and Person and Act are one and indivisible."[104] Burgess captures Torrance's ontological emphasis about Jesus's intercession well when he notes, "In His being He *is* intercession for us, He *is* our advocate."[105]

Second, Torrance shows how the ontological nature of the ascended Jesus's intercession is teleologically oriented toward communion with the Father.[106] Torrance is rather brief in his explication of this aspect, but Milligan's works offers insights that help readers understand that Torrance is indeed intending to communicate something that is teleological in nature. Torrance notes that "Christ is the eternal Leader of our prayer and intercession, in which he makes himself the true content and sole reality of the worship and prayer of man."[107] Torrance then unpacks how all through his life Christ exemplified such a perfect communion with the Father; it is this aspect that Christ in his ascension welcomes other human beings to experience as well.[108] Says Torrance, "That is the prayer which Jesus *eternally* is before the face of the Father and in God himself where he ever lives in active

---

100. Torrance, *Space, Time, and Resurrection*, 115–16.

101. Torrance, *Space, Time, and Resurrection*, 115.

102. Torrance, *Space, Time, and Resurrection*, 115–16. On p. 116n13, Torrance quotes from Milligan, *Ascension*, 160, for a substantiation of the ongoing nature of Jesus's ontological intercession as follows: "The Intercession and the Offering cannot be separated from each other. The offering is itself a continuous intercession; the continuous intercession implies the offering as a present thing."

103. Fergusson, "Ascension of Christ," 98.

104. Torrance, *Space, Time, and Resurrection*, 116.

105. Burgess, *Ascension in Karl Barth*, 119–20.

106. Torrance, *Space, Time, and Resurrection*, 116.

107. Torrance, *Space, Time, and Resurrection*, 116.

108. Torrance, *Space, Time, and Resurrection*, 116.

intercession and prayer for us."[109] Torrance's statement is rather enigmatic, but it is quite probable that Torrance has the following statement of Milligan in mind:

> "Intercession" is a much wider word than prayer. That prayer is included under the term is not for a moment to be denied, but we are not to limit it to prayer. We are to understand it of every act by which the Son, in dependence on the Father, in the Father's name, and with the perfect concurrence of the Father, takes His own with Him into the Father's presence, in order that whatever He Himself enjoys in the communications of His Father's love may become also theirs.[110]

In other words, Torrance is perhaps agreeing with Milligan that Jesus's heavenly intercession continues even after "the humblest believer needs His aid,"[111] because the teleological orientation to prayer is much grander—nothing less than intimate communion with the Father, and this is something that requires Jesus's eternal intercession.[112]

Third, Torrance explains how Jesus's intercession for humankind is worked out practically, in two specific ways: "in terms of *substitution* as well as *representation*."[113] By these two terms Torrance intends to communicate that the ascended Jesus does for humankind what they could never do for themselves—he offers perfect worship and prayer to the Father as a human *for* humankind.[114] As such, Torrance declares, "But as substitute as well as representative he acts in our place and offers worship and prayer which we could not offer, yet offers them in such a vicarious way that while in our stead and on our behalf they are made to issue out of our human nature to the Father as our own worship and prayer to God."[115]

Torrance goes on to explain how the ascended Christ's perfect prayers to the Father are credited to humankind through the work of the Spirit.[116] Says Torrance, "Through the Spirit Christ's prayers and intercessions are made to echo in our own, and there is no disentangling of them from our weak and stammering and altogether unworthy acts of devotion."[117]

---

109. Torrance, *Space, Time, and Resurrection*, 116.
110. Milligan, *Ascension*, 152.
111. Milligan, *Ascension*, 150.
112. Milligan, *Ascension*, 152.
113. Torrance, *Space, Time, and Resurrection*, 116.
114. Torrance, *Space, Time, and Resurrection*, 116–17.
115. Torrance, *Space, Time, and Resurrection*, 116–17.
116. Torrance, *Space, Time, and Resurrection*, 117.
117. Torrance, *Space, Time, and Resurrection*, 117.

While Torrance does not go into further detail, Milligan proves especially insightful when he avers that the ascended Jesus and the Holy Spirit both function as intercessors, albeit one externally and the other internally, but together work in harmony to bring about the desired outcome in the believer's life.[118] The Holy Spirit, for Milligan, cements the work of Christ in the heart of the believer: "The second [Holy Spirit] brings the Redeemer in such a manner home into our hearts that, in the innermost depths of our nature, we see and judge and feel with Him; that His requests for us become our prayers for ourselves; and that the unity of Father, Son, and redeemed humanity is in Him completely realised."[119] Torrance uses these insights to shed light on how to understand "Eucharistic worship and prayer" and "the Lord's Prayer."[120] Both acts of worship, for Torrance, are to be grounded in Christ's ontology—which includes the cross and the ongoing work of Christ in heaven.[121] Torrance is keen to avoid any form of Pelagianism in one's understanding of prayer or the Eucharist.[122]

Christ alone is "our Mediator and Advocate," Torrance insists, and in the process chooses thought-provoking language to communicate Christ's ongoing intercession: "the pleading of a sacrifice which by its very nature is offered on our behalf and in our place and in our stead, so that it is not we but Christ himself who here stands in for us."[123] Burgess rightly notes that Torrance does not wish to convey any notion of "Jesus 'repeating' the sacrifice of the cross, nor of any addition to the work of the cross—there is one offering made once for all."[124] Fergusson points out that Torrance's language treads precariously on dangerous terrain; he explains,

> It is of course quite difficult to present this notion of heavenly priesthood without appearing to lapse into an anthropomorphic or even Arian account of the Father-Son relationship, as if the ascended Christ were a unique member of the heavenly council, a kind of chief executive whose function was to plead celestially on our behalf with the chairman of the board. The imagery is risky here, but Torrance is quite adamant that if we properly integrate the person and work of Christ, then we have to commit to expressing such notions, hazardous though they are and

---

118. Milligan, *Ascension*, 159–60.
119. Milligan, *Ascension*, 159–60.
120. Torrance, *Space, Time, and Resurrection*, 117.
121. Torrance, *Space, Time, and Resurrection*, 117.
122. Torrance, *Space, Time, and Resurrection*, 117.
123. Torrance, *Space, Time, and Resurrection*, 117.
124. Burgess, *Ascension in Karl Barth*, 120.

prone to misinterpretation. His point is that the ascended Christ is the same acting subject who is with us and for us in all that he does. He does not cease to be our advocate upon his ascension, but he must be understood as exercising this function in a different mode.[125]

In other words, Fergusson insists that for Torrance there is a symmetry between the work of Christ before and after ascension, because Christ is still the same person. He is an "advocate" in heaven as opposed to being one on earth.[126]

### 2.3.3 *The Eternal Benediction of the Ascended Jesus*

In a brief exposition, Torrance includes three integral aspects that he believes exegetes the blessing that the ascended Jesus pours out on his people.[127] First, Torrance explains that the ascended Jesus blesses his people by "sending down upon us the presence of the Holy Spirit."[128] Torrance makes it a point to underscore that this blessing, which can be found in Luke's vivid rendering—"the lifting up of his hands in blessing upon the disciples"— does not just remain words, but manifests itself in real life: "Pentecost is the content and actualization of that high priestly blessing."[129] Second, Torrance reasons, though not as lucidly as one would like, that the blessing the ascended Jesus brings to full realization is foreshadowed by the "Aaronic blessing of God's people after the completion of the sacrificial liturgy on the Day of Atonement" and also "Melchizedek's blessing of Abraham."[130] Torrance believes that the beginning and ending of the book of Revelation testify to the magnanimity of Christ's blessing of his people.[131] While he does not elucidate this insight further, one can be quite confident that he is

---

125. Fergusson, "Ascension of Christ," 97–98.
126. Fergusson, "Ascension of Christ," 98.
127. Torrance, *Space, Time, and Resurrection*, 117–18.
128. Torrance, *Space, Time, and Resurrection*, 117.
129. Torrance, *Space, Time, and Resurrection*, 118. This stress on blessing through words and the fulfillment of these words are also stressed by Milligan, *Ascension*, 162, when he explains that a believer receiving a blessing from God "believes that His Father in heaven desires to shower down blessings with a full hand upon all His creatures. But this is not enough. In the weakness of our nature we need to see the channel opened by which the blessing is conveyed, and to behold, as it were, the streams which actually convey it."
130. Torrance, *Space, Time, and Resurrection*, 117–18. Cf. Milligan, *Ascension*, 163–65.
131. Torrance, *Space, Time, and Resurrection*, 118.

referring to Milligan's emphasis on how the Aaronic blessing is eschatologically realized, as the book of Revelation testifies: "'The Lord make His face to shine upon thee, and be gracious unto thee,'—and is it not one of the privileges of the New Jerusalem of which all saints are citizens, that 'they see their Lord's face, and that His name is on their foreheads'?"[132] Third, Torrance highlights how the blessing of the Holy Spirit results in the outpouring of the spiritual gifts to members in the body of Christ, and also leads to intimate communion with the risen and ascended Lord.[133] Importantly, these gifts of the Spirit that Christ bestows enables the church to participate in Christ's work in such a way that there is harmony.[134] The point Torrance wants to underscore is "the one Priesthood of Christ," such that the church never thinks of itself as replacing Christ as priest, but only reflecting Christ's priesthood "in a secondary sense" in all her works.[135]

### 2.3.4 Torrance's Broader Corpus

#### 2.3.4.1 LITURGICAL ASPECTS

Torrance sheds further light on the necessity of Christ's eternal priesthood in an essay entitled "The Mind of Christ in Worship: The Problem of Apollinarianism in the Liturgy."[136] He points readers to this essay to encounter a detailed (and nuanced) argument for why it is necessary for Christ to eternally offer "prayer and intercession" for human beings, rather than leave human beings to pray and intercede to God on their own.[137] In essence, the argument of the essay can be summarized as a clarion call against the dangers of an Apollinarian christological influence on Christian worship.[138] In other words, if Christ is devoid of a human mind, then he is not fully human; consequently, there would be negative soteriological and liturgical

---

132. Milligan, *Ascension*, 163.
133. Torrance, *Space, Time, and Resurrection*, 118.
134. Torrance, *Space, Time, and Resurrection*, 118.
135. Torrance, *Space, Time, and Resurrection*, 118. On p. 118n17, Torrance interprets *basileion* in 1 Pet 2:5, 9, "as an adjective" and not "as a noun," with the result that "'royal priesthood'" [noun] is translated with the adjectival rendering: "a priesthood in the service of the King"; while Torrance believes the noun form of the word can be used, he does not believe that this reading can resort to "patristic support for such a translation."
136. Torrance, *Theology in Reconciliation*, 139–214.
137. See Torrance, *Space, Time, and Resurrection*, 116n14.
138. Torrance, *Theology in Reconciliation*, 139–214.

ramifications.[139] The soteriological consequences of Apollinarianism are clearly highlighted, when Torrance states, "By teaching that Christ was not really *homoousios* with us in the wholeness of our human being, sharing with us our rational human soul, Apollinarianism damages 'the complete economy' of salvation."[140] It is the liturgical consequences that Torrance seeks to bring to the surface in his whole essay, and he uses insights from Athanasius and Cyril to substantiate his claims against Apollinarianism.[141] What then are these liturgical consequences?

Torrance clearly distills these negative liturgical consequences in the following explanation:

> If Jesus Christ in his human mind does not worship the Father with us and on our behalf, then his priestly ministry becomes absorbed in the majesty of his Godhead, and we are left without an effective mediation from mankind towards the Father . . . we are inevitably thrown back upon ourselves to offer our own worship to the Father, worship of our own devising, although it may be worship for the sake of Christ, motivated by him and patterned on his earthly example, rather than worship mediated and shaped through his priesthood.[142]

If indeed Christ does not continue to worship the Father in his humanity in a vicarious manner, then Torrance argues that either human beings, institutions, or even the sacraments will try to fill the void and step in Christ's place.[143] All of these forms of mediation, however, will fail miserably, because ultimately through them "worship becomes psychologically motivated and oriented, and ends up by being not much more than an expression of cultural relativism and pluralism."[144] The antidote to these human attempts to replace the intercession of Christ, Torrance declares, is found in a robust theological understanding of the "*vicarious humanity* of Christ."[145] Undergirding this theological conviction, for Torrance, is a Trinitarian understanding of how Christian worship ought to be conceptualized.

---

139. Torrance, *Theology in Reconciliation*, 139–214.

140. Torrance, *Theology in Reconciliation*, 148.

141. See sections 2 and 3 of the essay where Torrance unpacks relevant insights from Athanasius and Cyril, respectively. See Torrance, *Theology in Reconciliation*, 151–56; 156–85.

142. Torrance, *Theology in Reconciliation*, 204.

143. Torrance, *Theology in Reconciliation*, 204–8.

144. Torrance, *Theology in Reconciliation*, 205.

145. Torrance, *Theology in Reconciliation*, 209.

This Trinitarian understanding of Christian worship is rooted in what can be called a christological ontology.[146] In other words, Christ fully identified with human beings in the incarnation, and the salvation he wrought for humankind was ontological in nature and therefore doctrinally thoroughly anti-Apollinarian. Stated differently, since Jesus so completely identified with human beings, he brings salvation and, importantly in his own person, ongoing mediation for humankind to the Father.[147] If christological ontology is the grounds for Christian worship, pneumatology is the means by which Christ's ongoing worship is appropriated to humankind.[148]

Torrance illuminates this pneumatological aspect by underscoring that it is the same Holy Spirit that lived in Jesus that now lives within the believer, and therefore Jesus's own "prayer and worship of the Father are made to echo in us and issue out of our life to the Father as our own prayer and worship."[149] The christological and pneumatological aspects of worship, for Torrance, leads to a third important corrective: "Jesus Christ is himself our prayer and worship."[150] This is an understanding of worship that is thoroughly participatory in nature and completely opposes thinking of worship as a human enterprise.[151] Torrance explains this well: "Really to pray to God, therefore, is to pray with Christ who prays with us and for us, and to pray with him is to pray his prayer, the prayer of his life which he offered in our place and on our behalf, and in which through union with Christ in the one Spirit we are made continually participant."[152]

Torrance provides a helpful patristic formulation of prayer that is "at once Trinitarian and Christocentric" and he goes on to state that "they expressed [it] by bringing together as mutually complementary the formulae, *From the Father, through the Son, and in the Spirit*, and *To the Father, through the Son, and in the Spirit*."[153] What is important to understand about this ancient Trinitarian formulation of worship, Torrance underscores, is the centrality of the mediation of the Son, who has two natures, divine and human.[154] It is precisely "through his divine-human constitution as the incarnate Son [that he] mediates the Word of God to man and the word of

---

146. Torrance, *Theology in Reconciliation*, 208.
147. Torrance, *Theology in Reconciliation*, 208.
148. Torrance, *Theology in Reconciliation*, 209.
149. Torrance, *Theology in Reconciliation*, 209.
150. Torrance, *Theology in Reconciliation*, 209.
151. Torrance, *Theology in Reconciliation*, 209.
152. Torrance, *Theology in Reconciliation*, 209.
153. Torrance, *Theology in Reconciliation*, 210.
154. Torrance, *Theology in Reconciliation*, 210.

man to God."[155] There are three crucial words that illuminate the mediation of Christ in prayer, for Torrance: "Through, with and in Christ"—these are key words that highlight that it is actually *"through the mind of Christ"* that one prays—"i.e. through Jesus himself as worshipper of God, and worshipper in our place."[156] Anything less than such a thoroughgoing emphasis on Christ's mediation, Torrance warns, will only lead to mere verbal confession to the role Christ plays in prayer without any actual substance.[157] Christ's role is central in mediating worship, because all human attempts, even at their best are muddled with self-interests of one kind or another, and only Christ's worship is pure and can grant one complete confidence that his worship is acceptable to the Father.[158] Torrance honestly asks for introspection: "Who does indeed come before God without ulterior motives of some kind corrupting his intention? But to worship and pray through, with and in Christ is to worship God for God's sake, with the perfection of true worship which Christ is, and not in some secret way for our own sake."[159] Torrance's emphasis on the vicarious humanity of Christ has been instrumental in revitalizing a theology of worship in the church, evidenced by the number of works in scholarship on this subject.[160]

### 2.3.4.2 Eucharistic Aspects

Torrance directs readers to other sources where he explicates the ongoing priestly ministry of Jesus in relationship to the Eucharist.[161] With respect to the ascension and in consonance with the thoroughly christological emphasis on the liturgical aspects mentioned above, the Eucharist, for Torrance, must be understood in dynamic and participatory ways.[162] The participa-

---

155. Torrance, *Theology in Reconciliation*, 210.
156. Torrance, *Theology in Reconciliation*, 211.
157. Torrance, *Theology in Reconciliation*, 211.
158. Torrance, *Theology in Reconciliation*, 211–12.
159. Torrance, *Theology in Reconciliation*, 211–12.
160. James Torrance shares the same view as Thomas Torrance, and together the Torrance brothers' theology of the vicarious humanity of Christ has resonated with many contemporary scholars, evidenced in their publications which range from pastoral theology to liturgical studies. For more, see J. B. Torrance, "Vicarious Humanity of Christ" and *Worship*. For some works inspired by the Torrance brothers' theology, see Navarro, *Trinitarian Doxology*; Fach, "Answering the Upwards Call"; Redding, *Prayer and the Priesthood*.
161. See Torrance, *Space, Time, and Resurrection*, 115n11 and 117n15.
162. See Torrance, *Theology in Reconciliation*, 118–20.

tory aspects of the Eucharist are clearly evidenced when Torrance explains that

> the eucharistic *anamnesis* is thus not merely something which we do by way of remembrance in consciousness, word and deed of the historical self-offering of Jesus Christ once and for all on the Cross, but is something we do in and through the real presence of the whole Christ who constitutes himself in his sacrificial death and justifying resurrection, its objective effectiveness and eternally enduring reality, so that the bread which we break and the cup of blessing which we bless are communion (*koinonia*) in the body and blood of Christ and the eucharistic offering of Christ to the Father which we make through him is communion (*koinonia*) in his own sacrificial self-offering to God the Father.[163]

The dynamic aspect of the Eucharist underscores the reality of Christ's presence in it, which, for Torrance, can only be explained in mysterious and miraculous terms.[164] He clarifies that Christ's presence in the Eucharist is different from his earthly presence or his glorified presence, but maintains that Christ's "real presence" is what one encounters in the Eucharist: "But it is nevertheless the real presence (*parousia*) of the whole Christ, not just the presence of his body and blood, nor just the presence of his Spirit or Mind, but the presence of the actual Jesus Christ, crucified, risen, ascended, glorified, in his whole, living and active reality and in his identity as Gift and Giver."[165]

Torrance goes on to highlight that the best explanation for such a presence of Christ in the Eucharist is that it is a miracle that human words cannot capture: "How he is thus present is only explicable from the side of God, in terms of his creative activity which by its very nature transcends any kind of explanation which we can offer."[166] When Torrance emphasizes that Christ's actual presence is mediated by the Holy Spirit, he is underscoring its miraculous and mysterious aspects: "That is what is meant by saying that he is really present *through the Spirit*, not that he is present only as Spirit, far less as some spiritual reality, but present through the same kind of inexplicable creative activity whereby he was born of the Virgin Mary and rose again from the grave."[167]

---

163. Torrance, *Theology in Reconciliation*, 118–19.
164. Torrance, *Theology in Reconciliation*, 119–20.
165. Torrance, *Theology in Reconciliation*, 119.
166. Torrance, *Theology in Reconciliation*, 119.
167. Torrance, *Theology in Reconciliation*, 119–20.

Torrance rejects the arrogation of worship as a human enterprise; his outlook on the Eucharist is very similar. "Because it really is the presence of the Lord Jesus in his living, creative reality, in his personal self-giving to us, it is a presence over which we have no kind of control, ecclesiastical, liturgical or intellectual."[168] While the Eucharist promises to communicate the same "kind of presence" that the early disciples encountered, the means ("form") by which Jesus is met in this act is certainly different.[169] Until the eschaton, however, it is in the Eucharist that disciples are to encounter Jesus "in the closest and most intimate way . . . in anticipation of his unveiled form when he will come again in great power and glory."[170]

## 2.4 The Ascended Jesus as Prophet

Torrance programmatically shapes his whole exposition on the present ministry of the ascended Jesus through the *triplex munus* to highlight Jesus as both "Subject and Content" of the kingship, priesthood, and the prophetic aspects.[171] Jesus, explains Torrance, is "Prophet in a unique sense, for he is in himself the Word he proclaims just as he is himself the King of the Kingdom and the Priest who is identical with the Offering he makes."[172] The ascension, for Torrance, is the point at which Jesus's prophetic ministry comes to a climax, as in the case of his kingship and priestly ministry.[173] He clearly notes this when he writes, "It is in that identity of Word of God and Word of man that Christ's prophetic ministry is fulfilled."[174]

However, this does not mean that Jesus's prophetic ministry is over and done with. Jesus is not static in his ascension, but continues to be active and dynamic, personally working as king, priest, and prophet. Torrance uses Mark 16:19–20 to illuminate the way Jesus continues to actively work as prophet: "Here we have a statement about the relation between the Church's proclamation of Christ and the activity of Christ himself in that proclamation where, through their common objective and dynamic content, the proclamation of the Gospel in the name of Christ and Christ's own proclamation are one and the same."[175]

168. Torrance, *Theology in Reconciliation*, 120.
169. Torrance, *Theology in Reconciliation*, 120.
170. Torrance, *Theology in Reconciliation*, 120.
171. Torrance, *Space, Time, and Resurrection*, 118–19.
172. Torrance, *Space, Time, and Resurrection*, 119.
173. Torrance, *Space, Time, and Resurrection*, 119.
174. Torrance, *Space, Time, and Resurrection*, 119.
175. Torrance, *Space, Time, and Resurrection*, 119.

Torrance illustrates this oneness between Jesus's proclamation about himself and the church's proclamation about Jesus through "the New Testament concept of *kerygma*."[176] The role of the Holy Spirit is crucial in synchronizing Christ's message and the church's message, but no less central is Christ's own active work in allowing for this to be a possibility in the first place.[177] Says Torrance, "It is Christ's own *kerygma*, his self-proclamation, which through the Spirit he allows to be echoed and heard through the preaching of the Church, so that their *kerygma* about Jesus Christ is made one with his own *kerygma*."[178] Importantly, Torrance notes that the "apostolic office" in a unique and "once for all" fashion has faithfully passed on Jesus's *kerygma* through their own words about Jesus bequeathed in "the saving Word of God" to the generations to come.[179] Even when the apostles' message is faithfully proclaimed or taught, "it is Christ himself the incarnate and risen Word who is mightily at work, confronting men and women with himself and summoning them to believe and follow him."[180]

Torrance continues his exposition of the prophetic ministry of the ascended Christ by making two important observations.[181] First, he highlights the kingly aspects of this prophetic ministry: "The ascension is not only the bearing of that Word up before the Face of the Father, but that Word accepted and honoured by God, that Word fully installed in the divine Kingdom, sent back to earth through the Spirit and by means of the Church proclaimed to all nations and all ages."[182] While emphasizing the kingly aspects of the prophetic office of the ascended Christ, Torrance wants to make clear that *who* Jesus is, is still crucial to the prophetic message of Jesus.[183] In other words, the message that is proclaimed is still about a person, and it is the person, Jesus, who is proclaiming this message: "It is Word of forgiveness now finally actualized by Act of God in the Cross and Resurrection, Word that is itself Act of God, but it is Word in which the historical Jesus Christ and the eternal Word of God are in indissoluble union."[184] It is through the proclamation of this message by the church that Jesus exercises his dominical rule over the earth, says Torrance: "The Church's

---

176. Torrance, *Space, Time, and Resurrection*, 119.
177. Torrance, *Space, Time, and Resurrection*, 119.
178. Torrance, *Space, Time, and Resurrection*, 119.
179. Torrance, *Space, Time, and Resurrection*, 119.
180. Torrance, *Space, Time, and Resurrection*, 119.
181. Torrance, *Space, Time, and Resurrection*, 120–22.
182. Torrance, *Space, Time, and Resurrection*, 120.
183. Torrance, *Space, Time, and Resurrection*, 120.
184. Torrance, *Space, Time, and Resurrection*, 120.

proclamation of the Gospel becomes thus the *sceptre*, as Clement of Rome called it, through which the risen and ascended Christ rules over the nations and all history."[185]

Second, Torrance asserts that the relationship between the ascended Christ and the church on earth functions in a way that is "sacramental" and "contrapuntal."[186] In other words, Christ is actively involved in and through the ministries of the church, but this does not mean that the church takes center stage and displaces Christ.[187] The "'sacramental relation'" between Christ and the church is illuminated through the analogy of "Head" and "Body," by which is meant that Christ is "King and Head of the Church."[188] What this amounts to is a profound assurance that the work of Christ was not just something that happened in the past (through the ministry of the apostles he commissioned to faithfully communicate the message of Christ through the Scriptures or to form the body of Christ that proclaimed his message to others), but the work of Christ is ongoing.[189] This is so because "he continues to pour out special gifts for ministry" to the church but also makes the gospel proclamation of the church redound as his own.[190] Torrance not only wants to assure the church of Christ's presence, but seems to want to remind the church that her mission is *always* only one of reflecting Christ to the world, and not replacing him:

> Thus the mission of the whole Church as the Body of Christ on earth and in history is called through the Spirit, as it were, into contrapuntal relation to the heavenly ministry of Christ, King, Priest and Prophet, yet in such a way that the Church cannot draw attention to itself, for the patterns of its life and work on earth have their significance entirely and only in directing the world away to the risen and ascended Lord himself.[191]

The exhortation to the church is very clearly stated by Torrance.

---

185. Torrance, *Space, Time, and Resurrection*, 120–21.
186. Torrance, *Space, Time, and Resurrection*, 121–22.
187. Torrance, *Space, Time, and Resurrection*, 121–22.
188. Torrance, *Space, Time, and Resurrection*, 121.
189. Torrance, *Space, Time, and Resurrection*, 121.
190. Torrance, *Space, Time, and Resurrection*, 121.
191. Torrance, *Space, Time, and Resurrection*, 122.

## 2.4.1 Torrance's Broader Corpus

Torrance's emphasis on the integral relationship between the ascended Christ and the church has already been underscored in the section above. In other places, he illuminates how the integral relationship between Christ and the church needs to be viewed in terms of their distinction as well. For instance, in his work entitled *Royal Priesthood* he stresses the importance of maintaining a distinction between Christ and the church lest the church seek to usurp Christ.[192] Torrance declares,

> The ministry of the Church is in no sense an extension of the ministry of Christ or a prolongation of certain of His ministerial functions. That is the view that leads to very wrong notions of Eucharistic Sacrifice as an extension of Christ's own priestly sacrifice in the Eucharist, and to wrong notions of priesthood as the prolongation of His Priesthood in the ministry: and behind it all lies the notion of the Church as an extending or prolonging of the Incarnation, and sometimes, as in certain Roman expositions, there even lurks the heretical idea of the reincarnation of Christ in the Church through the Spirit regarded as the soul of the Church.[193]

Torrance provides two points of clarification to avoid such negative theological and practical consequences.

First, Torrance warns against ontologically confusing Christ and the church: "There can be *no relation of identity* in part or in whole between the ministry of the Church and the ministry of Christ."[194] Second, Torrance cautions against placing Christ against the church: "The ministry of the Church is *not another ministry* different from the ministry of Christ, or separable from it."[195] Torrance believes that the Roman Catholic "view of the ministry" tends to succumb to the danger of ontologically confusing Christ with the Church, while "the so-called 'sectarian' view of the Church or ministry" is guilty of placing Christ against the church.[196] Both the relationship and distinction between Christ and the church are premised, for Torrance, as highlighted above, on the order of priority in which Christ is always central

---

192. Torrance, *Royal Priesthood*, 37.
193. Torrance, *Royal Priesthood*, 37.
194. Torrance, *Royal Priesthood*, 37.
195. Torrance, *Royal Priesthood*, 37.
196. Torrance, *Royal Priesthood*, 37. Cf. Fergusson, "He Ascended into Heaven," 41–42.

and the church is always secondary.[197] Says Torrance, "From beginning to end it is a relation of subordination and obedience. The Church participates in Christ's ministry by *serving* Him who is Prophet, Priest, and King."[198]

## 2.5 Section Summary

In this section, Torrance's use of the *triplex munus* as a framework for thinking about the present ministry of the ascended Jesus was explored in detail. Torrance does not explicate the details of Jesus as king; however, he does emphasize that the full demonstration of Jesus's kingship is muted for the present time to give people time to repent and get ready for the eschatological judgment when Jesus will be revealed in all his kingly glory. The priesthood of Jesus is expounded in detail by Torrance. The integral relationship between the person and work of Christ comes to the fore in Torrance's threefold explication of this theme. The prophetic ministry of the ascended Christ highlights the active agency of Christ in the ongoing ministry of the church.

Each of the three aspects of Torrance's explication of the *triplex munus* will be constructively developed in what follows. First, Jesus's kingship in light of the ascension is mostly embryonic in Torrance's theology. Therefore, it will be developed further vis-à-vis the theme of victory, specifically as it relates to his doctrine of sanctification. This will be done through a dialogue with Wesleyan theology. Second, Torrance's exposition of Jesus's priesthood in his ascension contains a critique of Barth's exposition of the same theme. This aspect will be highlighted to show Torrance's reservations with Barth's theology on this point. Third, in Torrance, the prophetic ministry of the ascended Jesus is integrally tied to his doctrine of Scripture. It will also be acknowledged that a legitimate lacuna in Torrance's theology is the lack of in-depth exegetical expositions of biblical books.

---

197. Torrance, *Royal Priesthood*, 37. Fergusson puts this point well when he explains that, for Torrance, "the church engages in the ministry of Christ in a manner that is appropriate to its derivative status as his body." For more, see Fergusson, "He Ascended into Heaven," 43–44.

198. Torrance, *Royal Priesthood*, 37.

## 3. THE PRESENT MINISTRY OF THE ASCENDED CHRIST: A CONSTRUCTIVE DEVELOPMENT

### 3.1 Jesus as Ascended King and the Doctrine of Sanctification

Torrance must be commended for allowing the doctrine of the ascension to shape his exposition of the *triplex munus*. He reorders the traditional sequence found in the *triplex munus* from "Prophet, Priest and King," to "King, Priest and Prophet," in light of the centrality of Jesus as king because of the ascension.[199] While the kingly aspects of Jesus's ascended ministry is minimally expounded in comparison to that of the priestly and prophetic aspects,[200] to be fair to Torrance, he alerts his readers to the fact that all his discussion on the *triplex munus* is shaped by the predominance of the kingship of Jesus, which then provides meaning to the priestly and prophetic areas of Jesus's ministry.[201] One can fault Torrance for not providing a more substantial account of Jesus as king in his ascension, but one cannot critique Torrance for not beginning to explore the frontiers of theology in light of the ascension. However minimalist Torrance's account may be, it still provides important desiderata on thinking about the ascension vis-à-vis the three offices of Christ, and in the process distinguishes his theology from other Reformed expositions that primarily expound the *triplex munus* in light of the earthly ministry of Jesus.[202] Gregory Liston judges classical and contemporary Reformed theology to manifest such a theological shortcoming:

> In most of these expressions, and particularly in the Reformed catechisms, the focus is on Christ's earthly session and its implications for us. There is, in contrast, less emphasis on Christ's heavenly session, Christ's continuing role as prophet, priest, and king, and the relevance of that to our current ecclesial existence. As such, most expressions of the *munus triplex* view it within the bounds of fallen time, rather than exploring it through an intrinsically eschatologically focused framework. . . . Most recent Reformed expositions of the *munus triplex* . . . focus . . . on Christ's earthly session, particularly his death, and then as a

---

199. Torrance, *Space, Time, and Resurrection*, 106.

200. See Torrance, *Space, Time, and Resurrection*, 112, where Torrance discusses the kingly aspects of the ascended Jesus in less than a page.

201. Torrance, *Space, Time, and Resurrection*, 106–7.

202. See Liston, "Eschatology," 325–27, where he states that Reformed theologians such as John Calvin, Louis Berkhof, Donald McKim, Daniel Migliore, and Robert Sherman mainly explore the *triplex munus* from the vantage point of Jesus's earthly ministry.

consequence they (sometimes) go on to consider the implications of these offices for us now.[203]

Torrance stands out among Reformed theologians for the way he begins to think about the *triplex munus* in light of the ascension, but Liston contends that the kingly aspect of Christ's ministry is embryonic in comparison to the priestly and prophetic aspects.[204] Liston is agreeing with and echoing reservations that other scholars such as Baxter Kruger and Dick Eugenio have noted; therefore, he is not wrong to make such an observation.[205] Liston also, commendably, provides important scaffolding for a constructive theological account of the kingly ministry of Jesus that takes eschatology seriously, and as such his work provides a helpful way to fill certain gaps in Torrance's theology.[206]

Nonetheless, Torrance's account of the kingship of Jesus in his ascension is not devoid of important theological insights, even if they are present only in seed form. There is one key idea in Torrance that Liston's impressive constructive and conceptual work has missed, namely, that for Torrance Jesus is the *suffering-yet-victorious* king.[207] In his ascension, Torrance insists, Jesus exercises his kingship in a manner that is consistent with who he is and what he accomplished through the cross and resurrection: "Christ Jesus crucified and risen is on the Throne—of that the Christian must never doubt. Jesus, yes, he Jesus, is now at the right hand of God holding the reins of the world in his hands, the hands that bore the imprint of the nails hammered into them on the cross."[208] When he further elucidates this point, Torrance proclaims,

> The fact that it is Jesus of Nazareth, Jesus who suffered under Pontius Pilate, Jesus who was nailed to the Cross at Golgotha, who reigns there, the fact that his Ascension guarantees to us what his Incarnation revealed, that *God is like Christ*, and *Christ is God* in his actuality among men, means that the hands which rule and guide the wheels of providence are in the hands that have been pierced and scarred at Calvary![209]

---

203. Liston, "Eschatology," 325–26.
204. Liston, "Eschatology," 329, 336.
205. Liston, "Eschatology," 336. Cf. Kruger, "Self-Knowledge of God," 325; Eugenio, Communion, 139.
206. Liston, "Eschatology," 336–43.
207. Torrance, *Space, Time, and Resurrection*, 112.
208. Torrance, *Doctrine of Jesus Christ*, 194.
209. Torrance, *Doctrine of Jesus Christ*, 194.

Torrance asserts that the ascended Jesus still carries his wounds with him.[210] Therefore, he wants to underscore that the same Jesus who suffered and was victorious is now in his ascension exercising his kingly ministry.[211] Torrance also mentions the wounds of Christ in other contexts, but he does not theologize about it. However, there is sufficient warrant to do so because he explicitly connects the kingship of Jesus with the wounds that still mark Jesus's ascended body. Peter Widdicombe helpfully narrates the theological reception history of the wounds of Christ by noting how it resonated well particularly with "patristic and medieval theologians," and goes on to provide the following theologically salient insight:

> However transformed in glory, Christ is not to be thought of as dehominised and the evidence of his history as the incarnate and suffering human being is not to be erased. For the earlier theologians, the reign of Christ in all its fullness is signified by the retention of the marks. Suffering and sinful humanity indeed finds itself in the Son at the right hand of the Father and it can see there the evidence that the divine heart has and continues to beat with compassion for humanity in its continuing brokenness. It is the enduring presence of the marks of the wounds in heaven that testifies to the divine engagement with the sinful human condition, in both judgment and mercy, which in turn is the basis of our response of thankfulness.[212]

Widdicombe's exposition on the theological significance of the wounds of Christ sheds light on an important yet underdeveloped theme in Torrance's theology. Since Torrance wishes to highlight the manner in which Jesus currently exercises his kingship as the suffering and victorious Lord, Widdicombe's insights are particularly germane and can serve as a development of embryonic ideas in Torrance.

Dick Eugenio concurs with the general observation about the neglect, in Torrance, of the kingship of Jesus, in comparison to the priestly and prophetic aspects of the *triplex munus*. Particularly lacking, Eugenio contends, is sufficient exploration of how Jesus as king relates to the lives of Christians today: "He [Torrance] does not elaborate [on] the important implications of Christ's vicarious victory over sin and death for Christians now."[213] Christ's

---

210. There are also other places in Torrance's corpus where he highlights this theme in other contexts. For more, see Torrance, *When Christ Comes*, 26; Torrance, *Conflict and Agreement*, 2:138–39.

211. Torrance, *Doctrine of Jesus Christ*, 194.

212. Widdicombe, "Wounds and the Ascended Body," 154.

213. Eugenio, *Communion*, 139.

kingship, for Torrance, is integrally connected to the theme of victory, and it is this insight that can serve to address critiques such as the ones leveled against Torrance by Eugenio and others.[214] Contemporary ecumenical exchanges between Wesleyan and Torrancean scholars provide one clear way of addressing this critique against Torrance. Through these exchanges there are clear solutions to redressing a gap in Torrance's theology of Jesus's kingship more generally, but also specifically with relation to the ascended Jesus and the kingly aspect of the *triplex munus*.

Wesleyan theologian Thomas Noble, for instance, finds in Torrance's theology of "ontological" sanctification grounded in Christ's holiness an important corrective to an overemphasis on the "subjective" aspects of sanctification that he finds in his own Wesleyan tradition.[215] "It is not simply a matter of our personal faith and love and consecration," emphasizes Noble, further stressing, "it is first of all a matter of the action of God in Jesus Christ, particularly in 'Christ crucified.' That is the side that Pietistic evangelicals (including Wesleyans) are always in danger of forgetting."[216] What Noble goes on to state, after he has underscored the priority of basing Christian holiness on Christ's holiness, is equally important because it does not neglect the "subjective aspect" of sanctification: "But the other side of the coin is that salvation not only has the ontological, corporate, objective, 'once-for-all' aspect: it also has the relational, personal, subjective aspect."[217] While ontological sanctification is certainly a strength in Torrance's theological arsenal, it is no secret that subjective sanctification is a lacuna. Andrew Purves clearly acknowledges such a limitation in Torrance's theology, after insisting that it is not merely functional but deeply relational: "Perhaps Torrance could have developed this further, and especially perhaps robustly in the direction of a deeper understanding of the doctrine and process of sanctification."[218] Alexandra Radcliff interprets Torrance's reticence not to an aversion of the subjective aspects of sanctification but as something symptomatic of the theological trajectory he represents: "Although T. F. was

---

214. See Liston, "Eschatology," 336; See also Eugenio, *Communion*, 139.

215. Noble, *Holy Trinity*, 156. Cf. Van Kuiken, "All of Him," 35, who explains that Noble's book has been significant from an ecumenical point of view because he "has shown that the Torrancian doctrines of ontological healing and total substitution are bedrock on which Wesley's doctrine may be built." See also Radcliff, *Claim of Humanity*, 129n28: "Noble seeks a reappraisal of Wesley's doctrine of sanctification by doing what he perceives Wesley failed to do: the rooting of subjective sanctification in the objective Person and Work of Christ."

216. Noble, *Holy Trinity*, 156.

217. Noble, *Holy Trinity*, 156.

218. Purves, *Exploring Christology*, 100–101.

remarkably encouraging about the exploration of the subjective nature of sanctification, both he and J. B. are characteristic of their Reformed tradition in largely avoiding the subject."[219]

Van Kuiken practically demonstrates specific ways in which the Torrancean and Wesleyan traditions can mutually enrich each other with what is best in their respective theological convictions and practices.[220] In this spirit of ecumenical reciprocity, Van Kuiken promises, "Torrance enriches Wesley by stressing the objectivity and unity of salvation in Christ, especially in the doctrine of ontological healing. These emphases can help Wesleyans to put down deep dogmatic, theo-ontological, and Christological roots, finding nourishment and stability instead of rotting away from moralism or blowing about in the winds of theological vagaries and spiritual neuroses."[221] In a similar attitude, Wesley's principal blessing to Torrance's followers would be to effectively counter the dangers that can exist in a "strongly objective theological approach [which] is to drift into intellectualism and spiritual lethargy, if not antinomianism—to become but a deep-rooted stump."[222] Van Kuiken clarifies that Torrance himself is not guilty of such an assessment, but since "the tendency remains, latent and liable to emerge in a weaker soul or later generation," Wesley's exhortation "to pursue Christlikeness of inward and outward life to the praise of God's grace," is particularly relevant for Torrance's followers.[223]

To add more specificity to this exhortation, Van Kuiken believes that Wesley's ability to put in place organizational structures to facilitate discipleship and spiritual formation in his followers can be a model for Torrance's followers to inculcate as a way to address issues of personal formation that can be neglected in Torrance's theology.[224] In particular, Wesley developed "discipleship groups" that were "patterned after his *ordo salutis*, with groups for 'seekers' (to use today's parlance), new converts, those pursuing entire sanctification, backsliders (anticipating today's Alcoholics Anonymous)."[225] These structures not only enabled the longevity of the Methodist movement in a time when similar movements began but did not have the "staying power" to endure for generations, but it also "preserved their members

---

219. Radcliff, *Claim of Humanity*, 126. She gives a plausible reason for the Torrances' reticence on p. 127: "This lack of exploration could perhaps be attributable to their following the concern of their Reformed tradition to avoid works-righteousness."

220. Van Kuiken, "All of Him," 33–38.

221. Van Kuiken, "All of Him," 33–34.

222. Van Kuiken, "All of Him," 34.

223. Van Kuiken, "All of Him," 34.

224. Van Kuiken, "All of Him," 34, 36.

225. Van Kuiken, "All of Him," 36.

from subjectivism and promoted spiritual growth."[226] Van Kuiken then goes on to add that "Torrancians may adapt Wesley's system to nurture spiritual growth rooted in Christ's total substitution."[227]

While there are ways to address the critique leveled against Torrance's inadequate emphasis on the personal implications of the kingship of the ascended Jesus, there are others who perceive a serious shortcoming in terms of relevant teaching on a wider level—that address issues related to the cosmos and society. Baxter Kruger, for instance, contends that Torrance's theology neglects integrating Jesus's kingship and its impact on the whole cosmos: "There is not very much emphasis in Torrance's theology upon the kingly work of Christ viewed in terms of the restoration of the whole creation and specifically the restoration of man's relation to the creation."[228] John Webster believes that there is a lacuna in Torrance's theology, especially in comparison with Karl Barth, when it comes to its contribution to ethics: "Barth thought of the Reformed tradition as a kind of theocentric humanism, with a double theme of divine and human action; Torrance more naturally gravitated to the theology of human participation in Christ, leaving less space for ethical considerations."[229] Whether or not Torrance is guilty of neglecting ethics is open to debate. Chapter 6 will explore this theme in detail.

## 3.2 Jesus as Ascended Priest and Torrance's Critique of Barth

Torrance and Barth share many similarities in their respective theologies in general and the doctrine of the ascension in particular.[230] Torrance, however, insisted to Barth himself that there were certain areas in his exposition of the priestly ministry of the ascended Christ where they differed:

> I then ventured to express my qualms about his account of the ascended Jesus Christ in *CD* IV.3, in which Christ seemed to be swallowed up in the transcendent Light and Spirit of God, so that the humanity of the risen Jesus appeared to be displaced by what he called "the humanity of God" in his turning toward us. I had confessed to being astonished not to find at that point

---

226. Van Kuiken, "All of Him," 36.
227. Van Kuiken, "All of Him," 36.
228. Kruger, "Self-Knowledge of God," 325.
229. Webster, "Thomas Forsyth Torrance," 427. Webster does not make this comment in the context of Jesus's kingship in Torrance's theology, but it is still germane to the discussion at this point.
230. Burgess, *Ascension in Karl Barth*, 109–10.

in Barth's exposition a careful account of the priestly ministry of the ascended Jesus in accordance with the teaching of the Epistle to the Hebrews about the heavenly intercession of the ascended Christ, which would have been fully consonant with Barth's anticipatory references to the high-priestly ministry of Christ in *CD* IV.1 (cf. "The Verdict of the Father") and with his persistent emphasis on the vicarious humanity of Christ. What might appear to be a "suspicion of Docetism" in what Barth had written about the ascended humanity of Jesus inevitably raised questions in some quarters about how he really regarded the humanity of the pre-resurrection Jesus![231]

Barth averred that he did not intend to neglect the priestly ministry of the ascended Christ in his theology, and even asked Torrance "to rewrite those parts of *CD* IV to make them consistent with the rest of his theology!"[232] Barth's acknowledgement to Torrance suggests that he recognized the merits of Torrance's critique.

Andrew Burgess, however, in his recent study on Karl Barth's theology of the ascension, does not believe that Torrance's critique of Barth is valid.[233] In his final analysis, he insists that "Torrance's theology of the ascension does not appear to have caused him actually to diverge from Barth in his description of the incarnation, nor even to any large degree in his vision of Jesus' ascended ministry."[234] While Burgess admirably compares and contrasts both Barth and Torrance on the ascension, interestingly he chooses not to critically explore two areas where both theologians diverge in their views—the Eucharist and eschatology.

Torrance and Barth's differing perspectives of eschatology vis-à-vis the ascension will be explored in chapter 6. At this stage, their views on the Eucharist and the ascension will be briefly analyzed. Burgess correctly observes that "Torrance . . . places a greater emphasis than Barth upon the eucharist as a fundamental place of Jesus' presence to the church during the age of His heavenly session."[235] He goes on to controversially note, "Although he [Torrance] attends to it in various places, the eucharist does not appear to wield any significant influence over Torrance's ascension theology."[236]

---

231. Torrance, *Karl Barth: Theologian*, 133–34.
232. Torrance, *Karl Barth: Theologian*, 135.
233. Burgess, *Ascension in Karl Barth*, 109–34.
234. Burgess, *Ascension in Karl Barth*, 133.
235. Burgess, *Ascension in Karl Barth*, 110.
236. Burgess, *Ascension in Karl Barth*, 110.

David Fergusson and George Hunsinger would strongly disagree with Burgess's assessment. Fergusson argues that while Barth and Torrance shared a commonality in their theologies of the ascension, they parted ways in their views on "the doctrine of church, sacraments, and ministry."[237] Importantly, contra Burgess, Fergusson insists that the above loci, including the sacraments, "are crucially related to his [Torrance's] account of the ascension."[238] Hunsinger lavishly praises Torrance's work on the sacraments by stating that he is able "to bring Calvin and Barth together into a brilliant new synthesis. . . . The result is surely the most creative Reformed breakthrough on the sacraments in twentieth-century theology, and arguably the most important Reformed statement since Calvin."[239] In a later work, Hunsinger attributes the main inspiration for his theological views on the Eucharist, not to Karl Barth, but to T. F. Torrance and Alasdair Heron.[240]

Admittedly readers will want an explanation from Hunsinger, especially because he is "so steeped in Barth's theology."[241] To such readers, he responds as follows: "The most general answer is that I wish to align myself with the trajectory established by Thomas F. Torrance and Alasdair Heron, who have blazed a trail before me, moving not only with Barth and through Barth on the eucharist, but also beyond and against him."[242] More specifically, Hunsinger relies on Torrance over Barth on the Eucharist, because he contends that "Barth arguably failed to exploit the full potential of his theology regarding the eucharist."[243] Hunsinger believes that Torrance filled in the gap that was present in Barth's theology of the Eucharist, and therefore he relied on his work as a resource in his own theological construction.[244]

Fergusson explains the various theological resources Torrance relied on to enable him to develop a unique theology of the Eucharist in comparison to that of Barth:

> Torrance was a longstanding member of the Scottish Church Society, founded in the late Victorian period by leading figures

237. Fergusson, "Ascension of Christ," 95.
238. Fergusson, "Ascension of Christ," 95.
239. Hunsinger, "Dimension of Depth," 159–60.
240. Hunsinger, *Eucharist and Ecumenism*, 15.
241. Hunsinger, *Eucharist and Ecumenism*, 15.
242. Hunsinger, *Eucharist and Ecumenism*, 15.
243. Hunsinger, *Eucharist and Ecumenism*, 15.
244. Hunsinger, *Eucharist and Ecumenism*, 17: "The full contemporaneity of Christ's person in his work here and now, and of his work in his person, would have to take place, for Barth, primarily through Word and Sacrament. Yet it fell to T. F. Torrance, Barth's student, to make the connection that his mentor never quite managed to carry through."

such as Milligan, John McLeod, and James Cooper. The goals of the society included a more Catholic reading of the Reformed tradition that sought liturgical renewal, frequent celebration of the Lord's Supper, and a Calvinist (as opposed to a Zwinglian) account of sacramental grace and the real presence of Christ in the eucharistic elements. It is this configuration of influences that enabled Torrance to move beyond Karl Barth in some important respects. In particular, his commitment to the ministry of the ascended Christ made present by the Holy Spirit led to a stronger ecclesiology, sacramentalism, and eschatology than we find in Barth himself. This is apparent in works such as *Royal Priesthood* and also in those mild criticisms he ventures of Barth.[245]

Fergusson's insights shed helpful light on Torrance's critique of Barth on the ascension and the priesthood of Christ. Paul Molnar, however, provides a mediating approach to this debate. He reasons that both Torrance and Barth are guilty of inconsistencies in their theologies.[246] Molnar contends that Torrance was not consistent in the area of "natural theology," while for Barth "the sacraments" were an area of "some inconsistency."[247] However, Molnar believes that if the two theologians had the time to "discuss these issues today," it is highly likely that they would have agreed "that a more consistent focus on the grace of God in Christ, the giver of grace, is and should be the main focus of both sacramental theology and systematic theology itself."[248] In other words, Molnar maintains that the result of a sustained dialogue between both theologians would have provided avenues for self-correction of their own theologies in ways that were consistent with their overall theological convictions. With this said, it must be mentioned that Barth and Torrance's theological anthropologies also differed, and it is this area that is underexplored in comparative studies of both theologians. This issue will be addressed in chapter 6.

## 3.3 Jesus as Ascended Prophet and Torrance's Doctrine of Scripture

Torrance emphasizes the active agency of the ascended Jesus in his exposition of the prophetic aspect of the *triplex munus*, as a section above has

---

245. Fergusson, "Ascension of Christ," 96.
246. Molnar, "Torrance and Karl Barth," 84.
247. Molnar, "Torrance and Karl Barth," 84.
248. Molnar, "Torrance and Karl Barth," 84.

clearly highlighted.[249] While Torrance does not specifically attribute this theme to Karl Barth, it is clearly a unique aspect of Barth's work on the prophetic ministry of Jesus.[250] A central feature of the office of prophet that Barth is highlighting is the dynamic nature of God's revelation: "Revelation takes place in and with reconciliation. . . . As God acts in it, He also speaks. Reconciliation is not a dark or dumb event, but a perspicuous and vocal [one]."[251] John Webster helpfully illuminates Barth when he explains, "To speak of Jesus as prophet is to speak of him as the immediate agent of the knowledge of himself: he is literally, self-proclaiming."[252] In other words, the prophetic aspect of Jesus's ministry is grounded in the agency of Jesus himself. Importantly, with reference to the ascended Jesus (and indeed to the return of Jesus), Barth exclaims that one encounters him even today:

> It cannot be the case, then . . . where our relationship to Jesus Christ can only be indirect, where it can be reduced to a mere looking back to His past presence and action and forward to His future. . . . There can be no question of Jesus Christ being even temporarily directed in His absence to let Himself be represented by an honoured Christianity and the holy Church. . . . Jesus Christ cannot be absorbed and dissolved in practice into the Christian *kerygma*, Christian faith and the Christian community. He cannot be replaced by Christianity. He remains sovereign even in this respect. There is no pause or vacuum in the exercise of His prophetic function. He Himself is fully present and active.[253]

Barth's theology of the *triplex munus* at this point stands out from the "older Protestant dogmatics," explains Webster, wherein the office of prophet was either undermined or viewed only in terms of appropriating the benefits associated with Jesus's ministry on earth.[254] Torrance, like Barth, seeks to highlight a similar point.

Torrance, however, utilizes Mark 16:19–20 to illustrate his point.[255] For Torrance, the prophetic office is integrally related to his doctrine of Scripture, as Joseph Sherrard explains, "Torrance's unique contribution to

---

249. See section 2.4 above for more on this point.

250. See Barth, *Church Dogmatics*, 4/3.1:3–367; Webster, *Barth*, 131–37; Liston, "Eschatology," 329–32.

251. Barth, *Church Dogmatics*, 4/3.1:8.

252. Webster, *Barth*, 131.

253. Barth, *Church Dogmatics*, 4/3.1:349–50.

254. Webster, *Barth*, 131. Cf. Liston, "Eschatology," 330–31.

255. See section 2.4 above for more on this point.

the prophetic office is to begin his description of the office with the apostolic foundation of Holy Scripture. Rather than focusing upon the ecclesial act of preaching, he instead traces this act to its fundamental grounding upon Holy Scripture."[256] Some contemporary theological exegetes commend Torrance's interpretation of the Mark 16 passage, especially because of the connection it makes between the ascended Christ and his prophetic ministry.[257] Gerald O'Collins has recently argued that Torrance's interpretation of Mark 16:19–20 is far superior to the work of biblical exegetes like Francis Moloney because they tend to limit the interpretation of the two verses (Mark 16:19–20) to "mere authorisation" of Jesus's disciples to fulfill certain tasks without the presence of Jesus, when in fact the message of the text, particularly v. 20, unmistakably points to "Christ who actively proclaims the message."[258] O'Collins concludes his assessment by giving Torrance's interpretation his stamp of approval: "It is the power of the Lord *who works with them* that enables them to carry out their mission successfully. Torrance, rather than Moloney, correctly respects the full force of what the Markan addition states about the prophetic activity of the risen and ascended Christ."[259] Historically, however, Torrance's interpretation of the biblical text has at times been severely scrutinized.

Torrance's method of biblical interpretation is theological in nature, and he acknowledges elsewhere that he depends on Kittel's *Theological Dictionary of the New Testament* for his own theological appropriation of various biblical words.[260] Essentially, Torrance wants to argue against *container* notions of interpreting the Scriptures, wherein one believes that biblical words exhaustively contain in themselves all the truths they are meant to communicate.[261] Instead, Torrance offers a theological view of biblical interpretation that "does not focus myopically, as it were, upon the words and statements themselves, but *through* them on the truths and realities they indicate beyond themselves."[262] Stated differently, Torrance is keen to view the Scriptures not as the end goal of revelation, but as the means by which one is led to know God.[263] Drawing inspiration from Calvin's works, Torrance avers that "the Holy Scriptures are the *spectacles* through which we are

---

256. Sherrard, *T. F. Torrance*, 184.
257. See O'Collins, "Thomas Torrance."
258. O'Collins, "Thomas Torrance," 175.
259. O'Collins, "Thomas Torrance," 175.
260. Torrance, *Royal Priesthood*, x.
261. Torrance, *Reality and Evangelical Theology*, 64–65.
262. Torrance, *Reality and Evangelical Theology*, 64.
263. Torrance, *Reality and Evangelical Theology*, 65.

brought to know the true God in such a way that our minds fall under the compelling power of his self-evidencing Reality."[264] Not all are impressed by Torrance's overarching vision of biblical interpretation and theological exegesis. James Barr, for instance, finds Torrance's assertion that "In Hebrew the terms for ascension and oblation are the same: עֹלָה" to be fundamentally flawed.[265]

Barr mounts a four-point counter argument and does not shy away from dismissing his senior Edinburgh colleague's claim. First, Barr alleges that Hebrew grammar testifies against Torrance because there is a different word for ascension—namely "ma'ᵃleh," which does not mean the same thing as "'olah," or sacrifice.[266] Second, Barr contends that equating "ascension and oblation"[267] just does not work because it lacks specificity in distinguishing between "'olah," which denotes "a *burnt* offering," and "oblation," which can mean "other sacrificial offerings."[268] Third, Barr insists that there is no precedent in the reception history to justify the connection Torrance makes between "ascension and oblation."[269] Barr contends, "There [is no] evidence that 'olah was etymologized as 'ascent' in the biblical period," nor for that matter in the Septuagint or the "Aramaic and Syriac versions."[270] Fourth, Barr asserts that even the book of Hebrews rejects Torrance's proposal because it "thinks of the ascension as similar to the entry of the High Priest to the holiest place," but importantly eschews what Torrance avers when it maintains that the entrance "was not connected with the 'olah but with the blood of a totally different type of sacrifice."[271] Barr's eventual assessment of Torrance's overall approach to biblical interpretation, and specifically with respect to the ascension, is unmistakably negative. He pronounces his judgment by declaring it to be "most probably gratuitous and worthless."[272]

Torrance is aware of and acknowledges the legitimacy of certain aspects of Barr's stern critique, while insisting that his own overall method is theologically sound because it acknowledges that biblical "words and statements" are not the terminal locus but the means by which one encounters

---

264. Torrance, *Reality and Evangelical Theology*, 64–65. Torrance refers to Calvin's *Institutes* 1.6.1 and 14.1, among other references from Calvin's work for his use of the analogy of the scriptures as "spectacles."

265. Torrance, *Royal Priesthood*, 39n2; Barr, *Semantics of Biblical Language*, 151–52.

266. Barr, *Semantics of Biblical Language*, 151.

267. Torrance, *Royal Priesthood*, 39n2.

268. Barr, *Semantics of Biblical Language*, 151–52.

269. Torrance, *Royal Priesthood*, 39n2.

270. Barr, *Semantics of Biblical Language*, 152.

271. Barr, *Semantics of Biblical Language*, 152.

272. Barr, *Semantics of Biblical Language*, 152.

"the realities beyond which they are meant to direct us."[273] John Webster's assessment of Torrance's doctrine of Scripture, perhaps, more accurately reflects its strengths and weaknesses when he praises its overarching theological richness but points out that the lack of detailed exegetical engagement with the biblical text remains one of its shortcomings.[274] Webster avers,

> The text does not, of course, make the Word comprehensively available or transparent; but the Word's relation to the text is more than asymptotic, and so to read the text as natural sign *is* to hear the divine Word in (not only behind or beneath) its textual surface. And if this is so, then, once again, theology may be encouraged to adopt a more commentarial rhetoric, to "notice the sequence of the words" and so to be vouchsafed divine revelation. It was Torrance's achievement to have expounded—with characteristic zeal and decisiveness—the dogmatics, semiotics and semantics of scripture, the commentarial application of which remains an unfinished task.[275]

Webster's assessment is fair and more nuanced than Barr's. Torrance's doctrine of Scripture, however, needs to be bolstered through a more in-depth engagement with his wider corpus and by bringing him into dialogue with other theologians on this point.[276]

## 3.4 Section Summary

In this section, Torrance's theology vis-à-vis the *triplex munus* was constructively developed in the following manner. Jesus as king was shown to have clear implications (through the theme of victory) to Torrance's doctrine of sanctification. Since Torrance's emphasis on sanctification stresses the *objective* aspects more than the *subjective* aspects, it is evident that this issue needs to be addressed. Through an existing ecumenical dialogue between contemporary Wesleyan and Torrancean theology, it was suggested that both can address weaknesses in their respective theologies. Torrance clearly critiques Barth in his explication of Jesus as priest in his ascension. Molnar, however, explains that both theologians had gaps in their theologies and

---

273. Torrance, *Royal Priesthood*, x.

274. Webster, "T. F. Torrance," 62–63.

275. Webster, "T. F. Torrance," 62–63.

276. Cf. Backfish and Owen, "Torrance and Biblical Theology," which focuses on exploring T. F. Torrance's biblical theology. Several articles engage various aspects of Torrance's theological interpretation of Scripture and provide helpful suggestions on how to explore his doctrine of Scripture in more detail.

would have benefited from further interaction with each other on the areas of their theological divergence. Jesus as prophet is deeply interconnected with Torrance's doctrine of Scripture. James Barr, in particular, sternly critiques Torrance's exegesis, but this section avers that John Webster's assessment of Torrance is more accurate, because he recognizes both strengths and weaknesses in Torrance's theological engagement with the biblical text.

## 4. CRITIQUE

### 4.1 Jesus as Ascended King

With regard to Jesus as ascended king, the following question becomes pertinent and will be addressed in chapter 6: Does Torrance's emphasis on Jesus as King address issues of ethics and politics?[277] Torrance's approach to the kingship of the ascended Jesus pushes the frontiers of theology in ways that some other Reformed theologians do not; however, in the final analysis, Torrance's focus is more epistemological and methodological than theological. Two major critiques related to the kingship of the ascended Jesus will need to be addressed in the next chapter. First, even sympathetic readers of Torrance's theology conclude that his exposition of the ascension focuses more on an individual's relationship with God rather than on the corporate, ethical, political, and global implications. Fergusson, for example, maintains that Torrance underscores the "vertical rather than [the] horizontal" aspects, or that he neglects the "ethical and political significance" of the ascension.[278] With Todd Speidell and Jerome Van Kuiken, this work will argue that there are resources in Torrance's theology to sufficiently address the criticism that Fergusson and others have leveled against Torrance.[279]

---

277. See section 2.3.1, "Critique #7," in chapter 6 for more on this point.

278. Fergusson, "Ascension of Christ," 106–7. Cf. Ziegler, "Doctrine of the Ascension," 30–31, in the context of Jesus's ascended Kingship in Torrance's theology makes a similar observation: "Except in passing, Torrance has little to say about *Christus Victor*, Christ triumphing over the powers (Col 2:15). Also lacking is any serious reflection upon the relation of Christ's kingship to 'the kings of the earth'—governments and civil authorities. The absence of significant discussion of these real life issues is a problem in Torrance's collection of works. One could be left with the impression that Christ's kingship has little relevance to our space-time world."

279. See Speidell, "Soteriological Suspension"; Speidell, *Fully Human in Christ*. See also Van Kuiken, "'Not I, but Christ,'" 252–56.

## 4.2 Jesus as Ascended Priest

On Jesus as ascended priest, the following question will be addressed in chapter 6: Does Torrance affirm the need for Jesus to be an eternal priest?[280] Torrance provides a substantial account of Christ's priesthood in his ascension, and for this he is commended because "Christ's priesthood is not just something he has done, but something that he is continuously doing."[281] While it is hard to find fault with Torrance's articulations on the ascended Christ's priestly ministry, one can quibble and ask if he clearly pushes the discussion far enough. Torrance does not consistently address the question about whether Jesus would have been the mediator between God and human beings irrespective of human sin.[282] Correspondingly, while Torrance affirms the *eternal mediation* of Christ, he does not elaborate on its necessity. These aspects will be addressed in chapter 6.

## 4.3 Jesus as Ascended Prophet

With respect to Jesus as ascended prophet, the following question will be addressed in chapter 6: Does Torrance specifically address how the prophetic ministry of the ascended Jesus is connected to pneumatology and preaching?[283] The role of the Holy Spirit is crucial in understanding the way Torrance conceptualizes the ministry of Jesus as prophet in his ascension. Joseph Sherrard helpfully summarizes the key aspects involved in Torrance's vision of the prophetic ministry of the ascended Jesus as follows: "God's Word to humanity, the perfect word from humanity back to God that is Jesus' perfect obedience, and finally the post-ascension mediation of that accomplished work by the Holy Spirit."[284] This would seem to suggest that Torrance's theology has a robust pneumatology; however, not all are convinced. Fergusson, for example, contends that the Holy Spirit's role in Torrance's theology is rather insular and not actively theologized beyond the walls of the church:

> Admittedly, a correlative account of the Spirit as indwelling and enabling may be less developed here—a similar deficit is apparent in John McLeod Campbell—and interpreters of Torrance

---

280. See section 2.3.2, "Critique #8," in chapter 6 for more on this point.
281. Liston, "Eschatology," 334.
282. Cf. Molnar, *Thomas F. Torrance*, 118n76. This view is known as the *Scotist Hypothesis* or the doctrine of the Primacy of Christ.
283. See section 2.3.3, "Critique #9," in chapter 6 for more on this point.
284. Sherrard, *T. F. Torrance*, 150–51.

may require to think further about this in the future to avoid charges of Christomonism. In his characterization of the two hands of God—Word and Spirit—the work of the first tends to outweigh the second. This in turn may lead to an underdeveloped sense of the Spirit as active in the world outside the community of the church.[285]

Fergusson's criticism is shared to varying degrees by other scholars as well,[286] but, among others, scholars from the Pentecostal tradition are increasingly engaging with Torrance's work and therefore there will be no dearth of ideas to redress this lacuna in Torrance's theology.[287]

## 5. CONCLUSION

This chapter examined Torrance's theological use of the *triplex munus* as a framework from which to think of the present ministry of the ascended Christ. The kingship of Jesus, it was noted, is central to interpreting the significance of the ascension, for Torrance. Jesus is the suffering-yet-victorious king; and while both suffering and victory mark the nature of Jesus's kingship for Torrance, the former takes precedence until the eschaton; while the latter is real, it is currently mostly muted because a full revelation of the kingship of Jesus will entail the final judgment, and since God is gracious, he is giving people time to repent and be ready for that day. The priesthood of Jesus in light of the ascension, according to Torrance, it was observed, is illuminated by three aspects. The first, *endless self-oblation*, by which he emphasizes the ontological and teleological nature of salvation as fulfilled in Christ's ascended human life that is both victorious and vicarious as well as one which has reached its ultimate telos by offering his life as a thanksgiving to God. The second, *eternal intercession*, through which he highlights: (a) how the person of Jesus is intrinsic to his work of intercession; (b) that the goal of this prayer is nothing short of intimate communion with the Father; and (c) that Jesus's prayers and worship on behalf of and in the place of humans is essential because it is not something human beings could ever accomplish on their own. The third, *eternal benediction*, which for Torrance signals the way Jesus concretely blesses his people by sending the Holy Spirit on them, resulting in various gifts being bestowed on the church, which are to be exercised in submission to the unique Priesthood of Christ, and never with the desire to usurp what belongs only to Jesus. The prophetic

---

285. Fergusson, "He Ascended into Heaven," 45.
286. Cf. Habets, *Theosis*, 140; Lee, *Living in Union*, 316.
287. Cf. Yom, *Number, Word, and Spirit*, 85–126.

ministry of Jesus vis-à-vis the ascension, for Torrance, entails the conviction that when the gospel is proclaimed by the church, it is Christ himself who, through the Holy Spirit, is encountering those who are hearing the message. In other words, Christ is not static but active and dynamic. The Scriptures play a key role in illuminating the prophetic office of the ascended Christ because therein lies the faithful testimony about Christ, and when it is proclaimed in the church, Christ uses it to reveal himself to people.

Constructive theological exploration of Torrance's contribution to the *triplex munus* sought to develop the largely embryonic insights related to the kingship of Jesus. Torrance is critiqued for not connecting Jesus's kingship to the lives of Christian believers, but in this section, it was observed that Torrance's emphasis on connecting Jesus's kingship to the theme of victory—over Satan, sin, and evil—promises to shed further light on his doctrine of sanctification. Through a dialogue with Wesleyan theology that stresses *subjective* sanctification, which is a weakness in Torrance's *objective* sanctification emphases, it was noted that both traditions (Wesleyan and Torrancean) can mutually supplement their weaknesses by learning from the strengths of the other. Such a dialogue promises to offer important resources to expand Torrance's minimalistic emphasis on the doctrine of sanctification, even while offering potential correctives to the Wesleyan traditions tendency to neglect the objective foundation for sanctification in Christ.

The priesthood of Jesus marks a high point in Torrance's reflection of the *triplex munus* in light of the ascension. While there are few reasons to quibble with Torrance on this point, it is important to note Torrance's critique of Karl Barth on the priestly ministry of Jesus. It was observed that while Torrance and Barth share many similarities in their theologies of the ascension, Torrance does indeed part ways with his *Doktorvater* on the priestly ministry of the ascended Jesus. The prophetic ministry of the ascended Christ, for Torrance, is grounded in a doctrine of Scripture, which functions not as the terminal locus but as a means to point to Jesus. For some, Torrance's doctrine of Scripture is grounded in sound meta-theological convictions, but weak in the details of biblical exegesis, and while this critique is a valid and necessary one, it was also observed that Torrance's interpretation of select passages at times excels in comparison to some biblical exegetes (for example, Mark 16:19–20). Torrance's doctrine of Scripture needs to be bolstered, it was noted, through a more in-depth engagement with Torrance's wider corpus and by bringing him in dialogue with other theologians on this point. The next chapter will critically evaluate and constructively build on Torrance's theology of the ascension.

# 6

# A Critical Appraisal and Constructive Account

## 1. INTRODUCTION

TORRANCE'S THEOLOGY OF THE ascension is a holistic account of an underexplored theological locus. There are unique theological insights into the *ontology*, *spatiality*, and *present ministry* of the ascended Christ that remind the reader that one is engaging with the work of a theologian who is unafraid to charter theological frontiers. He also manages to integrate theology with worship, so that even a subject as seemingly esoteric as the ascension is shown to be integrally relevant to the church and the world. There is something in his theology for the scientist, the theologian, and the lay Christian, provided each is willing to work hard to engage with his work. The scope of Torrance's work on the ascension is truly impressive and worthy of emulation. Critics and sympathetic readers alike share an admiration for what Torrance has accomplished in his exposition on the ascension. The preceding chapters have provided a detailed overview, critical commentary, analysis, and suggestions for further investigation on the three areas of focus within the ascension in Torrance. Each of the chapters has also highlighted areas that deserve closer critical scrutiny. This chapter will critically engage nine specific criticisms leveled against Torrance's theology of the ascension in the preceding chapters, three within each subsection (*ontology*, *spatiality*, and *present ministry*).

Chapter 3, "The Ontology of the Ascended Christ," highlighted the need to interrogate Torrance on the following aspects: (1) Does Torrance's theological anthropology affirm an eschatological existence for human beings? (2) Does Torrance make clear distinctions ontologically between Christ and the church? (3) Does Torrance's Christology avoid succumbing to some form of kenoticism? Chapter 4, "The Spatiality of the Ascended Christ," underscored the need to investigate the following questions: (4) Does Torrance's theology suffer from an overrealized individual eschatology? (5) Does Torrance have an embryonic Trinitarian spatial theology that can be developed? (6) Does Torrance provide specific details about the location of the ascended Christ? Chapter 5, "The Present Ministry of the Ascended Christ," stressed the need to examine the following subjects: (7) Does Torrance's emphasis on Jesus as King address issues of ethics and politics? (8) Does Torrance affirm the need for Jesus to be an eternal priest? (9) Does Torrance specifically address how the prophetic ministry of the ascended Jesus is connected to pneumatology and preaching? Each of the nine issues provide avenues to clarify Torrance's account of the ascension, as well as constructively build on his theology to provide a more holistic account of the ascension.

## 2. CRITIQUING TORRANCE'S THEOLOGY OF THE ASCENSION

In his 2018 keynote address to the T. F. Torrance Theological Fellowship, Jeremy Begbie correctly captures what is contained in Torrance's *Space, Time, and Resurrection* (a text that contains Torrance's mature writings on the ascension) through the word "vision," which he goes on to qualify as something that is "comprehensive and compelling," and not to mention "audacious."[1] This word *vision* helps one to appreciate as well as to critique Torrance in a manner that is fair and sympathetic. In other words, Torrance is offering a *vision*, not an exhaustive treatment of the subject of the ascension. John Webster sheds further light on the nature of Torrance's theological writing when he explains how "on occasions, analytical and logical order, as well as elegance and economy of phrasing, were compromised in the rush of ideas."[2] Most of the criticisms leveled against Torrance can be explained by Begbie's and Webster's perceptive comments about the nature of Torrance's scholarship. In other words, Torrance is primarily criticized for either being unclear or for leaving many subjects in an embryonic form. The lack of clarity at points seemingly suggests that Torrance is affirming

---

1. Begbie, "Incarnation, Creation, and New Creation," 02:23–02:58. Cf. the published version of this keynote address in *Participatio*: "Incarnation, Creation, and New Creation."

2. Webster, "Thomas Forsyth Torrance," 429.

views that are contrary to his overarching theological position, and the lack of sufficient exploration on some subjects leave the reader disappointed, but to Torrance's credit there are sufficient seed ideas that can be developed. At the outset, one must acknowledge that while all the criticisms leveled against Torrance help to sharpen his already robust contribution to scholarship on the ascension, none of the criticisms suggests that Torrance's theology needs to be overhauled. The next section will therefore examine nine specific kinds of criticisms that function like checkpoints to help readers of Torrance's theology on the ascension to pause, reflect, and carefully consider major concerns as well as opportunities for refinement and constructive development.

## 2.1 Ontology of the Ascended Christ: A Critical Appraisal

Torrance's exposition of the ontology of the ascended Christ has a direct bearing on doctrines such as theological anthropology, ecclesiology, and Christology. The Chalcedonian doctrine plays an important role in helping Torrance stay away from collapsing Christology into theological anthropology or ecclesiology (although these may collapse back the other way in his theology). In other words, Christ retains his humanity in his ascension in a manner that avoids any kind of *Monophysite* conceptions of fusing Christ's divinity into his ascended humanity, or his ascended humanity into the church, or even for that matter false notions of deifying humankind at the eschaton. Christ remains both human and divine in his ascension, the church remains distinct from the ascended humanity of Christ but integrally related to it, and humans remain *human* at the eschatological culmination of God's purposes. Not all are convinced that Torrance has succeeded in providing a robustly orthodox theology of the ascension vis-à-vis theological anthropology, ecclesiology, and Christology. With regard to theological anthropology, Nathan Hitchcock asks those influenced by Barth's theology, and by implication Torrance, to examine whether Barth's negation of humanity as *human* at the eschaton would apply to them as well. For ecclesiology, Stanley MacLean wonders whether Torrance has an eschatologically deficient ecclesiology that elides the distinction between Christ and the church. When it comes to Christology, Andrew Burgess accuses Torrance of an ontologically deficient Christology that must succumb to a form of *kenoticism* because of the distinctive role the ascension plays in uniting God with humankind in his theology. Each of these criticisms deserves careful attention, and in what follows, they will be critically interrogated.

## 2.1.1 Critique #1: Non-Existent Eschatological Anthropology?

Nathan Hitchcock warns readers "about the disappearance of the human" in Karl Barth's theology of the resurrection.[3] Hitchcock locates himself in Barth's corpus to sustain his argument, but he cautions theologians for whom Barth is a kindred spirit to ask whether a similar assessment cannot be made of their theologies as well.[4] Unsurprisingly, Hitchcock lists Torrance among many other theologians who may be susceptible to the weaknesses endemic to Barth's eschatology, particularly because he shares with Barth and other theologians "a full-fledged doctrine of glorification based on participatory categories."[5] While Hitchcock does not offer a sustained argument against Torrance and others who share many commonalities with Barth's theology, his critique provides helpful criteria to assess Torrance's theological anthropology. Hitchcock's critique of Barth also helpfully locates the discussion in eschatology, which is a locus of theology that is not sufficiently interrogated when comparing Barth's and Torrance's theologies of the resurrection and ascension. Burgess, for instance, concludes his comparative study of both theologians on the ascension by maintaining "we hold that the difference between Barth and Torrance is not great."[6] However, Burgess's investigation into Barth's theology of the ascension vis-à-vis Torrance's lacks a critical scrutiny of eschatological loci that are dependent on Jesus's resurrection—not least the future of humanity in the eschaton. Hence, after summarizing Hitchcock's arguments against Barth, the focus will shift to discerning whether there is any warrant to believing Torrance's theology suffers from the malaise Hitchcock unexpectedly discovers in Barth.

Principally, Hitchcock identifies three major themes in Barth's theology of the resurrection: (1) "'lifting into divine duration,' that is, *eternalization*"; (2) "'removal of the veil,' that is, *manifestation*"; and (3) "'raising into union with God,' that is, *incorporation*."[7] Within the theme of *eternalization* in Barth, Hitchcock detects "*the problem of continuity*"—for both the risen Jesus and the eschatological human being.[8] At issue is whether there is any tensed existence in the resurrection, according to Barth, and after a thorough investigation, Hitchcock insists that neither Jesus nor human beings

3. Hitchcock, *Karl Barth*, 184.
4. Hitchcock, *Karl Barth*, xv.
5. Hitchcock, *Karl Barth*, xv.
6. Burgess, *Ascension in Karl Barth*, 133.
7. Hitchcock, *Karl Barth*, 73.
8. Hitchcock, *Karl Barth*, 184.

experience a temporal *after*, after the resurrection.[9] An "omnitemporal" theology of time shapes Barth's understanding of Jesus's resurrection existence, explains Hitchcock, which means that Jesus is given the "freedom to dwell contemporaneously with every time."[10] Grounding his conclusions primarily from an engagement with Barth's mature theology in *Church Dogmatics* IV, among other places, Hitchcock concludes that the risen Jesus has no "*ongoing* history" but only a "*concluded* history with resurrection *duration*."[11] The destiny of humankind is not too hopeful either, avers Hitchcock, given Barth's view of death spelled out in *Church Dogmatics* III as something that is positive and his endorsement of the termination of human existence at one's death.[12] Hitchcock is unconvinced that one can find in Barth any real temporal future for humankind, evidenced in his summative assessment: "[Barth's] doctrine of the resurrection of the flesh has a strange odor of timelessness" deeply embedded within it.[13]

With respect to *manifestation*, Hitchcock notices "*the problem of creatureliness*," in which, arguably, both the resurrected Jesus and the eschatological human shed most of their distinctively human attributes for divine qualities.[14] Hitchcock, in other words, believes that Barth's theology of the resurrection dangerously gravitates toward Eutychianism.[15] Hitchcock prosecutes his case by arguing that Barth's Christology, while formally Reformed, is materially Lutheran, evidenced through three themes that are native to Lutheran soil.[16] First is an emphasis on the oneness rather than the differences between the natures in Christ; second, an acknowledgment of a nonsequential reading of the states of Christ's humiliation and exaltation; and third, an interpretation of *communicatio idiomatum* in which the human nature is infused with "divine properties" and is thereby ontologically

---

9. Hitchcock elaborates on this point in chapter 3 of his work. For more, see Hitchcock, *Karl Barth*, 74–108.

10. Hitchcock, *Karl Barth*, 81, 83.

11. Hitchcock, *Karl Barth*, 87–88. Hitchcock substantiates this claim by referring to Barth, *Church Dogmatics*, 4/1:316, and on p. 88n37, by pointing readers to theologians like T. F. Torrance and Colin Gunton who echo reservations about the continuing priestly ministry of Jesus in Barth's theology.

12. Hitchcock, *Karl Barth*, 94–102. Hitchcock points readers to *Church Dogmatics*, 3/2:624, where Barth writes, "There is no question of the continuation into an indefinite future of a somewhat altered life. The New Testament hope for the other side of death is very different from that. What it looks forward to is the 'eternalising' of this ending life."

13. Hitchcock, *Karl Barth*, 107.

14. Hitchcock, *Karl Barth*, 184.

15. Hitchcock, *Karl Barth*, 145. By charging Barth with Eutychianism, Hitchcock follows Farrow. For more, see Hitchcock, *Karl Barth*, 145n56.

16. Hitchcock, *Karl Barth*, 115–21.

transformed.[17] Barth's theo-logic of the resurrection, Hitchcock maintains, entails the conviction that "the human fulfils creatureliness—by becoming divinized!"[18] This inevitably posits a resurrection wherein only "something flesh-*like*" is revivified, not the flesh *in toto*.[19]

The theme of *incorporation*, Hitchcock insists, ends up with "*the problem of particularity*," wherein there is an elision of the identities of God and human beings.[20] In other words, Hitchcock charges Barth with "eschatological panentheism," which he clarifies is not something Barth ever endorsed so he ameliorates his critique, but nevertheless suggests that it is an inevitable outcome of his mature theological views.[21] Hitchcock reasons that Barth's panentheism, or more accurately "panen*christ*ism,"[22] is the culmination of a theological journey of collapsing the distinct identities of persons: "the resurrection . . . into the Spirit, the Spirit . . . into the risen Son, and, ultimately, all humanity is subsumed into Christ's eschatological corpus."[23] Cumulatively, each of these three arguments convince Hitchcock that there is no future for humankind in Barth's eschatology.[24]

Assessing the soundness of Hitchcock's formidable critique of Barth is not the focus of this work; but it should suffice to say that he is not alone in making such an argument.[25] How would Torrance's theology respond to the three main critiques that Hitchcock levels against Barth's eschatology: (1) the removal of time, (2) the removal of bodies, and (3) the removal of distinct individual identities? It would be unfair to begin a rebuttal without first acknowledging that Torrance's theological anthropology in general, and specifically with reference to eschatology, is underdeveloped.[26] While

17. Hitchcock, *Karl Barth*, 117–19.

18. Hitchcock, *Karl Barth*, 144. Hitchcock's claim that Barth's theological anthropology amounts to a form of divinization is a counterintuitive one, since Barth expressed a strong dislike for deification. Cf. Neder, "Barth on Participation," 352: "If Barth is a critic of all existing models of deification, he is so as an insider to the discussion, as someone who agrees with the validity and importance of the questions, and who intends to think the issue through from its dynamic center in Jesus Christ."

19. Hitchcock, *Karl Barth*, 146.

20. Hitchcock, *Karl Barth*, 184, 149.

21. Hitchcock, *Karl Barth*, 149, 164–66, 169, 179.

22. Hitchcock, *Karl Barth*, 181.

23. Hitchcock, *Karl Barth*, 181.

24. Hitchcock, *Karl Barth*, 184.

25. Cf. Cortez, *Resourcing Theological Anthropology*, 245–58, particularly 253–58.

26. Kim, *Person*, xiv, readily acknowledges that there are some in-depth studies on Torrance's theological anthropology but they "are limited in number." Eric Flett reasons that this lacuna exists "because Torrance's creative powers were never turned fully upon the subject matter [theological anthropology] as a whole." For more, see Flett, *Persons*,

more work needs to be done to develop embryonic insights in Torrance into a robust theological anthropology,[27] one can confidently provide a Torrancean response to the three accusations Hitchcock charges Barth with, and insist that while Barth may be guilty, Torrance is certainly not.

With respect to (1) the removal of time at the eschaton, one can counter this allegation on behalf of Torrance by underscoring the consistency with which he affirms the importance of time in his theology. Apart from briefly entertaining the early Barth's emphasis on the "'eternity/time' dialectic"[28] as a young theologian, Torrance unequivocally affirms the importance of time in his theology. As for the ascension, in his 1938–39 Auburn lectures, he underscores the importance of time when he exclaims, "Time is real for eternity and therefore is not illusory."[29] Even in his mature writings Torrance echoes a similar sentiment when he declares, "In the risen Jesus, therefore, creaturely space and time, far from being dissolved are confirmed in their reality before God."[30] Torrance is reticent in providing too many details about eschatological realities like the new heavens and the new earth, but he goes out of his way to underscore the existence of time in the new creation: "Eternity will not be a timeless monotone but an eternity with time at the heart of it."[31] It is clear, therefore, that there is no removal of time in Torrance's eschatology. What about the removal of bodies at the eschaton?

This second issue, (2) the removal of bodies, unlike the first one answered above, cannot be addressed so easily because some Torrancean scholars have suspiciously wondered whether human beings retain their distinct identities as *humans* within Torrance's theology of *theosis*. Kye Won Lee, for instance, asks whether Torrance's theological anthropology is guilty of monophysitism:

> Torrance strongly rejects the notion of divinization through union with Christ and instead argues for the Greek notion of *theosis*. Contrary to this, he sometimes states that union with Christ means "the exaltation of man to be a partaker of the life and love that God is, and thereby to be a partaker of *divine*

---

*Powers, and Pluralities*, 117. In contemporary scholarship, perhaps, Habets's *Theosis* comes closest to articulating a broad theological vision of human beings vis-à-vis eschatology under the overarching theme of *theosis*.

27. See Woznicki, *Christological Anthropology*. Ziegler and Habets, "Theological Anthropology," has several illuminating essays on Torrance's theological anthropology.

28. MacLean, *Resurrection*, 87.

29. Torrance, *Doctrine of Jesus Christ*, 192.

30. Torrance, *Space, Time, and Resurrection*, 127. See also pp. 87–96.

31. Torrance, *Apocalypse Today*, 176.

*nature.*" Having said this, one may wonder how one cannot be divinized or deified when one partakes of divine nature.[32]

Habets rightly critiques Lee for not considering the diversity of words Torrance uses to communicate *theosis*, such as "participation, engrafting, spiritual union, sacramental union and cognitive union," among others.[33] Since Lee only examines "*union* and *communion*" in his study of Torrance, Habets contends that such a focus "is unable to appreciate how Torrance can reject a *form* of divinisation/deification and yet endorse a *doctrine* of *theosis*."[34]

In the context of evaluating Torrance's doctrine of divine simplicity, Sang Hoon Lee concludes with a mixed assessment, claiming that Torrance's doctrines of the ascension and time vis-à-vis the passibility and impassibility of God contravene divine simplicity, while his doctrine of relational space does not undermine divine simplicity.[35] Essentially, Lee is arguing that Torrance's doctrines of the ascension and time make theological claims that alter the "perichoretic Being"[36] of God—in the case of the ascension by allowing "corporeal elements" and with respect to time by positing "temporal" aspects "into the eternal Being of God."[37] It is evident that Lee interprets Torrance's doctrines of the ascension and time in a Lutheran-like way, specifically by allowing human attributes to be posited to God's being and vice versa, and in doing so is confusing the natures with the person. Torrance, however, is a *Reformed* theologian steeped in patristic theological convictions and grounds his doctrine of the person of Christ in the "hypostatic union," which confines itself to the "*inconfuse, immutatabiliter, indivise* and *inseparabiliter*" perimeter.[38]

32. Lee, *Living in Union*, 317.

33. Habets, *Theosis*, 109.

34. Habets, *Theosis*, 108. It must be noted that Calvin, too, accepted certain expressions of theosis, while rejecting Osiander's version of theosis. Therefore, there is a precedent in what Torrance was doing. For more, see Habets, *Theosis*, 101–2.

35. See Lee, "Doctrine of Divine Simplicity," 199–200, where he summarizes his argument as follows: "Torrance's construal of divine simplicity does not fully accord with the traditional one that rejects any form of introduction of creaturely composites or contingency into the Being of God. And yet, taking his Trinitarian notion of space into account . . . for Torrance, the one God embraces the created elements into himself through Christ without vitiating his oneness: God comprehensively comprehends the creaturely others in his indivisible oneness."

36. Lee, "Doctrine of Divine Simplicity," 209.

37. Lee, "Doctrine of Divine Simplicity," 210.

38. See Habets, *Theosis*, 116, where Habets notes that Torrance accuses Roman Catholics and Lutherans of the sixteenth century for transgressing the four-point Chalcedonian regulations that interpret the "hypostatic union."

With respect to time vis-à-vis the passibility/impassibility debate, it is key to understand that while Torrance may sound inconsistent on this point, the overarching framework under which he operates makes clear distinctions between the immanent and economic Trinity, and also affirms the *extra Calvinisticum*. Both entail that any contrary sounding statements are "functioning at the economic level only."[39] Torrance's emphasis on the *hypostatic union* and the *extra Calvinisticum* is missing from Lee's analysis, and so, while some passages from Torrance can be read in the ways that Lee suggests, a more faithful reading of Torrance's entire corpus along with foundational theological impulses (Reformed and patristic) would have prevented one from coming to Lee's conclusions.[40] It cannot be overemphasized therefore that "Torrance asserts in unequivocal terms that human beings remain human beings, even in *theosis*."[41] This would undercut any attempt to read Torrance's theology as one that denies human bodies at the eschaton.

Given a Torrancean rebuttal of points (1) and (2) above, one would be hard pressed to find any concerns related to (3), the denial of distinct individualities at the eschaton. Torrance expressly rejects panentheism when he underscores God's freedom from human beings: "For he does not need relation to us to be what he is as the living acting God,"[42] and from the world: "There is no necessary relation between God and the world which he has freely created, for God does not need the world to be God."[43] While one would have expected Torrance to flesh out his eschatology in more detail, his sermons testify unequivocally to his robust affirmation of a distinct embodied existence for human beings:

> There are people who imagine that in eternity all personalities are swallowed up and lost in God, that all temporal distinctions, and all that is finite and individual, melt into the infinite. That may be the view of some heathen Nirvana, but it is certainly not the teaching of the Christian faith. . . . The Christian hope is

---

39. Habets, *Theosis*, 86.

40. It must be emphasized that Torrance adopts a Reformed perspective on this issue, which affirms a *communio idiomatum*, wherein the attributes of each nature are rightly said to apply only to the person of the Son; whereas, in the Lutheran understanding, it is the *communicatio idiomatum*, which applies the attributes of one nature to the other nature and vice versa. For more, see Habets, "Fallen Humanity," 41n97. This insight also helps shed light on why Torrance would not compromise God's being or human ontology by allowing any mixing of divinity with humanity and vice versa.

41. Habets, *Theosis*, 128.

42. Torrance, *Christian Doctrine of God*, 4.

43. Torrance, *Christian Doctrine of God*, 207.

fulfilled only in a new heaven and a new earth peopled with human beings living in holy and loving fellowship with God, with one another, and in harmony with the fullness of creation.[44]

Each of the three critiques Hitchcock levels against Barth, therefore, does not apply to Torrance. While more work is required to develop a well-rounded theological anthropology from Torrance's corpus, one will find clearly distinguishable embodied humans at the eschaton in such a theology.

### 2.1.2 Critique #2: Eschatologically Deficient Ecclesiology?

Stanley MacLean outlines an argument that Torrance's eschatology elides the distinction between Christ and church.[45] The root cause for such a tendency, MacLean avers, lies in Torrance's prioritization of his christological hermeneutic over the testimony of Scripture, which he attempts to prove by scrutinizing "the theme of judgment" in Torrance's eschatology.[46] MacLean builds his argument by summarizing key insights from Torrance's ecclesiology, after which he expresses his main concern. MacLean correctly notes that "the Body of Christ" is a central analogy Torrance uses to underscore the *ontology* as well as the *teleology* of the church.[47] In other words, the relationship between Christ and the church is not symbolic but "a concrete ontological reality"; while at the same time acknowledging that there is "an eschatological reality" to the church's existence in which she "still has to become the Body of Christ."[48] At issue, for MacLean, is a twofold concern: (1) about Torrance's theology and (2) about the theological terms that Torrance adopts.[49]

With respect to (1) theology, MacLean contends that "Torrance presses this Body image too far, so that the relationship between the Christ and the church becomes too close."[50] This belief leads MacLean to conclude that at the interface of Christology, ecclesiology, and eschatology, "the net effect of . . . [Torrance's] procedure is that the doctrine of final judgment is left debilitated."[51] MacLean is of the view that there is no place for a "final judg-

---

44. Torrance, *Apocalypse Today*, 176–77.
45. MacLean, *Resurrection*, 196–97.
46. MacLean, *Resurrection*, 196.
47. MacLean, *Resurrection*, 196.
48. MacLean, *Resurrection*, 196.
49. MacLean, *Resurrection*, 196–97.
50. MacLean, *Resurrection*, 196.
51. MacLean, *Resurrection*, 196.

ment" in Torrance's theology because Christology dominates the discussion so much that the suffering of Christ on the cross is construed to mean "that the final judgment is already past."[52] If one were to posit a future judgment on the church in Torrance's theology, MacLean insists, it will be as perplexing as maintaining that "Christ [is] judging his own body."[53]

MacLean then goes on to argue (2) that Torrance's use of the language of "*anhypostasis/enhypostasis*" in his ecclesiological discussions confirms his views about the collapse of the church into Christ and the inability to create space for eschatological judgment.[54] "The *anhypostasis* and *enhypostasis* assert Christ's substitutionary atonement for the church. Yet this means that the church has no *per se* existence except in the person of Christ."[55] Ultimately, this notion, MacLean asserts, stresses ontology to such an extent that there is no room for teleology, and consequently no logic to a future judgment for humankind before God.[56]

MacLean's arguments against Torrance's eschatology vis-à-vis the final judgment can be summarized in a threefold manner as: (1) a hermeneutical argument, (2) a theological argument, and relatedly (3) a theological-linguistic argument. To be fair to MacLean, he articulates his critique at the end of his important study on the historical development of Torrance's eschatology, and perhaps, does not wish to or have space to provide an in-depth justification for his views.[57] Nonetheless, while MacLean's overall project on Torrance's eschatology is an impressive and much-needed one, his three arguments against Torrance's eschatology are unfairly critical of Torrance and at points even inaccurate.

Paul Molnar clearly addresses points (1) and (2) of MacLean's critiques.[58] In response to (1), the hermeneutical argument that claims that Torrance prioritizes Christology over Scripture, Molnar argues that in following Christ to understand eschatology (and all aspects of theology), Torrance is actually being biblical: "Torrance's doctrine of the church as the body of Christ is exactly right because it is so thoroughly Christocentric."[59] Molnar is on sound biblical and theological grounds when he argues in this fashion,

52. MacLean, *Resurrection*, 197.
53. MacLean, *Resurrection*, 196.
54. MacLean, *Resurrection*, 197.
55. MacLean, *Resurrection*, 197.
56. MacLean, *Resurrection*, 197.
57. Shepherd, "Body of Christ," 29, correctly observes that "these critiques are not extensively elaborated upon" by MacLean. Cf. MacLean, *Resurrection*, 195–99, where he outlines various critiques against Torrance.
58. For more, see Molnar, "Introduction," li–lii.
59. Molnar, "Introduction," li.

and therefore one cannot but concur with his assessment. As for (2), the theological argument that Torrance ignores the distinction between Christ and the church, Molnar insists that MacLean has misread Torrance on this point. Specifically, Molnar contends that MacLean "fails to take account of the reasons why Torrance rejected identifying the church as Christ's body with Christ as its head"; and this oversight on MacLean's part is revealed when he concludes that a final judgment for Torrance can only mean a judgment of Christ.[60] Molnar counters the charge that the final judgment is coterminous with Christ's judgment on the cross by clarifying Torrance has room for *both* an emphatic declaration that "reconciliation, justification and redemption are in reality completed events in the life, death, resurrection and ascension of the coming Lord," *and* for a future judgment of the church.[61] Molnar rightly points readers to *Space, Time, and Resurrection* to underscore the existence of an eschatological judgment in Torrance's theology.[62] In an important article entitled "What Is the Church?," Torrance is perhaps most categorical in enunciating his theology of eschatological judgment, and in so doing challenges the very foundation of arguments such as MacLean's:

> He will come again as Judge, and judgment will begin at the House of God, begin at the Church. Therefore the Church is summoned to cast itself under His judgment, to bring all that it has done and failed to do to the feet of its Lord in humble confession that it may be cleansed and forgiven, and all that is wrong put away. The Church is also summoned to cast all its hope upon the Advent of Christ, for He will come not only to judge the quick and the dead but to renew His creation and to present the Church to Himself at last as a pure and spotless Bride. It is the Advent which reminds the Church that although it is already one Body with Christ through the Spirit, it has yet to be made one Body with Him in the consummation of His Kingdom. Until then the Church is the Bride of Christ waiting for the great Marriage Supper of the Lamb, and can only live in that expectation and hope.[63]

Considering this clear testimony from Torrance himself, it would be very hard to sustain MacLean's claim that there is no room for a final judgment in Torrance's eschatology. What about (3), Torrance's use of the *an/*

60. Molnar, "Introduction," li–lii.

61. Molnar, "Introduction," lii.

62. Molnar, "Introduction," liin187, where he points readers to *Space, Time, and Resurrection*, 157–58, for an explication of a future judgment of believers in the theology of Torrance.

63. Torrance, "What Is the Church?," 15.

*en-hypostasis*? Does this really undermine the church's distinct ontological existence, as MacLean claims? Since Torrance appropriates the *an/en-hypostasis* from its christological context into ecclesiology, it is essential to interpret its meaning christologically.[64] Robert Walker helpfully does this when he explains, "The church owes its very being and life entirely to the *anhypostatic* act of God in Christ, but in Christ the church is *enhypostatically* real *in Christ*, real in being, life, and very humanity in him."[65] It would be wrong to construe Torrance's use of the *an/en-hypostasis* as ontologically conflating Christ with the church because he explicitly rejects such a conception: "It is really so theologically wrong to speak of the Church as the extension of the Incarnation as if it could be the prolongation of Christ Himself."[66] But, more importantly, it is wrong because Torrance's ecclesiology is grounded in the Lordship of Christ over his church, and when the use of *an/en-hypostasis* is understood in that context, it cannot but entail that "Christ is the Church means that He is also the Head and Lord of the Church, and that the Church is only His servant."[67] While Torrance's eschatology certainly needs to be expounded and articulated in more detail, each of the three criticisms that MacLean charges Torrance with can be adequately rebutted.

### 2.1.3 Critique #3: Ontologically Defective Christology?

Andrew Burgess accuses Torrance of *kenoticism* because he believes that to affirm the ascension, not the cross, as the culmination of the atonement leads to the following conundrum: "If the new humanity is only joined to the life of God in Jesus' ascension, is Jesus' divinity in some way reduced so that His humanity is not to be regarded as united to the life of God? Or, is the union of His two natures in some way imperfect until the ascension?"[68] In other words, since Torrance believes that it is only at the ascension that "our humanity in Christ is taken up into the full Communion of Father, Son and Holy Spirit in life and love,"[69] Burgess maintains that one cannot but cast aspersions about the sanctity of Jesus's being or of his relationship with

---

64. See Walker, "Innovative Fruitfulness," 198, where he explains that Torrance initially appropriated the *an-en-hypostasis* in 1954, but did so "cautiously." On p. 198n42, Walker explains Torrance's reticence by noting that since Torrance was exporting something that was more at home in Christology, he wanted only "to introduce the novelty of the application with care."

65. Walker, "Innovative Fruitfulness," 199.

66. Torrance, "What Is the Church?," 9.

67. Torrance, "What Is the Church?," 9.

68. Burgess, *Ascension in Karl Barth*, 128–29.

69. Torrance, *Space, Time, and Resurrection*, 133.

the Father during the incarnation.[70] To this end, Burgess asks some probing questions:

> How is it that Jesus' humanity is only (fully) united to the life of God in His ascension? The reading of Jesus' history involved appears to require that some aspect of Jesus' being as the eternal Son is either given up or put aside in the incarnation, and then taken up again in the ascension. Indeed it might imply that what Jesus gives up is the fullness of His relationship to the Father, as this would explain the claim that it is only the ascension that fully unites humanity to God in Christ. All this appears to cast a troubling light back upon Jesus' incarnate life prior to the ascension. To take this line of thought further, if our humanity is not united to God's life in the very fact of the incarnation, then what must we say of Jesus' being?[71]

Burgess sheds further light on his critique when he identifies a possible resolution to the conundrum he poses, but then believes that even that in the final analysis fails. He writes, "The solution to the difficulty initially appears to lie in Torrance's formulation of the matter in terms of *new* humanity in Christ—meaning thereby humanity as perfected through the life-acts of Jesus, and in particular His death."[72] However, Burgess reckons that even with such a response it becomes hard not to question the legitimacy of the hypostatic union during the interim period (between incarnation and ascension) and therefore Torrance has no room for escape: "That Jesus only presents a new humanity before the Father in the ascension still appears to cast a shadow over the unity of God and humanity throughout the incarnation."[73] While Burgess finds Torrance's view on Jesus's ontology problematic, he believes Barth is able to circumvent such a critique by subscribing to the view that it is not at the ascension that our humanity in Christ is finally united to the Triune God, but "*throughout* His incarnation" it was true of Jesus—he "presents the Father with perfect human obedience at every turn."[74] How does one provide a Torrancean response to Burgess's forceful critique?

Three specific responses can be made to address the heart of Burgess's critique. First, one can argue that Torrance is being biblically and theologically grounded when he argues that the ascension is the climax of the atonement, and therefore the problems Burgess envisions against his theology

70. Burgess, *Ascension in Karl Barth*, 126.
71. Burgess, *Ascension in Karl Barth*, 126.
72. Burgess, *Ascension in Karl Barth*, 126.
73. Burgess, *Ascension in Karl Barth*, 126.
74. Burgess, *Ascension in Karl Barth*, 126.

do not apply. When Torrance argues in such a fashion, he can be said to follow William Milligan who subscribes to the view that the Old Testament atonement ritual did not conclude with the animal's death but with the presentation of the animal's blood in the holy of holies; with this theological framework as the background, one must view the cross as part of the atonement with the ascension being its climax.[75] In a more recent work on the ascension vis-à-vis the atonement, Burgess acknowledges the contribution of David Moffitt's exegetical work, which is essentially in agreement with Milligan's and Torrance's theological views on the subject. Writes Burgess,

> An important addition to the conversation comes from recent discussion of Jesus's ascension and atoning work as High Priest in Hebrews. . . . Moffitt examines the strong emphasis in Hebrews on Jesus's self-offering as culminating in the heavenly sanctuary. . . . Central to his work is the argument that in Old Testament sacrificial liturgy the death of the animal was not the culmination but a necessary step in the movement, with the offering of the "life" of the animal in the sanctuary marking the peak of atoning action. So Jesus's ascension to the Father as the "lamb who was slain" and presentation of his life as sacrifice, in the true sanctuary, mark the peak of his atoning work.[76]

Based on this insight, one must at least acknowledge that Burgess's initial critique of Torrance is greatly ameliorated, given that there is a strong biblical and theological basis for Torrance's view.

Second, one can assert that Torrance's theology of the incarnation does not undermine the hypostatic union when his emphasis on the *fallen* humanity of Christ is properly understood.[77] Torrance clearly affirms that Jesus took on a *fallen* human nature in the incarnation: "Although he assumed our fallen and corrupt humanity when he became flesh, in assuming it he sanctified it in himself, and all through his earthly life he overcame our sin through his righteousness, our impurity through his purity, condemning sin in our flesh by the sheer holiness of his life within it."[78] Torrance's use of the *an/en-hypostasis* helps shed light on how Jesus's human *nature* was *fallen*, but his *person* was sinless:[79] "The doctrine of *anhypostasia and enhy-*

---

75. See Milligan, *Ascension*, 139. Cf. Torrance, *Space, Time, and Resurrection*, 114.

76. Burgess, "Ascension," 379.

77. For more on the *fallen* humanity of Christ in Torrance's theology, see: Van Kuiken, *Christ's Humanity*; Chiarot, *Unassumed Is the Unhealed*; Cameron, *Flesh and Blood*.

78. Torrance, *Space, Time, and Resurrection*, 53.

79. See McFarland, "Fallen or Unfallen?," 399–415, who also uses the distinction between *nature* and *person* to make sense of the fallenness of Christ's human nature, but the sinlessness of his person.

*postasia* (put together as one concept) helps us . . . to understand or express how God the Son was made in the likeness of our flesh of sin, and yet was not himself a sinner. . . . He assumed our corrupt and estranged humanity, but in such a way as at the same time to heal and sanctify in himself what he assumed."[80] In other words, Torrance's insights enable one to affirm *both* the fallenness of Christ's human nature, but also the sinlessness of his person.

Oliver Crisp, a former fierce critic of the *fallenness* view, now concedes that Torrance's position is actually tenable, and furthermore provides a solution to the ongoing debate about Christ's human nature by allowing for an affirmation of *anhypostatic fallenness* but *enhypostatic sinlessness*.[81] In other words, Crisp explains, "The Word of God may assume a human nature that would be constitutionally fallen in abstraction from the act of assumption, so to speak, but that is 'healed' of its fallen state—including the removal of original sin—through the very act of assumption by means of which the Word hypostatically unites himself to his human nature."[82] Crisp correctly identifies a theology of *anhypostatic fallenness* but *enhypostatic sinlessness* in Torrance's work and helpfully shows how it can provide a resolution to the ongoing debate between the *fallen* and *unfallen* views of the human nature of Christ.[83] However, Torrancean theologians will also rightly argue that Crisp has only identified one aspect within Torrance's thinking on the matter.

There is in Torrance's theology *both* an emphasis on the immediate healing of human nature at the incarnation *and* a continual healing of human nature through the course of the incarnate life of Christ.[84] Thomas Noble, for example, brings out this dual aspect in Torrance's thinking very forcefully: "Christ assumed our common 'sinful flesh' from his mother, and while it was still 'fallen' in him during his earthly life in the sense that it suffered from infirmities, temptation, and mortality, yet it was sanctified and so sinless from the moment of conception."[85] Noble goes on to add: "What must also be said, however, is that while the humanity of Christ was sinless, his sanctification of humanity was not finished at the point of his

---

80. Torrance, *Incarnation*, 231–32.

81. See Crisp, "On the Vicarious Humanity," 238. This view shares similarities with Darren Sumner's position. For more, see Sumner, "Fallenness and *Anhypostasis*." Sumner uses the phrase "*anhypostatic* fallenness" on pp. 195 and 209.

82. Crisp, "On the Vicarious Humanity," 238.

83. In an earlier work, Crisp argues against the *fallenness* position. For more, see Crisp, "Did Christ?"

84. Torrance, *Space, Time, and Resurrection*, 53.

85. Noble, "Incarnation and Atonement," 186.

human birth."[86] Theologians studying Torrance's view on this dual aspect (of immediate and continual healing of human nature) differ on whether Torrance's position is sound.

Kevin Chiarot contends that it is unsound because, for example with reference to "Christ's will," he believes it entails that it is "perfectly obedient, perpetually condemned, progressively sanctified, and increasingly in conflict with the will of God."[87] Unsurprisingly, he identifies such a view as "not coherent."[88] Jerome Van Kuiken, however, believes that Torrance's view is sound and that Chiarot does not read Torrance accurately, because he wrongly applies "what Torrance says of corporate humanity (i.e. that it is genuinely rebellious and sinful) to Christ's own humanity."[89] Van Kuiken goes on to explain how Christ's humanity can be both immediately sanctified at the incarnation and also continually sanctified through the course of Christ's life: "Christ's progressive sanctification does not negate his full sanctification at conception, for he does not become holier; rather, his full holiness extends itself into ever-new situations."[90] While a fuller exploration of this debate will take us beyond the scope of this project, it is possible that Torrance could have articulated his view more clearly to avoid being misread. There are other nuances to the debate, however, that must be briefly highlighted.

Noble believes that instead of focusing on the difference between the fallen "nature" and sinless "person" of Christ, it is better to highlight the distinction between being "fallen" and "sinful."[91] He does this in order to alert readers to the fact that Torrance did not share Edward Irving's views on the incarnation, wherein Christ "was free of actual sin," but "in his human birth the Son took our 'constitutional sin,' the law of sin and death at work in the flesh."[92] Such a conclusion, Noble argues, legitimately elicits criticisms of Irving, namely, that he was "compromising the sinlessness of Christ."[93] Noble's stress on distinguishing Torrance from Irving is important in the

---

86. Noble, "Incarnation and Atonement," 186.
87. Chiarot, *Unassumed Is the Unhealed*, 202.
88. Chiarot, *Unassumed Is the Unhealed*, 202.
89. Van Kuiken, *Christ's Humanity*, 40.
90. Van Kuiken, *Christ's Humanity*, 40.
91. Noble, "Incarnation and Atonement," 186.
92. Noble, "Incarnation and Atonement," 186. Noble here draws on and points readers to Van Kuiken, *Christ's Humanity*, 12–21, for an accessible overview of Edward Irving's views on this subject.
93. Noble, "Incarnation and Atonement," 186.

ongoing debate about what kind of human nature Christ assumed in the incarnation.[94]

Third, one must clearly distinguish between *Christ's* humanity and the *rest of humankind*. Sandra Fach makes such an argument when she responds to Burgess's critique by noting that he does not pay sufficient attention to Torrance's distinction between Jesus's own humanity and the rest of humankind.[95] In other words, she contends that Torrance argues in the way he does to make a "soteriological" point, while Burgess interprets him in an "ontological" manner, which is why many problems ensue.[96] Fach writes, "Barth's claim that Christ's ontological reality is no different post-ascension is not contentious. But fallen humanity is in need of perfection in order to stand in the presence of God. Objections that centre on how an understanding of soteriological 'events' may compromise Christ's ontological status miss the point."[97] Fach continues her rebuttal to Burgess (and Barth) by underscoring the neglect of Heb 2:10: "It was fitting that God for whom and through whom all things exist, in bringing many children to glory, should make the pioneer of their salvation perfect through suffering."[98] According to Fach, Burgess himself recognizes such an emphasis when he seemingly concedes that: "Jesus' work of perfecting humanity is not complete until the drama of atonement has been fully played out—that is, the perfection of humanity is not finalised until dramatic coherence is brought to Jesus' life by His obedient death—but that does not mean that Jesus' humanity prior to the ascension is not perfect."[99] Fach counters Burgess by asking:

---

94. See Van Kuiken, "Sinless Savior," 339n60, where he notes that theologians such as Donald Macleod, Stephen J. Wellum, Michael Allen, and Katherine Sonderegger do not sufficiently distinguish between the views of Edward Irving on the one hand and Thomas F. Torrance and Karl Barth on the other hand. Relatedly, see also the point Van Kuiken makes about the ongoing relevance of Irving in the debate. On p. 338, Van Kuiken argues that in the debate between the "fallen" and "unfallen" views on Christ's human nature it is important to "*leave Irving behind.*" By this he means that Irving may be a "fascinating figure" but he is "a red herring in the current fallenness debate and an albatross around the necks of more recent fallenness theologians, whether hung there by themselves or their opponents. Rather than trying to rehabilitate him or appealing to him as a protomartyr for the cause, today's fallenness proponents would serve themselves better by explicitly severing ties with his heterodox stance." There is wisdom in both Noble's clarification and Van Kuiken's exhortation.

95. Fach, "Answering the Upwards Call," 224.

96. Fach, "Answering the Upwards Call," 224. Cf. Farrow, *Ascension and Ecclesia*, 241–54, who criticizes Barth for a similar shortcoming.

97. Fach, "Answering the Upwards Call," 224.

98. Fach, "Answering the Upwards Call," 225.

99. See Fach, "Answering the Upwards Call," 225, where she critically interacts with Burgess, *Ascension in Karl Barth*, 127.

"But what about 'our' humanity—and is this not the humanity that Jesus assumed? Fallen humanity is in need of perfection. If fallen humanity is made perfect at the point of the incarnation, then the events of Jesus' life are rendered meaningless."[100]

Douglas Farrow also responds to both Barth and Burgess in helpful ways, stating that Barth's theology of the ascension "unites the doctrine of the two states and that of the two natures into a unified theory of the incarnation, such that the being of 'the one Jesus Christ' is understood in terms of two simultaneous and mutually qualifying movements—the humiliation of God and the exaltation of man."[101] Fach helpfully illuminates Farrow's main criticism of Barth by clarifying that Farrow is not against a theology that holds the person and work of Christ closely together, but he finds fault with the extension of it into a theology where "Christ's history goes around in circles."[102] Fach grounds her critique of Barth in what Farrow emphasizes: "The divine descent/human ascent scheme simply cannot accommodate the wholeness of priestly action."[103] In other words, given such a theological position, it becomes almost impossible to make meaningful sense of the heavenly intercession of Christ; as Fach exclaims, "There is no room to explore the distinct nature of Christ's mediatorial role as a result of the ascension."[104] Farrow's response to Burgess is more forceful. He contends that Burgess obsesses over ontology and completely misses not only the distinction between "ontology" and "soteriology," but also the teleological role the ascension and return of Christ play in pointing to the Spirit's work of bringing the story of salvation to its ultimate culmination.[105]

> What is not complete before his ascension, indeed before his parousia, is the work of preparing our humanity for the fullness of the gift of the Spirit.... What follows from it is the capacity to distinguish soteriology from ontology; or, better, to distinguish one kind of soteriology from another, by respecting the difference between man's need for God qua creature and his need qua sinner. That, and the capacity to tell a story that is and remains a *human* story, about human suffering and triumph, precisely

---

100. Fach, "Answering the Upwards Call," 225.
101. Farrow, *Ascension and Ecclesia*, 244.
102. Fach, "Answering the Upwards Call," 226.
103. Farrow, *Ascension and Ecclesia*, 252.
104. Fach, "Answering the Upwards Call," 226.
105. Farrow, review of *Ascension in Karl Barth*, 207–8.

as a story about God with us and about our own "deification" in the Spirit.[106]

Overall, Burgess must be commended because his work advances theological discussion on the ascension in important ways by highlighting an underemphasized theme in Barth's theology, but also by bringing Barth into dialogue with key theological interlocutors in Thomas F. Torrance, Douglas Farrow, and Robert Jenson.[107] His critique of Torrance raises important questions and concerns, for which one can respond with a sound Torrancean rebuttal, as the above subsection demonstrates.

## 2.2 Spatiality of the Ascended Christ: A Critical Appraisal

Having examined Torrance's ontology of the ascended Christ through the first three critiques, it is appropriate at this stage to scrutinize Torrance's spatiality of the ascended Christ in the next three critiques (#4–6). Torrance's exposition on the spatiality of the ascension affirms the humanity of Christ in a manner consistent with Reformed theological convictions as opposed to Lutheran ones. Three levels of thought undergird Torrance's contribution to the ascension vis-à-vis space and time: a christological level, a Trinitarian level, and an epistemological level that provides important desiderata for how to use theological language in ways appropriate to theological mysteries like the ascension. The christological aspect is infused with unique soteriological insights about how the ascension guarantees that heaven is a place that can be inhabited by human beings, as well as eschatological concerns that underscore the full realization of God's purposes in a new heaven and a new earth. It is this eschatological aspect, specifically individual eschatology, that is troubling for some, because it seems to suggest a form of an overrealized eschatology. The Trinitarian aspect of Torrance's thought emphasizes perichoresis in a manner that highlights the intimacy within the Trinity as well as the distinct identity of each person, all of which have implications for humankind and creation. Admittedly, Torrance's thought with regard to Trinity and space and time is nascent and in need of further constructive development. The epistemological aspect conveys how theological language can be used to accentuate both how the ascension is spatial and temporal but also beyond the human categories of space and time with reference to this fallen creation. Artistic language, or in other words language that recognizes mystery after a certain point in theology,

---

106. Farrow, review of *Ascension in Karl Barth*, 207–8.
107. See Burgess, *Ascension in Karl Barth*, 109–87.

is key to properly understanding Torrance's contributions in this area. For some, however, Torrance's language is rather vague and inadequate because he does not provide specific information about where Christ is located in his ascension. Each of these criticisms needs to be engaged with, and at points certain modifications to Torrance's thought will be accepted to fill some gaps in his theology.

### 2.2.1 Critique #4: Overrealized Individual Eschatology?

Torrance clearly affirms both a *proleptic* and an *expectant* eschatology. In other words, he insists that Jesus's resurrection has already brought in new creation in the midst of old creation,[108] but he also recognizes that the full realization of "the new creation in Christ is hidden from us," because if it were fully revealed it would mean the final judgment and all the consequent entailments that come along with it.[109] Overall, Torrance affirms both the *already* and *not yet* aspects of biblical eschatology, but with respect to individual eschatology, his view seems to conflate the *not yet* with the *already*. While Torrance does not name his view, others have associated it with an *instantaneous resurrection* position.[110]

*Prima facie*, Torrance's view on individual eschatology seems to affirm an instantaneous resurrection.

> When the believer dies, he goes to be with Christ and is in his immediate presence, participant in him and made like him. That is to each believer the *parousia* of Christ to him. Yet when this is regarded on the plane of history and of the on-going processes of the fallen world, the death of each believer means that his body is laid to sleep in the earth, waiting until the redemption of the body and the recreation of all things at the final *Parousia*. Looked at from the perspective of the new creation there is no gap between the death of the believer and the *parousia* of Christ, but looked at from the perspective of time that decays and crumbles away, there is a lapse in time between them.[111]

On closer examination, however, Torrance nuances his position to affirm either an immediate resurrection (from the perspective of the believer who has died) or an interim period (from the perspective of the loved one

---

108. For more, see Torrance, *Conflict and Agreement*, 1:304–15.
109. Torrance, *Space, Time, and Resurrection*, 98.
110. Yates, "Immediate or Intermediate?," especially pp. 315–17.
111. Torrance, *Space, Time, and Resurrection*, 102.

who remains on this fallen earth), as Stephen Travis's interpretation confirms.[112] Travis explains, "Torrance is able to suggest that when the believer dies he goes to be with Christ (*cf.* Phil. 1:23) and receives his resurrection body. From *his* perspective there is no gap between his death and Christ's parousia. But from the perspective of those who live on in time, there is an interval between his death and the parousia—hence the texts which speak of a still future general resurrection."[113]

Within the context of *Space, Time, and Resurrection*, in which the above passage is found, Torrance points readers to Emil Brunner's work for an exposition that is kindred to his, with the important caveat that he rejects Brunner's "docetic conception of the resurrection."[114] Principally, Brunner believes that Paul in his letter to the Philippians affirms both an immediate encounter with the Lord after death and a resurrection at the eschaton, without any "attempt to harmonize them" nor any intention to communicate that there is a "contradiction between the [two] statement[s]."[115] In effect, Brunner believes in an immediate resurrection of believers after death because they are no longer in "the earthly" space-time continuum characterized by "a before and an after and intervals of time which embrace centuries or even millenniums."[116] In other words, this is a *relational* accounting of the issue of death, resurrection, and the interim period: from God's perspective, resurrection happens instantaneously; but from a fallen human perspective, there is a long interim period.[117] Says Brunner, "The date of death differs for each man, for the day of death belongs to this world. Our day of resurrection is the same for all and yet is not separated from the day of death by intervals of centuries—for these time-intervals are here, not there in the presence of God, where 'a thousand years are as a day.'"[118]

Torrance, too, arguably is highlighting a similar point—namely, a *relational* way of thinking about the issue. Andrew Purves helpfully illuminates the meaning of Torrance's vexing passage by stating that Torrance is using a "differential view of time" as a way of thinking about the postmortem state of human beings.[119] In another context, he further expounds the meaning of this passage by asserting that it is in the final instance mysterious how one

---

112. Travis, *Christian Hope*, 111–12.
113. Travis, *Christian Hope*, 111–12.
114. Torrance, *Space, Time, and Resurrection*, 102n14.
115. Brunner, *Eternal Hope*, 151.
116. Brunner, *Eternal Hope*, 152.
117. Brunner, *Eternal Hope*, 152.
118. Brunner, *Eternal Hope*, 152.
119. Purves, "End of Ministry," 281.

can simultaneously affirm an interim period after death and an immediate resurrection.[120] While Purves's explanation might be the best way to answer the meaning of Torrance's view on the postmortem state of believers, not all are convinced by its theological acuity.[121]

John Yates, for example, believes Torrance's position entails an instantaneous resurrection, wherein "all the dying (and all the living) participate in the events of the End together" because they experience their resurrection timelessly.[122] Such a view, according to Yates, is "theologically" and "philosophically" deficient for the following reasons: (1) it ruptures biblical eschatology by viewing the culmination of God's purposes in the "timeless," not the "temporal" realm; (2) it transgresses the boundaries of theological anthropology by ascribing exclusively divine qualities like "atemporality" to a human being; (3) it contravenes sound philosophical thinking by viewing the resurrection as a "'timeless change,'" straining credulity in the process because transformation can only happen "in time"; (4) it severs the "continuity" between the body at death and the resurrection body of the believer by maintaining an instantaneous resurrection; and finally (5) it undermines the biblical testimony and the orthodox Christian belief that Jesus's body was in the tomb for three days before he was resurrected.[123] Is Yates's analysis correct, and if so, how can Torrance's theology respond to criticisms that are associated with the instantaneous resurrection view?

Two specific responses can be given to Yates's critique. First, one must clarify that Torrance is only being suggestive not dogmatic when he writes about the postmortem state of the believer.[124] This is clearly evidenced when he acknowledges that "it is impossible for us to think completely together the two times [fallen time and new creation time] in which we are involved, yet we may discern something of how the two 'moments' fall together in our being in Christ."[125] Yates himself acknowledges this point when he notes that "Torrance is not altogether clear here," before moving on to infer his

---

120. In a discussion about his chapter "The End of Ministry," Purves clarifies the meaning of Torrance's passage about the postmortem state of the believer vis-à-vis his/her resurrection when he explains that Torrance "taught a differential view [of time]. Namely, that in tick-tock time, when we die, we're dead, but in God's time, in the twinkling of an eye, we are raised with Christ. And it's holding that together. We're holding together something that can't be thought." For more, see Purves, "Purves-Handbook," 1:03:53–1:04:24.

121. Cf. Yates, "Immediate or Intermediate?," 315–17.
122. Yates, "Immediate or Intermediate?," 315.
123. Yates, "Immediate or Intermediate?," 316–17.
124. Torrance, *Space, Time, and Resurrection*, 102.
125. Torrance, *Space, Time, and Resurrection*, 102.

meaning and then critique it.[126] This lack of clarity on Torrance's part is important to note as it may assist one in sympathetically evaluating his view on the post-mortem state of believers.

Relatedly, it is no secret that the theme of eschatology in general is rather embryonic in Torrance, and therefore, one must be careful about inferring too much from brief statements that Torrance makes. Stanley MacLean sheds light on the *ad hoc* nature of Torrance's eschatology by explaining that "there is the elusiveness of his eschatology" and goes on to add that "Torrance did not leave us with a systematic treatment of the subject."[127] In fact, he goes on to note that "the traditional 'four last things'—the *resurrection, last judgment, heaven and hell*—are peripheral to his eschatology."[128] Two aspects of Torrance's theology can account for this lack, among other reasons, and MacLean's insights are once again helpful: (1) the christological aspect and (2) the methodological aspect. With regard to Christology, MacLean observes that in Torrance's eschatology "christocentrism" is key, which means that "eschatology for Torrance has to do with the *parousia* (presence and coming) of Christ, and this entails his redeeming work in history and in the church."[129] In terms of methodology, the pursuit of a *scientific theology* "helps to explain why Torrance does not tell us much about heaven and hell, the final judgment, and life in the new creation—the traditional fare of eschatology. Our scientific knowledge of these things is severely restricted."[130] In light of the fact that there is insufficient evidence in Torrance's eschatology[131] to draw strong conclusions, it would be wise to ameliorate the tone of the criticisms addressed to Torrance on this point.

Second, while acknowledging that one must be circumspect about judging Torrance's eschatology (specifically, the postmortem state) too harshly, there is no harm in conceding that Torrance's discussion about "eternity" is seemingly contradictory.[132] MacLean correctly observes that while Torrance affirms time for the incarnation and the ascension of Jesus, he seems to undermine it for the return of Christ:

> In fact, the ascension of Christ refers to the movement of all human "conditions"—including time—into eternity, within the realm of "God's sovereign purpose." But if this is really the

---

126. Yates, "Immediate or Intermediate?," 315.
127. MacLean, *Resurrection*, 190.
128. MacLean, *Resurrection*, 195.
129. MacLean, *Resurrection*, 191.
130. MacLean, *Resurrection*, 200.
131. See MacLean, *Resurrection*, 190.
132. MacLean, *Resurrection*, 21. Cf. Torrance, *Doctrine of Jesus Christ*, 197.

nature of the case, then Torrance is stuck with an inconsistency. The effect of the second advent does not correspond to the effect that the incarnation and ascension had on time. How can one say that eternity "has no present, past or future" and thus must "gather" these all up at the end, if the God in Christ represents eternity, and the ascension of Christ is the sign that eternity is forever united to time? It seems that the significance of the ascension for the second advent is not commensurate with its christological and soteriological significance.[133]

While there is insufficient data in Torrance's theology to draw strong judgments, one must hold him accountable for the suggestive comments he makes and question whether they are always helpful or even consistent with what he states elsewhere in his corpus. MacLean's critique is therefore justified, and while it is beyond the scope of this present work to interrogate it, a more robust account of Torrance's eschatology would need to tackle such issues. The issues both Yates and MacLean raise, however, may be attributable to a residue of what MacLean regards as an early "triumphalistic"[134] eschatology that Torrance did not entirely expel from his later theology. One cannot be certain of this conclusion, given Torrance's reticence in providing a more robust eschatology, but it seems plausible. Since Yates's critique remains, however, one must map a way forward for Torrance studies.

One must preface the following constructive suggestion by emphasizing that Torrance would reject it because it goes against his theological ethos. Torrance would often utter the words "clapping our hands upon our mouth" when confronted with theological mysteries that he felt no need to explore.[135] Arguably, Torrance is doing something similar with regard to individual eschatology; nonetheless, since his suggestions seemingly affirm an instantaneous resurrection, leading to numerous theological issues, one is forced to offer a corrective to this aspect of his theology.

N. T. Wright offers conceptual clarity that is missing in Torrance's thought regarding individual eschatology when he affirms an *interim period* after death, which he calls "'life after death,'" which is followed by the final resurrection, which he calls "'life *after* 'life after death.'"[136] Wright believes

---

133. MacLean, *Resurrection*, 21. Cf. Torrance, *Doctrine of Jesus Christ*, 197.

134. MacLean judges Torrance's early eschatology to be "triumphalistic." For more, see MacLean, *Resurrection*, 35, 36, 46.

135. See chapter 4 for more on this point. One instance, among many others, where Torrance uses this phrase is *Christian Doctrine of God*, 210.

136. Wright, *Resurrection*, 30–31. See also Wright, *Surprised by Hope*, which includes material from his 2005 Didsbury lectures given at Nazarene Theological College, Manchester. The lecture series was entitled "Life After Life After Death."

the intermediate state is a period characterized by disembodiment, while the resurrection is to "a fresh living embodiment."[137] Torrance would affirm a corporeal resurrection, but may find it hard to accept a period of postmortem disembodiment because of his strong antipathy towards dualistic conceptions of defining a human being.[138] Therefore, while Wright's contributions to the discussion about the postmortem state of the believer may offer a helpful corrective that would shield Torrance from critiques such as Yates's, there is a need for a more Torrancean account.

Habets provides such an account when he builds on biblical foundations and Torrance's theological anthropology to develop a constructive view on the intermediate state of the believer that is neither *monistic* nor *dualistic*.[139] On the basis of passages such as Luke 23:43; 16:19–31; and 2 Cor 5:8, Habets believes Scripture testifies to the reality of an intermediate state; while passages such as Matt 10:28 lend credence to "the distinction between body and soul."[140] But most importantly from accounts such as the transfiguration (Matt 17:3–9), Habets believes one can make a strong case for an "*embodied* and conscious" existence in the intermediate state because that is how Moses and Elijah are presented.[141] In contradistinction to both *monism* and *dualism*, Habets offers what he calls "anthropological *duality*" in which "a human is a materialized unitary being."[142] In other words, intrinsic to defining a human being is to have both body and soul on earth, in the intermediate state, and at the resurrection;[143] consequently, at death there is no separation of the soul from the body but the reception of a "temporary body" that during the parousia will "be replaced with a perfect resurrection body like Christ's (Phil 3.21)."[144] Habets's account is arguably a consistent application of Torrance's Christology and theological anthropology, which may not directly address the intermediate state but is certainly building on explicitly Torrancean theological instincts.[145] Whether

137. Wright, *Resurrection*, 30–31.

138. Cf. chapter 3 for more on the holistic account of a human being in Torrance's theology, wherein a human being comprises of both "body and soul." For more, see Torrance, *Christian Frame of Mind*, 35.

139. See Habets, "Naked but Not Disembodied," 33–50. *Monism* offers an account of the human that does not distinguish between body and soul, whereas *Dualistic* accounts make a clear distinction between body and soul.

140. Habets, "Naked but Not Disembodied," 47–48.

141. Habets, "Naked but Not Disembodied," 47–48.

142. Habets, "Naked but Not Disembodied," 48.

143. Habets, "Naked but Not Disembodied," 33.

144. Habets, "Naked but Not Disembodied," 48–49.

145. Habets, "Naked but Not Disembodied," 39, where he notes that Torrance's

or not Habets is persuasive is something that can be investigated further, but by adopting his view as a possible answer to the question about the intermediate state, Torrance's theology can circumvent Yates's critique, and also fill in certain gaps in Torrance's theology in ways that are arguably consistent with his overall theology.

### 2.2.2 Critique #5: Embryonic Trinitarian Spatiality?

Sang Hoon Lee correctly notes that neither Torrance nor scholarship that is Torrancean in nature has developed a robust doctrine of "divine simplicity."[146] A similar assessment can be made with regard to Torrance's doctrine of Trinitarian spatiality, which is explained in less than one statement in Torrance's mature work on the ascension.[147] Nonetheless, with phrases such as "communion of the Persons" and "mutual indwelling of the Father, Son and Holy Spirit," Torrance's conception of space influenced by the doctrine of the Trinity is pregnant with meaning.[148] At one level this lack of discussion on the spatiality of the Trinity is surprising given Torrance is quintessentially described as a "Theologian of the Trinity";[149] but on another level this is to be expected because Torrance's exposition on God's relationship to space and time with respect to the incarnation and ascension focuses predominantly on epistemological issues.[150] Readers of Torrance's theology, therefore, face the difficult task of gleaning disparate insights from Torrance's oeuvre in order to construct a coherent doctrine of Trinitarian spatiality.

Torrance's conception of *three levels of theology* can be used to develop a doctrine of Trinitarian spatiality, in inverse order. In other words, instead of moving in an ascending order of conceptualization, as Torrance prescribes, one will be moving in a descending order, from the highest level down to the lower levels of theology.[151] Such a task is perilous because one

---

theology focuses more on the resurrection. By implication, Habets intends to convey that Torrance neglects theologizing on the intermediate state. Habets, however, finds Bloesch, *Last Things*, to be a helpful dialogue partner about the intermediate state.

146. Lee, "Doctrine of Divine Simplicity," 199. This doctrine argues that one cannot view God's Triune being as a composition of various *parts* that makes up a whole.

147. See Torrance, *Space, Time, and Resurrection*, 131.

148. See Torrance, *Space, Time, and Resurrection*, 131.

149. See Molnar, *Thomas F. Torrance*, 31.

150. Cf. Torrance: *Space, Time, and Incarnation*, 4; Torrance, *Space, Time, and Resurrection*, xi.

151. Cf. Torrance, *Ground and Grammar of Theology*, 156–59, for a helpful overview of and commentary about the relevance of these levels in Torrance's theology. In relation to broader theological scholarship, see Myers, "Stratification of Knowledge."

can easily collapse the immanent Trinity into the economic Trinity, but if this danger can be avoided, one is still tasked with theologizing about the spatiality within the immanent Trinity with minimal theological resources in Torrance. However, while exercising extreme caution and proceeding with proper humility, one can still make a provisional constructive attempt, because Torrance provides promising embryonic insights that can be developed. To aid in the following theological construction, Sang Hoon Lee, Jeremy Begbie, and John Inge, among others, offer illuminating theological proposals that can be adapted, especially in ways that correspond to the *ontological, theological,* and *doxological* levels of Torrance's theology.[152]

### 2.2.2.1 RELATIONAL SPACE AT THE ONTOLOGICAL LEVEL

In the context of explicating Torrance's doctrine of divine simplicity, Lee correctly observes that *perichoresis* is foundational to how Torrance envisions "divine space" or how God is related to spatiality, typically referred to as *Trinitarian space*.[153] Lee's interpretation of Torrance's use of *perichoresis* accurately portrays the relational, as opposed to competitive, ways in which it is to be understood: "divine fullness is room for others in the Trinity, the three persons do not compartmentalize the one space of God but secure the undividedness of the space that God himself is."[154] In other words, Lee is emphasizing Torrance's refusal to think of God's intra-Trinitarian space in terms of a container needing to be filled with three different parts in order to be full, or in order to comprise a whole being. Instead, Lee avers that Torrance's "concept of divine space secures and safeguards the unicity of God,"[155] which he insists must mean that "even in the generation and procession, God does not become partite: divine plenitude is uncountably 'one' and indivisibly whole."[156] Importantly, such a conception amounts to an orthodox Trinitarian theology, which denies heresies such as *tritheism* or *modalism*. As Torrance's theology clearly demonstrates: God is "One Being Three Persons,"[157] and Lee does well to capture this central Torrancean insight when he declares that "God's fullness remains indivisibly and wholly

---

152. See Lee, "Doctrine of Divine Simplicity," 208–13; Begbie, "'Semblance More Lucid'"; Inge, *Christian Theology of Place*.
153. Lee, "Doctrine of Divine Simplicity," 209.
154. Lee, "Doctrine of Divine Simplicity," 209.
155. Lee, "Doctrine of Divine Simplicity," 208.
156. Lee, "Doctrine of Divine Simplicity," 212.
157. This is the subtitle of Torrance's mature theological writing on the Trinity. For more, see Torrance, *Christian Doctrine of God*.

one as the absolute and perfect plenitude in his embrace of other persons."[158] Lee finds some of Torrance's affirmations about the ascension vis-à-vis the Triune being of God to be problematic,[159] but he finds no problems with the conception of Trinitarian space Torrance promulgates.[160] Torrance's articulations on the spatiality of the Trinity are pitched at a meta-theological level, and helpfully guard against heretical conceptions on the one hand and *container* conceptions on the other. Relational space at the *ontological* level is to be viewed as a space suffused with a simultaneous *oneness* and *otherness*. The challenge, therefore, is to allow such a Trinitarian conception of space to percolate to the *economic* level, and Jeremy Begbie's insights are especially helpful in this regard.

### 2.2.2.2 Relational Space at the Economic Level

Jeremy Begbie contends that certain insights from music theory uniquely enhance and guard against errors in theological discussions about space at the ontological and the economic levels.[161] Begbie believes that spatiality discussed through one's sight, or what he calls "visual perception" is fraught with limitation because there is no room for distinctiveness, but only scope for "juxtaposition and mutual exclusion."[162] Such an environment fosters "zero-sum games" according to Begbie, by which he means that: "the more of one thing . . . [leads to] the less of another."[163] A theology that is bent on seeing all the nuances involved in the spatiality of the Trinity will find it difficult to "comprehend how there can be irreducible threeness and oneness."[164] In contrast to the "visual" model, Begbie offers an "aural" perspective, which is basically one that enters spatial theologizing through sound or through one's ears.[165] Such a view takes the Trinitarian spatial discussion to terrain that is fruitful because there is no room for "receptacle" kinds of thinking about God and space.[166] God's relationship to space need not be conceptualized in terms of *a priori* views of space such as a "receptacle" that contains "both God and world" or one that contains "the

---

158. Lee, "Doctrine of Divine Simplicity," 212.
159. See Lee, "Doctrine of Divine Simplicity," 201–3.
160. See Lee, "Doctrine of Divine Simplicity," 208–14.
161. Begbie, "'Semblance More Lucid.'"
162. Begbie, "'Semblance More Lucid,'" 22.
163. Begbie, "'Semblance More Lucid,'" 22.
164. Begbie, "'Semblance More Lucid,'" 23.
165. Begbie, "'Semblance More Lucid,'" 23–33.
166. Begbie, "'Semblance More Lucid,'" 31–32.

Trinitarian Persons."[167] Instead, through salient insights from the theory of music, one can conceptualize Trinitarian space in a way that is more specific to the "self-presentation of the triune God."[168]

Such a belief is grounded in the conviction that "aural space" can better account for both oneness and distinctiveness, evidenced through the example of how two different musical notes on one piano can both be heard as two distinctive notes: "In this aural environment, two distinct entities, it would seem, can occupy the same space at the same time and yet be perceived as irreducibly distinct."[169] Therefore, by building on musical insights from Victor Zuckerkandl, Begbie believes one can account for the nuances of Trinitarian space in the following ways. (1) Through Zuckerkandl's concept of "'interpenetration' of sounds in our aural perception," Begbie explains how one can better account for the Triune *oneness* and *threeness* in a way that eschews notions of "God possessing 'parts'" because "the three heard notes are not parts of a whole, they *are* the whole."[170] (2) Through Zuckerkandl's concept of "'coming from' / 'coming toward'" as something that describes what music "*is*," Begbie avers that one can illuminate how "self-giving" is an intrinsically Trinitarian act that does not entail giving up one's being; or in other words, there is no "self-evacuation of one for the sake of the other" in the act of giving oneself to the other.[171] (3) Through Zuckerkandl's concept of the "'order of auditory space,'" Begbie insists that one is better able to encounter "the *mutual enlivening* of the Trinitarian Persons."[172] By this, he means the relationality that characterizes the essence of the Triune being and "the *uncontainability* of this mutuality," which for Begbie communicates how the Holy Spirit can be viewed as the overflow "of the mutual love of Father and Son."[173]

Begbie offers such a model as a proposal for how one can conceptualize Trinitarian space, but along the way he also provides helpful pointers on how one can use such insights to theologize about spatiality at the economic level. Two aspects are especially pertinent. First, he does not believe there is a univocal relation between how the persons of the Trinity relate to one another immanently and spatial relations at the economic level.[174] In order

---

167. Begbie, "'Semblance More Lucid,'" 31.
168. Begbie, "'Semblance More Lucid,'" 32.
169. Begbie, "'Semblance More Lucid,'" 23.
170. Begbie, "'Semblance More Lucid,'" 32.
171. Begbie, "'Semblance More Lucid,'" 32.
172. Begbie, "'Semblance More Lucid,'" 33.
173. Begbie, "'Semblance More Lucid,'" 33.
174. Begbie, "'Semblance More Lucid,'" 26.

to avoid such a dangerous correspondence, he encourages various spatial relations like "intra-Trinitarian relations, the relation of Creator and creature, divine and human in the hypostatic union, Christ and church, and the relations between persons in the church" to be explored in "assiduously differentiated" ways.[175] In other words, arguably, Begbie is guarding against collapsing God into human categories on the one hand and elevating human beings to the level of God on the other hand.

Second, Begbie identifies several benefits of theologizing about space through "aural" rather than "visual" categories because for him the latter represents containment and competitive models, whereas the former fosters genuine relationality. In "visual" models of spatiality, theologically, "God's relation to the world" will be conceived in oppositional categories; "'Transcendence' will tend to be opposed to 'immanence'"; "divine and human agency" will be pitted against each other; "contractual models of salvation will find a ready home"; and among other concerns, "human freedom will tend to be envisaged primarily as freedom *from* the other (whether divine or human)."[176] In an "aural" model one can better account for various relationships in ways that do justice to the distinctiveness and nuances of various persons and relations, and therefore, for Begbie, such a non-competitive model is to be preferred. The challenge of conceiving how such a spatial conception at the economic level can percolate to the *doxological* level remains, and it is here that John Inge's contribution is relevant.

### 2.2.2.3 Relational Space at the Doxological Level

John Inge's *A Christian Theology of Place* provides a biblical and theological exploration of the importance of "place" in God's interactions with people in his world, in order to correct the academic and practical neglect of "place" in "Western society."[177] Inge contends that such a disregard of "place" is actually "dehumanizing" and seeks to redress this issue by working toward "a recovery of a sense of place in Western society."[178] Inge's constructive contribution is built on the testimony of the Old and New Testaments and the reception history of the significance of places where God has encountered people in Christian tradition.[179] Inge's study convinces him that "place" is an important biblical theme but should be understood

---

175. Begbie, "'Semblance More Lucid,'" 26.
176. Begbie, "'Semblance More Lucid,'" 22–23.
177. Inge, *Christian Theology*, ix.
178. Inge, *Christian Theology*, xi.
179. Inge, *Christian Theology*, 33–123.

in a "relational"[180] manner, by which he means that "God, people, and place cannot be separated" in thinking theologically about place.[181] Among many other theologians' work, Inge also draws on Torrance's insights on how the incarnation shapes a theology of space that is *relational* when he acknowledges, "Developing Torrance's approach . . . the incarnation implies that *places are the seat of relations or the place of meeting and activity in the interaction between God and the world.*"[182] Inge insists that while Scripture and Christian tradition point to the importance of certain places, one can also develop a theology of "place in general," but in a way that takes into account the provisional and eschatological nature of places.[183] In other words, one must recognize how places are "penultimate" because they are not the end in themselves—"They point towards our ultimate destiny which is to be *implaced*, where the nature of the places in which we will find ourselves will be a transfigured version of the places of the here and now."[184] It is the Christian hope in resurrection that, for Inge, points to the eschatological fulfillment of places in this world.[185]

While Inge's work on place is not grounded on Trinitarian space (space at the *ontological* level), it is a remarkably insightful study on place from an *economic* and *doxological* standpoint, to use Torrance's categories. Inge's work is relevant in developing Trinitarian spatiality in Torrancean ways at the *doxological* level because he specifically interacts with Torrance, uses categories that are congruent with Torrance's theology, but also because he recognizes, as would Torrance, both the provisionality and eschatological nature of places. Inge's work is an excellent display of rich theology made accessible.

At one place, he concretely suggests how a theology of place is relevant today by noting how "all churches could operate as a shrine," which for him means "that church buildings would enhance the capability of the Christian community to live out their prophetic and priestly ministry to the secular world."[186] Such a conviction about the importance of the place in which the church exists, Inge insists, would enable the church to challenge

---

180. Inge, *Christian Theology*, 78–88.

181. Inge, *Christian Theology*, 79.

182. Inge, *Christian Theology*, 57. Inge is here adapting insights from Torrance's *Space, Time, and Incarnation*, 67. For more, see Inge, *Christian Theology*, 52.

183. See Inge, *Christian Theology*, xi, 141.

184. Inge, *Christian Theology*, 141.

185. Inge, *Christian Theology*, 141–43.

186. Inge, *Christian Theology*, 122.

"secular assumptions of late modernity and find openings to faith."[187] Inge's contribution to a theology of place in general, and specifically vis-à-vis the church, resonates well with Torrance's own convictions, evidenced, among other things, in his pursuit of an ecumenical theology that longed to be embodied in practice, not just remain at the theoretical level.[188] In other words, Torrance wanted the church to concretely embody unity because he believed Trinitarian theology would accept nothing less.[189]

Torrance, like Inge, would affirm a strong theology of place, which is grounded in the incarnation, and ultimately realized in "a new heaven and a new earth."[190] While Torrance does not develop all the ways in which a theology of place can be worked out in practice, as Inge does, the ontological theology that Torrance espouses, arguably, is consistent with the economic and doxological applications that Inge provides. The *doxological* theme that emerges from Inge is the importance of places in God's economy, which should be the basis for Christians to value places now as well as long for its eschatological fulfillment in the new creation. These themes would sit well with Torrance's Trinitarian convictions and clearly demonstrate how his embryonic conceptions of spatiality influenced by the Trinity can be articulated at the *doxological* level in ways that are easily accessible to the church.

### 2.2.3 Critique #6: Unclear Spatial Language?

Analytic theologian Oliver Crisp in a recent work entitled *Analyzing Doctrine: Toward a Systematic Theology* critiques Torrance for not providing a detailed response to the question of where the ascended body of Jesus is.[191] More accurately, Crisp critiques Torrance in a secondary manner, while addressing his main criticism to Robert Jenson's answer to the question: "to where did Christ's body disappear?,"[192] which he finds both inadequate and theologically problematic.[193] Nonetheless, Crisp also finds fault with Torrance's answer: "To be fair to Jenson, he is hardly the only theologian that does not provide an unambiguous response to this question. This is also true

---

187. Inge, *Christian Theology*, 122.

188. See Torrance, *Theology in Reconciliation*, 9.

189. Torrance, *Theology in Reconciliation*, 9, where he grounds his ecumenical pursuit in his Trinitarian convictions.

190. Torrance, *Apocalypse Today*, 176–77.

191. Crisp, *Analyzing Doctrine*, 229n38.

192. Crisp, *Analyzing Doctrine*, 229.

193. Crisp, *Analyzing Doctrine*, 219, 229.

of Torrance in *Space, Time, and Resurrection*."[194] Crisp makes an important observation on Torrance's theology of the spatiality of the ascension that deserves critical engagement, but before doing so, it is important to provide some important context for the overall point Crisp is seeking to make.

Crisp takes Jenson to task on two issues: (1) a concern that Jenson ends up with "a doctrine of multiple incarnations" when he totally equates the Son with Jesus, and after the resurrection, of Jesus with the Eucharist and church;[195] and (2) a concern that Jenson does not provide a satisfactory reason for "Christ's missing body on Easter Day."[196] With regard to (1), Crisp believes that Jenson is indeed guilty as charged, but with some additional explanation this criticism could be significantly ameliorated.[197] Since Torrance is certainly not guilty, nor likely to be charged of such a thing, a detailed elaboration on this point is unnecessary.[198] Point (2) applies to both Jenson and Torrance, and therefore will be critically interrogated in what follows.

Crisp summarizes Jenson's whole approach to the resurrection as follows: "He attempts to reframe the doctrine so that the postresurrection body of Christ is *whatever makes Christ available to us*."[199] In light of such a framework, Crisp is dissatisfied with Jenson's main reason for affirming an empty tomb, namely, for fear that "Christ's body would have become a relic had it remained in the tomb on Easter Day."[200] Crisp believes such an answer is not grounded in a conviction that the resurrection entails an empty tomb.[201] Since Jenson still faces the problem of how to account for the location of the resurrected body, Crisp goes on to provide four possible options, which will be discussed in what follows, that can provide a more satisfactory answer.[202] While these options provide important "repair"[203] work for Jenson's account which is faulty, Crisp believes only his fourth option provides a correction to the faults present in Jenson's theology. Therefore,

194. Crisp, *Analyzing Doctrine*, 229n38.

195. Crisp, *Analyzing Doctrine*, 219. For the whole analysis of this point, see pp. 219–28.

196. Crisp, *Analyzing Doctrine*, 219.

197. For this specific remedy, see Crisp, *Analyzing Doctrine*, 228.

198. Torrance's clear distinctions between the immanent and economic trinity, together with his affirmation of the *extra Calvinisticum*, would militate against such an equation. For more on why Torrance does not equate the ascended Christ with the church or Eucharist, see chapter 3.

199. Crisp, *Analyzing Doctrine*, 218.

200. Crisp, *Analyzing Doctrine*, 229.

201. Crisp, *Analyzing Doctrine*, 229.

202. Crisp, *Analyzing Doctrine*, 231.

203. Crisp, *Analyzing Doctrine*, 231.

even for Torrance, while this fourth option does not remedy any glaring faults in his theology, it nonetheless expands on insights that are embryonic in his theology by helpfully making sense of the location of Christ's ascended body.[204] Before critically engaging with option four, the first three views will be briefly summarized.

The first two options make sense of where Christ's resurrection body is by getting rid of it, either for option (1) through annihilation, or for option (2) through breaking up the body into many parts that are "scattered over a particular region of space-time."[205] Both these options are unhelpful, explains Crisp, because (1) entails denying the reality of Christ's "incarnate" existence from "the moment at which his corpse is annihilated and the blessing of the elements at the next Eucharist";[206] and (2) entails affirming the existence of the resurrected "human body" in theory only, not in practice because all the elements of the body exist but no longer as a cohesive whole.[207] The third option tries to account for where the resurrected body is by locating it in the eschatological future, or in other words by affirming that the resurrection body "is not present in our frame of reference" from the ascension to the *parousia*.[208] While option (3) can make good sense of where the resurrection body is vis-à-vis the Gospel accounts and modern science, it does so with the risk of giving up immediate access to Christ because he is now "at a great distance from where he began," as well as undermining the existential dividends of the priestly ministry of the ascended Christ because it "cannot be given anything like a straightforward or realist interpretation."[209] All these three options therefore are to be rejected, leaving the reader with the option that according to Crisp is the best—option (4).[210]

The fourth option is like the third, but without the imposition of a "temporal" separation between Christ and the rest of humankind. In this view, Crisp suggests how the resurrection body can be located somewhere

---

204. See Crisp, *Analyzing Doctrine*, 218, where Crisp clearly states that for Torrance the resurrection of the body is central to his whole theology—simply put, no resurrection = no salvation, for Torrance.

205. Crisp, *Analyzing Doctrine*, 231.

206. Crisp, *Analyzing Doctrine*, 231.

207. Crisp, *Analyzing Doctrine*, 232. In addition, for the second option, there is the added conundrum because of its inability to clarify the relationship between the Son and the "dispersed elements of his human body postresurrection," and his relationship "to the eucharistic elements postresurrection."

208. Crisp, *Analyzing Doctrine*, 232–33.

209. Crisp, *Analyzing Doctrine*, 233.

210. Crisp, *Analyzing Doctrine*, 234.

and yet remain a human body by positing its existence in another "dimension" altogether.[211] Crisp insists that such a view is superior to the third option because it has explanatory power and existential appeal:

> This is where OPTION 4 has an advantage over OPTION 3. Imagine that our space-time continuum is a kind of growing four-dimensional block. At the leading face of the block are the present temporal events. God could remove Christ's human nature from the block at a certain moment in time, from a certain place (say, the moment at which his human body is hidden from the sight of the apostles at the ascension). He could transpose Christ's human nature to another adjacent block—one that in a sense overlaps the present block but is distinct because it occupies a different set of dimensions to our own. His human nature could continue to exist in this adjacent block, tracking in parallel with the moments that elapse in the spatiotemporal block in which we exist, until at the eschaton his human nature is returned to our block by divine action.[212]

Crisp is drawing insights from a *hyperspace* theory promulgated by Hud Hudson to make sense of where the resurrected body could be.

Hudson's theory makes sense of the location of the resurrected and ascended body by proposing that it exists in a real four-dimensional place that is related to, but not accessible to humans in our three-dimensional existence.[213] The benefits of such a theory, Hudson contends, are manifold, but can be summed up as follows:

> A body moving ana or kata could leave its clothes or burial robes without taking them off, could vanish from a dinner table without a trace, and could appear in a locked room without passing through its windows, doors, or walls. In short, a body free to move in hyperspace could be positioned just inches away, yet remain undetectable for days on end, and could enter and leave our own three-space with exactly the ease and abruptness that is attributed to the risen Jesus.[214]

This fourth option provides an important corrective to Jenson's theology of the resurrection and arguably an expansion of insights to Torrance's theology.

211. Crisp, *Analyzing Doctrine*, 234.
212. Crisp, *Analyzing Doctrine*, 234.
213. For more, see Crisp, *Analyzing Doctrine*, 234–35; see also Hudson, *Metaphysics of Hyperspace*, 204.
214. Hudson, *Metaphysics of Hyperspace*, 204.

One must commend Crisp for engaging with Hudson's work and uniquely appropriating insights from a metaphysical theory into systematic theology.[215] Arguably, Crisp's use of *hyperspace* as an explanation for where the resurrected and ascended body of Jesus is corresponds well with Torrance's *relational* account of space and time.[216] Two reasons can be offered to justify this view. First, Torrance's language about "heaven" corresponds well to the *hyperspace* theory. This is clearly evidenced in Torrance's positive appropriation of Karl Barth's use of the term: "'Heaven' in biblical language is the sum of the inaccessible and incomprehensible side of the created world, so that, although it is not God himself, it is the throne of God, the creaturely correspondence to his glory, which is veiled from man, and cannot be disclosed except on his initiative."[217]

While neither Torrance nor Barth uses the language of *hyperspace* to explain what heaven is, Barth's language about heaven and in turn Torrance's use of it potentially contains important elements of Hudson's *hyperspace* theory in seed form. Second, the way N. T. Wright uses Torrance's insights on *relational* space and time to construct a view about *heaven* confirms that it is congenial to Hudson's theory on *hyperspace*. Wright commends Torrance's *relational* conception of space and time vis-à-vis the ascension to readers and goes on to explain that "heaven and earth in biblical cosmology are not two different locations within the same continuum of space or matter. They are two different dimensions of God's good creation."[218] One can argue that Wright is extending Torrance's insights on *relational* space and time in his interpretation about what *heaven* is. These two reasons suggest that the *hyperspace* theory is amenable to Torrance's theology of *relational* space and time.

Admittedly, Torrance himself would not have approved of the method adopted above, namely, extending his insights through analytic theology, as Torrance was content with *mystery* as the answer to some theological subjects.[219] Furthermore, Torrance's distinction between "dogmatism" and "dogmatics" illuminates why he would generally disapprove of analytic kinds of theologies.[220] Torrance approves of "dogmatics" because for him it

---

215. Cf. Hill, "Incarnation, Timelessness, and Exaltation," 14, where he explains why theology may not be as keen as philosophy to incorporate insights from *hyperspace* as an explanation of where the ascended body of Jesus is.

216. See Torrance, *Space, Time, and Resurrection*, 126–30, especially 129n8.

217. See Torrance, *Space, Time, and Resurrection*, 129n8, where he quotes Barth from *Church Dogmatics*, 3/1:453.

218. Wright, *Surprised by Hope*, 111.

219. See chapter 4 for more on this subject.

220. See Torrance, "Reformed Dogmatics."

is a "science," categorized by an attitude of submission to the "subject-matter in its own nature";[221] whereas he eschews "dogmatism" because he contends that it is in essence a form of "*a priori* reasoning."[222] Analytic theology, for Torrance, would resemble a form of *dogmatism* that is "scholastic . . . [and] designed to pose and solve a theoretical problem."[223] Nevertheless, lest one think that Torrance has nothing but antagonism toward "dogmatism," he does recognize some strengths even in an approach that he rejects:

> In spite of this, it must be admitted that . . . even in its form of abstractive knowledge and propositions, [it] is well worth studying, not only for its richness of content and remarkable trains of thought as different doctrines are pursued to their end with care and exactness, but also for the determined way in which the writers seek to ground the substance of their thought upon the biblical revelation and draw it out in closely reasoned statements and coherent patterns. Theology of this kind has a sterling quality and a rational force that are markedly absent from much modern writing. What has so often been derided as scholastic "hairsplitting" is in fact often a praiseworthy endeavour after systematic precision in which every attempt is made to see that no problem is left unexamined.[224]

Torrance may indeed reject Crisp's analytic theological method, but from what he appreciates about "dogmatism" above, one could argue that he does value theological scholarship that strives to be meticulous and clear, and therefore there is some Torrancean warrant for the constructive proposal that is being offered here.

The Torrancean constructive use of *hyperspace* will need to be used in a defensive manner, only for illustrative purposes, in order to show how one can make a credible biblical and scientific case for the ascension of Christ in a manner that retains his humanity. Torrance's refusal to provide more details on the spatiality of the ascended Jesus can be construed by some theologians as both inadequate and uninspiring. However, by adopting something like Crisp's constructive use of *hyperspace*, Torrance will certainly forestall critics who think he may not have wrestled sufficiently with a difficult topic and therefore dismiss his insights on this subject.[225]

221. Torrance, "Reformed Dogmatics," 153.
222. Torrance, "Reformed Dogmatics," 155.
223. Torrance, "Reformed Dogmatics," 154.
224. Torrance, "Reformed Dogmatics," 156.
225. Cf. Ben Myers, comment on Myers, review of *Ascension in Karl Barth*: "As a minimal requirement for theological statements, though, I think Bultmann is right: any

## 2.3 The Present Ministry of the Ascended Christ: A Critical Appraisal

Since Torrance's ontology and spatiality of the ascension have been examined in the six critiques above, this third and final section will evaluate Torrance's views on the present ministry of the ascended Christ. Torrance commendably explored the work of Christ as King, Priest, and Prophet in the light of the ascension, and while he pressed the frontiers of theology with respect to the priestly ministry of Christ and to a certain extent the prophetic ministry of Christ, his exploration of Jesus's kingship is still emerging. David Fergusson lauds several aspects of Torrance's theology of the ascension, but finds fault with the lack of ethical and political implications in his work. This aspect relates directly to Jesus's kingship in his ascension and, therefore, will be explored in detail in what follows. Torrance's articulation of Jesus's priestly ministry with regard to the ascension is a robust account, and critics find little fault with it. Torrance presents Jesus as continuing to exercise his priestly ministry, but arguably one can ask whether he has sufficiently extended his theology *retrospectively* and *prospectively*. This section uses Torrance's tacit approval of the *Scotist hypothesis* in order to make a Torrancean case for the need for Jesus to function as priest/mediator eternally. Torrance's exposition of Jesus as prophet with respect to the ascension is integrally connected to pneumatology and preaching. However, David Fergusson, among others, wonders whether Torrance's pneumatology in general needs to be given more attention in his theology, and Joseph Sherrard avers that the relationship between the prophetic ministry of Jesus and the church's preaching is not given a detailed exposition. The following section will explore these aspects.

### 2.3.1 Critique #7: Underdeveloped Doctrine of Jesus's Ascended Kingship?

Torrance's expositors readily acknowledge that he has not developed a robust doctrine of the ascension vis-à-vis Jesus's kingship.[226] David Fergus-

---

statement that isn't intelligible (within the basic framework of what we know about the world) has to be thought through more deeply. . . . We need to re-think 'space' and 'time' from the standpoint of Jesus' resurrection/ascension (this is perhaps one of the most urgent tasks for contemporary theology). But the account of space and time that we come up with can't simply be a mythology—it has to cohere with what we already know from other sources about space and time." By using *hyperspace* as one possible explanation for where the ascended Jesus is, Torrance can circumvent the force of this criticism.

226. Cf. Liston, "Eschatology," 333, 336; Sherrard, *T. F. Torrance*, 171–78; Ziegler, "Doctrine of the Ascension," 30–31.

son, in the context of assessing Torrance's overall theology of the ascension, identifies what he believes to be a significant lacuna in Torrance's writings on the ascension, namely, "the relative absence of the ethical and political significance of the ascension," which is all the more conspicuous because these subjects are "given . . . prominence in Barth."[227] Fergusson's main critique of Torrance is clearly addressed at, first, the lack of ethics, which he explains as follows:

> For Torrance, the divine-human relation tends to be largely a private one, although his strong sense of the corporate nature of worship might have taken him in a different direction . . . the important relations and movements in Torrance are, as it were, vertical rather than horizontal. His occasional excursions into Christian ethics tend to be confined to areas of private rather than social morality—for example, marriage and abortion.[228]

Furthermore, second, the lack of sociopolitical implications of the ascension, which Fergusson reasons is a justified critique because

> only occasionally does he give hints about the wider sociopolitical significance of the ascension—for example, we are told that we cannot be pessimistic about the world since it is loved by Christ. . . . There is little about social justice, human equality, or the peaceable kingdom. The focus is generally doxological rather than ethical, whereas the royal Psalms and Jesus' teaching of the kingdom point to ways in which these can be integrated. In this respect, Nicholas Wolterstorff's writings on the ethical and political dimensions of the Reformed liturgy and Oliver O'Donovan's political theology provide an important complement to Torrance's doxological treatment of the ascension.[229]

Both issues Fergusson raises are important in addressing areas of Torrance's thought that need to be bolstered. In recent scholarship a few Torrancean scholars have risen to the occasion and provided helpful ways of extending Torrance's insights into subjects such as ethics and politics in ways that address how Jesus's kingship is to be understood in light of the ascension. In what follows, the focus will be on providing Torrancean insights on how Jesus as the ascended king should inform the subjects of ethics and politics.

---

227. Fergusson, "Ascension of Christ," 106.
228. Fergusson, "Ascension of Christ," 106.
229. Fergusson, "Ascension of Christ," 106–7.

## 2.3.1.1 JESUS'S KINGSHIP AND ETHICS

Fergusson's critique of Torrance about the lack of ethics can be understood in one of two ways. First, one can interpret Fergusson's critique in a restricted manner, primarily as a contrast between Barth and Torrance. Or, second, Fergusson can be understood to be making a comprehensive assessment of Torrance's theology. Since Fergusson himself does not expand upon his criticism of Torrance, one cannot be dogmatic and pigeonhole him into either of the two interpretations. However, because he references Barth in the immediate context of his quotation[230] and uses John Webster's overarching critique of Torrance on ethics to substantiate his own criticism,[231] it is likely that there is some truth in both interpretations. With respect to Torrance and Barth on ethics, it is widely acknowledged that Barth devotes more space to ethics than does Torrance in his theology.[232] Todd Speidell forcefully rebuts the more comprehensive claim that Torrance's theology undermines ethics, but even he is willing to acknowledge, along with those who knew Torrance well, that Barth contributed more content to the subject of ethics than did Torrance.[233] Fergusson is right, therefore, to contrast Torrance with Barth and find the latter's contribution to Christian ethics to be more substantial.

With respect to the broader assessment of whether Torrance's theology undermines ethics, one can summarily respond along with Speidell that two

---

230. It would seem like Fergusson is only comparing Torrance to Barth on ethics and is not making a more general assessment of Torrance's overall theology. This would seem to be the best interpretation based on the available evidence. For more, see Fergusson, "Ascension of Christ," 106.

231. See Speidell, "Soteriological Suspension," 57, where he recounts how "Fergusson cited John Webster's criticism that Torrance 'neglected ethics,'" as the basis for his own critique. Therefore, one could justifiably interpret Fergusson to be providing a general assessment of Torrance's overall theology.

232. Two representative examples should suffice to make this point: Molnar, *Incarnation and Resurrection*, 150, where he acknowledges that both Barth and Torrance ground ethics in the person and work of Christ, but also notes that "Torrance does not develop his thought on this subject explicitly with respect to Christian ethics in any sense as thoroughly as Barth has"; and McGrath, *Thomas F. Torrance*, 112n1, where he refers to two monographs written by John Webster (*Barth's Ethics of Reconciliation* and *Barth's Moral Theology: Human Action in Barth's Thought*) to substantiate the following observation: "Barth addressed some issues on which Torrance has not chosen to focus in depth, such as the foundations and structure of Christian ethics."

233. Speidell, "Soteriological Suspension," 60, attributes the following observation to Alasdair Heron and David Fergusson, both of whom explain that one reason that Barth's contribution to ethics is more substantial than Torrance's is because "unlike Karl Barth in Basel, T. F. Torrance in Edinburgh taught theology and not ethics, the latter being relegated to New College's Dept. of Christian Ethics and Practical Theology."

factors within Torrance's theology would counter such a view. (1) Theology and ethics are deeply integrated in all of Torrance's theology: "*One can read the entirety of Torrance's body of work as a theology of reconciliation on all levels of life: personal, social, historical, political, and cosmic.*"[234] (2) Theology and ethics are explicitly addressed in his brief expositions on the following five issues: (a) "Ministry of Women," (b) "God-Language," (c) "Abortion," (d) "Telling and Doing the Truth," and (e) "Law."[235]

Jerome Van Kuiken builds on Speidell's analysis of Torrance's contribution to ethics by evaluating it through the prism of "the Decalogue," which is "one standard summary of biblical ethics" and notes that only two main themes from the Decalogue are missing in Speidell's account: "sexual" ethics and "economic" ethics.[236] Van Kuiken observes that Torrance's broader corpus includes brief expositions on both sexual and economic ethics. In the case of the former, it is briefly addressed through written works on the Christian ordinance of marriage (which is an endorsement of the "male-female union" as central to the definition of marriage), and a Christian response to homosexuality (wherein he rejects the practice of homosexuality but encourages the church to accept the person).[237] In the case of economic ethics, Van Kuiken points readers to Torrance's ministerial practices that Speidell captures so well, such as regular Bible studies with his church members that helped both Torrance and his congregants to apply the Scriptures to real-life situations.[238] During one of the monthly Bible studies on the Sermon on the Mount, a church member felt compelled to raise his worker's wages, and Van Kuiken uses this as an instance to show how Torrance's theology practically addressed issues germane to economic ethics.[239] Therefore one can be confident in concluding, according to Van Kuiken, that "Torrance has covered the main loci of biblical ethics," even if it is done in a minimalistic manner.[240]

234. Speidell, "Soteriological Suspension," 64.

235. See Speidell, "Soteriological Suspension," 83–89, where he uses the following works from Torrance to explicate Torrance's explicit contribution to Christian ethics: *Ministry of Women*; "Christian Apprehension"; *Soul and Person*; *Christian Doctrine of Marriage*; and *Juridical Law*.

236. Van Kuiken, "'Not I, but Christ,'" 254.

237. Van Kuiken, "'Not I, but Christ,'" 254–55. Van Kuiken points readers to the following works where Torrance expounds his view on Christian marriage and a Christian response to homosexuality, respectively: *Christian Doctrine of Marriage*; and "Thomas Torrance Responds," 323–24.

238. Van Kuiken, "'Not I, but Christ,'" 254, where he refers readers to Speidell, "Soteriological Suspension," 78.

239. Speidell, "Soteriological Suspension," 254.

240. Van Kuiken, "'Not I, but Christ,'" 254–55.

Furthermore, when Torrance's theology as a whole is viewed as a combination of theology and ethics, as Speidell insists, then Van Kuiken believes one can notice "a profound ethical vision" in the foreground of many of Torrance's theological discourses; namely his "special scholarly concerns with reconciling Christianity and science," his desire to bridge "the churches' divisions through ecumenical dialogue," and to foster reconciliation "between Christians and Jews."[241] While Fergusson is right to note that Torrance does not have sufficient expositions on ethics, there are more ethically-focused themes in Torrance, albeit in embryonic form, than Fergusson has acknowledged, and more work needs to be done to bolster Torrance's contribution to ethics.[242] According to Van Kuiken, one area ripe for further investigation is Torrance's own life and legacy.[243] While one would have to be wary of the danger of a hagiography, there is nevertheless scope for critical reflection on how Torrance's "Christian living, not just his writings" offers insights on the subject of Christian ethics.[244]

### 2.3.1.2 Jesus's Kingship and Politics

Fergusson is right to point out that Torrance's theology of the ascension does not contain substantial implications for political issues. Joseph Sherrard concurs with Fergusson's assessment,[245] but goes on to explain, analyze, and provide corrective suggestions on how Torrance's theology can better engage with political issues.[246] Sherrard draws insights from Torrance's article entitled "Service in Jesus Christ"[247] to explain Torrance's views on a political issue—namely, the relationship between church and state.[248] For Torrance, Sherrard notes, there is to be *no* relationship between church and state, fundamentally, because the former is called to "service," and the latter is known to exercise excessive "power" to accomplish good in the world, leaving no

---

241. Speidell, "Soteriological Suspension," 255.

242. To be fair to Fergusson, his article "Ascension of Christ" is based on a lecture given to the Thomas F. Torrance Fellowship, and therefore he perhaps chose to condense his criticism. Fergusson's doctoral student Kim, in *Person*, 124–39, makes a case for the existence of embryonic themes in Torrance that are related to Christian ethics.

243. Van Kuiken, "'Not I, but Christ,'" 255.

244. For more, see Van Kuiken, "'Not I, but Christ,'" 255–57.

245. See Sherrard, *T. F. Torrance*, 171n115.

246. Sherrard, *T. F. Torrance*, 163–79, especially 168–79.

247. For more, see Torrance, *Gospel, Church, and Ministry*, 140–61.

248. Sherrard, *T. F. Torrance*, 168–71; cf. Torrance, *Gospel, Church, and Ministry*, 140–61.

middle ground.[249] In Torrance's thinking, Sherrard correctly insists, "Christian service and worldly government exist in opposition to one another."[250] Sherrard is surprised that Torrance's own theological resources—such as (1) the shared responsibility the church and state have toward "service," (2) the recognition that God has entrusted a lesser and derivative form of authority to the "state or . . . temple" to rule in a godly manner, and (3) the inevitability of the sinful use of this authority by the state or the church but the defeat of this wickedness through "Christ's kingly work"—are not all utilized to develop a theology "of the positive exercise of authority for rulers, the state, or even the church."[251]

Sherrard provides a two-point analysis that sheds light on why Torrance does not make any allowances for how the church and state can use power.[252] First, from an article entitled "The Church in the World," Sherrard concludes that for Torrance the church and the state represent two mutually exclusive kinds of worlds—the former, "new creation," the latter, the "old order."[253] Both these worlds represent two diametrically opposed ways of thinking and living, and therefore even when the church does not live up to her calling to be a representative of "new creation," she is still commissioned to oppose the state, whose tendency to abuse power is an ever-present danger.[254] Second, the reordering of the *triplex munus* after the ascension from prophet, priest, king, to *king, priest, prophet* is a clear declaration that the ascended Christ is already king, but "the Kingly reign is now hidden, exercised only by way of the priestly office and in the sphere of the church."[255]

On the basis of keen insights that Torrance makes in *Space, Time, and Resurrection* and *Royal Priesthood*, Sherrard correctly notes that the period between the ascension and the return of Christ is defined by Jesus's kingship, but (1) in a "hidden" manner, (2) manifested through the "priestly office," (3) seen "provisionally . . . in the . . . church," when she (4) participates "in the kingly office" of the ascended Christ, who exercises his kingship through "the priestly office."[256] In other words, kingship only belongs

---

249. Sherrard, *T. F. Torrance*, 168–70.

250. Sherrard, *T. F. Torrance*, 170.

251. Sherrard, *T. F. Torrance*, 169–71. In this section, Sherrard is gleaning insights from Torrance's *Atonement* volume, especially pp. 30–32.

252. Sherrard, *T. F. Torrance*, 171.

253. Sherrard, *T. F. Torrance*, 171. Sherrard is drawing insights from select portions of Torrance's essay entitled "The Church in the World," in *Gospel, Church, and Ministry*, 74–84.

254. Sherrard, *T. F. Torrance*, 172.

255. Sherrard, *T. F. Torrance as Missional Theologian*, 174.

256. Sherrard, *T. F. Torrance*, 174.

to the ascended Jesus, and even when it is visible through the church it is to be seen through priesthood more than kingship.[257] Cumulatively, Sherrard notes that both these reasons lead Torrance to view the church and state in "sharp contrast" to each other.[258] Since Torrance evacuates the state from having any function in his theology, Sherrard legitimately wonders whether Torrance actually undermines the biblical testimony that grants a "limited" kind of "authority . . . to the state" until the *parousia*.[259] Sherrard is keenly aware that Torrance is articulating a theology in line with Barth in order to avoid the catastrophic consequences of marrying church and state, but he insists that "Torrance overcorrects in a way that goes beyond his theological mentor."[260] Sherrard's assessment concurs with Fergusson's identification of the problem in Torrance's theology of the ascension vis-à-vis politics; he goes on to provide two theological correctives that are mostly in line with Fergusson's own constructive suggestions.

Sherrard provides a (1) "christological correction" and (2) an "eschatological correction" to Torrance's theology that he believes will allow fruitful theological engagement with political issues.[261] Christologically, Sherrard believes the Reformed concept of the *extra Calvinisticum* can help address the tendency in Torrance's theology to limit Christ's kingship to the domain of the church.[262] Sherrard gleans insights from Heiko Oberman to note that "for Calvin the *extra* also meant *extra etiam ecclesiam*."[263] In other words, just as Calvin used the *extra* to highlight how the Son was present in Jesus but not in a way that undermined the Son's ubiquity, similarly through the "*extra etiam ecclesiam*," Sherrard notes (through Oberman's reading of Calvin) how the kingship of Christ is not limited to his church but extends "over the [whole] world."[264] Sherrard correctly observes that the use of the *extra Calvinisticum* in this manner consistently extends Torrance's theology

---

257. Sherrard, *T. F. Torrance*, 174.

258. Sherrard, *T. F. Torrance*, 174.

259. Sherrard, *T. F. Torrance*, 174. Sherrard notes Rom 13 and 1 Pet 2:13–17 as a couple of examples that clearly show that the state is entrusted with legitimate authority from God, and he believes that one would find it hard to reconcile these passages with Torrance's overall theology.

260. Sherrard, *T. F. Torrance*, 174.

261. Sherrard, *T. F. Torrance*, 175–79.

262. Sherrard, *T. F. Torrance*, 175–76.

263. Sherrard, *T. F. Torrance*, 175. Sherrard is summarizing insights from Oberman, "'Extra' Dimension," 64.

264. Sherrard, *T. F. Torrance*, 175. Cf. Oberman, "'Extra' Dimension," 64.

in helpful ways, provided there is no "improper use of the *logos asarkos*" attached to it.[265]

Sherrard also contends that Torrance's theology of Jesus's kingship in light of the ascension is a manifestation of an overrealized theology, and therefore gleans insights from Oliver O'Donovan in order to provide an "eschatological" corrective.[266] Eschatologically, therefore, Sherrard believes Torrance's theology of the ascension correctly underscores the reality of Jesus's present kingship, but does not work out the details of how Jesus is king until the *parousia*. This is where he believes that O'Donovan provides insights that can supplement what is missing in Torrance; namely, through an understanding of the ascension as a "bridge" between the incarnation and new creation, one can begin to think of how the state should function in this interim period.[267] When such a theological approach is adopted, it has the benefit of allowing "a limited function" to the state without undermining the Lordship of Christ.[268] Cumulatively, both these correctives, avers Sherrard, provide Torrance's theology with the resources to articulate a political theology where the scope of Christ's reign is universal, and worked out with clear expectations for how the state should govern in the interim period, so that the church can either work with the state in certain areas or express dissent when the state transgresses its boundaries.[269]

Sherrard and Fergusson provide keen insights to bolster Torrance's theology of Jesus's kingship vis-à-vis ethics and politics, but an area that both these theologians do not highlight is the promise James Torrance's life and praxis offer to supplement T. F. Torrance's theology (notwithstanding the political differences there may have been between them) in this area.[270] It is important to note that James Torrance's theology is unique in and of itself, but it can enhance T. F. Torrance's political and ethical theology not because of a biological kinship, but because of a kindred theological outlook and vision. Arguably, T. F. Torrance's theology focuses on issues at a meta-level with respect to ethics and politics, while James Torrance clearly

---

265. Sherrard, *T. F. Torrance*, 176.

266. Sherrard, *T. F. Torrance*, 176–77.

267. Sherrard, *T. F. Torrance*, 176–77. On p. 177n135, Sherrard acknowledges his dependence on O'Donovan, *Desire of the Nations*, 143, for the insight on how the ascension is a "bridge" between the present world and the world to come.

268. Sherrard, *T. F. Torrance*, 177.

269. Sherrard, *T. F. Torrance*, 177.

270. I want to thank Jerome Van Kuiken who, during the 2021 Torrance Virtual Workshop-Retreat, suggested the promise of James Torrance's theology to supplement T. F. Torrance's theology with respect to Jesus as ascended king. Cf. Habets et al., "Current Trends," 09:50–11:24.

articulated a praxis-oriented political and ethical theology. The combined theology of the Torrances would provide a robust theological desideratum to politics and ethics, but also one that percolates into salient issues in the world, church, and culture.[271]

### 2.3.2 Critique #8: Permanent Priesthood of Christ?

Torrance is rightly commended for providing a "rich understanding of Christ's eschatological priestly office."[272] With Liston, one has to agree that Torrance's exposition of the priesthood of Christ in light of the ascension stands out in classical and contemporary Reformed theology, where luminaries such as John Calvin, Louis Berkhof, Donald McKim, Daniel Migliore, and Robert Sherman all expound the *triplex munus* primarily in light of the earthly ministry of Jesus.[273] In other words, especially with regard to the priestly ministry of the ascended Jesus, Torrance does not just work with a "then-to-now logic" as many of his Reformed colleagues, but works with "an eschatological lens,"[274] which focuses on how Jesus's "present" priestly ministry has implications for the church.[275] It is hard to find fault with Torrance's account of the priesthood of Jesus vis-à-vis the ascension, but arguably Torrance could have extended his exposition of Jesus as priest into eternity. Stated differently, Torrance does not utilize resources within his theology to develop a robust theology of the priesthood of Jesus that will last into eternity. In what follows, one can employ Torrance's tacit support for the *Scotist hypothesis* in order to make a case for the priestly ministry of Jesus as something that will last forever.

---

271. The following resources briefly highlight the promise James Torrance's theology offers to issues of politics and ethics: A. J. Torrance, "Introduction"; Newell, "Stuttgart Declaration of 1945."

272. Liston, "Eschatology," 333.

273. For references to the Reformed theologians, see Liston, "Eschatology," 325–27; for an overview of Torrance's theology of Jesus's priesthood vis-à-vis the ascension, see pp. 332–36.

274. Liston, "Eschatology," 327. Liston also correctly explains that Torrance expounds the prophetic ministry of Jesus in a similar way, but does not work out the implications of Jesus's kingship through an "eschatological" perspective. For more, see pp. 332–33, 336–43.

275. Liston, "Eschatology," 335–36.

## 2.3.2.1 SCOTIST HYPOTHESIS AND TORRANCE SCHOLARSHIP

The Scotist hypothesis affirms two things: first, that sin was an efficient, not primary, cause for the incarnation; and consequently, second, the incarnation would have happened even if the fall had not occurred.[276] Torrance scholars acknowledge the difficulty of interpreting Torrance's own views on this subject, but end up claiming that a wider reading of his theology necessitates either rejecting it or accepting it with certain qualifications. Paul Molnar believes Torrance would reject it, but acknowledges that Torrance's position is "somewhat ambiguous" because in his reading Torrance simultaneously rejects and affirms it.[277] Molnar reads Torrance's rejection and affirmation of the Scotist hypothesis through the following statements.

> *Torrance's Rejection*: "Because God *is* Love, we cannot and may not try to press our thought speculatively behind that Love to what might have happened, had not the fall taken place. . . . We can no more do that than we can think beyond the ultimate Being of God in his inner divine Life."[278]

> *Torrance's Affirmation*: "while clapping our hands upon our mouth, without knowing what we say, we may nevertheless feel urged to say that in his eternal purpose the immeasurable Love of God overflowing freely beyond himself which brought the creation into existence would have become incarnate within the creation even if we and our world were not in need of his redeeming grace."[279]

Molnar recognizes the challenge of interpreting Torrance on this subject, but categorically insists that a wider reading of Torrance would necessitate a rejection of the Scotist hypothesis.[280] His argument, perhaps, would be that since Torrance only seems to affirm the Scotist position once in his entire corpus, there is insufficient warrant to argue that he held the view. Added to this, Molnar may argue that in every other instance in his work, Torrance affirms a view that contradicts the Scotist position. Furthermore, in his written work, Molnar contends that Torrance would reject the Scotist hypothesis because it lends itself to "speculate" on theological subjects,

276. See Habets, "First Things First," 343–64.
277. Molnar, *Thomas F. Torrance*, 118n76.
278. Torrance, *Christian Doctrine of God*, 210.
279. Torrance, *Christian Doctrine of God*, 210.
280. Molnar, *Thomas F. Torrance*, 118n76.

whereas Torrance would prefer to focus on "the love of God actually revealed in the incarnate Word."[281] With respect to the passage where Torrance seems to affirm the Scotist position, Molnar asserts that there is a better interpretation that does not lead to the conclusion that he was affirming the Scotist view. Says Molnar, "Nonetheless, it seems quite clear that Torrance does not really want to go beyond the love of God actually revealed in the incarnate Word and so he does not in fact speculate about matters as they 'might have been.' He really sticks to the love of God revealed in the incarnation and that is why for him incarnation and atonement are inseparably related."[282]

Myk Habets, however, believes that Torrance's theology does affirm the Scotist view because one can find a shift in Torrance's thinking from his early theology found in the Auburn Lectures where he rejects the Scotist view to his mature theology where he affirms it.[283] Habets reasons that Torrance's "thought thus developed considerably in this area, largely due to his later interest in Athanasian theology, contingency, and the vicarious humanity of Jesus Christ."[284] Nevertheless, Habets concurs with Molnar insofar as he recognizes that in Torrance there is an "equivocation on the issue."[285] He nonetheless avers that there is sufficient warrant to believe that Torrance would affirm the Scotist hypothesis, but in a "modified" manner.[286] Habets maintains that a distinction must be made between the Scotist "thesis" and Scotist "hypothesis," wherein the former argues from the actual event of the incarnation and insists that it happened principally because of "the supreme love of God," not human "sin";[287] while in the latter, there is an extension from thinking about the actual to the realm of the "hypothetical," with the contention that Christ would have become incarnate "even if Adam had not sinned."[288] Habets believes that Torrance's theology affirms both the "thesis" and "hypothesis," but with the qualification that "the former [is] asserted positively and the latter [is] asserted tentatively."[289]

---

281. Molnar, *Thomas F. Torrance*, 118n76, points readers to Torrance's *Divine and Contingent Order*, 134–35, to substantiate his argument.

282. Molnar, *Thomas F. Torrance*, 118n76.

283. Habets, "First Things First," 358n58, substantiates his claim of a change in Torrance's theological position by pointing readers to Torrance, *Doctrine of Jesus Christ*, 154; and *Christian Doctrine of God*, 210. On p. 357, Habets describes Torrance's *Christian Doctrine of God* as "his *magnum opus*."

284. Habets, "First Things First," 358n58.

285. Habets, *Theosis*, 194.

286. See Habets, *Theosis*, 28n40; Habets, "First Things First," 357–61.

287. Habets, "First Things First," 347.

288. Habets, "First Things First," 350.

289. Habets, "First Things First," 360.

Since Torrance maintains both that "creation is proleptically conditioned by redemption" and that it is "proleptically conditioned by the incarnation,"[290] it would seem that Habets's reading of Torrance is justified on the subject of the Scotist hypothesis, but with Habets one must exercise caution and not be dogmatic.[291] The constructive account below will first highlight why Torrance's theology would affirm the Scotist hypothesis, which will be followed by an extension of the theo-logic of the Scotist hypothesis into an affirmation of the need for Christ's priestly ministry to be eternal in nature.

### 2.3.2.2 TORRANCE AND THE *SCOTIST HYPOTHESIS*

Myk Habets believes that Torrance's theology would affirm the Scotist hypothesis and substantiates his claim with a fourfold argument.[292] Cumulatively, (1) the ontological divide, (2) the epistemological gap, (3) the transformational intent, and (4) the *Imago Christi* lend credence to his argument.[293] Each of these four points can be explained as follows. By (1) the "ontological barrier," Habets explains that for Torrance the "ontological divide" between the "Creator-creature" is unbridgeable.[294] Says Habets, "God himself had to become human without ceasing to be divine in order to raise humanity up to participate in the Triune communion."[295] He goes on to explain that for Torrance this "ontological divide" could only be bridged by "Christ and the Holy Spirit," and also, importantly points out that Adam's sin only exacerbated this chasm; it did not create it in the first place.[296] With regard to (2), the "epistemological barrier between humanity and God," this point can be illuminated by an undergirding principle in Torrance's theology that Habets rightly points to, namely, "'Since only God can really know God, we may know him only as he reveals *himself* to us *through* himself.'"[297] In other words, human beings cannot on their own initiative know God, without God taking the first initiative to reveal himself, and in this instance Habets highlights how Torrance goes even further by underscoring how only God can reveal God.

290. Torrance, *Christian Doctrine of God*, 210.
291. Habets, "First Things First," 360.
292. Habets, "First Things First," 357–61.
293. Habets, "First Things First," 358–61.
294. Habets, "First Things First," 358.
295. Habets, "First Things First," 358.
296. Habets, "First Things First," 358.
297. Habets, "First Things First," 359; cf. Torrance, *Mediation of Christ*, 115.

By point (3), Habets observes that Torrance wishes to communicate the "saving significance of the incarnation," or in other words, the transformational intent: "Transformation of men and women into glorified saints" was part of God's original design for his creatures.[298] Importantly, Habets asserts that this transformational intent of fashioning human beings into the likeness of Jesus "was and is the divine intention for men and women regardless of human sinfulness."[299] Finally, point (4) relates to Torrance's "anthropology," which Habets points out is undergirded by a christological destiny: God created human beings with Christ in mind, more specifically with the goal of "conformity to an archetype—Jesus Christ," therefore the incarnation was necessary.[300] While each of these four points makes a strong cumulative case for the necessity of the incarnation irrespective of human rebellion and sin in Torrance's theology (i.e., the Scotist hypothesis), they would need to be slightly altered to apply to the necessity of the eternal priesthood of the ascended Jesus.

### 2.3.2.3 *Scotist Hypothesis* and the Eternal Mediation of Christ

Jesus's eternal priesthood or mediation would be necessitated for points (1) and (2) above for similar reasons. There is an unwittingly popular assumption that at the eschaton, human beings will be so transformed that they no longer need the mediation of Jesus Christ. Such a view is arguably also present in theological scholarship, not least in the works of theological giants in the Reformed tradition such as John Calvin.[301] This is, however, certainly not Torrance's view, which comes across clearly in doxological contexts.[302] Jesus is needed as a mediator between God and human beings in eternity, not because there will be sin that needs to be atoned for, but because the ontological and epistemological divide will still exist between God and human beings. In other words, since God remains *divine* and humans remain *human* and there is no intermingling between the two, therefore, Jesus and

---

298. Habets, "First Things First," 360.

299. Habets, "First Things First," 360. This point can be contentious in theological scholarship, but it is arguably important to Torrance, and as such is important to the overall argument of this research as well.

300. Habets, "First Things First," 360.

301. Cf. Calvin *Institutes* 1:2.14.3; *First Epistle*, 327. See also chapter 1 for a brief explication of the debate within Reformed theology on the role that Christ as mediator will (or will not) continue to play in the eschaton.

302. See chapter 5 for an explication of this theme in Torrance's theology. Cf. Torrance, *Apocalypse Today*, 183.

the Holy Spirit will always be needed to bridge the ontological divide and epistemological chasm between God and human beings that Habets rightly points to, with regard to the incarnation.

Torrance does not explicitly argue in the way that Wayne Grudem does, but he may not be averse to endorsing what Grudem mentions about one important aspect of what bodily resurrection existence will be like in the new creation:

> Since God is infinite and we can never exhaust his greatness (Ps. 145:3), and since we are finite creatures who will never equal God's knowledge or be omniscient, we may expect that for all eternity we will be able to go on learning more about God and about his relationship to his creation. In this way we will continue the process of learning that was begun in this life, in which a life "fully pleasing to him" is one that includes continually "increasing in the knowledge of God" (Col. 1:10).[303]

Grudem's insights[304] apply very clearly to the ontological and epistemological divide between God and humankind, and helpfully illuminate why (1) and (2) would continue into eternity, necessitating the eternal mediation of Christ.

Furthermore, with regard to points (3) and (4), Jesus Christ will be needed even in eternity because the process of being conformed into the likeness of Jesus is an *eternal* one.[305] It is important to decouple the need for an eternal transformation from any notion of human sin, and Habets does this in a different context, in answering how there will be growth and development even in the eschaton.[306] Principally, Habets insists that human ontology even when it is not stained by sin, as will be the case in heaven, will necessitate development and progress: "The nature of creaturely perfection means we will continue to change and develop, and continue to be perfected in a multitude of ways."[307]

---

303. Grudem, *Systematic Theology*, 1162.

304. Grudem is in accord with the views of Gregory of Nyssa. Cf. Gregory of Nyssa, *Life of Moses* 1:3–10, but especially 1:10: "For the perfection of human nature consists perhaps in its very growth in goodness."

305. See Habets, *Heaven*, 50–52. On p. 52, Habets highlights how the eschatological life in the new creation will be characterized by "eternal progress and perfecting," and as a movement from "glory to glory." While Habets does not state it in this context, arguably he is theologically expositing 2 Cor 3:18: "And we all, with unveiled face, beholding the glory of the Lord, are being transformed into the same image from one degree of glory to another. For this comes from the Lord who is the Spirit" (ESV).

306. Habets, "Theosis," 147.

307. Habets, *Heaven*, 50.

Elsewhere, Habets sheds more light on why there will be an eternal process of growth when he explains Christlikeness as a pursuit to be like God.[308] Since the ontological difference between God and human beings will never be bridged, the pursuit to be like God will never obtain; however, humans can "become God-like" when they imitate God as he is in his Triune being.[309] Essentially, the argument is best summarized as follows: "God is dynamic, God is community, God is relational. If we are made in that image, which Jesus Christ bears uniquely and then we are in that image of Christ who is the image of God, then in eternity, we can never exhaust that being of God. We emulate, we imitate it, we partake of it, which means . . . we are always chasing after God."[310] Since Christlikeness = Godlikeness, therefore, it is an eternal pursuit.[311] Given that Christ manifests the image of God perfectly, human beings in eternity will continue to learn from him and grow into his image.

### 2.3.3 Critique #9: Prophetic Ministry Loosely Connected to Pneumatology and Preaching?

The role of the Holy Spirit and preaching are both central to Torrance's account of the prophetic ministry of the ascended Jesus, but arguably both of these aspects are underemphasized in Torrance. The importance of both pneumatology and preaching vis-à-vis the prophetic ministry of the ascended Christ is evidenced when Torrance underscores that "the ascension is not only the bearing of that Word up before the Face of the Father, but that Word accepted and honoured by God, that Word fully installed in the divine Kingdom, *sent back to earth through the Spirit and by means of the Church proclaimed to all nations and all ages.*"[312] Sherrard helpfully summarizes Torrance's theology of Christ as ascended prophet through the phrase "triple mediation," by which he observes three kinds of mediation taking place in the prophetic office: "[1] God's Word to humanity, [2] the perfect word from humanity back to God that is Jesus' perfect obedience, [3] *and finally the post-ascension mediation of that accomplished work by the Holy Spirit.*"[313] Sherrard also correctly observes that for Torrance the prophetic

---

308. Habets, "Theosis," 147.
309. Habets, "Theosis," 147.
310. Habets, "Theosis," 147.
311. Habets, "Theosis," 147.
312. Torrance, *Space, Time, and Resurrection*, 120.
313. Sherrard, *T. F. Torrance*, 150–51.

ministry in light of the ascension is "ongoing" and "exercised primarily through the church's preaching."[314]

Scholarship on Torrance, however, notes the underemphasis of both pneumatology and preaching. Fergusson, for example, in the context of highlighting the important role the ascended Christ continues to play in worship, avers that the Holy Spirit's role in Torrance's theology is rather insular and not actively conceptualized beyond the walls of the church:

> Admittedly, a correlative account of the Spirit as indwelling and enabling may be less developed here—a similar deficit is apparent in John McLeod Campbell—and interpreters of Torrance may require to think further about this in the future to avoid charges of Christomonism. In his characterization of the two hands of God—Word and Spirit—the work of the first tends to outweigh the second. This in turn may lead to an underdeveloped sense of the Spirit as active in the world outside the community of the church.[315]

Fergusson's critique would equally apply to the prophetic ministry of the ascended Christ in relation to pneumatology, as other Torrancean scholars have identified pneumatology as an area that is not as developed in Torrance's theology.[316] With regard to a theology of preaching, Sherrard rightly observes that there is "a relative lack of reflection upon the actual act of preaching," in Torrance.[317] Both of these criticisms are important and deserve closer scrutiny.

### 2.3.3.1 Prophetic Ministry and Pneumatology

Fergusson's critique of Torrance's pneumatology can be divided into two aspects: (1) an inadequate emphasis on the *person* of the Holy Spirit and (2) an insufficient exploration of the *work* of the Holy Spirit.[318] Both of these aspects deserve a thorough critical investigation that is beyond the scope of this work.[319] However, one can respond to the first critique which finds Tor-

---

314. Sherrard, *T. F. Torrance*, 151.
315. Fergusson, "He Ascended into Heaven," 45.
316. Cf. Habets, *Theosis*, 140; Lee, *Living in Union*, 316.
317. Sherrard, *T. F. Torrance*, 189.
318. Fergusson, "He Ascended into Heaven," 45.
319. Torrance, "Thomas Torrance Responds," 312, acknowledges that he has "not devoted a special work to the doctrine of the Holy Spirit" in comparison to how he has explored "the Father and the Son" but contends on pp. 312–14 that he has explored central aspects of the person and work of the Holy Spirit in different parts of his corpus.

rance's articulation of the person of the Holy Spirit to be lacking by noting that Torrance believes biblical fidelity and theological correctness requires one to describe the Holy Spirit in a way that always points to Christ and the Father, not to himself.[320] Torrance therefore insists that the very being of the Holy Spirit necessitates pointing away from himself: "He [Holy Spirit] is the invisible Spirit of truth sent from the Father in the name of the Son, not in his own personal name as the Holy Spirit, and thus does not speak of himself but speaks of the Father and of the Son what he receives from them."[321]

Elsewhere Torrance emphasizes, "By his very mode of being as Spirit of Spirit he hides himself from us behind the Father in the Son and behind the Son in the Father, so that we do not know him face to face in his own ὑπόστασις."[322] Therefore, in response to the charge of "Christomonism" that Fergusson exhorts Torrance scholars to seriously consider, one can respond by noting what Gary Deddo underscores about Torrance's pneumatology in general: "This approach actually corresponds to the nature of the subject matter, the Holy Spirit. It reflects the ineffable and self-effacing nature of the Spirit whose ministry is to shed light on everything else rather than to be in the spotlight."[323] Torrance himself approves Deddo's observation.[324]

One can also respond to the second critique that finds Torrance's explanation about the details of the work of the Holy Spirit sparse by insisting that Torrance is not interested in explaining the inner workings of mystery.[325] In other words, for Torrance, as Deddo observes, many "how" type of questions are answered with a *who* answer: "For the Holy Spirit itself is the answer to the ultimate 'how' questions we might ask. How was Jesus

---

Some places where Torrance engages in exploring the doctrine of the Holy Spirit are: *School of Faith*, xcv–cxxvi; *God and Rationality*, 165–92; *Theology in Reconstruction*, 209–58; *Trinitarian Faith*, 191–251; *Christian Doctrine of God*, 59–67, 147–55, 185–94. For secondary scholarship, which is minimal, see Deddo, "Holy Spirit"; Colyer, *How to Read*, 211–41; Molnar, *Thomas F. Torrance*, 187–217; Habets, "You Wonder Where."

320. Torrance, *Trinitarian Faith*, 211–12. On pp. 211–12n99, Torrance points to several passages from the Gospel of John to substantiate his claim; namely, "John 14.16f, 25f; 15.26f; 16.13f." He also cites selections from the works of theologians such as Athanasius, Hilary, Didymus, Cyril, Epiphanius, and Gregory of Nyssa to support his view. The specific passages he refers to are as follows: "Athanasius, *Ad Ser.*, 1.20; 3.1; *Con. Ar.*, 1.15; 3.44; Hilary, *De Trin.*, 7.20; 8.20; Didymus, *De Sp. St.*, 30–38; Cyril of Jer., *Cat.*, 16.14; Epiphanius, *Haer.*, 48.12; 62.4, 7; 69.18, 34; 74.1, 4, 6, 9ff; 76.4, 7; *Anc.*, 6ff, 11, 73, 120; Gregory Nyss., *De Sp. St.*, Jaeger, 3.1, p. 108, etc."

321. Torrance, *Trinitarian Faith*, 211.

322. Torrance, *Trinitarian Faith*, 212.

323. Deddo, "Holy Spirit," 103–4.

324. See Torrance, "Thomas Torrance Responds," 312.

325. Deddo, "Holy Spirit," 105–6.

conceived in the womb of Mary? By the Holy Spirit!"[326] Deddo therefore states that Torrance underscores "the agency of the Holy Spirit" in a Western intellectual milieu that interprets reality "in terms of impersonal, causal, or instrumental means."[327] When read through such a perspective, one can respond to Fergusson's critique that one does not find too many details about how the Holy Spirit works in the world by noting that Torrance's overarching emphasis in his pneumatology is to provide a "radical critique" and corrective to tendencies that undermine "the centrality of agency for theological description."[328] Therefore, Fergusson is right to find many details missing, but nonetheless, with Deddo, one can affirm that Torrance has provided a "foundation" upon which others can build a biblical and theologically robust pneumatology that distills the specific ways in which the Holy Spirit is working in the world today.[329]

Not all are convinced by Deddo's charitable reading of Torrance on this point. Theologians such as Myk Habets, Aaron Yom, and Alexandra Radcliff, for example, can be said to want to take Torrance's theology further in the realm of pneumatology. Acknowledging that Torrance's theology does have a pneumatology, especially with a stress on the Trinity and epistemology, the specific criticism revolves around the lack of pneumatology in his exploration of other theological loci.[330] Habets, for example, believes that Torrance does not sufficiently explore how pneumatology plays a role in "the life of Christ" and "the Christian life" in general.[331] He substantiates his argument with respect to Christology as follows:

> In his discussion of *enhypostasia* and *anhypostasia*, and other christological themes, Torrance speaks of the Holy Spirit regularly but fails adequately to incorporate a pneumatological discourse. By positing too great an emphasis on the agency of the divine Word on the human nature of Jesus, as opposed to a relation mediated by the Holy Spirit, Torrance implicitly makes the human nature of Christ merely instrumental. It would be too much to suggest that Torrance's christology is docetic or Apollinarian, but his lack of pneumatology in this area does risk bringing him to the brink of such a failing.[332]

---

326. Deddo, "Holy Spirit," 105–6.
327. Deddo, "Holy Spirit," 106.
328. Deddo, "Holy Spirit," 106.
329. Deddo, "Holy Spirit," 106–9.
330. See Habets, "You Wonder Where."
331. Habets, "You Wonder Where," 53.
332. Habets, *Theosis*, 71.

In another place he sheds further light on the lack of pneumatology with respect to the life of a Christian: "A robust pneumatology would be evident in a detailed discussion of the incarnational dynamics of Jesus' life, in a study of the cross, in issues of practical theology, and most especially, in detailed discussion of the Christian life."[333] Therefore, in their own ways Habets, Yom, and Radcliff seek to offer a corrective to Torrance's pneumatology.

Habets and Yom do this from a methodological perspective, the former through his contribution to a *Third Article Theology*,[334] while the latter does this by bringing Torrance into dialogue with noted pneumatologist Amos Yong in order to develop a "pneumatological imagination,"[335] by which Torrance's theology can more easily discern the work of the Spirit in the world today.[336] Radcliff's work is arguably a dogmatic work that seeks to discern how Torrance's theology of sanctification can be better informed, among other ways, by pneumatology.[337] In light of both kinds of perspectives on Torrance's pneumatology, one can agree that more work is needed to develop his theology in constructive dialogue with others in the field of pneumatology.

### 2.3.3.2 Prophetic Ministry and Preaching

Sherrard correctly observes that Torrance's main concern is to ground the church's preaching in the Scriptures, which Christ uses to faithfully communicate his *own* message.[338] Essentially, Sherrard notes that for Torrance it was imperative "to emphasize the immediacy of Christ's communication to the church not first by way of the church's preaching but instead in the word of Scripture itself."[339] The central leitmotif of preaching that Torrance wanted to communicate was that when the Scriptures were preached, it

---

333. Habets, "You Wonder," 50.

334. See Habets, "Prolegomenon," 19; Yom, *Number, Word, and Spirit*; Radcliff, *Claim of Humanity*.

335. Yom, *Number, Word, and Spirit*, 86.

336. See Yom, *Number, Word, and Spirit*, 85, where he contends that "pentecostal-pneumatological imagination opens up Torrance's revelatory-realist paradigm to the constructive and critical dimensions of human spirituality while acknowledging the imperative of thinking scientifically and the necessity of engaging reality objectively."

337. See Radcliff, *Claim of Humanity*, 192–93, where she highlights the need for a better understanding of pneumatology in Torrance's emphasis on the humanity of Christ vis-à-vis the doctrine of sanctification.

338. See Sherrard, *T. F. Torrance*, 186, where he correctly summarizes Torrance, *God and Rationality*, 152.

339. Sherrard, *T. F. Torrance*, 186.

was Christ himself who was being communicated.[340] Drawing on Webster's critique of Torrance's doctrine of Scripture, wherein the former finds "extended exegesis"[341] lacking, Sherrard points out that a similar "criticism can also be applied to preaching."[342] More specifically, Sherrard explains that just as Torrance, according to Webster, "does not linger over the textual sign, fearing, no doubt, that this may arrest the movement of hermeneutical intelligence in pressing through to the *res*,"[343] similarly one does not find details about the preaching act in Torrance because of a fear that "Christ's agency in speaking through the text" will be compromised.[344] Torrance's account of the act of preaching is only given "a slim description" in his theology, and according to Sherrard, what would be helpful is an explanation of how exactly "Christ's own prophetic proclamation" corresponds to the church's preaching.[345]

With regard to specific aspects of preaching, Sherrard points to Karl Barth's theological contributions to this subject as a better in-depth resource.[346] From Barth's work on *Homiletics*, Sherrard observes that Torrance, unlike Barth, does not reflect upon the following: "The definition of the sermon, the necessity of expository preaching, and the way that the preacher's speech should relate to, reflect, and honor the biblical passage."[347] Sherrard draws such a conclusion after assessing Torrance's explicitly preaching-oriented resources such as *Preaching Christ Today* which he believes lack the kind of depth of insight that one finds in Barth.[348] He goes on to insist along with Webster that Torrance merely chose not to focus on such subjects, not that his theology is inimical to them, by making it a priority "to establish the direct connection between Jesus Christ, the apostolic deposit of faith, and the church's encounter with the ascended Christ in its preaching."[349]

Sherrard is correct to make this observation, but recent Torrance scholarship is noticing that Torrance's sermons themselves can serve as a

340. See chapter 5 for an explication of this theme. But see also Torrance, *Atonement*, 323, which Sherrard is drawing from in formulating his own views in *T. F. Torrance*, 187.

341. Webster, *Domain of the Word*, 110.

342. Sherrard, *T. F. Torrance*, 189.

343. Webster, *Domain of the Word*, 110.

344. Sherrard, *T. F. Torrance*, 189.

345. Sherrard, *T. F. Torrance*, 189.

346. Sherrard, *T. F. Torrance*, 190.

347. Sherrard, *T. F. Torrance*, 190. Sherrard is here summarizing key aspects of Barth's reflection on the specific aspects of preaching from Barth, *Homiletics*.

348. Here, Sherrard refers to Torrance, *Preaching Christ Today*, 1–40.

349. Sherrard, *T. F. Torrance*, 190.

means to better understand aspects of his theology that do not come to the fore in some of his academic works.[350] Dick Eugenio, for instance, observes that while not contradicting his overarching theological views, Torrance emphasizes different theological aspects to provide correctives to the differing audiences he had in mind.[351] Eugenio insightfully notices in the context of his study on Torrance's soteriology that "in his published writings, he [Torrance] was consciously engaging the existentialist understanding of salvation prevalent in the evangelical movement that emphasizes human decision in the salvific process. In his dealings with his parishioners, however, he was engaging a group of people deeply rooted in federal Calvinism that emphasizes divine fiat at the expense of human responsibility."[352] Therefore, to each respective audience, Torrance was accentuating different theological truths to redress what he believed were the default errors that needed to be excoriated.[353] Eugenio's insights along with recent work on Torrance's theology in his preaching[354] suggest that there is a need to explore Torrance's preaching in order to discover specific aspects of his theology of preaching. Barth's work on preaching does stand out, but Torrance's work needs to be investigated further, by using a wider corpus that includes his unpublished sermons. This is a task that is needed to further Torrance scholarship in ways that helpfully provide nuance and perspective on aspects that are arguably latent in his published work.

## 3. CONCLUSION

This chapter interrogated Torrance's theology of the ascension through nine specific criticisms. Each of these critiques served as a checkpoint that enabled readers to pause and carefully evaluate the merits of the criticisms leveled against Torrance. Furthermore, these critiques served as opportunities for further refinement and constructive development of an already robust contribution to a theology of the ascension. Criticisms 1–3 related to the *ontology* of the ascended Christ, 4–6 focused on issues specific to the *spatiality* of the ascended Christ, and finally, 7–9 examined concerns related to the *present ministry* of the ascended Christ. Specifically, *Critique #1* focused on Torrance's theological anthropology in eschatological perspective,

---

350. See Eugenio, *Communion*, 208.
351. Eugenio, *Communion*, 208.
352. Eugenio, *Communion*, 208.
353. Eugenio, *Communion*, 208.
354. Cf. Habets, "*Theologia Is Eusebia*," 259–76. See also chapter 6 of Navarro's *Trinitarian Doxology*, 113–41, where he explores "T. F. Torrance and Preaching."

examining whether he acknowledged human existence in the eschatological future and concluding with the affirmative. *Critique #2* scrutinized whether Torrance is guilty of eliding the differences between Christ and the church, specifically with respect to the eschatological judgment. Torrance, notwithstanding criticism to the contrary, does affirm a clear distinction between Christology and ecclesiology, and also maintains that the church will face a future judgement. *Critique #3* investigated whether Torrance is guilty of compromising Christ's ontology by having to succumb to a form of kenotic Christology because he maintains that it is only at the ascension that humanity is united to God. Torrance, it was argued, is not guilty of a kenotic Christology because he makes a distinction between Christ's own humanity and the rest of humankind, the former is "fallen" but "sinless" from the point of conception onward, but the latter is in need of healing and restoration, which is fully realized in principle only in the ascension (and will be realized in practice at the eschaton).

*Critique #4* considered whether Torrance's theology is an expression of an overrealized individual eschatology because it seemed to affirm an instantaneous resurrection, and concluded that it was. To avoid a plethora of conundrums, it was suggested that Torrance could have affirmed an intermediate state that was not disembodied to be faithful to his nondualistic theology, but also to circumvent the force of the criticism targeted at his theology on this point. *Critique #5* acknowledged that Torrance did not develop a robust Trinitarian spatial theology, and suggested through nascent insights in Torrance one could develop a well-rounded Trinitarian spatiality by using the *three levels of theology*, in inverse order. *Critique #6* probed Torrance's theological language with respect to the location of the ascended Christ and concluded that a more specific answer was required to avoid accusations of being vague. Through the *hyperspace* theory, which explains heaven as another "dimension," it was argued that one could provide an answer about the location of the ascended Christ. While Torrance does not explicitly endorse such a theory, it was argued that it was similar to his own views about where heaven is, and therefore a legitimate extension of his own thought.

*Critique #7* studied whether Torrance was indeed guilty of neglecting to expound Jesus's kingship in a way that addressed ethics and politics. Surprisingly, while there is not much explicit material within Torrance in both areas, there were sufficient ethically-relevant works in Torrance, and with some modifications to his theology, along with key dialogue partners, politics could be addressed more substantially as well. *Critique #8* pondered whether Torrance had sufficiently expounded a theology of the eternal priesthood of Christ and reasoned that he did not. Using the *Scotist hypothesis*, it was argued, one could extend Torrance's theology of the priesthood both *retrospectively* and *prospectively*. Finally, *Critique #9* reviewed the concern about the lack of specific information about the how the prophetic ministry of the ascended Christ relates to pneumatology and preaching. Torrance's focus was on providing a "foundation" in this area, and the conclusion of this section highlighted the need for more work in this area.

Cumulatively, all nine criticisms, positively, highlight the relevance of Torrance regarding various facets of contemporary thinking about the ascension. Not all of Torrance's answers are satisfactory because he has not expounded the details of various aspects pertinent to a theology of the ascension. However, he has provided a sound theological, epistemological, and constructive work on the ascension. The next chapter will summarize the study and highlight areas for further exploration within Torrance's theology of the ascension.

# 7

# Critical Conclusions

## 1. UNIQUE CONTRIBUTION TO SCHOLARSHIP

THIS WORK EXAMINES THE doctrine of the ascension in the thought of T. F. Torrance and demonstrates how his *holistic* account took into consideration the *ontology*, *spatiality*, and *present ministry* of the ascended Jesus. Beginning with his mature theological writings in *Space, Time, and Resurrection*, and supplemented by other writings across his vast theological oeuvre, the intricate details that constitute Torrance's holistic account of the ascended status of Christ have been examined. Specifically, his holistic account of the ascension includes concrete declarations, grounded in biblical and theological convictions, with implications for other doctrines, and several avenues for constructive development.

Torrance's theology of the ascension has been rightly recognized as a modern theological classic. This study shined the spotlight on a theologian who is often neglected. While there have been some articles and book chapters on Torrance's theology of the ascension, this study offers the first monograph devoted to the topic. Methodologically, this work aimed to be true to Torrance's own approach to theology. In other words, it aimed to be a study in *constructive dogmatics*, wherein the goal was not just to interpret carefully Torrance's theology of the ascension but also to develop constructively his theology in critical dialogue with contemporary theological interlocutors. This is arguably what Torrance did in his own theology, and this work sought to follow him in adopting such a method. The intended outcome of such an approach has been the constructive development of embryonic Torrancean insights as well as refinement and clarification of Torrance's theology in certain areas.

On the ontology of the ascended Jesus, Torrance's views were shown to align more with Augustine's theological anthropology than with Gregory of Nyssa's. This is because Torrance (like Augustine) affirmed a gendered eschatological existence for humankind rather than a humanity that is devoid of gender at the eschaton. Furthermore, regarding ecclesiology, Torrance made it a point to avoid theological conceptions that viewed the "Body of Christ" as a biological entity with Christ as "head" and the church as the "body." Through a critical interaction with contemporary Lutheran theologian Ian McFarland on the theology of the "Body of Christ," it was shown that there is a way to advance ecumenical dialogue between Torrance and Lutheran theology on the subject of the *totus Christus*. McFarland promises to be an important dialogue partner for Torrancean scholars on the *totus Christus* because he linguistically and verbally affirms the intricate relationship between the "head" and "body" without ending up with a conception that is a biological entity. Torrance would find much to commend here. Finally, about Christ's corporeality in his ascension, it was established that Torrance would not support any difference between so-called Lukan perspectives and Pauline interpretations on the subject. For Torrance, the ascended Christ is a corporeal human being, free from any kind of corruption and decay.

On the spatiality of the ascended Christ, christologically, it was shown that a strong case can be made to expand Torrance's affirmation of the *extra Calvinisticum* as a heuristic for the ascension as well as the incarnation. This is important not only because it arguably represents Torrance's own views on the subject, but more importantly in order to avoid reading Torrance in Lutheran ways (as some contemporary scholars do) rather than as a Reformed theologian. From a Trinitarian perspective, Torrance does not offer a detailed exposition of how to conceptualize space in the light of the Trinity. However, his emphasis on both the *oneness* and the *threeness* of the Triune God unmistakably affirms genuine relationality between God and human beings, which then provides a vision and an exhortation for how human beings are to relate to each other with mutuality and reciprocity. With respect to epistemology and theological language, an analysis of Torrance's rhetoric showed that he utilizes the category of mystery at several key places in his theology, which this work has identified as *artistic* language. A study of Torrance's rhetoric on the ascension in juxtaposition to specific aspects of C. S. Lewis's rhetoric revealed that like Lewis, Torrance's work can also be said to be a work of theological art and beauty. Theologically analyzing Torrance's rhetoric promises to pay rich dividends in the future.

On the present ministry of the ascended Christ, Torrance's emphasis on the kingship of Jesus vis-à-vis the theme of victory was explicated to address an embryonic area of his theology—namely, the doctrine of sanctification. This was done through a dialogue with Wesleyan theology in order to address weaknesses endemic within their respective theologies. Torrance's theology could benefit from the strengths of Wesley's subjective emphasis on sanctification, and Wesley's theology could stand to gain from Torrance's objective focus in his doctrine of sanctification. This exchange underscored the ecumenical potential that exists within Torrance's theology on the subject of sanctification. Concerning the priesthood of Christ, Torrance's critique of Barth on this point, as well as the ecclesiological and sacramental emphases in his theology that arguably are not adequately present in Barth, provide areas of contrast between his *Doktorvater* and himself. With respect to the prophetic ministry of Jesus, Torrance's views are grounded in his doctrine of Scripture. While Torrance's corpus does not contain detailed exegesis of biblical texts, it was stated that his interpretation of select passages (such as Mark 16:19–20) stand out as noteworthy contributions to biblical and theological exegesis. More work is needed, however, to provide substantial exegetical engagement with the text of Scripture from Torrance's perspective. This is a task for future Torrance scholars to take up.

## 2. CRITIQUING A THEOLOGICAL GIANT

Critiquing a theological giant such as Torrance is a daunting task, but this work has sought to commend as well as critique Torrance. Chapter 6 offered a substantial critical evaluation of Torrance's doctrine of the ascension in relation to interconnected themes, such as theological anthropology, ecclesiology, Christology, eschatology, Trinity, theological use of language, Jesus's kingship in relation to ethics and politics, Jesus's priesthood vis-à-vis questions like the *Scotist hypothesis*, and finally, the implications of Jesus's prophetic ministry for pneumatology and preaching. With the twofold goal of listening to criticisms as well as refining Torrance's theology where relevant, this exercise flagged many areas for legitimate critique and other areas for promising constructive development.

From a critical perspective, doctrinally, while eschatology was noted as one of Torrance's strengths, it is not inappropriate to critique him because he seemingly affirms an instantaneous resurrection, thereby contradicting his overall *proleptic* and *expectant* eschatology. By affirming a non-dualist embodied intermediate state, Torrance's theology, it was argued, can circumvent numerous criticisms. Furthermore, although Torrance develops a robust christological account of the ascension, there are some aspects that are neglected, not least pneumatology and his doctrine of Scripture. Recent studies on Torrance redress these lacunae and provide helpful ways forward in Torrance scholarship with respect to both theological loci. Theological language, it was emphasized, was an area that sheds new insights on Torrance's articulation of the ascension; but even in this area, at times, Torrance does not provide sufficient details, leaving aspects of his theology unclear. By showing Torrance's theology to be open to a scientific explanation such as *hyperspace*, his theology can substantiate the claim of an ascended body that is located somewhere, thereby circumventing critiques of intellectual vagueness.

There were many promising areas for a constructive development of Torrance's theology, but some of the more prominent ones were: the need to compare and contrast Torrance's and Barth's theological anthropologies vis-à-vis eschatology; the need to study Torrance's writings from a rhetorical perspective with respect to *artistic/mystery* language; the need to develop a Torrancean theology of ethics and politics that takes the best of Torrance's meta-theological framework and James Torrance's extension of such a framework into a praxis-oriented theology; the need to expand Torrance's Reformed theological convictions on the *extra Calvinisticum* as a heuristic for the ascension; and finally, the need to examine the eternal role of Jesus as the exclusive high priest and intercessor between God and humanity. Each of these areas were explored in this study and attempts were made to develop constructive accounts. Others can take up these aspects and build structures from the scaffolding that were offered here.

Commendably, Torrance has demonstrated a willingness to confront theological frontiers with a robust theological account of the ascension in an intellectual environment that is ready to sacrifice the doctrine because it is unpalatable to modern scientific sensibilities. Torrance serves as a rigorous theological interlocutor to any of his critics because he is able to holistically construct a doctrine of the ascension that simultaneously affirms a *realist* theology of the ascended body, which is located in heaven as a corporeal body, while currently engaging humanly in a ministry of priestly intercession, prophetic declaration, and ascended kingship. Torrance is able to do this without succumbing to literalism (space travel), demythologization (metaphorical reading), or Pelagianism (human effort-based sanctification and glorification), and therefore, his construction deserves a wide critical engagement.

## 3. STRENGTHS AND POTENTIAL WEAKNESSES

The strengths of this study are found in its detailed exposition, constructive development, and critical analysis of Torrance's theology of the ascension with respect to the ontology, spatiality, and present ministry of the ascended

Christ. The goal has been to learn from Torrance so that one could build on what he has produced, and through the focus on constructive dogmatics, several underexplored areas in Torrance scholarship were highlighted, developed, and identified for further expansion.

A perceived weakness of this work could be that it was not *constructive* enough, since it did not focus enough on questions pertaining to the details of the eschatological future—questions such as what resurrection bodies will be like, what the new heavens and new earth will look like, and whether human beings will see God face to face (and what that could even mean), to name but a few. Since this study focused on the risen and ascended humanity of Christ, the scope was limited to the ascension, and only suggestively explored various aspects about the eschatological future. Further exploration on eschatology is needed; this study offers a foundation for such work to happen.

For want of space, this research has not explored the resonances of Torrance's theology with contextual theologies. However, this is an important area that deserves more in-depth reflection by Torrance scholars. Veli-Matti Kärkkäinen persuasively demonstrates the need for constructive theology in today's context to be conversant with global theologies; a theology that chooses not to engage with contextual issues is inadequate.[1] Therefore, future studies can take up this theme and explore it in an in-depth manner.[2]

## 4. TO CONCLUDE: A MISSIONAL LAST WORD

Torrance's entire theology is energized by a commitment to missions, and therefore, perhaps, the most important resonance for theology is missiological in nature. The period between the ascension and the return of Christ, for Torrance, is for the purpose of proclaiming the gospel, so that people can hear and respond to the message of Jesus Christ, the incarnate, risen, and ascended Lord. It is hoped that this study on the ascension will

---

1. Karkkainen, *Constructive Christian Theology*; Heltzel et al., *Dialogic Evangelical Theology*.

2. A dialogue between Torrance and Christian theology in India is ripe for further critical exploration. I have begun this exploration in John, "Torrance and Global Evangelicalism"; John, "Chalcedon and Indian Christologies." Some other helpful resources that will aid in understanding some of the challenges and opportunities with respect to the ascension in the Indian Christian theological context, so that a more fruitful dialogue can take place with Torrance's theology, are: George, *Jesus Beyond Borders*; George, "Christological Reflections"; Stubbs, "Resurrection"; Abraham, "Indian Pentecostal Christology"; Boyd, "Some Indian Christian Interpretations"; Bennema and Bhakiaraj, *Indian and Christian*; Thomas, "High Priestly Christology."

encourage further theological studies on the doctrine that are both theologically robust and missiologically grounded, just as Torrance himself was throughout his life.

The ascension is a crucial doctrine, integrally related to the Incarnation. When it is underemphasized, it results in an impoverishment of our theology of Christ, the church, human beings, and all that is to come (eschatology). Torrance's theology offers a compelling vision and holistic doctrine of the ascension that, notwithstanding its flaws, deserves a careful and detailed examination, as this study has provided. It is hoped that Torrance's theological vision of the ascended Christ will impact the minds, hearts, and lives of many, so that we all can stand on the shoulders of giants and perceive more than our theological forebears. May such added sight lead to a more faithful living and a winsome proclamation of the message of the risen and ascended Christ. Torrance has enriched my understanding in this area by being my literary *Doktorvater*. It is my hope that the insights I offer in this study will be of help to others.

# Bibliography

Abraham, Shaibu. "Ordinary Indian Pentecostal Christology." PhD diss., University of Birmingham, 2011.
Allen, Michael. *Grounded in Heaven: Recentering Christian Hope and Life on God*. Grand Rapids: Eerdmans, 2018.
———. "A Heaven on Earth Perspective." In *Four Views on Heaven*, edited by Michael Wittmer, 115–35. Grand Rapids: Zondervan Academic, 2022.
———. "On Bavinck, the Beatific Vision, and Theological Practice." *Reformed Faith & Practice* 7 (2022) 57–62.
———. "The Visibility of the Invisible God." *Journal of Reformed Theology* 9 (2015) 249–69.
Allen, Michael, and Scott R. Swain, eds. *Christian Dogmatics: Reformed Theology for the Church Catholic*. Grand Rapids: Baker Academic, 2016.
———. *Reformed Catholicity: The Promise of Retrieval for Theology and Biblical Interpretation*. Grand Rapids: Baker Academic, 2015.
Anderson, Ray S. "Reading T. F. Torrance as a Practical Theologian." In *The Promise of Trinitarian Theology: Theologians in Dialogue with T. F. Torrance*, edited by Elmer M. Colyer, 161–84. Lanham, MD: Rowman & Littlefield, 2001.
———. *Theology, Death, and Dying*. Eugene, OR: Wipf & Stock, 2012.
Arles, Siga. "The State of Mission Studies in India: An Overview and Assessment of Publications and Publishing." *International Bulletin of Missionary Research* 34 (2010) 156–64.
Backfish, Elizabeth H. P., and Paul Owen, eds. "Torrance and Biblical Theology." Special issue, *Participatio* 8 (2020).
Baker, Mark D., and Joel B. Green. *Recovering the Scandal of the Cross: Atonement in New Testament and Contemporary Contexts*. Downers Grove, IL: InterVarsity, 2000.
Baker, Matthew. "The Place of St. Irenaeus of Lyons in Historical and Dogmatic Theology According to Thomas F. Torrance." *Participatio* 2 (2010) 5–43.
Barr, James. *The Semantics of Biblical Language*. New York: Oxford University Press, 1961.
Barth, Karl. *Church Dogmatics*. Vol. 4/2, *The Doctrine of Reconciliation*. Edited by G. W. Bromiley and T. F. Torrance. Translated by G. W. Bromiley. London: T&T Clark, 2004.
———. *Church Dogmatics*. Vol. 4/3.1, *The Doctrine of Reconciliation*. Edited by G. W. Bromiley and T. F. Torrance. Translated by G. W. Bromiley. London: T&T Clark, 1961.

---. *Homiletics*. Translated by Geoffrey W. Bromiley and Donald E. Daniels. Louisville: Westminster John Knox, 1991.

Bauman, Michael. "Thomas Torrance." In *Roundtable Conversations with European Theologians*, 109–18. Grand Rapids: Baker Book House, 1990.

Begbie, Jeremy. "Incarnation, Creation, and New Creation: T. F. Torrance and a Theological Re-visioning of the Arts." *Participatio* 11 (2023) 61–79.

———. "Incarnation, Creation, and New Creation: What T. F. Torrance Offers to a Theological Re-visioning of the Arts." Keynote Lecture delivered at the 2018 Thomas F. Torrance Theological Fellowship Annual Meeting, August 18, 2019. https://www.youtube.com/watch?v=h00w9X_or-4.

———. "'A Semblance More Lucid'? An Exploration of Trinitarian Space." In *Essays on the Trinity*, edited by Lincoln Harvey, 20–35. Eugene, OR: Cascade, 2018.

Bennema, Cornelius, and Paul Joshua Bhakiaraj, eds. *Indian and Christian: Changing Identities in Modern India*. Bangalore: SAIACS, 2011.

Billings. J. Todd. "The New View of Heaven Is Too Small." *Christianity Today*, February 15, 2018. https://www.christianitytoday.com/ct/2018/february-web-only/new-view-of-heaven-too-small-resurrection-hope.html.

———. *Union with Christ: Reframing Theology and Ministry for the Church*. Grand Rapids: Baker Academic, 2011.

Bloesch, Donald G. *The Last Things: Resurrection, Judgment, Glory*. Downers Grove, IL: InterVarsity, 2004.

Boersma, Hans. "Neo-Calvinism and the Beatific Vision: Eschatology in the Reformed Tradition." *Crux* 56 (2020) 25–29.

———. *Seeing God: The Beatific Vision in Christian Tradition*. Grand Rapids: Eerdmans, 2018.

———. "Thomas Aquinas on the Beatific Vision: A Christological Deficit." *TheoLogica* 2 (2018) 129–47.

Boyd, Robin H. S. *An Introduction to Indian Christian Theology*. Delhi: ISPCK, 1979.

———. "Some Indian Christian Interpretations of the Resurrection." *Indian Journal of Theology* 17 (1968) 49–61.

Brunner, Emil. *Eternal Hope*. Translated by Harold Knight. Philadelphia: Westminster, 1954.

Bryan, David K., and David W. Pao, eds. *Ascent into Heaven in Luke-Acts: New Explorations of Luke's Narrative Hinge*. Minneapolis: Fortress, 2016.

Burgess, Andrew. "Ascension." In *T&T Clark Companion to Atonement*, edited by Adam J. Johnson, 377–80. London: Bloomsbury T&T Clark, 2017.

———. *The Ascension in Karl Barth*. Aldershot: Ashgate, 2004.

Calvin, John. *The First Epistle of Paul the Apostle to the Corinthians*. Edited by David W. Torrance and Thomas F. Torrance. Translated by John W. Fraser. Grand Rapids: Eerdmans, 1960.

———. *Institutes of the Christian Religion*. Edited by John T. McNeill. Translated by Ford Lewis Battles. 2 vols. Louisville: Westminster John Knox, 2006.

———. "John Calvin to the Reader." In *Institutes of the Christian Religion*, edited by John T. McNeill, translated by Ford Lewis Battles, 1:3–5. Louisville: Westminster John Knox, 2006.

Cameron, Daniel J. *Flesh and Blood: A Dogmatic Sketch Concerning the Fallen Nature View of Christ's Human Nature*. Eugene, OR: Wipf & Stock, 2016.

Chiarot, Kevin. *The Unassumed Is the Unhealed: The Humanity of Christ in the Christology of T. F. Torrance*. Eugene, OR: Pickwick, 2013.
Collver, Albert B. "The Person of Christ as Confessed by the Session." *Logia* 11 (2002) 9–15.
Colyer, Elmer M. *How to Read T. F. Torrance: Understanding His Trinitarian and Scientific Theology*. Downers Grove, IL: InterVarsity, 2001.
Cortez, Marc. *Christological Anthropology in Historical Perspective: Ancient and Contemporary Approaches to Theological Anthropology*. Grand Rapids: Zondervan, 2016.
———. *Resourcing Theological Anthropology: A Constructive Account of Humanity in the Light of Christ*. Grand Rapids: Zondervan, 2017.
Crisp, Oliver D. *Analyzing Doctrine: Toward a Systematic Theology*. Waco, TX: Baylor University Press, 2019.
———. "Did Christ Have a Fallen Human Nature?" *International Journal of Systematic Theology* 6 (2004) 270–88.
———. *Divinity and Humanity: The Incarnation Reconsidered*. Cambridge: Cambridge University Press, 2007.
———. "Methodological Issues in Approaching the Atonement." In *T&T Clark Companion to Atonement*, edited by Adam J. Johnson, 315–34. London: Bloomsbury T&T Clark, 2017.
———. "On the Vicarious Humanity of Christ." *International Journal of Systematic Theology* 21 (2019) 235–50.
———. "T. F. Torrance on Theosis and Universal Salvation." *Scottish Journal of Theology* 74 (2021) 12–25.
Davies, Oliver. *Theology of Transformation: Faith, Freedom, and the Christian Act*. Oxford: Oxford University Press, 2013.
Dawson, Gerrit. *Jesus Ascended: The Meaning of Christ's Continuing Incarnation*. London: T&T Clark, 2004.
Deddo, Gary W. "The Holy Spirit in T. F. Torrance's Theology." In *The Promise of Trinitarian Theology: Theologians in Dialogue with T. F. Torrance*, edited by Elmer M. Colyer, 81–114. Lanham, MD: Rowman & Littlefield, 2001.
Ellis, Brannon. *Calvin, Classical Trinitarianism, and the Aseity of the Son*. Oxford: Oxford University Press, 2012.
Eugenio, Dick O. *Communion with the Triune God: The Trinitarian Soteriology of T. F. Torrance*. Eugene, OR: Pickwick, 2014.
Fach, Sandra. "Answering the Upwards Call: The Ascended Christ, Mediator of Our Worship." PhD diss., King's College, University of London, 2008.
Farrow, Douglas. *Ascension and Ecclesia: On the Significance of the Doctrine of the Ascension for Ecclesiology and Christian Cosmology*. Grand Rapids: Eerdmans, 1999.
———. *Ascension Theology*. London: T&T Clark, 2011.
———. "Resurrection and Immortality." In *The Oxford Handbook of Systematic Theology*, edited by John Webster et al., 212–35. Oxford: Oxford University Press, 2015.
———. Review of *The Ascension in Karl Barth*, by Andrew Burgess. *International Journal of Systematic Theology* 7 (2005) 205–8.
Fee, Gordon D. *The First Epistle to the Corinthians*. Grand Rapids: Eerdmans, 1987.
Fergusson, David. "The Ascension of Christ: Its Significance in the Theology of T. F. Torrance." *Participatio* 3 (2012) 92–107.

———. "Barth and T. F. Torrance." In *The Wiley Blackwell Companion to Karl Barth*. Vol. 2, *Barth in Dialogue*, edited by George Hunsinger and Keith L. Johnson, 657–68. Chichester: Wiley-Blackwell, 2020.

———. "He Ascended into Heaven: The Ascension and Agency of Christ in the Theology of T. F. Torrance." In *What Is Jesus Doing? God's Activity in the Life and Work of the Church*, edited by Edwin Chr. Van Driel, 27–46. Downers Grove, IL: InterVarsity, 2020.

———. "Thomas F. Torrance as a Scottish Theologian." In *T&T Clark Handbook of Thomas F. Torrance*, edited by Paul D. Molnar and Myk Habets, 37–50. London: Bloomsbury T&T Clark, 2020.

Finley, John. "The Metaphysics of Gender: A Thomistic Approach." *Thomist* 79 (2015) 585–614.

Fleming, John V. "Literary Critic." In *The Cambridge Companion to C. S. Lewis*, edited by Robert MacSwain and Michael Ward, 15–28. Cambridge: Cambridge University Press, 2010.

Flett, Eric G. *Persons, Powers, and Pluralities: Toward a Trinitarian Theology of Culture.* Eugene, OR: Pickwick, 2011.

———. "Priest of Creation, Mediators of Order: The Human Person as a Cultural Being in Thomas F. Torrance's Theological Anthropology." *Scottish Journal of Theology* 58 (2005) 1–23.

Gaine, Simon Francis. "The Beatific Vision and the Heavenly Mediation of Christ." *TheoLogica* 2 (2018) 116–28.

———. "Thomas Aquinas and John Owen on the Beatific Vision: A Reply to Suzanne McDonald." *New Blackfriars* 97 (2016) 432–46.

Garland, David E. *1 Corinthians*. Grand Rapids: Baker Academic, 2003.

George, Samuel. "Christological Reflections from India." In *Christian Theology: Indian Conversations*. Vol. 1, *Dogmatic Themes*, edited by Samuel George and P. Mohan Larbeer, 99–115. Bangalore: BTESSC, 2016.

———. *Jesus Beyond Borders: Towards a "Glocal" Christology*. New Delhi: Christian World Imprints, 2016.

Gordon, Bruce. *Calvin*. New Haven: Yale University Press, 2009.

Gordon, James R. *The Holy One in Our Midst: An Essay on the Flesh of Christ.* Minneapolis: Fortress, 2016.

Green, Joel. "What You See Depends on What You Are Looking for: Jesus's Ascension as a Test Case for Thinking About Biblical Theology and Theological Interpretation of Scripture." *Interpretation* 70 (2016) 445–57.

Gregory of Nyssa. *The Life of Moses*. Translated by Abraham J. Malherbe and Everett Ferguson. New York: Paulist, 1978

Grudem, Wayne. *Systematic Theology: An Introduction to Biblical Doctrine*. Grand Rapids: Zondervan, 1994.

Habets, Myk. "The Essence of Evangelical Theology." In *The Trinitarian Faith: The Evangelical Theology of the Ancient Catholic Church*, by Thomas F. Torrance, vii–xxxii. 2nd ed. London: Bloomsbury T&T Clark, 2016.

———. "The Fallen Humanity of Christ: A Pneumatological Clarification of the Theology of Thomas F. Torrance." *Participatio* 5 (2015) 18–44.

———. *Heaven: An Inkling of What's to Come*. Eugene, OR: Cascade, 2018.

———. "Naked but Not Disembodied: A Case for Anthropological Duality." *Pacific Journal of Baptist Research* 4 (2008) 33–50.

———. "On Getting First Things First: Assessing Claims for the Primacy of Christ." *New Blackfriars* 90 (2009) 343–64.

———. "Prolegomenon: On Starting with the Spirit." In *Third Article Theology: A Pneumatological Dogmatics*, edited by Myk Habets, 1–20. Minneapolis: Fortress, 2016.

———. Review of *The Holy Spirit as Bond in Calvin's Thought: Its Functions in Connection with the extra Calvinisticum*, by Daniel Y. K. Lee. *International Journal of Systematic Theology* 17 (2015) 240–43.

———. "*Theologia Is Eusebia*: Thomas F. Torrance's Church Homiletics." In *T&T Clark Handbook of Thomas F. Torrance*, edited by Paul D. Molnar and Myk Habets, 259–76. London: T&T Clark, 2020.

———. "Theological Interpretation of Scripture in Sermonic Mode: The Case of T. F. Torrance." In *Ears That Hear: Explorations in Theological Interpretation of the Bible*, edited by Joel B. Green and Tim J. Meadowcroft, 43–69. Sheffield: Sheffield Phoenix, 2013.

———. *Theology in Transposition: A Constructive Appraisal of T. F. Torrance*. Minneapolis: Fortress, 2013.

———. *Theosis in the Theology of Thomas Torrance*. Farnham: Ashgate, 2009.

———. "Theosis: Participation in the Divine Nature." In *Trinitarian Conversations*, edited by Michael D. Morrison, 2:138–48. 6th ed. Charlotte, NC: Grace Communion International, 2019.

———. "Who's in Heaven?" *Baptist* 127 (2011) 7, 13.

———. "You Wonder Where the Pneumatology Went? Thomas F. Torrance and Third Article Theology." *Participatio* 10 (2022) 33–55.

Habets, Myk, et al. "Current Trends in Torrance Studies." Panel Discussion during the 2021 Torrance Virtual Workshop-Retreat, August 2, 2021. https://vimeo.com/582317568.

Hardy, Daniel W. "T. F. Torrance." In *The Modern Theologians: An Introduction to Christian Theology Since 1918*, edited by David F. Ford, 163–77. 3rd ed. Malden, MA: Blackwell, 2005.

Harris, Mark. "Science, Scripture, and the Hermeneutics of Ascension." *Theology and Science* 12 (2014) 201–15.

Heltzel, Peter G., et al., eds. *The Dialogic Evangelical Theology of Veli-Matti Kärkkäinen: Exploring the Work of God in a Diverse Church and a Pluralistic World*. Lanham, MD: Fortress Academic, 2022.

Heron, Alasdair. "T. F. Torrance in Relation to Reformed Theology." In *The Promise of Trinitarian Theology: Theologians in Dialogue with T. F. Torrance*, edited by Elmer M. Colyer, 31–49. Lanham, MD: Rowman & Littlefield, 2001.

Hesselink, I. John. "A Pilgrimage in the School of Christ—An Interview with T. F. Torrance." *Reformed Review* 38 (1984) 49–64.

Hill, Jonathan. "Incarnation, Timelessness, and Exaltation." *Faith and Philosophy* 29 (2012) 3–29.

Hitchcock, Nathan. *Karl Barth and the Resurrection of the Flesh: The Loss of the Body in Participatory Eschatology*. Eugene, OR: Pickwick, 2013.

Hoeffer, Herbert. "Gospel Proclamation of the Ascended Lord." *Missiology* 33 (2005) 435–49.

Holmes, Christopher R. J. *Ethics in the Presence of Christ*. London: T&T Clark, 2012.

———. "Last Things." In *The Oxford Handbook of Reformed Theology*, edited by Michael Allen and Scott R. Swain, 609–22. Oxford: Oxford University Press, 2020.
Holmes, Stephen R. "Reformed Varieties of the *Communicatio Idiomatum*." In *The Person of Christ*, edited by Stephen R. Holmes and Murray A. Rae, 70–86. London: T&T Clark, 2005.
Horton, Michael S. *People and Place: A Covenant Ecclesiology*. Louisville: Westminster John Knox, 2008.
Hudson, Hud. *The Metaphysics of Hyperspace*. Oxford: Oxford University Press, 2005.
Hunsinger, George. "The Dimension of Depth: Thomas F. Torrance on the Sacraments of Baptism and the Lord's Supper." *Scottish Journal of Theology* 54 (2001) 155–76.
———. *The Eucharist and Ecumenism: Let Us Keep the Feast*. Cambridge: Cambridge University Press, 2008.
———. "Foreword." In *T&T Clark Handbook of Thomas F. Torrance*, edited by Paul D. Molnar and Myk Habets, xiii–xvi. London: T&T Clark, 2020.
Inge, John. *A Christian Theology of Place*. Aldershot: Ashgate, 2003.
Jansen, J. F. "1 Cor. 15.24–28 and the Future of Jesus Christ." *Scottish Journal of Theology* 40 (1987) 543–70.
John, Stavan Narendra. "Chalcedon and Indian Christologies." *Modern Reformation* 30 (2021) 9–13.
———. "The Risen and Ascended Humanity of Christ in Thomas F. Torrance's Holistic Christology." PhD diss., OCMS/Middlesex University, 2022.
———. "T. F. Torrance's Theology of the Ascension: An Underappreciated Constructive Theological Masterpiece?" *Participatio* (forthcoming).
———. "Thomas F. Torrance's Theology of the Ascension: A Practical Theological Dogmatic Sketch." *Participatio* (forthcoming).
———. "Torrance and Global Evangelicalism: Some Potential Generative Exchanges with Contemporary Indian Evangelical Theology." In *Thomas F. Torrance and Evangelical Theology: A Critical Analysis*, edited by Myk Habets and R. Lucas Stamps, 308–25. Bellingham, WA: Lexham Academic, 2023.
Kärkkäinen, Veli-Matti. *A Constructive Christian Theology for the Pluralistic World*. 5 vols. Grand Rapids: Eerdmans, 2013–17.
Kelly, Anthony J. "The Ascension: Recollecting the Experience." *Australian E-Journal of Theology* 20 (2013) 81–93.
Kernohan, R. D. "Tom Torrance: The Man and the Reputation." *Life and Work* 32 (1976) 14–16.
Kim, Hakbong. *Person, Personhood, and the Humanity of Christ: Christocentric Anthropology and Ethics in Thomas F. Torrance*. Eugene, OR: Pickwick, 2021.
Kruger, C. Baxter. "Participating in the Self-Knowledge of God: The Nature and Means of Our Knowledge of God in the Theology of T. F. Torrance." PhD diss., University of Aberdeen, 1989.
Langdon, Adrian. *God the Eternal Contemporary: Trinity, Eternity, and Time in Karl Barth*. Eugene, OR: Wipf & Stock, 2012.
Lee, Kye Won. *Living in Union with Christ: The Practical Theology of Thomas F. Torrance*. New York: Peter Lang, 2003.
Lee, Sang Hoon. "The Doctrine of Divine Simplicity in T. F. Torrance's Theology." *International Journal of Systematic Theology* 23 (2021) 198–214.
Letham, Robert. "The Triune God, Incarnation, and Definite Atonement." In *From Heaven He Came and Sought Her: Definite Atonement in Historical, Biblical,*

*Theological, and Pastoral Perspective*, edited by David Gibson and Jonathan Gibson, 437–60. Wheaton, IL: Crossway, 2013.

Lewis, C. S. *The Allegory of Love: A Study in Medieval Tradition*. Oxford: Oxford University Press, 1958.

———. "Bluspels and Flalansfers: A Semantic Nightmare." In *Selected Literary Essays*, edited by Walter Hooper, 251–65. Cambridge: Cambridge University Press, 1969.

———. *The Discarded Image: An Introduction to Medieval and Renaissance Literature*. Cambridge: Cambridge University Press, 1964.

———. *English Literature in the Sixteenth Century, Excluding Drama*. Oxford: Clarendon, 1954.

———. *A Preface to Paradise Lost*. Oxford: Oxford University Press, 1983.

———. *Spenser's Images of Life*. Edited by Alastair Fowler. Cambridge: Cambridge University Press, 1967.

———. *Studies in Medieval and Renaissance Literature*. Edited by Walter Hooper. Cambridge: Cambridge University Press, 1966.

Lipner, Julius. "Avatāra and Incarnation?" In *Re-Visioning India's Religious Traditions: Essays in Honour of Eric Lott*, edited by David C. Scott and Israel Selvanayagam, 127–43. Delhi: ISPCK, 1996.

Liston, Gregory J. "Eschatology and the *Munus Triplex*: The Threefold Anointing of the Spirit in Time." *Journal of Reformed Theology* 14 (2020) 323–43.

Luoma, Tapio. *Incarnation and Physics: Natural Science in the Theology of Thomas F. Torrance*. Oxford: Oxford University Press, 2002.

MacLean, Stanley S. *Resurrection, Apocalypse, and the Kingdom of Christ: The Eschatology of Thomas F. Torrance*. Eugene, OR: Pickwick, 2012.

———. "'Salvation Is of the Jews': Thomas F. Torrance's Doctrine of Israel." *Pacific Journal of Theological Research* 15 (2020) 1–13.

———. "Thomas Torrance's Recovery of the Spatial Dimension of Eschatology." *Reformed Theological Review* 75 (2016) 189–206.

Magezi, Vhumani, and Christopher Magezi. "Christ Also Ours in Africa: A Consideration of Torrance's Incarnational, Christological Model as Nexus for Christ's Identification with African Christians." *Verbum et Ecclesia* 38 (2017) 1–12.

———. "Healing and Coping with Life Within Challenges of Spiritual Insecurity: Juxtaposed Consideration of Christ's Sinlessness and African Ancestors in Pastoral Guidance." *HTS Teologiese Studies/Theological Studies* 73 (2017) 1–12.

McDonald, Suzanne. "Beholding the Glory of God in the Face of Jesus Christ: John Owen and the 'Reforming' of the Beatific Vision." In *The Ashgate Research Companion to John Owen's Theology*, edited by Kelly M. Kapic and Mark Jones, 141–58. London: Routledge, 2016.

McFarland, Ian A. "The Body of Christ: Rethinking a Classic Ecclesiological Model." *International Journal of Systematic Theology* 7 (2005) 225–45.

———. "Fallen or Unfallen? Christ's Human Nature and the Ontology of Human Sinfulness." *International Journal of Systematic Theology* 10 (2008) 399–415.

McGrath, Alister E. *Thomas F. Torrance: An Intellectual Biography*. Edinburgh: T&T Clark, 1999.

Middleton, J. Richard. "Response to Michael Allen." In *Four Views on Heaven*, edited by Michael Wittmer, 142–48. Grand Rapids: Zondervan Academic, 2022.

Milgrom, Jacob. *Leviticus: A Book of Ritual and Ethics*. Minneapolis: Fortress, 2004.

Milligan, William. *The Ascension and Heavenly Priesthood of Our Lord.* London: Macmillan, 1892.

———. *The Resurrection of Our Lord.* New York: Macmillan, 1901.

Moffitt, David M. *Atonement and the Logic of Resurrection in the Epistle to the Hebrews.* Leiden: Brill, 2011.

———. "Atonement at the Right Hand: The Sacrificial Significance of Jesus' Exaltation in Acts." *New Testament Studies* 62 (2016) 549–68.

———. "Blood, Life, and Atonement: Reassessing Hebrews' Christological Appropriation of Yom Kippur." In *The Day of Atonement: Its Interpretation in Early Jewish and Christian Traditions*, edited by Thomas Hieke and Tobias Nicklas, 211–24. Leiden: Brill, 2012.

Molnar, Paul D. *Incarnation and Resurrection: Toward a Contemporary Understanding.* Grand Rapids: Eerdmans, 2007.

———. "Introduction to the Cornerstones Edition." In *Space, Time, and Resurrection*, by Thomas F. Torrance, xvii–lv. London: Bloomsbury T&T Clark, 2019.

———. "Rejoinder to Gary Deddo, Chris Kettler, and Alan Torrance." *Cultural Encounters* 8 (2012) 83–88.

———. "Thomas F. Torrance." In *The History of Scottish Theology.* Vol. 3, *The Long Twentieth Century*, edited by David Fergusson and Mark W. Elliot, 227–41. Oxford: Oxford University Press, 2019.

———. "Thomas F. Torrance and Karl Barth: Similarities and Differences." In *T&T Clark Handbook of Thomas F. Torrance*, edited by Paul D. Molnar and Myk Habets, 67–84. London: T&T Clark, 2020.

———. "Thomas F. Torrance and the Problem of Universalism." *Scottish Journal of Theology* 68 (2015) 164–86.

———. *Thomas F. Torrance: Theologian of the Trinity.* Farnham: Ashgate, 2009.

Muller, Richard, A. "Christ in the Eschaton: Calvin and Moltmann on the Duration of the *Munus Regium*." *Harvard Theological Review* 74 (1981) 31–59.

Mullins, R. T. *The End of the Timeless God.* Oxford: Oxford University Press, 2016.

Munchin, David. *Is Theology a Science? The Nature of the Scientific Enterprise in the Scientific Theology of Thomas Forsyth Torrance and the Anarchic Epistemology of Paul Feyerabend.* Leiden: Brill, 2011.

Murray, D. M. "Milligan, William." In *Dictionary of Scottish Church History and Theology*, edited by Nigel M. de S. Cameron et al., 565–66. Downers Grove, IL: InterVarsity, 1993.

Myers, Benjamin. Review of *The Ascension in Karl Barth*, by Andrew Burgess. *Faith and Theology*, January 29, 2007. https://www.faith-theology.com/2007/01/andrew-burgess-ascension-in-karl-barth.html.

———. "The Stratification of Knowledge in the Thought of T. F. Torrance." *Scottish Journal of Theology* 61 (2008) 1–15.

Navarro, Kevin J. *Trinitarian Doxology: T. F. and J. B. Torrance's Theology of Worship as Participation by the Spirit in the Son's Communion with the Father.* Eugene, OR: Pickwick, 2020.

Neder, Adam. "Barth on Participation in Christ." In *The Wiley Blackwell Companion to Karl Barth.* Vol. 1, *Barth and Dogmatics*, edited by George Hunsinger and Keith L. Johnson, 341–53. Chichester: Wiley-Blackwell, 2020.

Nesteruk, Alexei V. "Universe, Incarnation, and Humanity: Thomas Torrance, Modern Cosmology, and Beyond." *Participatio* 4 (2013) 213–39.

Newell, Roger. "Participatory Knowledge: Theology as Art and Science in C. S. Lewis and T. F. Torrance." PhD diss., University of Aberdeen, 1983.

———. "The Stuttgart Declaration of 1945: A Case Study of Guilt, Forgiveness, and Foreign Policy." In *Trinity and Transformation: J. B. Torrance's Vision of Worship, Mission, and Society*, edited by Todd Speidell, 157–74. Eugene, OR: Wipf & Stock, 2016.

Newton, William. "Why Aquinas's Metaphysics of Gender Is Fundamentally Correct: A Response to John Finley." *Linacre Quarterly* 20 (2019) 1–8.

Noble, Thomas A. *Holy Trinity: Holy People; The Theology of Christian Perfecting*. Eugene, OR: Cascade, 2013.

———. "Incarnation and Atonement." In *T&T Clark Handbook of Thomas F. Torrance*, edited by Paul D. Molnar and Myk Habets, 173–88. London: T&T Clark, 2020.

Oberman, Heiko. "The 'Extra' Dimension in the Theology of Calvin." *Journal of Ecclesiastical History* 21 (1970) 43–64.

O'Collins, Gerald. "Thomas Torrance, Mark 16:19–20, and the Ascended Christ's Prophetic Role." *Scottish Journal of Theology* 74 (2021) 168–76.

O'Donovan, Oliver. *The Desire of the Nations: Rediscovering the Roots of Political Theology*. Cambridge: Cambridge University Press, 1966.

Orr, Peter. *Christ Absent and Present: A Study in Pauline Christology*. Tübingen: Mohr Siebeck, 2014.

———. *Exalted Above the Heavens: The Risen and Ascended Christ*. London: Apollos, 2018.

Ortlund, Gavin. "Explorations in a Theological Metaphor: Boethius, Calvin, and Torrance on the Creator/Creation Distinction." *Modern Theology* 33 (2017) 167–86.

———. "Will We See God's Essence? A Defence of a Thomistic Account of the Beatific Vision." *Scottish Journal of Theology* 74 (2021) 323–32.

Palma, Robert J. "Thomas F. Torrance's Reformed Theology." *Reformed Review* 38 (1984) 2–46.

Park, Chan Ho. *Transcendence and Spatiality of the Triune Creator*. Bern: Peter Lang, 2005.

Philipose P. M., Philip Blesson. "A Critical Exploration of Onto-Relational Atonement Through the Work of Thomas F. Torrance." MTh Thesis, South Asia Institute of Advanced Christian Studies, 2015.

Prasadam, Ajit A. "Beyond Conscientization: James E. Loder's Transformational Model for Christian Education in the Indian Context and Beyond." PhD. diss., Princeton Theological Seminary, 2005.

Presa, Neal D. *Ascension Theology and Habakkuk: A Reformed Ecclesiology in Filipino American Perspective*. Cham: Palgrave Macmillan, 2018.

Purves, Andrew. "The End of Ministry: Thomas F. Torrance and Eschatology." In *T&T Clark Handbook of Thomas F. Torrance*, edited by Paul D. Molnar and Myk Habets, 277–90. London: T&T Clark, 2020.

———. *Exploring Christology and Atonement: Conversations with John McLeod Campbell, H. R. Mackintosh, and T. F. Torrance*. Downers Grove, IL: InterVarsity, 2015.

———. "Purves-Handbook." T. F. Torrance Discussion Group, December 10, 2020. https://vimeo.com/492652315.

———. *Reconstructing Pastoral Theology: A Christological Foundation*. Louisville: Westminster John Knox, 2004.

Radcliff, Alexandra S. *The Claim of Humanity in Christ: Salvation and Sanctification in the Theology of T. F. and J. B. Torrance*. Eugene, OR: Pickwick, 2016.

Radcliff, Jason Robert. *Thomas F. Torrance and the Orthodox-Reformed Theological Dialogue*. Eugene, OR: Pickwick, 2018.

Rae, Murray. "The Spatiality of God." In *Trinitarian Theology After Barth*, edited by Myk Habets and Phillip Tolliday, 70–86. Cambridge: James Clarke, 2012.

Rahner, Karl, and Joseph Schmitt. "Resurrection—Resurrection of Christ." In *Sacramentum Mundi Online*, edited by Karl Rahner. Leiden: Brill, 2016. http://dx.doi.org/10.1163/2468-483X_smuo_COM_003831.

Raj, Subin. "Why Jesus Is Not an Avatar: A Critique of the Indian Hindu and Christian Incarnation Idea of Jesus as 'Avatar' on the Basis of Nicene Affirmation for Future Missions." *Missio Apostolica* 22 (2014) 94–108.

Ramsey, Ian T. *Models and Mystery: The Whidden Lectures for 1963*. Oxford: Oxford University Press, 1964.

Ratzinger, Joseph. "Ascension of Christ." In *Sacramentum Mundi Online*, edited by Karl Rahner. Leiden: Brill, 2016. http://dx.doi.org/10.1163/2468-483X_smuo_COM_000320.

Redding, Graham. *Prayer and the Priesthood of Christ in the Reformed Tradition*. London: Bloomsbury T&T Clark, 2003.

Richardson, Kurt Anders. "Revelation, Scripture, and Mystical Apprehension of Divine Knowledge." In *The Promise of Trinitarian Theology: Theologians in Dialogue with T. F. Torrance*, edited by Elmer M. Colyer, 185–204. Lanham, MD: Rowman & Littlefield, 2001.

Ritchie, Bruce. *T. F. Torrance in Recollection and Reappraisal*. Eugene, OR: Pickwick, 2021.

Scandrett, Joel. "Thomas F. Torrance and Ecumenism." In *T&T Clark Handbook of Thomas F. Torrance*, edited by Paul D. Molnar and Myk Habets, 51–66. London: T&T Clark, 2020.

Schreiner, Patrick. *The Ascension of Christ: Recovering a Neglected Doctrine*. Bellingham, WA: Lexham, 2020.

Seamands, Stephen. *The Unseen Real: Life in the Light of the Ascension of Jesus*. Franklin, TN: Seedbed, 2016.

Seed, Caroline G., et al. "Thomas F. Torrance: Theology and Mission in Practice." *In die Skriflig* 50 (2016) 1–10.

Seim, Turid Karlsen. "The Resurrected Body in Luke-Acts: The Significance of Space." In *Metamorphoses: Resurrection, Body, and Transformative Practices in Early Christianity*, edited by Turid Karlsen Seim and Jorunn Økland, 19–39. Berlin: de Gruyter, 2009.

Shepherd, Albert L. "The Body of Christ: T. F. Torrance's Ecclesial Ontology." PhD diss., University of Aberdeen, 2015.

Sherrard, Joseph H. *T. F. Torrance as Missional Theologian: The Ascended Christ and the Ministry of the Church*. Downers Grove, IL: InterVarsity, 2021.

Sheth, Noel. "Hindu Avatāra and Christian Incarnation: A Comparison." *Philosophy East and West* 52 (2002) 98–125.

Sleeman, Matthew. *Geography and the Ascension Narrative in Acts*. Cambridge: Cambridge University Press, 2009.

Speidell, Todd. *Fully Human in Christ: The Incarnation as the End of Christian Ethics*. Eugene, OR: Wipf & Stock, 2016.

———. "The Soteriological Suspension of the Ethical in the Theology of T. F. Torrance." *Participatio* 5 (2015) 56–90.

Stein, Jock. "Editor's Introduction." In *Gospel, Church, and Ministry*, edited by Jock Stein, 1–24. Thomas F. Torrance Collected Studies 1. Eugene, OR: Pickwick, 2012.

Strobel, Kyle. "Jonathan Edwards' Reformed Doctrine of the Beatific Vision." In *Jonathan Edwards and Scotland*, edited by Kenneth P. Minkema et al., 163–80. Edinburgh: Dunedin Academic, 2011.

Stubbs, D. L. "Resurrection." In *Global Dictionary of Theology*, edited by William A. Dryness and Veli-Matti Kärkkäinen, 754–58. Downers Grove, IL: InterVarsity, 2008.

Sumner, Darren. "Fallenness and *Anhypostasis*: A Way Forward in the Debate over Christ's Humanity." *Scottish Journal of Theology* 67 (2014) 195–212.

Thiselton, Anthony C. *The First Epistle to the Corinthians*. Grand Rapids: Eerdmans, 2000.

Thomas, Matthew. "The High Priestly Christology of Hebrews as a Paradigm for an Indian Christology." *Bible Bhashyam* 27 (2001) 271–85.

Torrance, Alan J. "Introduction." In *Trinity and Transformation: J. B. Torrance's Vision of Worship, Mission, and Society*, edited by Todd Speidell, 1–16. Eugene, OR: Wipf & Stock, 2016.

———. "Reclaiming the Continuing Priesthood of Christ: Implications and Challenges." In *Christology, Ancient & Modern: Explorations in Constructive Dogmatics*, edited by Oliver D. Crisp and Fred Sanders, 184–204. Grand Rapids: Zondervan, 2013.

Torrance, David W. "Introduction: Discovering the Incarnate Saviour of the World." In *An Introduction to Torrance Theology: Discovering the Incarnate Saviour*, edited by Gerrit Scott Dawson, 1–22. London: T&T Clark, 2007.

———. "Thomas Forsyth Torrance: Minister of the Gospel, Pastor, and Evangelical Theologian." In *The Promise of Trinitarian Theology*, edited by Elmer M. Colyer, 1–30. Lanham, MD: Rowman & Littlefield, 2001.

Torrance, James B. "The Vicarious Humanity of Christ." In *The Incarnation: Ecumenical Studies in the Nicene-Constantinopolitan Creed A.D. 381*, edited by Thomas F. Torrance, 127–45. Eugene, OR: Wipf & Stock, 1998.

———. *Worship, Community, and the Triune God of Grace*. Downers Grove, IL: InterVarsity, 1996.

Torrance, Thomas F. *The Apocalypse Today*. London: James Clarke, 1960.

———. *Atonement: The Person and Work of Christ*. Edited by Robert T. Walker. Downers Grove, IL: InterVarsity, 2009.

———. *Calvin's Doctrine of Man*. Eugene, OR: Wipf & Stock, 2001.

———. "The Christ Who Loves Us." In *A Passion for Christ: The Vision That Ignites Ministry*, edited by Gerrit Dawson and Jock Stein, 9–21. Eugene, OR: Wipf & Stock, 2010.

———. "The Christian Apprehension of God the Father." In *Speaking the Christian God: The Holy Trinity and the Challenge of Feminism*, edited by Alvin F. Kimel Jr., 120–43. Grand Rapids: Eerdmans, 1992.

———. *The Christian Doctrine of God, One Being Three Persons*. London: Bloomsbury T&T Clark, 2016.

———. *The Christian Doctrine of Marriage*. Edinburgh: Handsel, 1992.

———. *The Christian Frame of Mind: Reason, Order, and Openness in Theology and Natural Science*. Eugene, OR: Wipf & Stock, 2015.

———. *Conflict and Agreement in the Church.* Vol. 1, *Order and Disorder.* Eugene, OR: Wipf & Stock, 1996.

———. *Conflict and Agreement in the Church.* Vol. 2, *The Ministry and the Sacraments of the Gospel.* Eugene, OR: Wipf & Stock, 1996.

———. "The Deposit of Faith." *Scottish Journal of Theology* 36 (1983) 1–28.

———. "The Distinctive Character of the Reformed Tradition." In *Incarnational Ministry: The Presence of Christ in Church, Society, and Family; Essays in Honor of Ray S. Anderson,* edited by Christian D. Kettler and Todd H. Speidell, 2–15. Colorado Springs, CO: Helmers & Howard, 1990.

———. *Divine and Contingent Order.* Edinburgh: T&T Clark, 1998.

———. *The Doctrine of Jesus Christ.* Eugene, OR: Wipf & Stock, 2002.

———. *God and Rationality.* Oxford: Oxford University Press, 1971.

———. *Gospel, Church, and Ministry.* Edited by Jock Stein. Thomas F. Torrance Collected Studies 1. Eugene, OR: Pickwick, 2012.

———. *Ground and Grammar of Theology.* Edinburgh: T&T Clark, 2001.

———. "Immortality and Light." *Religious Studies* 17 (1981) 147–61.

———. *Incarnation: The Person and Life of Christ.* Edited by Robert T. Walker. Downers Grove, IL: InterVarsity, 2008.

———. *Juridical Law and Physical Law: Toward a Realist Foundation for Human Law.* Eugene, OR: Wipf & Stock, 1997.

———. *Karl Barth: Biblical and Evangelical Theologian.* Edinburgh: T&T Clark, 1990.

———. *Karl Barth: An Introduction to His Early Theology, 1910–1931.* London: T&T Clark, 2000.

———. *Kingdom and Church: A Study in the Theology of the Reformation.* Eugene, OR: Wipf & Stock, 1996.

———. *The Mediation of Christ.* London: Bloomsbury T&T Clark, 1992.

———. *The Ministry of Women.* Edinburgh: Handsel, 1992.

———. "My Interaction with Karl Barth." In *How Karl Barth Changed My Mind,* edited by Donald K. McKim, 52–64. Eugene, OR: Wipf & Stock, 1998.

———. *Preaching Christ Today: The Gospel and Scientific Thinking.* Grand Rapids: Eerdmans, 1994.

———. *Reality and Evangelical Theology: The Realism of Christian Revelation.* Eugene, OR: Wipf & Stock, 2003.

———. "Reformed Dogmatics Not Dogmatism." *Theology* 70 (1967) 152–56.

———. "The Relation of the Incarnation to Space in Nicene Theology." In *The Ecumenical World of Orthodox Civilization.* Vol. 3, *Russia and Orthodoxy: Essays in Honor of Georges Florovsky,* edited by Andrew Blane, 43–70. The Hague: Mouton, 1974.

———. *Royal Priesthood: A Theology of Ordained Ministry.* 2nd ed. London: T&T Clark, 1993.

———. "Salvation Is of the Jews." *Evangelical Quarterly* 22 (1950) 164–73.

———. *The School of Faith: The Catechisms of the Reformed Church.* Translated and edited by Thomas F. Torrance. Eugene, OR: Wipf & Stock, 1996.

———. *Scottish Theology: From John Knox to John McLeod Campbell.* Edinburgh: T&T Clark, 1996.

———. "The Soul and Person, in Theological Perspective." In *Religion, Reason, and the Self: Essays in Honour of Hywel D. Lewis,* edited by Stewart R. Sutherland and T. A. Roberts, 103–18. Cardiff: University of Wales Press, 1989.

———. *The Soul and Person of the Unborn Child.* Edinburgh: Handsel, 1999.

———. *Space, Time, and Incarnation*. Edinburgh: T&T Clark, 1997.
———. *Space, Time, and Resurrection*. Edinburgh: T&T Clark, 1998.
———. "'The Substance of Faith': A Clarification of the Concept in the Church of Scotland." *Scottish Journal of Theology* 36 (1983) 327–38.
———. *Theological and Natural Science*. Eugene, OR: Wipf & Stock, 2002.
———. *Theological Science*. Oxford: Oxford University Press, 1969.
———. *Theology in Reconciliation: Essays Towards Evangelical and Catholic Unity in East and West*. Eugene, OR: Wipf & Stock, 1996.
———. *Theology in Reconstruction*. Eugene, OR: Wipf & Stock, 1996.
———. "Thomas Torrance Responds." In *The Promise of Trinitarian Theology: Theologians in Dialogue with T. F. Torrance*, edited by Elmer M. Colyer, 303–40. Lanham, MD: Rowman & Littlefield, 2001.
———. *The Trinitarian Faith: The Evangelical Theology of the Ancient Catholic Church*. 2nd ed. London: Bloomsbury T&T Clark, 2016.
———. "Universalism or Election?" *Scottish Journal of Theology* 2 (1949) 310–18.
———. "What Is the Church?" *Ecumenical Review* 11 (1958) 6–21.
———. *When Christ Comes and Comes Again*. Eugene, OR: Wipf & Stock, 1996.
Travis, Stephen H. *Christian Hope and the Future*. Downers Grove, IL: InterVarsity, 1980.
Tsoukalas, Steven. *Kṛṣṇa and Christ: Body-Divine Relation in the Thought of Śaṅkara, Rāmānuja, and Classical Christian Orthodoxy*. Milton Keynes: Paternoster, 2006.
———. "Theōsis: A Comparative Study of T. F. Torrance and Rāmānuja." *Journal of Hindu-Christian Studies* 30 (2017) 53–61.
Turretin, Francis. *Institutes of Elenctic Theology*. Vol. 3. Edited by James T. Dennison. Translated by George Musgrave Giger. Phillipsburg, NJ: Presbyterian and Reformed, 1997.
Tyler, Kate. *The Ecclesiology of Thomas F. Torrance: Koinōnia and the Church*. Lanham, MD: Fortress Academic, 2019.
Tyra, Steven W. "'Neither the Spirit Without the Flesh': John Calvin's Greek Doctrine of the Beatific Vision." *Archiv für Reformationsgeschichte* 111 (2020) 170–93.
Vale, Fellipe do. "Cappadocian or Augustinian? Adjudicating Debates on Gender in the Resurrection." *International Journal of Systematic Theology* 21 (2019) 182–98.
———. "Gender Identity: To Infinity and Beyond." *Pro Ecclesia* 32 (2023) 24–46.
Van Driel, Edwin Chr. "What Is Jesus Doing? Christological Thoughts for an Anxious Church and Tired Pastors." In *What Is Jesus Doing? God's Activity in the Life and Work of the Church*, edited by Edwin Chr. Van Driel, 1–23. Downers Grove, IL: InterVarsity, 2020.
———, ed. *What Is Jesus Doing? God's Activity in the Life and Work of the Church*. Downers Grove, IL: InterVarsity, 2020.
Van Kuiken, E. Jerome. "All of Him for All of Us: Christ's Person and Offices in John Wesley and T. F. Torrance." *Participatio* 4 (2018) 11–38.
———. *Christ's Humanity in Current and Ancient Controversy: Fallen or Not?* London: Bloomsbury T&T Clark, 2017.
———. "'Not I, but Christ': Thomas F. Torrance on the Christian Life." In *T&T Clark Handbook of Thomas F. Torrance*, edited by Paul D. Molnar and Myk Habets, 243–57. London: T&T Clark, 2020.
———. "Sinless Savior in Fallen Flesh? Toward Clarifying and Closing the Debate." *Journal of the Evangelical Theological Society* 64 (2021) 327–40.

Walker, Robert T. "Editor's Foreword." In Thomas F. Torrance, *Incarnation: The Person and Life of Christ*, edited by Robert T. Walker, x–xii. Downers Grove, IL: InterVarsity, 2008.

———. "Editor's Introduction." In Thomas F. Torrance, *Incarnation: The Person and Life of Christ*, edited by Robert T. Walker, xxi–lii. Downers Grove, IL: InterVarsity, 2008.

———. "The Innovative Fruitfulness of *an/en-hypostasis* in Thomas F. Torrance." In *T&T Clark Handbook of Thomas F. Torrance*, edited by Paul D. Molnar and Myk Habets, 189–206. London: T&T Clark, 2020.

Webb, Stephen H. *Re-figuring Theology: The Rhetoric of Karl Barth*. Albany, NY: State University of New York Press, 1991.

Webster, John. *Barth*. London: Continuum, 2000.

———. *Confessing God: Essays in Christian Dogmatics II*. London: T&T Clark, 2005.

———. *The Domain of the Word: Scripture and Theological Reason*. London: T&T Clark, 2012.

———. "T. F. Torrance on Scripture." *Scottish Journal of Theology* 65 (2012) 34–63.

———. "Thomas Forsyth Torrance: 1913–2007." *Biographical Memoirs of Fellows of the British Academy* 13 (2014) 417–36.

Wei, Jing. "The Theological Anthropology of Thomas F. Torrance: A Critical and Comparative Exploration." PhD diss., New College, University of Edinburgh, 2013.

Widdicombe, Peter. "The Wounds and the Ascended Body: The Marks of Crucifixion in the Glorified Christ from Justin Martyr to John Calvin." *Laval théologique et philosophique* 59 (2003) 137–54.

Wilkinson, David. *Christian Eschatology and the Physical Universe*. London: T&T Clark, 2010.

Willis, E. David. *Calvin's Catholic Christology: The Function of the So-Called Extra Calvinisticum in Calvin's Theology*. Leiden: Brill, 1966.

Woznicki, Christopher G. *T. F. Torrance's Christological Anthropology: Discerning Humanity in Christ*. London: Routledge, 2022.

Wright, N. T. "Reconciling the World? Theology and Exegesis in 2 Corinthians 5." In *A Sort of Homecoming: Essays Honoring the Academic and Community Work of Brian Walsh*, edited by Marcia Boniferro et al., 203–17. Eugene, OR: Pickwick, 2019.

———. *The Resurrection of the Son of God*. Minneapolis: Fortress, 2003.

———. *Surprised by Hope: Rethinking Heaven, the Resurrection, and the Mission of the Church*. London: SPCK, 2007.

Yates, John. "Immediate or Intermediate? The State of the Believer upon Death." *Churchman* 101 (1987) 310–22.

Yom, Aaron. *Number, Word, and Spirit: Rethinking T. F. Torrance's Theological Science from a Pneumatological Perspective*. New York: Peter Lang, 2018.

Ziegler, Geordie W. "The Doctrine of the Ascension in the Theology of T. F. Torrance." MTh thesis, University of Aberdeen, 2008.

———. *Trinitarian Grace and Participation: An Entry into the Theology of T. F. Torrance*. Minneapolis: Fortress, 2017.

Ziegler, Geordie W., and Myk Habets, eds. "Theological Anthropology." Special issue, *Participatio* 9 (2021).

# Index

Aaron, 141, 143, 150, 151
Abraham, 150
active obedience, 137
Alcoholics Anonymous, 165
Alexandria, 5n20
Allen, Michael, 10, 195n94
Ambrose, Isaac, 7n34
*anabaino* (to go up), 133
*analambano* (to take up), 134
analogical language, 108–9
Anglican Church, 16
*anhypostasis/enhypostasis*, 188, 189–90, 192–93, 233
animal sacrifice, 135n19, 142, 145–46, 192
Anselm, 6
anthropological duality, 203
anthropology, 228
Antioch, 5n20
Apollinarianism, 152
apophatic language, 110–11
*a priori* reasoning, 215
Aquinas, Thomas, 74, 137
artistic language, 112, 123, 197–98
ascension. *See* theology of the ascension
Athanasius, 6, 28, 47, 108–9, 152
atonement, 42n172, 112n163, 135–37, 138, 142–43, 191–92
Augustine of Hippo, 19, 32, 64, 72, 75–76, 81–82, 84, 240
avatāras, 46

bad time, 90n27
Baker, Matthew, 43
Barr, James, 172–73, 174

Barth, Karl
   on ascension of Jesus, 39–41, 113, 196
   Christology of, 182
   critique of, 82, 166–73, 177, 181
   on divine freedom, 77n154
   eschatological panentheism and, 183
   eternity/time emphasis of, 184
   ethics contribution of, 166
   on the Eucharist, 167, 168
   on heaven, 214
   on humanity of Jesus, 39–41
   influence of, 6, 15, 16, 24–25, 47
   panentheism of, 183
   on preaching, 235
   on priestly ministry of Jesus, 166–73, 177
   on prophetic ministry of Jesus Christ, 170
   realism of, 127
   on revelation of God, 170
   rhetoric of, 126–27
   theology of, 19–20
   theology of space of, 120
   theology of the resurrection of, 181–83
   on time, 104
   *triplex munus* of, 170
beatific vision, 5–6, 5n22, 6–7, 8
Begbie, Jeremy, 33, 129, 179, 205, 206–8
believers, 53, 68, 199, 234. *See also* human beings
benediction, 150–51, 176
Berkhof, Louis, 161n202, 224

Berkouwer, G., 9n39
*Biblical Commentaries* (Calvin), 32
biblical interpretation, 171–72, 177
Billings, J. Todd, 9
biological analogies, 76–78
biological procreation, 56, 73
birthing analogy, 68
blessings, 150–51
bodies, removal of, 184–85. *See also* resurrection
Boersma, Hans, 9, 10
Boyd, Robin, 46
Bruce, Robert, 6
Brunner, Emil, 199
Burgess, Andrew
    on Barth and Torrance comparison, 40, 167
    on the cross, 149
    on David Moffitt, 192
    on humanity of Jesus Christ, 195–97
    on intercession, 147
    on *kenotic* theory, 83, 180, 190–91
    on William Milligan, 143–44
Byzantine art, 92n37, 105–6, 123, 126

Calvin, John
    on ascension of Jesus, 38–39
    beatific vision and, 7–9
    church relevance of, 62
    criticism of, 9
    *duplex munus* of, 137
    on the incarnation, 88
    influence of, 6, 32–33, 38–39, 47, 171–72
    on kingship of Christ, 222
    symbiotic relationship in work of, 32
    theology of spatiality of the ascension, 31
    *triplex munus* and, 161n202, 224
    on work of Christ, 96
Campbell, John McLeod, 175–76
Chalcedonian Definition, 84
Chalcedonian doctrine, 180
Chiarot, Kevin, 87, 194
christocentrism, 201
Christology
    eschatology and, 97–98
    as ontologically defective, 190–97
    ontology of ascended Jesus and, 79–81, 180
    as prioritized over Scripture, 188–89
    spatiality of ascended Christ and, 87–94, 127, 128
    theological anthropology and, 50–51
    as theology theme, 27–28
Christomonism, 232
church
    *anhypostasis*/*enhypostasis* and, 189–90
    as body of Christ, 76, 187, 189
    earthiness to, 71
    encounter with Christ in, 78n164
    ethical implications of ontology of ascended Jesus for, 61–62
    Holy Spirit as mediator for, 93
    importance of place and, 209–10
    incarnational existence of, 60
    intercession of, 28, 59
    Jesus's ascension and, 57–62
    Jesus's relationship with, 71
    as meeting place of God, 93
    ministry of Christ in, 160n197
    ontology of, 187
    preaching in, 234–35
    proclamation of, 157–58
    relationship with ascended Christ and, 60–61, 77–78, 158, 159–60
    as rooted, 57
    Scripture and practices of, 57
    sectarian view of, 159
    service of, 220–21
    state and, 220–22
    structures as held loosely in, 58
Clement of Rome, 158
Collver, Albert, 3
Colyer, Elmer M., 18, 23
*communicatio idiomatum* (communication of properties), 113–14, 116, 182–83, 186

*communicatio operationum* (communication of operations), 116
*communio idiomatum*, 186
compositionalism, 117
constructive dogmatics, 11, 47, 239
container notion, 95
contingency argument, 73
contrapuntal relation of Jesus Christ, 158
Cooper, James, 169
Cortez, Marc, 72–73
Craig, John, 6
creation, 99, 129, 227
creatureliness, problem of, 182–83
Crisp, Oliver, 43–44, 129, 193, 210–14
critique, of Torrance's theology of the ascension
    embryonic Trinitarian spatiality and, 204–10
    eschatologically deficient ecclesiology in, 187–90
    introduction to, 179–80
    non-existent eschatological anthropology and, 181–87
    ontologically defective Christology and, 190–97
    on ontology of the ascended Christ, 180–97
    present ministry of ascended Christ in, 216–36
    on spatiality of the ascended Christ, 197–215
    unclear spatial language in, 210–15
cross of Jesus Christ, 107–8, 135n19, 189, 192. *See also* Jesus Christ
Cyril of Alexandria, 6, 137, 152

Day of Atonement, 150
death, 199, 202–3
Decalogue, 219
decay, 122
Deddo, Gary, 232–33
demythologization, 88–89, 107
discipleship groups, 165
disclosure models, 138
disembodiment, 203
divinization, 184–85

divine fullness, 205
divine simplicity, 204, 205
divine temporalism, 104
Docetism, 167
dogmatics/dogmatism, 214–15
doxological level, relational space at, 208–10
doxology, theology as, 23–24
dual affirmations, 99–100
dualism, 203
*duplex munus*, 137

ecclesiology, 28–29, 56–62, 76–78, 83, 187–90
economic ethics, 219
economic level, relational space at, 206–8
ecumenical theology, 16–17
Edwards, Jonathan, 7n34
Einstein, Albert, 86, 100n90
Elijah, 203
Ellis, Brannon, 9
Emmem, E., 8–9n39
emotions, 124–25
empty tomb, 66–67
endless self-oblation, 143–46
enthronement, 134
epistemic humility, 65
epistemology, 63–64, 105–12, 129
eschatological naturalism, 10
eschatological panentheism, 183
eschatology/eschaton
    *ad hoc* nature of, 201
    already and not yet aspects of, 198
    beatific vision and, 5n22, 7–8
    christocentrism of, 201
    christological aspect of, 201
    Christology and, 97–98
    denial of distinct individualities in, 186–87
    expectant, 198
    final judgment and, 187–88
    humankind at, 54
    importance of, 121–22
    judgment theme in, 187
    kingship of Jesus and, 223
    methodological aspect of, 201

eschatology/eschaton (continued)
    non-existent anthropology of, 181–87
    ontology of ascended Jesus and, 181–87
    overrealized individual, 198–204
    proleptic, 198
    realised, 98–99
    sexual differentiation at, 73–75
    spatiality of ascended Christ and, 97–99
    as theology theme, 29
    triumphalistic, 202
eternalization, 181
eternal mediation, of Jesus Christ, 228–30
eternity, 184
ethics, Jesus's kingship and, 218–20
Eucharist, 28–29, 60–61, 68–69, 71, 95, 154–56, 167
Eugenio, Dick, 162, 163, 236
Eutychianism, 4–5n20, 182
exaltation, 50–51, 134–35
expressionism, 127
*extra Calvinisticum*
    affirmation of, 105, 186
    ascension and, 92n37, 113–19, 130
    benefits of, 222–23
    presentation of, 87–88
    Reformed, Lutherans, and, 44–45
    relational conception of space and, 94–95

Fach, Sandra, 83, 195–96
the Fall, 73, 83–84, 106, 122
fallenness, 106, 193, 194–95
fallen space-time, 90
Farrow, Douglas, 37, 40, 81, 196, 197
Fergusson, David
    on church ministry, 160n197
    on emotive aspects, 124–25
    on ethics, 218, 220
    on the Eucharist, 168–69
    on *extra Calvinisticum*, 44–45, 76, 92n37, 113
    on heaven, 109
    on the Holy Spirit, 175–76, 233
    on Karl Barth, 47, 168
    on kingship of Jesus, 223
    on Lutheranism, 88
    on pneumatology, 231–32
    on theology of the ascension, 15, 40, 174, 216–17
    on Torrance's language, 111–12, 149–50
    on work of Christ, 147
    on worship, 142
final judgment, 187–88, 189
Finley, John, 74n138
Flett, Eric, 74, 183n26
Flint, Thomas, 117

gender, 11n55, 55–56, 72, 76
God
    blessings from, 150n129
    events of, 104
    existence of, 89–91
    face to face vision of, 8
    fullness of, 205–6
    interaction with human beings by, 89, 208–9
    knowing of, 18, 22–23
    love of, 111
    nature of, 90
    new creation and, 121
    ontological barrier and, 227
    perichoretic Being of, 185
    revelation of, 107, 170
    space and time of, 88, 100–101, 104, 121
    theological language for, 123–27
    transcendence of, 121
    will of, 194
*goel*, 136, 137
Gordon, James, 116–17
Gospel, proclamation of, 157–58
Gregory of Nyssa, 11n55, 72–76, 81, 84, 240
Grudem, Wayne, 229

Habets, Myk
    on anthropological duality, 203–4
    on Christ's humanity, 26–27
    on *communio idiomata*, 114

on divinisation, 53, 185
on doctrine of *theosis*, 43
on *extra Calvinisticum*, 118
on human ontology, 229
on the incarnation, 29
influence of, 9, 41n170
on the interpretation of Scripture, 31
on pneumatology, 233, 234
on Reformed theology, 6
on Scotist view, 226, 227
on spatial location, 108–9
on Torrance's language, 111
Hardy, Daniel, 14n1
Harris, Mark, 79
heaven, 92–93, 109, 118–19, 214
Heron, Alasdair, 6n25, 168
Hill, Jonathan, 105
Hinduism, 45–46
Hippolytus, 137
Hitchcock, Nathan, 82, 180, 181–83
Hoeffer, Herbert, 45
holiness, 164
Holmes, Christopher R. J., 3, 5–6
Holmes, Stephen R., 4–5n20
holy moments, 111
Holy Spirit
  active work of, 157
  as in the believer, 153
  benefits of, 52
  epistemological role of, 67–68
  incarnation and, 232–33
  indwelling of, 175–76
  intercession by, 149
  as mediator, 93, 155, 175
  oneness and, 108
  in prophetic ministry, 230
  role of, in Jesus as prophet, 232
  role of, in personally encountering Jesus, 36
*homoousion*, 105
Horton, Michael, 39
Hudson, Hud, 213–14
human beings
  as biologically differentiated as male and female, 55–56
  Christlikeness and, 230
  christological destiny of, 228
  composite of body and soul of, 54–55
  created time of, 104
  at the eschaton, 54
  exaltation of, 50–51
  fall of, 73, 83–84, 106, 122
  God's interaction with, 89, 208–9
  as human, 51–52
  immortality and, 54
  Jesus's intercession for, 146–50
  limitations of, 67
  ontological barrier and, 227, 229
  as participating in divine nature, 52–53
  perfection of, 195
  relationships of, 56
  resurrection of, 56, 80–81, 84, 199
  retainment of identity by, 184–85
  sexual differentiation of, 55–56, 73–75
  space-time of, 100–101, 104
  spiritual body of, 65–66
  *theosis* of, 29–30
humility, 110
Hunsinger, George, 24, 43, 168
*hupsoo* (to exalt), 134
hyperbole, 111
hyperspace theory, 213–14, 215
hypostatic union, 53, 121, 185, 186, 192

incarnation
  ascension and, 27, 87–89
  church and, 61, 76, 83, 190
  continuance of, 61
  deity of Jesus in, 27, 36
  fallen human nature in, 192
  goal of, 29, 50
  God's spatiality in, 92, 104–5
  healing at, 193
  humanity of Jesus in, 43, 49, 153, 194
  hypostatic union and, 192
  in Indian theological scholarship, 46
  Nestorianism and, 116–17
  as saving assumption, 75
  saving significance of, 228
  self-revelation of God and, 20
  theology of space and, 209
  time and, 97
  unified theory of, 196

incorporation, 181, 183
Indian theology, 45
Inge, John, 205, 208
*Institutes* (Calvin), 32–33
intercession, 28, 59, 146–50, 176
intermediate state, 203
Irenaeus, 37, 47
Irving, Edward, 195n94

Jansen, J. F., 8–9
Jenson, Robert, 77n155, 78n164, 197, 210–11
Jesus Christ
  as Advocate, 149
  as atoning sacrifice, 135n19, 136
  benediction of, 150–51, 176
  blessing from, 150–51
  centrality of, 24
  as composite substance, 117
  continuity of identity of, 139
  cross of, 107–8, 134, 135n19, 189, 192
  death of, 134, 142n72
  as deified by nature, 53
  empty tomb of, 66–67
  encountering, 78n164
  enthronement of, 134
  eternal mediation of, 228–30
  in the Eucharist, 28
  exaltation of, 134–35
  fallen or unfallen humanity of, 43–44
  as fulfillment, 91, 141, 146
  glorification of, 134
  holiness of, 164
  humanity of, 2–3, 25n72, 28, 43–44, 51, 70, 92, 98, 190–91, 194
  identity of, 139
  intercession of, 28, 59, 146–50, 176
  as Jew, 70–71
  as judge, 189
  *kerygma* of, 157
  kingship of, 27, 138–40, 157, 160, 162–64, 166, 174, 176, 177, 216–24
  as Lamb, 138
  as Lion, 138
  lordship of, 58, 139
  maleness of, 72
  mediation of, 5n22, 7, 8, 153–54, 175
  as Mediator, 149
  as New Man, 98
  obedience of, 137
  oneness of, 107
  *parousia* (presence and coming) of, 201
  perspective of, 59
  physical body of, 37, 38, 64
  as priest, 140–56, 160, 166–69, 175, 176, 224–30
  proclamation of, 157
  as prophet, 156–60, 169–73, 175–77, 230–36
  relationship with the church and, 60–61, 158, 159–60
  as representative, 148
  resurrection of, 62–63
  self-oblation of, 143–46, 176
  sinlessness of, 43–44, 193
  as sovereign, 139
  as substitute, 148
  suffering of, 162–63, 176
  as Temple of God, 87n7
  transfiguration of, 203
  vicarious humanity view of, 43–44
  vicarious life of, 28
  victory of, 58, 59, 66–67
  will of, 194
  wounds of, 163
  *See also* resurrection
John Chrysostom, 137
judgment, in eschatology, 187
justification, 111n163
Justin Martyr, 137

*kathizo* (to sit down), 133–34
Kelly, Anthony, 2
Kelly, Douglas, 2
kenoticism, 180, 190
kenotic theory, 83, 88–89
*kerygma*, 157
kingship
  ethics and, 218–20

of Jesus Christ, 27, 138–40, 157, 160, 162–64, 166, 174, 176, 177, 216–24
politics and, 220–24
*kipper*, 136, 137
Knox, John, 6, 69–70
Korff, F. W. A., 8–9n39
Kruger, Baxter, 162, 166

Lamont, Daniel, 19
Langdon, Adrian, 39
language
  analogical, 108–9
  apophatic, 110–11
  artistic, 112, 123, 197–98
  exaggerated, 111–12
  provocative, 111
  stratified, 109–10
  theological, for God, 123–27, 129
Lee, Kye Won, 184–85
Lee, Sang Hoon, 185, 204, 205–6
Letham, Robert, 111n163
Lewis, C. S., 42, 124, 125, 130–31, 240
Liston, Gregory, 161–62, 224
love of God, 111
Lutheran theology
  accusations of, 4–5n20
  on ascension of Christ, 44–45
  Christology of Barth in, 182
  *communicatio idiomatum* (communication of properties) in, 113–14
  criticism of, 76
  on the incarnation, 88
  on spatial theologies, 94–95

Mackintosh, Hugh Ross, 24
MacLean, Stanley, 71, 83, 98, 128, 180, 187–88, 201–2
Macleod, Donald, 195n94
manifestation, 181, 182–83
marriage, 219
McFarland, Ian, 76–77, 78, 240
McGrath, Alister, 14n2, 20
McKim, Donald, 161n202, 224
McLeod, John, 169
Melchizedek, 150

mercy seat, 134
metaphors, 42
Methodist movement, 165
Middleton, Richard, 10
Migliore, Daniel, 161n202, 224
millennium-time, 59
Milligan, William, 31, 80, 142, 143–45, 146, 169, 192
miracles, human limitations in understanding, 67
missionary theology, 21–22, 24, 243–44
modalism, 205
Model A, 117
Model T, 117
Moffitt, David, 134, 141–42, 192
Molnar, Paul
  on the ascension, 113
  on the church, 188–89
  on comparison of Torrance and Barth, 169, 173–74
  on God's relationship to space, 86
  influence of, 41, 43, 47, 83
  on Scotist hypothesis, 225–26
  on Torrance's ordination service, 33
Moloney, Francis, 171
Moltmann, Jürgen, 9n39
monism, 203
monophysitism, 89, 114, 180, 184–85
Moses, 141, 203
Muirhead, Ian, 61
Mullins, R. T., 104
music theory, 206
mystery, in theology, 110–11

Nestorianism, 4–5n20, 116–17
new creation, 98–99, 121, 122, 229
Newell, Roger, 124, 125, 126
Noble, Thomas, 164, 193–95

obedience, of Jesus Christ, 137
Oberman, Heiko, 222
O'Collins, Gerald, 171
O'Donovan, Oliver, 223
*'olah*, 172
oneness, 107, 130, 207, 240
ontological barrier, 227

ontology of ascended Christ
   biological differentiation of male and female and, 55–56
   Christology and, 62–71, 79–81, 83–84, 180
   composite of body and soul and, 54–55
   constructive development of, 72–82
   creaturely and finite at, 54
   creedal and theological sources regarding, 69–70
   critique of, 82–85, 180–97
   ecclesiology and, 56–62, 76–78, 83
   epistemology and, 63–64
   ethical implications for the church in, 61–62
   exaltation of human beings and, 50–51
   humans being humans and, 51–52
   introduction to, 4, 49–50
   Lukan, 79–81, 84–85
   overview of, 64–69, 240
   participating in the divine nature and, 52–53
   pastoral implications of, 70
   Pauline, 79–81, 84–85
   relationality and, 63–64
   relational space at, 205–6
   relationship between Christ and the church and, 60–61
   soteriology and, 196–97
   theological anthropology and, 50–54, 72–76, 82
   Torrance's broader corpus in, 53–54
Origen, 32, 35, 64
original sin, 193
Orr, Peter, 2
Orthodox Church, 16
Ortlund, Gavin, 109, 114
otherness, 79
Owen, John, 7, 7n34

*padah*, 136, 137
Palma, Robert J., 6n25
panenchristism, 183
panentheism, 183, 186
paper theology, 21

Park, Chan Ho, 86, 129
*parousia* (presence and coming) of Christ, 201
particularity, problem of, 183
passive obedience, 137
Pentecost, 118n196
perfection, time of, 106
*periochoresis*, 102–3, 205
picturing models, 138
place, as biblical theme, 208–10
Plato, 64, 81
pneumatology, 231–34
politics, kingship of Jesus and, 220–24
postresurrection, 212n207
prayer, 148, 153–54, 176. *See also* intercession
preaching, 230, 231, 234–36
present ministry of ascended Christ
   *anabaino* (to go up) in, 133
   *analambano* (to take up) in, 134
   benediction in, 176
   constructive development of, 161–74
   critique of, 174–76, 216–36
   doctrine of sanctification and, 161–66, 177
   endless self-oblation of Jesus Christ in, 143–46, 176
   *hupsoo* (to exalt) in, 134
   intercession of Jesus in, 28, 59, 146–50, 176
   introduction to, 4, 132–33
   *kathizo* (to sit down) in, 133–34
   kingship of Jesus Christ in, 138–40, 160, 162–64, 166, 174, 176, 177, 216–24
   lack, 218–20
   lack of ethics in, 217
   overview of, 176–77, 240–41
   priestly ministry of Jesus Christ in, 140–56, 160, 166–69, 175, 176, 177, 224–30
   prophetic ministry of Jesus in, 156–60, 169–73, 175–77, 230–36
   theological significance of words used for ascension in, 133–38
   underdeveloped doctrine of Jesus's ascended kingship in, 216–24

priesthood, 140–43
priestly ministry of Jesus Christ
   critique of, 175, 224–30
   critique of Barth in, 166–69
   endless self-oblation of Jesus Christ in, 143–46, 176
   eternal benediction of Jesus Christ in, 150–51, 176
   eternal intercession of Jesus Christ in, 146–50, 176
   Eucharistic aspects of, 154–56
   introduction to, 140–43
   liturgical aspects of, 151–54
   overview of, 176, 177
*prima facie*, 198
problem of creatureliness, 182–83
problem of particularity, 183
prophet, Jesus as, 156–60, 169–73, 175–77, 230–36
prophetic ministry, 231–36
propleptic theology, 121–22
Protestants, 17
provocative language, 111
Purves, Andrew, 164, 199–200

Quistorp, H., 9n39

Radcliff, Alexandra, 164–65, 233, 234
Radcliff, Jason, 17, 43
Rae, Murray, 120
Rahner, Karl, 92–93
Ramanuja, 45
Ramsey, Ian, 138
Ratzinger, Joseph, 92, 93
realised eschatology, 98–99
realised teleology, 98–99
realism, 127
reconciliation, 111n163
redemption, 90–91, 96, 99, 120–23, 137, 227
Reformation, 17
Reformed theology
   accusations of, 4–5n20
   on ascension of Christ, 44–45
   beatific vision and, 5–6, 5n22

*communicatio idiomatum* (communication of properties) in, 116
   on spatial theologies, 94–95
   theology of the ascension and, 5–11
   *triplex munus* and, 161–62
relational approach, 89–91, 94–95, 108, 126, 199, 214
relationality, 63–64, 102–3
relational ontology, 82
relational space, 205–10
resurrection
   ascension and, 62–63
   Barth's themes regarding, 181–83
   as basis for human resurrection, 93
   birthing analogy and, 68
   empty tomb of, 66–67
   eternalization and, 181
   final, 202–3
   gender at, 76
   human beings in, 56, 80–81, 84, 199
   incorporation and, 181, 183
   instantaneous, 198, 200
   interim period and, 198–99
   Jewish worldview and, 81
   living embodiment in, 203
   manifestation and, 181, 182–83
   physicality of bodily, 69
   unclear spatial language regarding, 210–15
rhetoric, 126–27
Ritchie, Bruce, 96–97, 122
Roman Catholic Church, 16, 159

sacramental relation of Jesus Christ, 158
sacraments, 168. *See also* Eucharist
sacrifice, animal, 135n19, 142, 145–46, 192
salvation, 96–97, 97n68, 98, 111n163, 164
sanctification, 161–66, 177, 193–94, 241
Scandrett, Joel, 42–43
scientific theology, 17–19, 22–23, 201
Scotist hypothesis, 216, 225–30
Scottish Church Society, 168–69
*Scottish Theology* (Torrance), 69–70

# INDEX

Scotus, John Duns, 6
second-person encounters, 77–78
Seim, Turid Karslen, 80–81
self-giving, 207
self-oblation, 143–46, 176
session, implications on earth and, 58
sexual differentiation, 55–56, 73–75
Sherman, Robert, 161n202, 224
Sherrard, Joseph, 16, 170–71, 175, 220–23, 230–31, 234–36
simple atemporalism, 105
sinlessness, 193
sin/sinfulness, 193, 194–95
Sonderegger, Katherine, 195n94
soteriology, 96–97, 102–3, 129, 196–97
space
- aural, 207, 208
- of God, 88, 100–101, 206–7
- importance of, 107–8
- overview of, 100–101
- redemption of, 120–21, 129
- relational view of, 89–91, 94–95, 126, 214
- teleological orientation of, 120–21
- Trinity and, 119–23, 207
- visual, 208

spatiality of ascended Christ
- analogical language of, 108–9
- apophatic language of, 110–11
- artistic language in, 123
- ascension and, 87–89
- Byzantine art and, 105–6, 123, 126
- Christology and, 87–94, 127, 128
- constructive development of, 113–28
- critique of, 128–29, 197–215
- embryonic Trinitarian, 204–10
- epistemology and, 105–12, 129
- eschatological debate regarding, 97–99
- exaggerated language of, 111–12
- *extra Calvinisticum* and, 113–19
- historical debate regarding, 94–95
- importance of space and time in, 107–8
- incarnation and, 87–89
- introduction to, 4, 86–87
- ontology and, 91–94
- overrealized individual eschatology and, 198–204
- overview of, 240
- redemption of space in, 120–21
- redemption of time in, 121–23
- relationality and, 102–3
- relational space and time and, 89–91
- soteriological debate regarding, 96–97, 129
- space and, 89–91, 119–23
- spatiality and, 87–94
- spatio-temporality and, 103–5
- stratified language of, 109–10
- theological language and, 105–12, 123–27, 129
- time and, 89–91, 119–23
- Torrancean construction of, 117–19
- Trinity and, 99–102, 119–23, 127–30
- as unclear, 210–15

Speidell, Todd, 174, 218–19
spiritual body, 65–66
spiritualization, of resurrected and ascended state, 64–65
stratified language, 109–10
subsistence, 117
suffering, 80

telos, time of, 106
thanksgiving, 146
theological anthropology, 29–30, 50–54, 72–76, 82
theological language, for God, 123–27
theology
- as apophatic, 25–26
- as constructive endeavor, 24–25
- as doxology, 23–24
- evangelical and doxological level of, 23
- higher theological level of, 23
- as missionary enterprise, 24
- as science, 22–23
- theological level of, 23
- Torrance's main contributions to, 22–26

theology of the ascension

as artistic, 41–42, 47
as biblical, 30–33
body of ascended Jesus in, 37, 38
Byzantine art and, 105–6
categorization of expositions on, 3–4
devotional aspects of, 15–16
emotive aspects of, 124–25
historical church and, 57–62
as holistic, 33–34, 48
implications on earth and, 58
incarnation and, 87–89
introduction to, 14–15, 30
kataphysic method of, 34–35
as modern theological classic, 239
neglect of, 1–5
non-dualistic method of, 35–36
overview of, 239–44
as patristic, 37–41
as personal, 36
potential for global theological dialogue regarding, 45–46
Reformed theology and, 5–11, 37–41
resurrection and, 62–63
as rich resource for ecumenical dialogue, 42–45
as scientific, 34–36
sociopolitical implications of, 217
theological significance of words used for, 133–38
*theosis*, theology of, 29–30, 52, 184–85
third-person encounters, 77, 78
Thomas Aquinas, 74, 137
time
  created, 104
  eternity and, 184
  of God, 88, 100–101, 104, 121
  importance of, 107–8, 184
  new, 122
  old, 122
  omnitemporal theory of, 182
  overview of, 100–101
  redemption of, 121–23, 129
  relational view of, 89–91, 94–95, 214
  removal of, at eschaton, 184

simultaneous operation of two different kinds of, 106–7
Trinity and, 119–23
uncreated, 104
Torrance, David W., 21
Torrance, James, 154n160, 223–24, 242
Torrance, Thomas F.
  accolades of, 14–15
  alignment of, 7
  Auburn lectures of, 70, 184, 226
  biblical interpretation method of, 171–72, 177
  Christian discipleship of, 15
  as Christian dogmatician, 87
  as dialogue partner, 11
  doctoral thesis of, 20
  doxology and, 23–24
  ecclesiology of, 28–29
  ecumenical theology of, 16–17
  ethical vision of, 220
  family background of, 16–17
  holistic account of, 4
  *homoousion* use by, 26n81
  influence of, 2
  lack of clarity by, 179–80
  main contributions to theology by, 22–26
  ministerial practices of, 219
  missionary theology of, 21–22, 24
  as pastorally academic, 20–21
  preaching of, 235–36
  as Reformed theologian, 6
  scholarship overview of, 14n2
  scientific theology of, 17–19, 22–23
  in Scottish Church Society, 168–69
  as theologian, 15–26
  theological anthropology of, 29–30
  theological convictions of, 16–22
  as theological giant, 241–42
  as theological scientist, 123
  transformative theology of, 20–21
  wholism of, 123–24
transfiguration, 203
transformative theology, 20–21
transphysicality, 66n92
Travis, Stephen, 199

Trinity
  coactivity of, 103
  oneness in, 130, 207, 240
  *periochoresis* and, 102–3, 205
  prayer and, 153
  self-giving by, 207
  space and, 119–23, 207
  spatiality and, 99–102, 119–23, 127–30
  as theology theme, 26–27
  threeness in, 130, 207, 240
  time and, 119–23
  worship and, 152–53
triple mediation, 230
*triplex munus*, 25n72, 132, 137, 160–64, 169–70, 173, 176–77, 224
tritheism, 205
Tsoukalas, Steven, 45
Turretin, Francis, 8n35
Tyler, Kate, 34

union argument, 73
universalism, 111n163

Vale, Fellipe do, 75, 76
Van Driel, Edwin Chr., 4
Van Kuiken, Jerome, 165, 174, 194, 219
van Ruler, A. A., 8–9n39
vision, defined, 179
visual perception, 206, 208

Walker, Robert, 30–31, 190
Watson, Thomas, 7n34
Webb, Stephen, 126
Webster, John, 120, 170, 173, 179, 235
Wellum, Stephen J., 195n94
Wesleyan theology, 164–66, 173
Widdicombe, Peter, 163
Wilkinson, David, 119, 121
Willis, E. David, 9n39
Wolterstorff, Nicholas, 217
World Council of Churches, 16
world history, interpretation of, 58
World War II, 139–40
worship, 152–53, 156, 231
Wright, N. T., 10, 66n92, 80–81, 128, 202–3, 214

Yates, John, 200–201, 202
Yom, Aaron, 233, 234
Yom Kippur, 142n72

Ziegler, Georgie, 74, 123–24
Zuckerkandl, Victor, 207

www.ingramcontent.com/pod-product-compliance
Lightning Source LLC
Chambersburg PA
CBHW022003220426
43663CB00007B/934